**The past, the present and the future
are really one: They are today.**

— *Harriet Beecher Stowe*

**We shall not cease from exploration,
and the end of all our exploring will be
to arrive where we started and
know the place for the first time.**

— *T.S. Eliot*

**Find a place inside where there's joy,
and the joy will burn out the pain.**

— *Joseph Campbell*

For my sister Debra's sons
—Jared, Ian, Jamin—
and my brother David's daughters,
Dena and Paige…

…and, moreover, for…

…all families everywhere,
regardless in what unexpected constellations
they might presently find themselves.

Roots of Darkness: One Family's Dreams and Nightmares in America
volume 1 of the pentalogy *Oceans of Darkness, Oceans of Light:
Our Family's Trials and Treasures in the New World*

Volumes 1, 2 and 3 are available as E-books and
available on-line via Amazon.com, etc.

author: Michael Luick-Thrams
with Anthony J. Luick and Gary Luick
copyright: © 2015 Michael Luick-Thrams
published on behalf of the TRACES
Center for History and Culture
ISBN 978-0-9857697-7-2

Contents

Prologue	5
Introduction	15
Part I: Rebels with Causes	23
Section 1: Bud & Phyllis (Thrams) Luick family	23
chapter 67: clash of cultures	26
chapter 68: winds of war	31
chapter 69: 'til blood flowed	38
chapter 70: against the grain	45
chapter 71: the fields ignite	50
chapter 72: whitie's world collapses	54
chapter 73: the rebellion spreads	60
chapter 74: hell an' back	66
chapter 75: revolution from within	78
chapter 76: war comes home	89
chapter 77: we all unravel	94
postscript: war's long shadows	99
Part II a: Warriors without Wars	105
Section 2: Donald & Charlotte (Juhl) Luick	105
chapter 56: the Big Thud	108
chapter 57: children of BOOM!	113
chapter 58: casualties of BUST!	117
chapter 59: best option imaginable	123
chapter 60: life's no holiday	127

chapter 61: wracked by darkness	135
chapter 62: a grinding poverty	139
chapter 63: wading into darkness	150
chapter 64: lust's lasting legacies	155
chapter 65: setting records straight	161
chapter 66: a fluid truth	168
postscript: series of surprises	173

Part II b: Warriors without Wars — 175

Section 3: George & Lorena (Jenison) Luick family — 175

chapter 50: two in one	178
chapter 51: the dutiful bigot	185
chapter 52: a lasting love	191
chapter 53: a "queer duck"	197
chapter 54: exorcising old demons	203
chapter 55: visiting vanished worlds	208
postscript: dark, indelible hues	211

Part III a: Children of Pioneers — 217

Section 4: Nick & Lottie (Moorehead) Juhl family — 217

chapter 46: an endless treadmill	220
chapter 47: fouling crowded nests	227
chapter 48: consuming one's own	234
chapter 49: an overdue autopsy	241
postscript: "This Everlasting Light"	246

Conclusions Volume I — 255

conclusion from the *persona*: my disrupted granny	256
postscript: into Everlasting Light	299

Supplements Volume I — 302

Parts III b and IV, with the second of three conclusions ("about the *populi*: my disappearing people") are in Volume II: *Chasing Restless Roots: The Dreams that Lured Us Across America*

Part V and VI, with the final conclusion ("for the polis: my derailed country"), plus
   Supplements
   Sources and Commentary, including footnotes and image registry
   Disclaimer and Acknowledgments
are in Volume III: *Tap Roots Betrayed: How Our Dreams Got Derailed in America*

both by the same author; further information at www.roots.TRACES.org

Prologue

my paternal grandmother, Charlotte (Juhl) Luick, in her living room

On the first of October 1962, Groucho Marx introduced Iowa-born Johnny Carson on national television. In turn, Carson welcomed Joan Crawford and Rudy Vallee, Tony Bennett, Tom Pedi, and the all-male African-American trio, the Phoenix Singers, as his first guests—and therewith took over hosting the *Tonight Show* for the next thirty years.

His opening monologue would become a staple of the nightly show with jokes lampooning the newsmakers of the day. One wonders what that first monologue, now lost, included. Did he mention that earlier that day, in strife-torn Mississippi, James Meredith had enrolled at all-white "Ole Miss" as the first student of color, escorted by a small army of U.S. marshals? Or that his first class—fittingly, Colonial History—was boycotted by more than a third of his registered class members due to the hue of their unwelcome classmate's skin?

Did Carson note that four Soviet Foxtrot submarines, armed with nuclear torpedoes, had departed bases in arctic Russia? Or that they were headed for the Caribbean in anticipation of a Soviet confrontation with the U.S. over the deployment of missiles in Cuba? If so, did Carson imagine that the world was about to stare all-out global destruction in the face—then escape it by a margin of hours?

A few days later—less explosively but leaving lasting ripples nonetheless—*Dr. No*, the first James Bond film, premièred in British cinemas, and the Beatles released their first single, *Love Me Do*. Also in October 1962: The U.S. suffered its first helicopter fatalities in Vietnam; China and India stumbled into war over their contested shared border; and, the reformist Second Vatican Council opened in Rome. In the jungles of Panama the Bridge of the Americas opened, uniting North and South America by land for the first time; the hold-no-punches play *Who's Afraid of Virginia Woolf* opened on Broadway; and, Hurricane Daisy pounded the coast of innocent Nova Scotia.

Closer to home, in Belmond, Iowa, Uncle Henry Luick's 73-year-old jaw continued to heal after a 20-something hitchhiker had broken it the previous July. Dena (Kramer) Riggins and her husband, Robert, opened the Sahara Supper Club alongside Highway 65, near Sheffield—the future site of my future uncle Bob Jones' secret life, which would fan my future Aunt Lorraine's decades-long misery. Also in October 1962, Lorraine (Luick) Jones' defiant kid sister, 18-year-old Sheranne Luick—who had just started learning about building beauty at La James School of Cosmetology in Mason City—was preparing to slip across the Minnesota border to secretly marry a fellow minor of whom her parents did not approve.

On the quieter maternal side of my extensive family, my grandparents, Elmer and Erma (Falcon) Thrams, were preparing to turn over Ashlawn Farm's operation to my young parents as of the New Year. And, Mom was in her eighth month of pregnancy with her third child—me. (Had Kennedy and Khrushchev not backed down, last-minute, from the brink of nuclear holocaust, I wouldn't be writing this now. And, you wouldn't be reading it: You wouldn't be alive today, either.)

Meanwhile, Aunt Della (Moorehead) Hughes True had been released after serving eighteen years in the Minnesota Reformatory for Women in Shakopee for two murders and was living per probation with her recently divorced (and about to divorce again) daughter, Beverly, in Florida. And, Della's niece, my paternal grandmother Charlotte (Juhl) Luick—who grew up with Della in the same household—was wearing sunglasses in her farmhouse's dimly lit living room. The picture shows her standing at the bottom of plank stairs I'd dream about for years as a child. They formed the structural core of a house that harbored scenes of crimes of the heart, not to mention at least one clearly codified in law books.

Dad and Mom, above, with Deb and Dave - and me "in the oven" still, at Ashlawn Farm, near Mason City, Iowa, in October 1962.
Newborn, right, is moi; curler-wearing Mom is holding me; David squats in front of TV showing duo figure skating; Grampa Donald's cowboy-booted foot shows on right, late winter 1962-63, on the Donald and Charlotte Luick farm near Thornton, Iowa.

When I study the photo of blindered Gramma now, after recent revelations of banal evils that my childhood self never could have imagined having happened in our family, I can only conclude that poor "Little Lottie" was doing her best to block out that which she could not bear to look at in the face. She could not endure what was right in front of her, would not go away, and was crushing her to her core.

I was three and a half years old when my paternal grandfather, Donald George Luick, dropped dead of a heart attack on Thornton's Main Street while eating an ice cream cone. It was a temperate, early-summer Iowa evening, Friday, 8 July 1966. He was 54 years old.

Over the almost half century since, I assumed that my few memories of Grampa Luick reflected more my own agenda-packed projections than any shreds of reality, given my immature age when he died. In the course of exploring the roots of my father's family, however, I recently uncovered (at age 51) just a few of its many secrets and lies. Though I didn't know the truth then, I feel vindicated now, that although a little tyke at the time I had accurately read our patriarch's aura.

Grampa Luick entering the corn crib on his and Gramma's farm

Still today, I can vividly recall that mysterious, speechless man floating along the shadowy, linoleum-floored living room of my Luick grandparents' farmhouse. That memory is triply uncomfortable to me. First, I feel a cool shudder go up my spine when I recall his image. Second, its implications are such sad ones. And, third, recalling it casts a gloomy pall over me.

As my family's self-appointed historian, I pride myself on recalling past events or settings factually, and on heroically refraining from editing them—positively or negatively—to suit my own needs or intentions. In this case, however, all indications are (and five older relatives have vouched for the accuracy of my recollections) that my child intuition—a sense that something murky and deeply disturbing happened in that house involving Donald, Charlotte & Co.—was spot on.

I now know this because revelations in numerous recent phone interviews or emails with Jones cousins—my deceased father's nieces—jibe with my own experiences. My cousin Barbara was born ten years, one month and eighteen days before me; her younger sister, Peggy, six years, ten months and nineteen days. When I forwarded to them the photo of Charlotte playing stationary hide-and-seek with troubling spirits in her austerely furnished living room, Jeanette (their kid sister, born in 1963, some eight months after me) responded

> Thanks! [Upon seeing this image] I could feel the cool linoleum, and even smell her house! I didn't think I remembered the farm that well, but I knew the spot instantly.

In turn, her older sister, Peggy, emailed back

> I also remember the exact spot and remember the house like the back of my hand. Over the years I would dream I was in the house. I could write a book about that house. Just about the house.

Peggy later clarified, in greater detail, what the repetitive images that visited her entailed:

> In my dreams, I would be driving out on those crazy Iowa gravel roads; lost and looking for grandma's farm. I would find the farm and be safe[.] I do remember feeling a bit scared standing at the base of the stairs looking up. I can't remember anything bad happening, but because of the turn in the stairs, you couldn't see all the way up. My [awake-state] memories collide with my dream memories so it is difficult to keep the 2 separated.

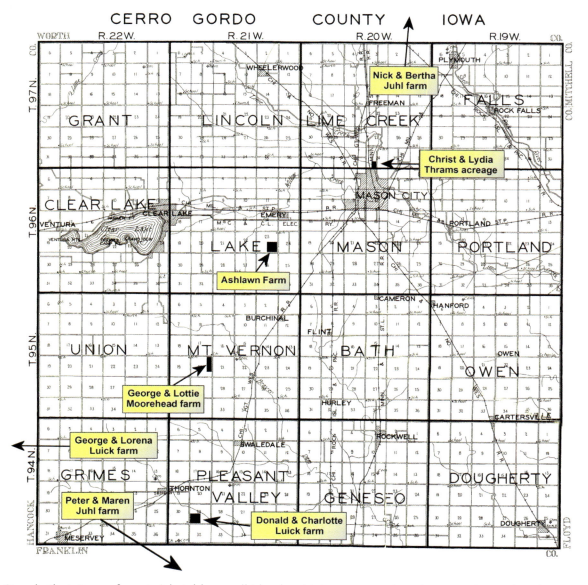

Struck that two of us Luick-Juhl grandkids should have recurring dreams about that house, and specifically that broken stairway, I wondered what personality or event that once was in it haunted us, years later. So, during a phone date with their older sister, I casually asked Barbara if—as opposed to me—she could remember the sound of Grampa Luick's voice. Assuming she did, as she was a maturing thirteen and a half rather than three and a half like me at the time of Donald's death at 54, she surprised me no small bit when she said "Well, no—now that I think about it, I don't."

Soon after that puzzling disclosure I dialed my two siblings—Debbie, seven years older than me, and David, four—and found, again, that neither could recall the sound of our paternal grandfather's voice. "Okay" thought I, "so, like, were we grandkids out ta lunch or sompthin' back then?"

David and Debbie Luick with our cousin Barbara Jones (top, center) playing dress-up, summer 1962

When, however, I asked Gary Luick—Donald's youngest first cousin—if he could remember my grandfather's voice, "Well" he responded slowly, "I really don't." A few weeks shy of his twenty-second birthday when Donald died, Gary added "Can't say I remember him talking."

By now both puzzled yet excited by the prospect that my childhood nightmares might have had something to do with the world around me than with any agitated demons inside me, I contacted my Gramma Luick's half-sister's (Cleo's) daughter, Janet, whose parents were with my grandparents when Grampa died. She swiftly confirmed my suspicion. As she carefully put it, "I didn't have anything against Donald, but whenever my folks would take me with them to visit Mom's half-sister, Charlotte, I always had a bad, dark feeling—as if there was something not right about that man."

"Really?" I grilled, pretending to be neutral, even disinterested.

"Oh" Janet didn't waver, "yes! There was no warmth, no sense that he had any time for me."

At that point the trans-Atlantic phone connection between Dresden, Germany, and Northwood, Iowa, seemed to go dead. "Jan?" I called out, thinking I'd lost her.

"Oh, I'm here" she shot back. "I was just asking myself if I'm thinking now that was how I felt then, or if that's how I really felt at the time."

"And" I prodded, "what'd ya come up with?"

"No" Jan said, "that's the unconscious feeling I really had."

"Can you recall the sound of Donald's voice, Jan?" I inquired further.

For a heavy moment the line again fell silent. Finally, she added "You know, I can't honestly recall that I ever heard your grandfather speak."

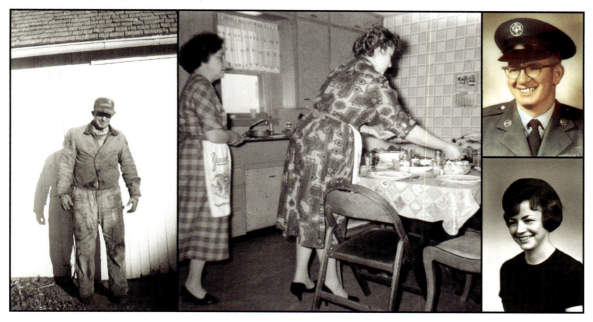

mute Grampa; Gramma and Mom at Christmas dinner, 1958; Gary Luick, 1962; Janet Gullickson, 1965

"Really?" I marveled, given that Jan was another seven years older than cousin Barbara, who was already considerably more aware than me at the time the man left our midst.

"Now Charlotte, she was *always* talkin'—but Donald" I could hear Jan wag her head by the slight swing in her voice, "he was a man of few, if any, words."

My grandmother's voice I, too, remember well.

———

When I was but a boy, Gramma Luick used to sit me down next to her on the worn-velvet, oak-leaf-green sofa and talk with—or at least, *to*—me. We'd "chat"—or at least, *she'd* expound—about everything and nothing for endless hours. By nature verbal and curious myself, I found it fun to listen to Gramma's cute stories and silly notions, of things or times long lost, of her working "for a dime an hour during the Depression" at stores along Rockwell's long Main Street, of being valedictorian of her "class o' '31" or of "drivin' the tractor through the cornfields, lookin' for lost cows."

As tactilely hungry as anyone, I enjoyed her scooping me up next to her, squeezing my smooth little body against her shrunken, diminutive frame. While relaying serial, seamless stories she'd scrunch up her face, purse her lips, wiggle her nose, then flutter and roll her eyes while rocking her head back and forth—like Charlie Chaplain playing a Hindu dancer. Gramma would mimic the characters she was describing and even act out—at least from the waist up, hands flying—the action she was conveying. Who needed to turn on the tellie when Granny was around?

At the same time, something felt subtly yet stubbornly wrong. On some long weekends or short weeks, I'd stay in that empty farmhouse with her, snippy Tammy—the short-tempered Shetland Collie that served as lone sentinel over the farmyard—and Susan, the glossy black cat that kept watch for rodents in the barn. When I awoke, I'd pad down the stairs, slink past the dining room buffet to the kitchen door and find Charlotte standing at the kitchen-sink window, holding court with herself. Perplexed by her incessant whispering to unseen entities, I'd slowly approach her and quietly ask "Who ya talkin' with, Gramma?" to which she'd reply "Oh, no one in partic'lar."

Greg Styles with his Great-Gramma Luick, 1996

Cousin Jeanette remembers "sleeping over in the summer, windows open for those summer breezes. The sound of clanking hog feeders would always lull me to sleep. [In the morning Charlotte] would feed us breakfast until we popped. Oatmeal? Sure. Toast? You bet. Pancakes? Why not? Grapefruit? Well... maybe with sugar on it. And her clear, plastic Kool-Aid Man pitcher was... the coolest. Kool-Aid poured into colored, tin cups. The best!" In response, our aunt, Sheranne, wrote "Jeanette that is so neat! I also remember the clanking hog feeders and the quietness outside - which I really miss!"

Dad was always sure to invite his widowed mother to join our innumerable horse-hunting trips, combing the Upper Midwest for replacement mares or a new stud. If Gramma noticed me noticing her staring out the window, muttering to herself in the backseat as we crisscrossed the American Heartland, she didn't seem to mind blatantly betraying her own odd self-talk. When she wasn't clasping my little-kid's hand, she was fingering the dusty Kleenex she always had crammed into her formless pocket or trap-like purse, wadding it, then unfolding and re-wadding it until that harassed piece of paper tissue disintegrated into a puff of powder. I wondered, all the while, who she was talking with—and why.

I could—and did—overlook my paternal grandmother's quirky habits, but had a much harder time forgiving feeling interchangeable. When I was with her I felt like the center of her compact universe—but likely so did the score of other kids I later found she'd "borrow" from their willing parents. I knew that my siblings took turns "stayin' with Gramma" so wasn't surprised when, for one, cousin Barbara reported going on the same grocery runs to Mabbs on Thornton's Main Street with Charlotte, eating the same cylindrical, orange-sherbet pop-ups, feeding dripping wash through the same clanking wringer in the basement or "helping" mow the lawn surrounding the asbestos-clad house. What gave me pause was when I found out that Jan Jacobsen, Grampa Donald's sister Voral's youngest of three, also "kept Charlotte company out on the farm" for stints at a time. That Gramma also "spent time" with her half-sister Cleo (Juhl) Gullickson, Cleo's husband Don and their young daughter, Janet, far afield from Thornton, in Northwood, took me aback, as that didn't fit her oft-repeated narrative "I had no siblings."

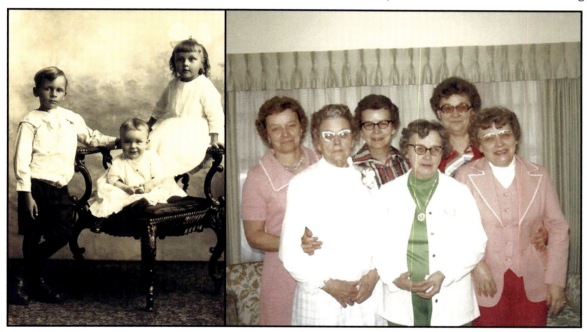

(l. to r.) Delbert, Cleo & Charlotte Juhl, circa 1918; Helen (Juhl) Johnson, Bertha (Hadsall) Juhl, Cleo (Juhl) Gullickson, Charlotte (Juhl) Luick, Hazel (Juhl) Troe & Edna (Juhl) Hanson: Bertha's 85th birthday, April 1978

When I asked Mom—now herself a grandmother of five—about her mother-in-law's revolving roster of juvenile guests, Phyllis didn't hesitate before rejoining

> Oh, the woman hated being alone. She'd 'stop by' on the way from Mason or The Lake on her way back to Thornton, then sit around an' sip an empty tea cup till it was 'too late to drive home in the dark' and spend the night. As if she didn't want to be alone, she'd do anything to avoid spending nights on her own there on that farm, in that empty house.

Although no joiner, Gramma did seem to be forever visiting one of her half-dozen half-sisters and step-mother or "goin' ta coffee" with any number of "friends" she'd then sit around afterwards and bad-mouth endlessly in their absence for their "chic shag rug" or "smart golf cart." Or, if she'd exhausted her list of excuses to visit us otherwise, she'd find some creeping malady that needed the trained medical attention she always avoided—and thus, happily, have another topic to dissect for hours with initially empathetic, but soon captive listeners eyeing the clock or nearest door.

———

Like everyone else in the family, as a kid I wasn't sure "what [was] the matter with Gramma" but assumed it had to do with me. I *was* sure, however, that the repetitive nightmares I had took place in Gramma's farmhouse. One involved a witch who waited for me at the crook of those stairs, beneath the lone stairwell window that, in reality, always had a mountain of dead flies heaped between the storm and the sash in an otherwise tidy house—as if Charlotte couldn't bring herself to sweep away the dead.

The scenario of the second nightmare unfolded always the same, always against a black background, in front of which appeared first a bright-blue square, then a blood-red triangle, followed by a yellow circle. The forms took turns coming from "off-stage." They made low-level thudding or shrill, squeaking noises as they slowly moved across a void, then silently swallowed the form that preceded them, until the universe fell dark again. This unsettling dream I had dozens of times; after each I awoke feeling afraid, empty and forsaken.

American Progress *by German-American painter Johann "John" Gast, 1872*

That these recurring nightmares arose out of my family's unreflective pursuit of the American Dream made me wonder, as a teenager coming of age during the nation's two-hundredth birthday, where the connection was: What had happened to us—what had we done, and thus become, while wandering around the New World for several centuries—that gave me this constant albeit vague feeling that something was amiss in my father's house?

The extreme discomfort, fear and desolation I felt in my father's family's home, in my paternal grandfather's presence and during the two, ever-repeating nightmares that haunted me for over a dozen years led me to seek relief from the subsequent deadly bleakness. In my search for plausible sources of our family's troubles in the New World, I discovered that what steered my grand-/parents' behavior most was least obvious or conscious, the deepest hidden and most sinister. To locate primal causes I could confront, then exorcise, I had to shift through decades, generations of accumulated emotional debris. The results of my lifelong search for release from all that now rest in your hands.

———

Introduction

A fortnight after Charles and Diana's fairy-tale royal wedding blue, white and red bunting still hung like long, saggy lace over Skipton's High Street. I had arrived in North Yorkshire at age 18 to attend venerable Ermysted's Grammar, one of England's last half-dozen state-run boys' schools. There, I boarded with a well-off young widow. Her veterinarian husband had dropped dead the previous year while biking cross-country through the Dales. Two of her three teenage children lived at home. The third, Matthew—set to study saddle-making upon his return to Britain—was to live in Pocahontas, Iowa, for the year I occupied his space.

Skipton's decorated High Street, August 1981; Jenny, Clare and Matthew Gully (surname altered) in garden

Through the plate-glass window in Matthew's room, I could see Pendle Hill. I had given up my family's generations-old spiritual home in Methodism a year earlier; shortly thereafter I found a new one among Quakers. This visible landmark summit, some 30 kilometers away, was said to have been the place where Quakerism had its beginning. Problem was, without a car, exploring that emblematic source of several Quaker institutional names remained nigh impossible.

Until, that is, I learned of a North Country Quaker Youth Pilgrimage to take place in Lancashire that fall of 1981. A group of young "Friends"—as Quakers are formally called—from England, Scotland, Ireland, California, Pennsylvania and (now) Iowa would explore the rainy, windswept region where the Society of Friends swiftly and resolutely arose in the mid-1600s. We were accompanied by the Quaker children's-book author, teacher, professional singer and peace activist, Elfrida Vipont (Brown) Foulds.

Elfrida holding her audience's rapt attention in one of North Country's oldest Quaker meeting houses

Though she'd turned 80 three months earlier, Elfrida didn't lag one moment as she guided us to ancient, vine-covered meeting houses, to the site of early Friends' imprisonment in Lancaster Castle and to their refuge at dark Swarthmoor Hall. At the end of it all, we stopped atop massive Pendle Hill, before trekking on to Firbank Fell.

Everywhere we turned, we observed oceans of darkness and oceans of Light!

Both Pendle Hill and Firbank Fell, far above the emerald pastures and quiet moors of rural Lancashire, impressed me deeply—as they had George Fox. One of Quakerdom's earliest weighty figures, he had found inspiration while on top of both mounts at the end of Whitsun ("Pentecost" in the U.S.) in June 1652. At Firbank Fell, he addressed a gathering of over a thousand "seekers" for three hours. Today, bolted to the rocky crag where he stood is a dull, weathered plaque. The uppermost line reads "LET YOUR LIVES SPEAK"—a central message of Fox to the people who already then called themselves "Publishers of Truth." Those simple words have guided me for more than thirty years, ever since that visit to Firbank Fell.

young Quakers taking breaks while hiking to and at Firbank Fell in Cumbria, near the Lancashire border

What is it that my life is "saying?" Or yours? What do others "hear" that we may or not intend to convey? Maya Angelou, the African-American writer, poet, actress and civil-rights activist, reminded us that "people will forget what you said, people will forget what you did, but people will never forget how you made them feel."

As I record select stories of the people who afforded me Life, I am mindful that whatever I relay will only be a glimpse—subjective and colored more by how our family made me feel than by what they might have said or done. In this way, the lives of our ancestors "speak" to us years or decades after they have died, whether or not they left behind many enduring traces of their one-time, earthly existence.

As first a willful child, then a soul-searching young man, I navigated my way through more than enough time with my parents and grandmothers to fill endless chapters with colorful, compelling details gathered from personal encounters. A central challenge in writing meaningful accounts about my grandfathers and further back, however, remains. Little of what I can write comes from my own experience. At the same time, with three exceptions my interpretation of what I have found over thirty-five years of research includes *no* fictionalizing: If I hadn't heard it, seen it, smelled it, read it, clipped it out or held it, it didn't make it into this story. (Proviso: I have altered five persons' names in consideration of their privacy.)

Still, while wanting to be true to factual events even as I expose the contradictory complexities rife in each human life, I'm not always certain what of interest, relevance or use to share about distant family members. Here is an example:

As far as I can remember, I met my great-grandfather George Michael Luick twice—once when I was about six at a Sunday afternoon Luick-family get-together in a musty rented hall on Thornton's deserted Main Street. The second time was when I was eleven years old, during a sojourn of a couple days as my family was returning from a trip to Yellowstone and Grand Teton National Parks via Cheyenne, Wyoming's renowned annual rodeo. We had stopped in Grand Island, Nebraska, to visit "Grampa George" and his second wife, Olga... and exactly there lies a gnawing question:

What to emphasize—and thereby eternalize—when writing about people I knew scarcely, if at all? What do I say about souls who have ceased to exist save for on a faded photo, in a scribbled entry in some forgotten census, on a tattered plat map or in a brittle obituary in some long-defunct newspaper?

George Luick, Grand Island, Nebraska; 1960s

Great-Grampa George (left), me, Dad, Dave and Deb, 1968; Olga, me, Dave, Grampa and Dad, 1974

The fact that George abandoned my great-grandmother Lorena and thereby left her destitute late in life, to die alone, an indigent charge of the State of Iowa, negatively affected several people's lives. Was that "necessary" or avoidable? Did he leave her with a semblance of dignity, I wonder, or nothing like it? And, what can be learned, in retrospect, from how those two beings came together, the 40 years of Life they shared, why and how they grew apart and, ultimately, how George eft Lorena to a solitary, sad and uncertain future? What can we learn for use in our own journey from their painful shared path?

All who knew George liked him, without qualification. Even my hyper-critical father and his gossipy mother spoke only well of their grandfather and father-in-law. And, in interviews some forty years later with my mother, sister and brother, my aunts Jeandelle and Sheranne, or others, no one reported anything but deep, heartfelt appreciation of the man. Each one I asked described him as a "kind, sweet, loveable old man." He would have been nearly 90 that summer of 1974 when I last saw him on the scorching Nebraska Plains. It seems we all *felt* exceptionally good in George's presence regardless of what he might have said or done in his life— including a stint serving as an affable terrorist in the 1920s.

Donald & sisters Voral, Velma & Jean, with George & baby Ricky, 1960

As *The Sound of Music*'s Captain von Trapp and Maria knew, "Nothing comes from nothing—nothing ever could," so the beatings from my father (which he'd recycled from his father) could only have come from somewhere. The lack of sexual boundaries which has plagued multiple generations of Luick men played out in George's life, too.

The question is how, with whom, when and with what consequences? (The man did leave his wife of 40 years to run away to Missouri with his neighbor's, after all.)

my grandfather's parents, George and Lorena (Jenison) Luick, early 1940s; on their son's farm, with Ring

If you ask George's grand- and great-grandchildren, he was the sweetest thing since honey—but what of substance do the memories of brief encounters with a tired geriatric say about the totality of one man's 90 years of Life? If you ask my five nephews and nieces about *their* "Grampa Luick" they'll likely also swoon about what a loving, loveable man he was. For my siblings and me, however, the indelible, unseen bruises he left in us even years later make it difficult (at least for me) to join their devoted chorus.

Is this not a dilemma for all of us when looking at another pilgrim's biography? (And, we're *all* pilgrims, stumbling our imperfect way along Life's endless, infinitely amazing path.) Especially when it is someone close to us or who we have loved, her or his life "speaks" to us of things, in ways that person may not have wished or intended. They may be inconvenient truths we may want to wish away but can do so only at our own loss. To acknowledge only the sweet and loveable is to forfeit the wisdom that invariably comes from being able to see, then possibly understand, the causes and effects that propel all our lives. We struggle to fully own not only the effects of others' actions on our lives, but the effects our actions have on others.

———

As I've gone through this same "struggle" while crafting this record, every Friday I have sent per installment "This Week's Words" to two-dozen readers in several countries for constructive feedback. One of the more astute and trusted—by the most improbable of coincidences a fellow Quaker historian and author also born in Iowa in 1962, who lives in my erstwhile adopted hometown of Berlin— protested each week "Michael, you always write from some moral standpoint, from some clear, black-and-white expectation of how the people populating your stories 'should' have acted or even lived, but rarely did. What is that unbending standard out of which you obviously operate, but never spell out?"

It's easy.

Mike Luick in the 4th grade, 1972

Take the nearest, youngest baby and pick it up into your arms. Listen to it gurgle, chortle or coo. Look into its eyes and *feel* the soul of that baby: How blemished or burdened is it, *really*? Not very, right? I know, as do you, that it is so, because there is hardly a baby ever born, anywhere, in any era, who doesn't arrive among us pure and free. Only after we land among those who've been walking around the planet for a while do we—longing to belong to those closest to us—allow ourselves to become troubled and fettered, too.

Child-murdering mothers and beast-bludgeoning fathers like the ones in my family are not born; they're bred. Too often, upon digging deeper, we find that they also were brutalized or beaten. As babies all of us appeared on this earth pure and free: We only later became tainted and constrained through repeated negative responses or implicit role-modeling from others—from other children but especially the adults around us. Their encumbrances and inhibitions became ours. They can remain ours to carry for years, even decades—and it's been my experience that only if we embrace them can we ever lay them down.

I cannot speak for my long-estranged-from-me siblings; I can only surmise how they internalized then later coped with the emotional burdens that we three Luick-Thrams kids inherited from our frustrated farmer father and our sweet-but-timid mother. Both my sister and brother turned to a

Donald with sisters Velma (left) and Voral, circa 1919

"born-again" Christianity that was foreign to our parents' home, while I turned to the opposite of fundamentalism—to the universalist worldview of the empirical spirituality embodied by many of the Quakers I met over time, in numerous countries, of various ages and conditions.

Little Debbie, 1960; Cary Grant in Alfred Hitchcock's 1959 Great-Plains thriller North by Northwest

My sister once said that had she gone on to study rather than marry and become a mother within months of leaving Clear Lake High, she would have liked to have studied psychology. I wish she had. Determined to erase some of the bad scripting we three received in the tense, emotionally confused-and-confusing environment at Ashlawn Farm, I consulted a small army of psychologists or even (only twice, out of desperation) psychiatrists, career counselors and life coaches, re-birthers, shamans or psychics, massage and reflexology therapists, priests, rabbis, mullahs, Buddhist monks and Catholic nuns. Had Deb become a shrink I would've saved a ton o' money had I been able to seek comfort and direction in-house, for cheap!

As it was, I came to the conclusion that most psychologists usually *became* one because, at least at first, they *needed* one. Still, to my friend Alan's feedback I say "there's no moral judgment there, since"—to briefly channel Albert Camus—"we all take turns being both victims and executioners. We are hurt early on and, until we understand the sources and causes of that trespass, we let the emotional pus of our unseen wounds ooze out onto the lives of others. We each, then, have the task, the responsibility of (ad)dressing our own wounds. It is a sort of damage-control asked of us as we temporarily occupy a space on a crowded, strained planet.

Luwarren "Bud," Phyllis, Debra, David and Michael Luick family: Christmas 1965 at Floyd home in Knoxville, Iowa; Easter mid-1990s at Ashlawn Farm; 18 December 2004 in Lincoln, Nebraska

some practical notes:

This chronicle begins with my parents and childhood home, then reaches back generation by generation, across the Atlantic and the ages. The lineages explored in a given section are presented in pedigree form at the beginning of that section, as well as detailed further in the footnotes at the end of volume III, *Tap Roots Betrayed*, which provide sources of specific, factual data or interpretive information. And, additional "outtake" texts and photos are available at www.roots.TRACES.org.

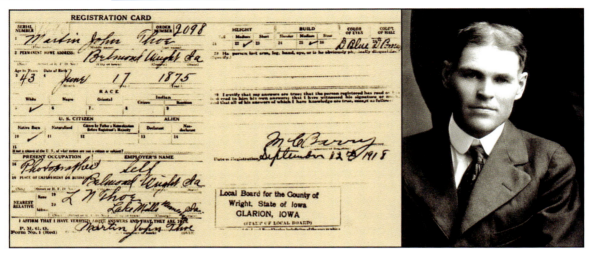

Martin John Thoe's World War I-era draft-registration card, 12 September 1918, and portrait, 1910s

use of special photograph collection:

Through the generous courtesy of the Belmond Historical Society, later sections of the first three volumes of this pentalogy feature images of rare quality by an obscure photographer, Martin John Thoe. Little is known about this enigmatic man other than the most basic of facts, which refuse to betray much of revealing value about him.

Born 17 June 1875 in Lake Mills, Iowa, of Norwegian stock, by 1908 he moved to Belmond, where he opened a photography studio by 1911 that survived into the late 1930s. By 1912 Thoe opened—with brother-in-law Harry Nordschow—also a car dealership on East Main. On 12 September 1918—less than two months before the fighting ended—the 43-year-old man registered for World War I. He died 4 July 1960 in Lake Mills, where he is buried.

The man and his singular photographic skills likely would have vanished with the tides of time had it not been for the massive tornado which destroyed much of downtown Belmond just as the Homecoming Day parade came to an end on 14 October 1966. In the aftermath of the monster storm (which claimed six lives and injured over 170), the people of the determined town hauled debris to the local dump by the truck load. One day, a worker found some wooden boxes full of antique glass negatives and brought them back into Belmond for closer inspection. Realizing the treasure that had been found, volunteers combed through the mountains of refuse and, in the end, recovered some seven thousand negatives and photos; more are stewarded in Iowa Historical Society's collection.

BHS member Don Bancroft provided me a sampling of less than a hundred of Thoe's thousands of images of the locals who populated the early-20th-century world my Luick-Jenison-Brooks ancestors and other relatives inhabited in Belmond, a community first settled by that extensive clan in the early 1850s. I have selected a few to illustrate the sort of hardy souls who transformed the prairie into what they deemed "civilization," the American Heartland that millions of Midwesterners have called "home" for almost two centuries.

The simple gift that lends the touch of friendship without the embarrassment of an obligation--

YOUR PHOTOGRAPH

The Thoe Studio

PART I
Rebels with Causes

Section 1:
Bud & Phyllis (Thrams) Luick family

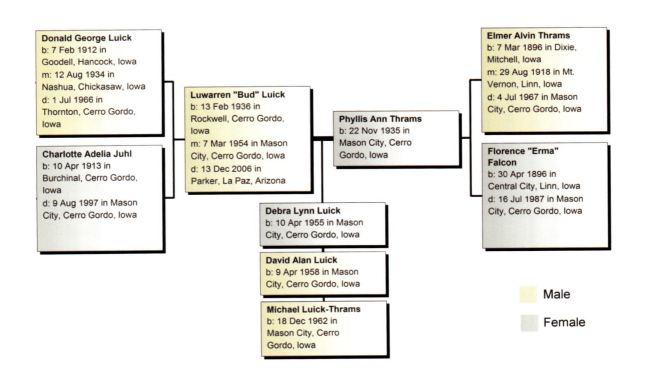

Luwarren Myrle Luick's nuclear family

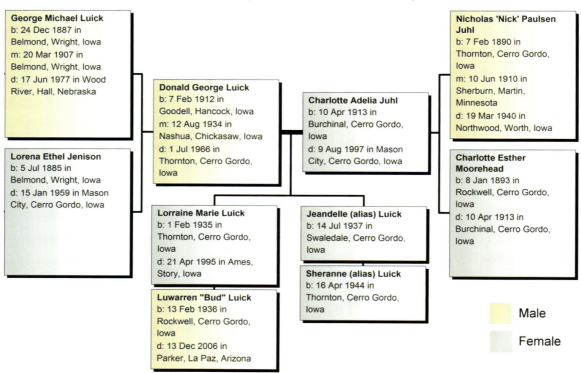

Phyllis Ann Thrams' nuclear family

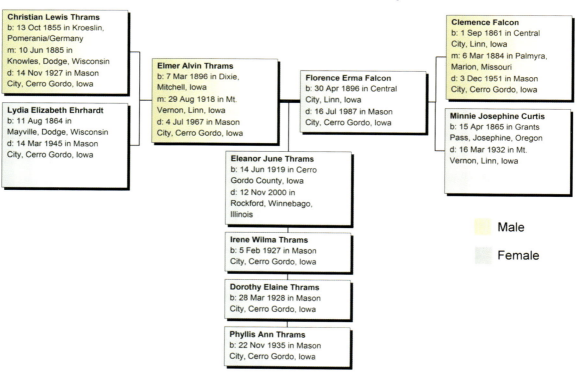

Luwarren Myrle "Bud" and Phyllis Ann (Thrams) Luick

born:	13 February 1936	22 November 1935
where:	Rockwell, Iowa/USA	Mason City, Iowa/USA
married:	7 March 1954	**where:** First Methodist Church, Mason City, Iowa/USA
died:	13 December 2006	
where:	Lake Havasu, Arizona/USA	

Looks truly can be deceiving. The below photo was taken in 1968 for Clear Lake's Methodist church directory. My siblings Debra and David, I and our parents, Bud and Phyllis, might have looked the part of the Happy Midwest Farm Family in days of yore, but lava swirled below the surface. All broke smiles except me when the photographer cracked a joke, then flashed the bulb while snapping his shutter. The cheery image captured on film belied the chaos and stress awaiting us behind the fake backdrop—and that fit the tenor of the times, if or not we knew it.

"Mike" (left), Dave, Phyllis, Deb and Bud Luick; Clear Lake United Methodist Church directory, 1968

Under the teachings of Confucius, ancient Chinese sages advised that "wise men [presumably wise women, too] understand the times in which they live." Apart from maybe some half-dozen shipwrecked souls scattered across South Pacific islands undetected and not yet rescued, no family, no person lives fully separate and untouched by the surrounding state of human affairs. Though we Luicks lived in semi-seclusion at isolated, well buffered Ashlawn Farm during the last gasps of a Victorian America unwilling to go gently, our lives were punctuated by social tumult. To grow up in the United States during the 1960s and early '70s was to tiptoe between anger and *Angst*—for me, in the barnyard as well as in the wider world that began just past the front gate. Although my family might have wished to have been spared the effects of events unfolding far beyond our protective prairies and our abilities to comprehend their meaning, we couldn't avoid feeling the rumblings of the political and social upheavals then afoot in the world.

The 1960s began quietly enough. At 70 the then-oldest U.S. president, grandfatherly Dwight Eisenhower (a Kansas Mennonite boy turned military man) surrendered the presidency to eager Jack Kennedy, at 43 then the youngest. This, though, Eisenhower did not do readily: before the election he told friends "I will do almost anything to avoid turning my chair and country over to [him]." This generational change, from cautious decorated general to confident junior senator, hinted at the transitions of power, passions and ideas that would shape the rest of the decade. We felt this tense, protracted transfer even in rural Iowa and in our own home. The struggle would be often ugly and claim many victims—innocent or not.

chapter 67: clash of cultures

Despite the twists and turns it eventually would take, what became Luwarren Myrle Luick's lifelong relationship with the Thrams family began with a flickering flirt. He unexpectedly met Phyllis Ann (his future mate) at the North Iowa Fair in summer 1952. It was the first year girls were allowed to keep and show livestock as 4-H projects. The few Lake Ambitious Vestae club-member girls showing stock that pilot year bedded their animals with those of the all-boy Lake Ambitious Feeders 4-H Club. Their appointed section of the fairground's open-sided cattle barn happened to be across the aisle from that of the Thornton Farmhands, a competing boys club.

As 16-year old "Phyl" curried her cross-bred Hereford heifer, she heard a playful "Oh, you're not doin' it right." She turned to see ebony-haired "Bud" from the Thornton Farmhands. He stood behind her, grinning. As he'd won a purple ribbon with his purebred, grand-champion Black Angus steer, she gladly surrendered the curry comb to the superior showman. "He did such a beautiful job grooming that calf," she'd recall, years later.

a Mason City banker buying Bud's champion steer at the North Iowa Fair winners' auction, August 1952

"I wish you could help me when we take our calves back into the ring to be auctioned," Phyllis teased. Ready to rise to the challenge, my future father then spent more time grooming her calf than his own—expertly, for Mom's white-ribbon heifer fetched only 50 cents less per pound than her would-be suitor's grand champion. Later, his father Donald scolded him for having "squandered [his] chances" on some unknown girl's behalf.

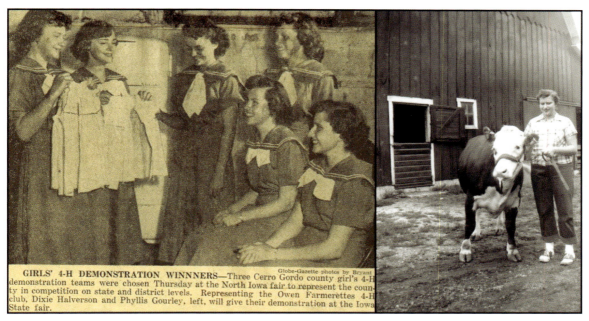

Phyllis at a 4-H demonstration (left photo, lower right) and with heifer in front of Ashlawn Farm's barn

Bud informed Phyllis "You owe me—big time!"

"What does that mean?" she teased coyly.

"You have to go on a date with me" he shot back. She promised him, that she would…

What the innocent teens from the prairie didn't consider, however, was that the melding of the Luick and Thrams clans might be a questionable project from the start. By the time my parents married in

1954, the Luicks had already roamed across the American landscape for over 120 years. Old Heinrich Luick had fled Stuttgart with two brothers for faraway *Amerika* due to a capital offense, and ever since the Luick clan had been headed by restless, often violent men who lurched from one post to the next. They towed along large, patchwork families and supported them with diverse work as, at various times: joiner-carpenter, surveyor, road grader, railway builder, canal digger, gold panner, stage or school-bus driver, delivery man, fruit picker, sheep shearer, cowboy, cattle puncher, butcher, restaurateur, soda jerk—almost every non-professional job imaginable except that of sailor or mercenary. Beyond each, typically short-term employment, Luick men dabbled in some sort of farming—even if only kitchen gardens or for niche markets. Even small-scale food production meant something could be scraped together to feed ever-hungry mouths.

Three of my mother's four grandparents hailed from families that had owned land in the United States for almost a hundred years. That rootedness lent ballast and temperance to decisions and actions alike. The Luicks, on the other hand, lived on the land of others as easy-come-easy-go tenants or subsistence sharecroppers. Beyond their lack of solid capital, though—or, rather, *because* of it—the Luicks differed from the Thramses in how, not just where they lived.

As youths, my mother and many of her relatives took music lessons built on Methodist hymns and classical airs. With few exceptions my father's people did not make much music—and when they did, as with great-great-grampa Louis' roadhouse foursome or Dad's high-school drumming stint, such efforts echoed ragtime or marching-band tunes.

Ah, the carefree '50s! While Jeandelle an' Bud marched with the Thornton High band, Phyl tickled ivory.

Charcoal drawing and fine woodworking stilled Grandpa Thrams' artistic itch; nimble-fingered crocheting, tatting and quilting kept his wife's hands productive even during Grandma's "free time." The Luicks, however, left no artistic heirlooms behind. Until 1959, they left no plumbing behind, either: The Thramses afforded themselves the luxury of running water—complete with a tub that could draw both hot and cold—and an indoor toilet thirty-four years before the Luicks did in their home, only a few miles away. While Grandma Thrams cooked on a gas-fueled stove since the 1920s, Gramma Luick toiled away on a smoky coal-or-cob burner until as late as the winter of 1959-60.

Grandma Thrams in a wartime home-safety demo photo; boarding an Amsterdam canal-tour boat, 1970s

By the time Grandma Thrams turned 83 she had been in every U.S. state save Alaska and had toured Europe twice. Travel for the stay-at-home Luicks seemed a necessary-but-joyless movement of bodies or goods from one site of failed attempts to the next—rarely a pleasure in itself. And, speaking of edifying pleasures: Thrams households all had well-stocked book shelves. At birthdays or holidays the gift of a book from Aunts Eleanor or Bernice could be assumed, and Mom read to us kids long beyond the age that many peers' parents had stopped. Gramma Luick once presented me with a mid-sized, dime-store globe for Christmas, but I don't remember getting a single title or seeing any books at her house except for a bible placed where all would notice it.

My folks came from families with fully different goals and concerns. As of the late 1800s, some half dozen of Mom's people had attended college. Conversely, had Dad mustered the mettle to earn his dreamed-of veterinarian degree, he would have been the first male in his lineage to study beyond high school. "Only playboys go to college" his father Donald taunted, so Dad's dream remained a fantasy and he embraced the alibi that Thornton High had failed to prepare him for college-level math and chemistry courses. "How'd we have found the money to study?" he argued later, to which Mom always nodded, having so jettisoned her own visions of becoming a home-economics teacher.

Dad (in dark sweater) at the center of his Thornton school class, during WWII; a veterinarian checks a dog

Bud and Phyllis always paid great heed to what their families thought and did. The problem was, the two clans moved in divided, divergent orbits. Thrams family reunions, for example, were grand affairs planned months in advance with dozens of immediate as well as distant relatives in attendance, who came from as far afield as New Jersey and North Carolina, Oregon and Arizona. Luick gatherings, in contrast, consisted of obligatory, last-minute holiday get-togethers, with Grampa and Gramma, their son and three daughters, in-laws and grandchildren on hand.

And, the food each family served spoke volumes about differing ideas of hospitality and style. At such fetes Grandma Thrams and her four daughters served mounds of meat with rounds of potatoes and vegetables, followed by a table full of homemade desserts. At Gramma Luick's house we picked through over-done roast and compilations of cottage cheese, iceberg lettuce and grated carrots entombed in watered down, mismatch-flavored Jell-O, capped with Cool- or, worse, Miracle-Whip, followed by sugary, store-bought pies.

Thrams-family picnic at Ashlawn Farm, summer 1963: standing, (l. to r.) Irene (Thrams) Floyd, me as infant, Marcia Hunt, Thurman Floyd, Bud & Dave Luick, Hank Bredenbeck, Phyllis (Thrams) Luick, Jack Hunt & Erma (Falcon) Thrams; seated, from the right, Elmer Thrams, Eleanor (Thrams) Hunt, Terry Hunt, and Steve Floyd

Whereas the Thrams' civic engagements gravitated toward the cultural, educational and spiritual, the Luicks' social activities were fewer and favored the practical. In January 2014 Phyllis recalled her parents and parents-in-law as having been involved in the following bodies; others didn't occur to her:

Elmer and Erma Thrams' civic affiliations…	**…and those of Donald and Charlotte Luick:**
Daughters of the American Revolution	Democratic Party of Cerro Gordo County
Iowa State College Extension Service	Lions Club of Thornton
Lake's Ambitious Vestae 4-H Club	Methodist women's circles
Methodist women's circles	National Farmers Organization
Order of the Eastern Star	Thornton Farmhands 4-H Club
Oweso [local farmwomen's] Club	Thornton School Board
District #5 Parent-Teachers Association	
Republican Party of Cerro Gordo County	

Erma & Elmer Thrams (3rd & 6th persons seated on table's left) at a banquet, mid-1950s

Random alphabetization of the two lists places the Thrams' membership in the Republican Party of Cerro Gordo County diametrically opposite the Luicks' affiliation with the Democratic one. That value-neutral coincidence perfectly reflects the central conflict between two families that shared little other than Methodism, 4-H and their offspring's choice in a mate. While the tee-totaling Thramses may have shunned card playing or dancing on Sundays, swearing and women publicly wearing pants as late as the 1940s, the Luicks showed few of the same prohibitions.

With their cumulative sins of assault and battery (Heinrich's long German shadow again), alcoholism (Gramma's father), incest (a creeping emotional cancer) and a hereditary weakness for adultery (read on), the Luicks may have had more fun than their comparatively staid counterparts, but they also held many hostages and left far more casualties. Yes, the Thramses aspired to—and, at times, affected—bourgeois notions of The Good Life, but at least the list of emotional landmines they passed from generation to generation was shorter and easier to erase through therapy.

―――

chapter 68: winds of war

A person's (or family's) thoughts and actions as seen outside his or her own four walls are only extensions of those taking place every day, every hour inside those walls. Coming from the Greek word for "the city," our burdened term "politics" refers to how one moves through one's community (these days, myopically seen as "the state"). It embodies how we juggle the needs as well as neuroses of others with our own, and how we share resources and potentials—or not.

Whether inner demons or societal saints were directing the two clans, the Thramses' and Luicks' political activism, then, reflected publicly what was flowing—or churning—inside them, privately. Steady-handed Grandma Thrams, for one, volunteered to staff local polling stations and draft boards for years, but never would have dreamed of parading her politics out on the streets—even as across the driveway hot-headed Dad was doing just that.

my mother's parents, Florence Erma (Falcon) and Elmer Alvin Thrams on Ashlawn Farm, 1950s

At the same time as the wholesome, contentment-lulled church directory photo of the "Luwarren Luick family" was going to print in some brightly-lit backroom, Dad and a handful of like-minded neighbors—including a new friend, fellow occasional activist Ben Muff—were going to bat in a dark shed, developing a daring and visible protest. Active in the nascent National Farmers Organization (the NFO), the men cobbled together a 4th of July [U.S. Independence Day] float. Ironically, their bold-yet-mute dissent featured a sawed-off plywood pyramid perched atop a trailer chassis—a stump resembling the structure on the back of the U.S. dollar bill, long claimed by some to hint at a secret, Illuminati-esque elite that "really runs America." After whitewashing it with thinned house paint, they hung alfalfa-green-and-stark-white NFO signs and stenciled inciting slogans in big, shiny-black letters on three sides, then trimmed their spectacle with eye-commanding bunting and crepe-paper streamers.

man in Rupert, Idaho with sign around neck, "We are only asking 2 [cents] a quart increase—NFO" while a family carries a sign reading "We like farming but can't do it for fun alone. Support NFO"

The motive behind Dad's and his cohorts' unorthodox demonstration was to support the 150,000 or so NFO members' hit-or-miss attempts to collectively bargain for higher, more stable commodity prices. The NFO's most result-yielding act had been the Holding Action of 1967, when that March member dairy producers withheld milk from the market for fifteen days, until a Federal judge issued a temporary restraining order. Ultimately the Johnson administration negotiated a settlement agreeable to the NFO leadership. By then, however, the organization's rank and file had acquired the tainted label of "radical" and thus became anathema to rural Americans made uneasy by urban unrest and jarring daily headlines from a distant jungle war. It was more than their intrinsically conservative natures could bear.

Blue Earth, Minnesota, family dumping milk, while women do same in Herkimer County, New York

Paradoxically, Dad and Mom had given up our small dairy herd a decade earlier, as had almost all of our neighbors. Furthermore, both the float's creation and its provocative showing seemed to take place without a long-range strategy. The parade goers lined up along Clear Lake's mile-long Main Street were waiting to see ever-smiling beauty queens and hear marching bands, to scramble for hard candy tossed in waves or to stand with covered hearts as surviving veterans dating back as far as to World War I solemnly filed by. They didn't come to be fed down-on-the-farm political fare.

NFO president Oren Lee Stanley answers questions at milk-pouring protest in Corning, Iowa, with signs with "Save our Family Farm from going down the Drain;" demonstrators (right) gathered outside milk-processing plant in St. Louis holding signs "Handlers let's make a deal. N.F.O." or "Have cow, will milk, but not for less" and "If you don't get milk, don't blame us, blame the processors"—all from mid-1960s

Despite their mostly unreceptive and non-responsive audience, Dad and associates felt ready to risk finger-wagging, head-shaking disapproval in order to shove a figurative fist in the face of a system they saw as stacked against them. After they and their clunky float had their day, however, they quietly backed that lumbering hulk into the dank, lightless lean-to attached to our ancient corncrib—and forgot it there.

NFO protest at White House with sign "Farmers get 15 [cents] for pork. What does your wife pay?"

Even as a clueless kid I sensed an air of impropriety about the whole affair. It was if my defiant dad and his accomplices were engaged in something clandestine, about which we youngsters should never speak. Later, when I was a teenager doing novice family-history research for the bicentennial, then again when I was a history student at Iowa State writing a biopsy of the 1980s farm crisis as seen through my family's experience, Dad consistently sidestepped my repeated inquiries about his own NFO-supporting father. He responded, if at all, with non-committal vagueness. Were his unresolved issues with that aloof, eerie figure too agonizing to allow Dad to speak freely about a man who clearly had caused him so much pain—or were Dad's passive-aggressive dismissals his way of protecting us kids from things too complex for us to understand or truths too harsh to bear?

Like so much in the collective Luick résumé, Dad's and his dad's, Donald's, NFO activities turned out to be too short-lived and too lone-wolf in nature to generate lasting gain. Still, any one of the multitude of causes Dad or Grampa Luick at one time or another espoused arose out of a generations-long tradition of fighting for underdogs—a predilection I inherited, have yet to shake, and likely never will.

———

Life, however, is not made up of social constellations and political passions alone. What most differentiated Bud and Phyllis from their parents when they married (at 18, still teenagers) were the technologies then at hand, coupled with a willingness to use them.

(back row) Irene, Dorothy & Eleanor; (seated) Elmer, Phyllis & Erma (Falcon) Thrams, circa 1945

For both sets of their parents, Bud and Phyllis' generation seemed alien from their own. Grandpa and Grandma Thrams had been born in 1896, one year before the downturn left by the Wall Street "panic" of 1893 finally faded in the face of returning capital. The future partners were only two years old when the re-ascendant United States entered war with Spain on manipulated grounds. After Spain, a centuries-long super-power, sued for peace within only ten weeks of the first shot, the U.S. annexed vast regions spread across half the globe. That coup ushered in what some would hail as the "American

Century," a colossus that provided an all-defining backdrop for the rest of Elmer and Erma's lives. Growing up in the prewar prosperity of what Europe celebrated as the "Belle Époque," Grandpa and Grandma Thrams reached adulthood knowing neither lasting want nor serious hardship. That, in an age where life still passed at a horse's pace: When they married in 1917 automobiles were so novel that Grandpa built their own—a motor mounted on four wheels, with a plank atop the gas tank as a seat.

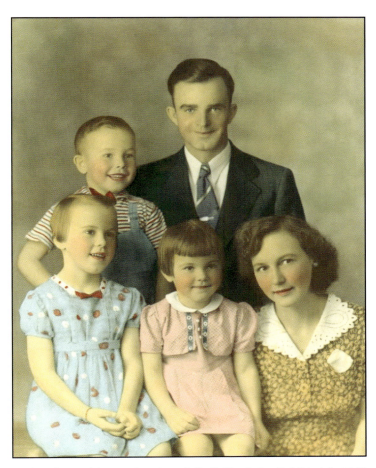

Bud and Donald; Lorraine, Jeandelle & Charlotte (Juhl) Luick, 1941

Similarly, but belonging to a generation later, my father's parents also grew up under radically different conditions from Bud and Phyllis. Born respectively in 1912 and 1913, Dad's father and mother were about to start school when the U.S. belatedly joined its European cousins in slugging out the First World War. By the time the Axis collapsed, Donald was not yet seven and his future bride, Charlotte, was just five and a half years old. They, too, spent childhoods marked by what seemed to be peace and endless economic boom—until, of course, the heady fiscal frenzy built on shaky credit and sham stock came crashing down as the two were to complete high school.

Still, so long as the '20s continued to roar all seemed well, as across the country unfettered consumption spun ever faster the wheels of an over-heated economy. Industrial production expanded. Urban as well as rural construction swelled. Between 1910 and 1930, the U.S. became fully automobilized; pavement elevated previous mud-and-dust byways into the first hard-surfaced highways. And, most intoxicating of all, there came an omnipresence of gadgets—radios and electrical appliances, along with cars, tractors, the first trans-continental passenger planes—and comforts such as running water and indoor toilets became the norm in most of the nation's cities.

Until, that is, all the gadgets in the world couldn't hold a cracked economy together any more. By then, though, Dad's still-single parents had come to assume Good Times would last for all time.

History, however, had different plans.

Born in the mid-1930s, Bud and Phyllis grew up under fundamentally different conditions from their parents. Even as they were learning to speak, they heard ever-louder talk of war clouds gathering over Europe. As tots, my parents were weaned on a steady diet of hawk, fed to them by Hitler & Co. and his Allied foes. As their only son, at age five Dad was forced to drive a tractor so his folks could cash in on wartime commodities prices even though he couldn't reach its pedals while sitting. And Mom, by the time she reached the first grade at Lake Township District #5's rural one-room school, spent recess with her classmates combing nearby ditches for milkweed silk with which to make airmen's parachutes. As a body, during recess and after school they collected scrap metal and bomb-bound kitchen fat.

Mom (behind tallest girl) and classmates with "Miss (Lillian) Neu" at Lake Township #5 during WWII

    Neither of my then-juvenile parents could escape being forever affected by the troubling tension of the times, by the intensity of the deadliest war that humanity had ever known. Pre-teens when it finally ground to an explosive end, my parents' early adolescence was filled with frightening images of nuclear mushroom clouds…

nuclear weapon test "Romeo" on Bikini Atoll, 27 March 1954

...and surrounded by scenes from Nazi concentration camps.

survivors liberated at Mauthausen concentration camp, 5 May 1945

In a kind of socio-psychological double-whammy, overnight my parents' first decade of deprivation born by the Great Depression, then dictated by wartime rationing and forced austerity, flipped into a flurry of postwar consumption. Having deferred gratification for more than a decade and a half of crippling unemployment followed by deadly global warfare, as the troops trundled home millions of Americans turned from public projects to private pleasures. Abruptly, Bud and Phyllis had to navigate an unfamiliar course from scarcity to satiation. At times, it overwhelmed them.

Marcia Hunt posing with her "Aunt Phyllis" and the family car in Ashlawn Farm's barnyard, circa 1950

My parents had spent their youth in an era of few consumer choices; as young adults they often agonized over even the simplest, low-cost purchases. After they married, our family was never really rich yet also seldom truly poor. Cash rarely flowed in our household; it trickled—from Dad's ragged, black-leather wallet. Coming from opposing cultural galaxies as they did, Mom's oft-touted "champagne taste on a beer budget" constantly collided with Dad's threadbare background.

An incorrigible ambience addict, the woman waded through waves of furnishing fads and dragged us kids with her into the ensuing moral muck. Mirroring the decorative tackiness of those dissonant times, we had no choice but suffer through her macramé and decoupage obsessions, as well as her pop-art phases—like when she plastered the bathroom with cadmium-red tulips and (mercifully, briefly) stuck yellow smiley faces to surfaces all throughout the house, then overran the kitchen with mushrooms of every conceivable shape, shade and size. (And, on the side, she secretly supplied her co-junkie, Grandma Thrams, with good-quality owl kitsch—in the form of statues, macramé, on porcelain, etc.)

When Dad, as the ultimate purse-string holder of her manic shopping sprees, caught Mom trying to sneak some new "must-have" adornment into our already overflowing house, he would stab the air in her direction with an angry index finger and spout loud words of disgust, then storm out the back door to "get some work done." Within seconds, however, Phyllis already could be found plotting her next covert purchase.

Initially, Mom's exposed transgressions would end in heartfelt promises of future self-restraint and spiritual reform. Later, however, as we all realized that her ornamentation addictions already had advanced to incurable stages, she began to hide her fixes. She would slip earth-toned 'shrooms hand-painted on battered bits of driftwood into the back of an overlooked buffet drawer—then simply wait for her ruse to be revealed.

Inevitably, while he dug in a drawer for a forlorn checkbook that once again had succumbed to my parents' eternal bookkeeping chaos, Dad would feel something suspicious under a stiff-ironed table cloth, grab it like some snapping, arch-backed crab under a stony river-bottom refuge, then whip it out into the disrobing light of day.

"What the hell is *this* piece o' crap?" he'd demand.

"Oh" Mom would respond truthfully, with cool but phony nonchalance, "that ol' thing? I've had it for months."

my parents in front of Mom's prized "rural rustica" mural in the living room at Ashlawn Farm, mid-1980s

———

chapter 69: 'til blood flowed

Bud and Phyllis' recurrent ambiguity toward—and palpable discomfort with—monetary matters complicated Dad's ambitions to modernize the technology that still ran the Thrams place when they took it over from Grandpa and Grandma in January 1963, a month after I was born. Dad strove to revolutionize how work and production at Ashlawn Farm would be fueled, to replace literal horsepower with petro-power. Until he retired, Grandpa Thrams had happily tapped a team of horses—an energy source already then decades out-of-date—to get heavy work done.

More times than not any hands-on work with an individual animal would end in someone getting a thorough beating—and it wouldn't be Dad. Debbie, but more typically David or, later, I would be ordered to hold a horse with a nose winch, stop a steer by the halter, or lock our clenched fingers under the base of a lamb's docked tail so that Dad could (respectively) trim its hooves, style its forelock for the fair, or de-worm its wooly little self. What normally began as a reasonable, benevolent mission almost always ended as an unreasonable, vicious contest of wills. By nature and in contrast to humans, animals can't be reasoned with—and their instinct for self-preservation is stronger than any winch, halter or teenager's scared-stiff, curled fingers.

David with prize-winning lambs at the North Iowa Fair, 1968; purple constituted the highest honor

Doctor Dad would start treating bestial insolence by threatening resistant four-legged patients with obscenities. If harsh words didn't work (which they hardly ever did) his remedial repertoire would graduate to confining them by applying several twists to an already torturously painful nose winch, pushing a "dumb animal" to the wall with a wire or plywood panel, knocking it to the ground and sitting on it or, bloodiest of all, knocking it unconscious. If all this failed to secure utter submission, he'd then attack the increasingly panicked animal with heavier weapons—first, a shovel. (Each season we must have gone through a half-dozen aluminum scoop shovels, reduced to scrap metal over some pitiable pig's head or unfortunate cow's backside.)

If that failed, Dad would grab an ax handle—at least one of which I remember him breaking over some skull. Or, he could whip scurrying little legs with a long rubber hose. Or, he'd poke a rebellious creature with an electric stock prod. Of course, during the application of amassing physical force, Dad's psychological pressure mounted, too. Swearing advanced to shouting, which then progressed to shrill screaming. By that stage, I felt like breaking free and running away myself.

During such horrific sieges I had the feeling Dad's knock-down-drag-out battles with livestock had little to do with the moment-by-moment reactions of an animal which happened to be "on" that day. Rather, with every stroke of a stinging lead rope or bruising ax handle against the flank, the back, neck or head of a miserable beast, I felt Dad's swelling fury had less to do with them and more to do with him. His bullying, his curses peppered with "damn you, you son-of-a-bitch" or "I'll show you" seemed targeted at something, at someone very much "present" yet eerily invisible. I wondered what fueled his blind fits—fear of being unable to cope? Did he dread being proved inadequate? Or, was it the litany of disappointments which filled not only his own résumé, but his father's, and his father's, and—?

Although he seldom tolerated us asking about or discussing Grampa Luick, Dad referred to his own father frequently—in brief, staccato references that betrayed Donald's occupying a permanent space in Dad's head, but hardly anything of telling substance about the man. His father's undying presence weighed on what was, in likely truth, Dad's tender, fragile heart.

Had Bud learned how to treat critters—how to treat anything or anyone, any experience or emotion—as Donald's involuntary apprentice? If so, at what price? I don't know, but there are clues. My brother once reported that Dad told him he would wake up shaken and sweat-soaked, having dreamt that his father had been standing at the foot of the bed.

———

Dad, though, was not the only Luick male who struggled with "father issues:" David and I did, too. Even as I braced my feet against blood-stained ground and clasped burning ropes to restrain flailing animals as Dad ordered, I agonized with them. With each lash or blow they suffered, I winced myself. Still, as much as witnessing their ordeal crushed my soul, I silently whispered thanks, that instead of me, they were "gettin' it." Oh, there was enough bottled-up ire boiling in Dad for me to get my daily dose later, but—mercifully, for me—beings more defenseless than his own dependents bore the brunt of Dad's deep, sorrow-born wrath.

We three kids tip-toed through our childhood days at Ashlawn Farm, never knowing what stray word or hurried move might set loose a cascade of swats, slaps or slugs. I don't remember Dad ever striking Deb, but the psychological warfare that flashed between the two of them felt total and overwhelming. David would get a kick in the pants but, like Debbie, he seemed to kowtow to our father in exchange for being allowed to slip away even while Dad's dirty mouth continued to spout clouds of curse-laced verbal assaults. And, as for me?

Deb and Dave didn't seem to mind, but Dad's steering our every move (at least at times, early on) drove me mad. Just study closely these two telling scenes at Ashlawn Farm in October 1962 (left) and summer 1963!

I fought back—eventually. Initially, though, I had no idea what had happened to the playful, affectionate "Daddy" I'd previously known—and that not knowing rendered me defenseless in the face of what as a dejected child seemed to me to be a livid lunatic.

My earliest memories of Bud Luick center around a beaming, doting young man lifting me to the ceiling—both of us content and relaxed. I'd giggle uncontrollably as he'd roll me back and forth between his big, sturdy hands, just below the ceiling. Then, making a swooshing sound between his upper dentures and lower teeth, he'd let me drop halfway to the floor. At first this sudden loss of support terrified me, but once I came to believe that Dad was there for me, that he'd always be there for me, I squealed with delight, pointed to the ceiling longingly and begged "play airplane wit' me again." Daddy gladly obliged—at first, anyway.

Grandpa Thrams with his team, & family on a bobsled ride: Irene, Elmer, Erma, Phyllis & "Dot"

Oh, Grandpa and Uncle Willard (his older brother and ghost business partner in farming) had long owned a simple tractor or two, plus the small-sized bolt-on equipment to match those engines-on-wheels. Still, Elmer clung to much-loved beasts with names like "Doc" and "Dolly" solely for romantic reasons. He loved working closely with such magnificent animals, the way they strode across the farmyard or field, how they moved so deliberately, so confidently, so loyally. Whether watching their muscles shudder to dislodge biting horseflies in summer or listening to them snort steaming breath into the frosty winter air as they pulled the bulky bobsled across the snow-covered fields, Grandpa remained fascinated by these docile giants long after other, less sentimental farmers had shipped theirs off to glue or dog-food factories.

Dad's push to mechanize his adopted farm wasn't because he didn't like horses; he loved them. As a boy, just after World War II ended, he was riding with his father one day on an errand near Estherville and recalled later how it broke his heart to see "pen after pen, as far as an eye could see, of big, strong, perfectly good draft horses waiting to be shipped off to…" at which his voice would trail off. Over the years, I heard Dad relay that remorseful anecdote repeatedly.

Little "Buddy" could ride a horse (or, in this case, a pony) soon after he could walk—like shown here, above left, around his familiy's farmyard. By the time he was a teen, Dad had mastered many of the equestrian arts needed not only to be a skilled rider (above right), but help us three kids (David at the North Iowa Fair, circa 1970, lower left) or future grandsons (lower right, from the left: Jared, Ian and Jamin Wass in the 1980s) master a few of our own.

My father's appreciation for horses (and Golden Retrievers) was so strong that even as a kid I sensed a deeper connection. I'd often follow him out to the pasture—typically late on summer evenings as the orange-glowing sun promised to set. When the scorching prairie air had cooled a bit Dad would carry a five-gallon, white-plastic pail "out ta give the horses a treat." He would dribble little mounds of molasses-covered oats with a touch of cracked corn in a broad circle around the slight rise between our barnyard and the one at Benners' Grove to the south. As the mares and their frisky colts trotted up to claim a mound or two, Bud would step backwards to the top of the rise, quietly set down the pail, then simply stand and watch "his" herd munch on the sticky grain. His equine prizes only stopped to stomp pesky gnats from their shins or swing their big chomping heads towards their flank to dislodge a particularly stubborn horsefly. A barely visible grin would then give way to a faint smile, as deep contentment won over Dad's entire face. At those moments, even kicked-about little Mike knew there had to be more than just darkness in the heart of a man who could so thoroughly appreciate such magnificent creatures.

the "hill" (it's Iowa after all!) south of Ashlawn Farm's building site, where Dad fed his horses treats

Reflecting what at least in the abstract was a love of animals, among Dad's rather few guarded possessions were two handed-down, hardbound husbandry books from the '20s. Whenever he reluctantly allowed me to turn the dog-eared pages, regardless of which livestock breed, need, distinguishing characteristic or disorder I might mention, Dad could give long discourses on it, retrieving details that had been etched into his mind since his youth.

My father's reverence for animal science—although frustrated by what he assumed was a permanent, perhaps even cursed inability to enter or pass college—translated into an exceptional respect he showed trained veterinarians. Whether we paid a rare visit to a vet's practice or, more typically, a vet made an on-site call to our barnyard, I can't remember contrary Dad ever openly contradicting a vet. Later, over a rushed sandwich lunch or seated at chronically late dinner, Dad would recount to Mom in exacting detail what a given vet had said and done. The very way he did it conveyed an awed deference.

The respect he had for those who doctored our animals, however, did not translate into respect for the animals themselves. In theory, Dad loved animals—but in practice? Not so much. Actually, he could identify so intrinsically with non-humans that he seemed to possess an extra sense, an ability to know what a given creature was feeling, thinking, planning. He knew in what direction she or he was about to head (handy when sorting market-ready individuals from herds), what that animal most would want to eat (helpful in selecting bait with which to lure renegades back to captivity), where a critter most likely would sleep (crucial to wisely investing costly bedding, as well as where not to ineffectively spread it)—and so on. The problem was, his empathy with the inner beings of quadrupeds was so accurate, so close to their essence, that he also often projected *his* feelings onto *them*. That was the point where raw misery really began.

———

From early on the "baby" of the family, I was at the receiving end of a hail storm of mixed emotional messages from kinfolk. On one hand, I was so cute that I actually would be paraded around for all to see and, presumably, adore. Long before I entered kindergarten, Grandma Thrams would dress me in a pastel pink, blue and yellow bunny suit and take me to "visit friends." My stubby, cottony tail bouncing behind me, I carried a plastic-grass-lined basket, filled (depending on the season) with chocolate Easter eggs or Brach's candy corn from the Ben Franklin five-and-dime store.

Our smile-sowing tours took us to many of North Central Iowa's "old folks' homes"—in those days mostly converted private houses that could accommodate a handful of seniors no longer self-reliant or whose families could not care for them. Often, the "staff" of such homes consisted of members of one family, perhaps with hired, part-time helpers—or not.

"Mike an' Daddy" in happier days, before our years-long duel began

The innate ham in me reveled in those outings—except, that is, for the odd uncomfortable moment, like when one confused codger kept asking "Who's that silly kid behind the stupid bunny mask?" He then pulled it down until he broke the elastic string, revealing my true identity—a shielded secret up until that humiliating instant.

Dad and Dave with Lassie (left) and my siblings with her puppies, winter 1961-62, near Swaledale, Iowa

All the attention indulged me antagonized the two people who should have been my closest allies, Deb and Dave. Well-matched in temperament and interests, they often seemed an unshakeable duo, a front I could rarely trump. Stripped of spiritual comrades, when my previously-loving father morphed into an ill-tempered fiend when I was about five years old, I had no idea what had happened or what I should do. I couldn't imagine that his mystifying transformation had to do with him rather than me; so, I assumed the latter—and suffered for it. (Even had I known the relevant facts, I would have been too young, too immature then to recognize a plausible connection: Dad was also five when his father stuck him on a tractor, just as Donald's father, George, had forced Grampa at age five to drive a team of horses in the fields, also at the start of a world war, in order to shore up a war-time labor shortage.)

Unlike for Dave, who received training wheels when it came time for him to learn to ride a bicycle, Dad refused to get me a pair. Instead, one afternoon (upon my fervent begging) he set me on the cherry red, banana-seated bike I'd received for Christmas. For a few strides he trotted alongside me to steady my bike, then shoved me off down the lane in the direction of the road gate. When he just kept on going—the other way, towards the barn—I yelled "Where ya goin', Dad?" then added "*Why* aren't you willing to help me?"

we three Luick-Thrams kids (me accompanied by my pal, Pooh) eye our booty, Christmas 1970

His non-answer then offers a possible clue now to the riddle that my father always posed for me. I could never ask merely "what" or "how" like most mortals; instead, I posed "why" questions. Problem was such probing nudged him towards truth. My unrelenting queries demanded he reach deeper, closer to the core of a matter. That is exactly what he, as a keeper of secrets, a victim of veiled occurrences, strove so adamantly to avoid: Relentless ghosts constantly bade my father to inviolate silence.

Ultimately, I wanted to understand, to name a thing, so I could better assign it a value. That also is likely what so vexed Dad about me. His other children willingly swallowed platitudes and accepted his mute shrugs sans protest, but I pressed for plausible explanations. This realization today offers me much comfort; it did not, however, console little Mike Luick then.

That first time I tried to ride a bike—involuntarily, solo—ended abruptly with me falling down and sharp-edged gravel sticking in my bleeding, scraped knee. As Ashlawn Farm seemed to be an island in an ocean of corn as far as one could see, I felt determined to master what I saw as my only available vehicle to freedom. Eventually—after tipping over more times than I could count—I took to peddling up and down the lane that led from our farmyard to the gravel road that beckoned me. Yes, I'd understood the trick of staying upright on a two-wheeler, but I'd not cracked the code of Dad's bizarre behavior, so felt like a helpless hostage.

To vent my frustration and mounting distress I took to both appealing to and cursing God—softly, under my breath, for I'd been taught that questioning or countering "His wishes" in any way was a sure ticket to hell.

"What have I done?" I'd plead, "Why does he hate me? *What* have I done?" I'd repeat endlessly: "*Why* does Dad hate me so?"

What did some abstract netherworld mean to me when I already felt like I was living in an emotional abyss every day, here on earth? It seemed hellish. Ironically, that inferno wasn't such a lonely place: I had plenty of company—among others, my own father. For one, was it a coincidence that I noticed changes in how Dad related to me over the year between when his father, Donald, unexpectedly dropped dead of heart failure in July 1966 and when lung cancer claimed his father-in-law, Elmer, a year later? And, that in Grandpa Thrams' absence the care of Elmer's worldly affairs was assumed by his wife Erma, the strong-willed mother-in-law whom Bud despised?

The way Dad interacted with the outer world, then, likely mirrored the way he danced with his disappointing, displeasing inner world. As those dynamics remained unnamed, he took those closest to him to unexplored emotional depths as unwilling backups. It became unbearable for us all, however, as those realms were dark, violent and destructive.

―――

chapter 70: against the grain

Even before the death of my maternal grandfather in 1967, the move to Ashlawn Farm in 1963 intensified what for my father constituted a career caught in a protracted, ever-faster downward spiral. When he and Mom first married (on Grandpa Thrams' 58th birthday, 7 March 1954) they moved into the hired hand's house at Ashlawn Farm, as Elmer had invited Bud to farm with him. The newlyweds' humble clapboard cottage sat across from the wide-windowed stucco farmhouse, home to collegial Grandpa and controlling Grandma Thrams.

Did my folks stay in the hired hands cottage, their first shared home, only one year because it had to be dug out from snowbanks bigger than the house? In any case, they endured one winter there, then moved.

Only 13 months later, after the birth of a daughter, Debra Lynn, on Easter Sunday 1955, the young couple moved to Doc and Norma Voetbergs' farm west of Thornton, some four miles from Dad's parents. (Whenever he referred to "the Voetberg place" years after my parents left it, Dad's glimmering eye betrayed vicarious pride that it belonged to "a well-known local vet[erinarian.]") There, Bud milked Guernsey cows, farrowed pigs and sometimes hauled livestock long-distance to packing plants in Saint Paul, Minnesota. Despite having recently become a new mother, Phyllis (whose name means "foliage" in Greek) grew a large garden, took care of chickens and washed heavy milking equipment—a monstrous chore. Donald often lent the young couple the use of his tractors or equipment. Charlotte and her new daughter-in-law shared gardening projects like canning or freezing corn. All seemed well.

(top left) Deb & Dave, Christmas 1959; Debbie with our parents on the Voetberg farm, 1956;
(bottom) house on Junior Edgington's farm near Swaledale; David on toy tractor, spring 1962

For six years Dad and Mom remained there, where in spring 1958 they had a son, David Alan. In 1961 they moved just over three miles to a site south of Swaledale, where they farmed per shares with "Junior" Edgington of nearby Sheffield. Within two years, however, they up-rooted all inventory and offspring again—this time "for good." Only time would tell if the move really was for "good"—or not—for with this move, by taking over Phyllis' family's home place between Mason City and Clear Lake, they forever fused the two families. Their experiment would test us all.

Once the windswept home to buffalo and the Native-American nomads who followed them, the piece of land later named "Ashlawn Farm" had been post-glacial, tall-grass prairie for about 10,000 years before Elijah G. Ford plowed open its root-knotted sod in 1856. After Christ Lewis Thrams (pronounced "Chris," born "Christian Ludwig") and his wife Lydia bought the farm 41 years later from a Yankee named Cruikshank, the Thramses further developed it per the practices, standards and technology of their time. They also brought to it lofty German-American ideals of agrarian life, traditions that arose over centuries in Central Europe and were imported by land-hungry emigrants seeking a New Canaan where they might realize their Old World dreams of land-owning autonomy.

Bud Luick's arrival a century after Elijah Ford's, then, marked a break with the overall flow of Ashlawn Farm's Euro-American experience to that point. Just as the old-order president (affable "Ike," their fellow Midwesterner for whom staunch-Republican Elmer and Erma had so enthusiastically campaigned) resisted a New England newcomer's taking over the reins of the world's then-most-powerful country, the transfer of Ashlawn Farm from the hands of Victorians to postwar moderns would not happen without friction or flare-ups. It would be a clash of irreconcilable systems: Fascinated by the large-scale technologies recently used in global warfare, Bud wanted to overturn Elmer's small-scale operation much as Elijah Ford had cut asunder the virgin prairie and, with that one incision, irreversibly separated the rich soil from its natural state.

Elmer Thrams on a harvest ring (ninth from the right on left photo) and harvesting hay (on far right)

Agriculture as Grandpa Thrams practiced it could have continued at Ashlawn Farm for centuries with little need for radical changes or massive inputs. The basically self-sufficient system Elmer had followed utilized largely horse and human power. Based on relationships—with animals, with other humans, with nature-determined weather patterns and capacities—it created little non-recyclable waste yet yielded enough food and fuel to sustain production into the next year, and the next, and the next. Grandpa cultivated most of his own crop seeds, for example, and avoided the use of chemicals—along with the binding credit farmers usually require to invest in such big-ticket inputs.

To sidestep the use of petroleum—the black devil of farmers' dependency on non-native means of production—the Thramses kept sheep busy instead of engaging lawn mowers; chickens scratched through "ripening" manure piles, thus helping to break down animal waste waiting to be returned to the fields, even as they foraged for their own fodder. In lieu of ever-stronger doses of antibiotics and herbicides, Grandpa mixed livestock and rotated crops, thus organically preventing the spread of parasites and weeds. And, the Thramses nurtured diversity at Ashlawn Farm: Wheat, sugar beets, oats, sorghum, hemp, hay and even peanuts complemented the corn-and-soybeans crop rotation that would become a soil-depleting norm within a generation.

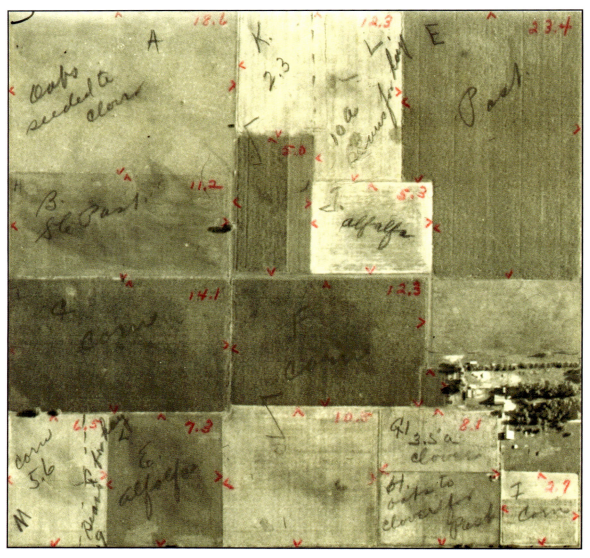
aerial view charting Ashlawn Farm's use of its quarter-section of prime Iowa loam, likely in the 1940s

The import-export-driven, external-input-based system Dad wished to establish would require massive amounts of exactly the things that his discredited predecessor had shunned: endless, ballooning loans; seas of petroleum-derived fertilizers, herbicides and pesticides; hefty hormones and high-powered antibiotics—in short, a costly chemical lab in the cornfield. Essentially, "controllable" petroleum derivatives were to eliminate uncontrollable people—family members, hired hands, local buyers… and Mother Nature herself. Like his dad, my Dad wasn't the most skilled in the Human Relations Department, so non-relationship-reliant agri-"business" seemed hands-down more attractive than the family-based agrarian *culture* industrial food production would replace. Unwittingly, Dad served as both cheerleader and foot soldier in a coup that, ultimately, would be his downfall—and ours.

The convention-bound farm folk of the Great American Middle West didn't disavow the time-tested practices and traditions of generations of our forebears, however, without context—or encouragement. I remember a night in the early '70s when our parents got all dressed up. Dad dug out his gray suit and splashed on some Old Spice; Mom wore her best Sunday dress and dabbed on her latest Avon acquisition. Rarely explicitly informed of our elders' intentions, we kids suspected "They're goin' ta meet God himself—or at least the Pres'dent!"

Mom, David (standing), me and Dad in our "Sunday best" for a church-directory portrait, mid-1970s

Leaving David and me alone—an act in itself that signaled something big was afoot—Dad and Mom drove off to the Surf Ballroom, where a dozen years earlier Buddy Holly had performed the night the music died. Giddy on freedom, we kids ate forbidden foods and watched scary movies until real, real late. Gosh, it must have been almost ten or even (gasp!) eleven o'clock when we saw the headlights of the old pink-and-brown Rambler Sedan come down the long driveway. We killed the lights, ran upstairs and dove under the covers.

Earl Lauer Butz (left) and one of his willing victims, Luwarren "Bud" Luick, at a tractor parade, circa 2000

The next morning—as they reviewed the previous evening's gala over several cups of Mom's ever-thin coffee—we discovered our parents hadn't had a meeting with God after all, but rather they had been in the weighty presence of the U.S. Secretary of Agriculture, Earl Lauer Butz. Dad recapped for us what President Nixon's messenger told the packed audience as they dined on prime Iowa corn-fed beef, compliments of the Cerro Gordo County Farm Bureau. A one-time Hoosier farmboy, Butz admonished the crowd to "get big or get out," to "go home and tear out the groves, pull down the fences and plant from fencerow to fencerow."

28 July 1973 issue of Iowa's Wallaces Farmer; *ad about corn pickers—and an example of its use*

Dad had reservations about handling the land "recklessly" but followed Butz' marching orders anyway: "The U.S.' food arsenal [was] going to feed the world!" Even I understood the basic message: It was a New Day for American agriculture. With Butz' unambiguous blessing, by the mid-'70s Dad and Mom had indeed plowed under the old cow lane that used to strike out across the fields from the barn (built by Great-Grandpa Christ Thrams soon after 1900). Dad recruited David and me to rip out fences and shave off our protective grove's overall area by a third. Assuming inordinate debt, the folks poured extensive concrete feedlots and constructed flashy emerald-green and stark-white metal sheds to house the hundreds of hogs and cattle they planned to fatten with increasing corn yields. Sown crops like oats and hay which relieve and enrich the soil between row-crop plantings became less and less common, not just at Ashlawn Farm but across the Midwest. Corn and soybeans shouldered out other grains as "cash crops" bound for Paris, Peking, Moscow and beyond. Sure enough, we was feedin' the world!

Then, the ground gave way beneath us, until we could hardly afford to feed ourselves—but I'll tell that wretched tale later.

———

chapter 71: the fields ignite

Remember: Despite its acrimonious twists and turns, what became my father's lifelong relationship with my mother's extensive family initially grew out of love.

Dad's Class of '53 ring; Phyllis Thrams (fourth from left) and Bud Luick about the time they met

My parents unexpectedly met at the North Iowa Fair in summer 1952. Young, baby-faced Bud bargained a date out of Phyllis after her heifer—the one he had groomed—fetched top dollar, and after his father berated him for neglecting his own Grand Champion steer for the sake of "some girl."

The next day—the last of that year's fair—Bud (whose nickname comes from the English word for "friend" or "brother") deliberately hung around the cattle barn until Phyllis showed up to do morning chores so he could ask "What you gonna do today?"

All senior 4-H girls then were expected, as proof of their culinary competence, to bake a 12-egg angel-food cake—a feat assumed too hard for younger girls. Set-to-graduate Phyllis had planned to pick up her white-ribbon angel-food cake in the home-economics building.

"Why don't you come home with me to eat that cake?" she offered as bait that Bud was happy to bite. On the trek to Ashlawn Farm, the humid summer heat reduced her fluffy creation to a flattened ruin that even Prince, Grandpa's German Shepherd, refused to eat.

Undaunted by the girl's bad-lucked baked goods, determined Bud asked "What ya gonna do now?"

Phyllis hesitantly dared share "I'm supposed to help my dad make hay this afternoon."

"Oh, I'll help" Bud bid.

"Well, you won't want to make hay like we do" she warned.

"Why not?"

"We use a team of horses—even though we *do* have a tractor."

"I'll have to see this" Bud laughed. Although he loved horses, he couldn't believe the Thramses still used a team to harvest hay. A harbinger of the rebellion to come, upon meeting the man who'd become his father-in-law a year and a half later, Bud convinced Elmer to use a tractor to pull the loose hay from the fields to the barn, where it would be lifted into the haymow by a set of ropes. As he likely intended, Phyllis felt immensely impressed by the young man's confidence, as well as his ability to win over reluctant Elmer.

Elmer Thrams putting loose alfalfa hay into the mow at Ashlawn Farm with a hay fork, 1950s

After that spontaneous first date, the teenage girl who one day would become my mother wasted no time inviting her new beau to soon join her and her parents on a trip to South Dakota to visit her Aunt Emma's family for a few days. Phyllis already had traveled with various uncles, aunts and cousins by car and even alone by train to both coasts, as well as around the Midwest. Bud had only been to Missouri to visit his paternal grandfather and the Danish-immigrant neighbor's wife with whom George Luick had run away some seven years earlier, so he readily accepted her offer of adventure.

teenage Bud Luick alone (left) and with his father, Donald (far right) and grandfather, George, in Missouri

Soon after the travelers arrived at the Lickingteller ranch near Newell, just east of the Montana border, the two sweethearts went for a stroll through the Big Sky Country scenery. When they returned, Aunt Emma (Erma's oldest sister) quietly inquired as to where they'd been.

"We just went for a walk over the prairie" Phyllis replied.

"Let me show you something." Emma led them to a corner of the room. She uncovered a big, blue enameled canning pot with white speckles. It was almost filled with rattle-snake rattles. "We killed each one of them on this place as of late" Emma explained. She advised them to take any more strolls with "the utmost of care."

Emma (Falcon) and George Lickingteller on their ranch in South Dakota, 1940s; buffalo herd and cowboy

For the young couple, "the utmost of care" was the last thing on their minds. They had just met, and according to Phyllis "It was love at first sight." Caught in fresh infatuation, she eagerly agreed when her cousin Jean Travis suggested the young folk dodge the old by taking a trip to Spearfish to attend a dance. A proper Victorian, Jean's father Quince (married to Emma and Erma's youngest sister, Nellie) and her Uncle Elmer insisted they drive the teens to what the worried fathers feared would be a wild shindig. The next day, Jean took Bud and Phyllis—sans chaperones—through the nearby Black Hills, into caves and to Mount Rushmore, which had been completed only eleven years before.

Back at the ranch, the men rustled Bud out of bed early to hunt elk, with the ironic explanation that although stalking the creatures out of season was technically illegal, it was decidedly safer than in season because there'd be no "inexperienced out-of-state hunters" lurking about to accidentally shoot them instead of a much-coveted elk bull.

South Dakota trapper's truck with assorted drying skins and young Bud, cleaning freshly caught fish

The ill-traveled boy from North Iowa had to adjust to numerous new conventions in South Dakota, including norms in hygiene that differed noticeably from those at home in Thornton. When his hostess told her husband to shave and get cleaned up for a festive family picnic, George informed her that he wouldn't do so until he'd finished haying for the summer, which would be in a few weeks. Emma and George's son Lewis, who later worked at a gold mine, always wore the same repertoire of clothes, every day, for years: spit-shined black cowboy boots, stiff-cuffed blue jeans, a black belt and black-and-red-checked shirt, topped with a black-felt cowboy hat. Beards and cowboy boots weren't the only novelties Bud encountered: The Lickingtellers routinely let their pet pony come into the house during meals like other families "out East" might a dog; that took Bud some getting used to.

George, Emma and Louis Lickingteller (back row), with unknown baby, Orlin and Enid (front row), 1940s

---

By 1952, when Phyllis took Bud out West for the first time, the Thrams-Falcon clan had been venturing into the area for more than sixty-five years. Her paternal grandparents had homesteaded in the center of what was then Dakota Territory, not far from the Missouri River, from 1885 until they could no longer stand serial hardships and fled their "soddie" in winter 1889 for the comforts of boom-town Pierre. In spring 1890, they retreated to North Iowa. Her maternal uncle, Will Falcon, had sought his fortunes, too, as a cattle rancher in South Dakota from 1910 till 1912. For that interlude he lured his sister Emma to cook and keep house when not helping with calving or cattle branding. Around the same time, one of Grandma Erma's countless cousins also tried his hand at dry-land farming near Lemmon—before he as well returned to "civilized" Iowa. Years later, in the 1940s, her widowed father, Clemence, invested his worldly worth in selling South Dakota real estate—only to finally give up and return to Iowa.

For wavy-haired Bud, though, South Dakota represented not a test of will but a magical escape into an unknown world. Under the enormous Western sky, he found one that gave him his first glimpses of Old-Frontier curiosities like "real" Native Americans and cowboys, wild buffalo and roaming elk, the barren Badlands as well as that nearby, quintessential tourist haven, kitschy Wall Drug.

my folks at Ashlawn Farm soon after they met, with unknown boy; Black Hills farm, mid-20th century

In the early Fifties, Phyllis and her future fiancé weren't the only ones fascinated by romantic images of the Great American West. The United States recently had turned its attention from blood-soaked battlefields which stretched from Europe to the South Pacific, from North Africa to the North Atlantic. Still traumatized from images of bestial Nazi death camps and the hovering specter of nuclear holocaust, the nation chose to look inward and backward in reflex to the horrors brought home from beyond its shores. The legendary stories of the West reassured Americans that their national character—arisen out of facing and overcoming adversity—was both pure and proven. In the history of settling their still-young country, they found Good Guys and Bad Guys aplenty to quiet their unsettled and unsettling quest for easy answers.

That summer of 1952 my parents-to-be were not yet victims of multi-million dollar marketing campaigns. It was still two years before Walt Disney would launch his Davy Crockett franchise—including several TV and film incarnations of the larger-than-life frontier man from Tennessee. The related ballad would sell more than ten million copies, and heavily hawked merchandise such as coonskin caps or other Crocket regalia more than $100 million. That all would mean little to Bud and Phyllis: They were in love, with the West and with each other. The self-isolating, consumption-drunk Howdy-Doody postwar world that afforded them carefree days of romping under sunny Dakota prairie skies, however, was a passing one. Even if they were happy to live apart from it, an increasingly complex and evermore interconnected world would, sooner than later, come and find them. Its unforeseen onset would feel to them like an all-out rebellion.

―――

chapter 72: whitie's world collapses

The controversial "'60s revolution" that supplanted the hands-in-pockets, head-in-sand Fifties wasn't so much a revolution as a quickening, the culmination of processes begun long before. Several differing but intertwined movements came to a head at once. Foremost may have been the growing demands to assure civil rights for African Americans, but not far behind came the push for full and equal rights for women; Native Americans; Latino migrant workers; gays and lesbians; the physically disabled; senior citizens... a maze of groups who felt the time was right to finally raise their voices and set down their feet. Having been relegated for too long to back rooms and back rows, they fought their way forward and seized the streets.

The plight of disadvantaged minorities—in the United States and most countries throughout the world—wasn't new. What was new was the militancy, the naked urgency of their combined calls for justice. The tone of social conversation shifted within a dizzyingly short time: The "Sir, might you please?" heard at the beginning of the decade morphed by its end into "Look here, Mother F****r!"

This domestic clamor played against a chorus of assassins' gunshots and the whistling of bombs falling over distant lands. Those glaring contradictions between claims of democracy at home and base war crimes in the Far East raised the shrill pitch of the times to unbearable levels. We heard the siren-like wailing even out on the Iowa prairie, even in the back of our big school bus.

Martin Luther King speaking at march on Washington, 28 August 1963

Lake District #5: hemp plant smokestack is visible left of tree; PTA Christmas party invitation—both 1940s

Freckled, feisty Debbie Theilen and her older sister Dawn lived in an old schoolhouse converted into a makeshift private home. It was one result of the fusion of Lake Township District #5 with Clear Lake schools in the mid-'50s, which meant we Luick kids would be bused to town to receive instruction rather than walk to class a mile away as Mom had. In turn, the converted schoolhouse yielded Mom two child-minding charges for a few summers.

The spirited Theilen girls came from laboring stock. As they had lived in rural Northern California, they ticked differently than we local yokels. One day, sitting on the back seat of the big yellow bus driven by Leonard Juhl (one of Gramma Luick's uncountable paternal cousins), Debbie casually cursed "niggers" to which I replied, aghast, "Debbie, those people are called 'negroes!'"

That term doesn't fit politically correct parlance today but then, as racial tensions burned out of control during riots in inner-city neighborhoods from Boston to Los Angeles, the word I'd learned at home for those whose skin was darker than ours was meant to show respect and good will. I do not know from where I inherited such sensibilities: I can't remember our parents openly preaching tolerance to us three children; it must have been by example.

Mom had told us stories that transcended mere tolerance. Already as a girl from lily-white North Central Iowa, she walked up to what was then a real but veiled racial barrier in Cerro Gordo County and poked her finger in its eye early on. As a teenager she befriended the daughter of Grandma's African-American podiatrist, Dr. Edward C. Martin. Like Mom, "bright and pretty" Cynthia attended Methodist youth camp at Clear Lake. One summer the two shared a cottage, then stayed in contact. Through their friendship, Phyllis learned about a family whose journey was radically different from her own.

"E.C." Martin's father had been born to a former slave in Belcher, Louisiana in 1874. At age seven, little Henry began to learn to read, which had been illegal for slaves before Emancipation. Later, as a young man working on a snag boat on the Mississippi River, he became injured and found treatment at a hospital in Dubuque. There, an African-American foot doctor befriended him and encouraged young Henry to attend a college in Chicago, to become a podiatrist. His son, Cynthia's father, followed his father's footsteps and in 1930 came to Mason City to replace an African-American podiatrist who had died, Dr. J.D. Reeler. In Iowa, Dr. Martin met his future wife, Berlina, a nurse. The couple built a large brick house on property her family owned just outside the city. Neighbors regarded them "as among the most well-to-do and best-loved residents of West Haven." The Martins had many friends.

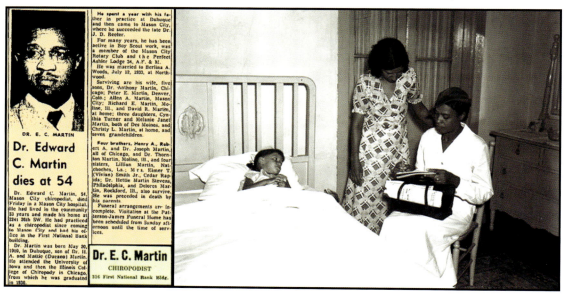

business ad (inset) and 17 July 1965 obituary for "Dr. Edward C. Martin;" His wife, Berlina, was a nurse.

My mother attended parties at her friend Ardith Millard's house on a farm between Mason City and West Haven, where Cynthia, her brother Edward Anthony or other members of the eight-child Martin family were present. "Tony" quickly caught piano-playing Phyllis' attention. She once had sheet music for *Blue Boogie* with her at Ardith's and loaned it to talented Anthony upon his keen request. Mom never got it back, but she figured "He could play that tune a whole lot better than me, so—"

The Martin children's parents encouraged them to follow Grandfather Henry's advice, to "Get an education. Once you have it, it can't be taken away from you." Cynthia and Anthony's younger brother, Allen, reported that in their family "failure was not an option." Anthony—as Mom knew "Edward A."—later remembered his father

> talking to each of [the children] when they were about 10. "He told us we were going to have to work twice as hard as other people to get recognition or status… I guess we all took it to heart." [His own philosophy was] "Whatever you want to be, be the best."

No activist, Phyllis said later that her strategy was simply to "act normal" when in the presence of the few minorities who lived in North Central Iowa during her youth. In both her childhood and mine 98 percent of Iowans counted as "white" in census figures. That has changed somewhat, but then most non-whites living in Cerro Gordo County were neither openly discriminated against nor fully integrated. Instead, they were simply sidelined.

Although headed by a doctor and a nurse, the Martin family lived in hardscrabble West Haven. In those days it was a mostly unpaved settlement on the "wrong side of the tracks" a mile or more southwest of Cerro Gordo's county seat. The family belonged to the "black" Union Memorial Methodist Church near East Park; however, the many Martin children did attend Mason City's public schools, where Mom's older sisters Irene and Dorothy went to high school and thought they fared well.* (Cynthia later died during an asthma attack in her 20s; Anthony practiced podiatry in Chicago and, later, in San Jose, California.)

Ester Walls' and Jovita Rodriquez' Mason City High graduation photos in Aunt Irene's album, 1944

[*To view an interview with Ruth and Ruby Haddix, African-American twins who grew up in Manly, Iowa and were denied access to their school prom at the Surf Ballroom in Clear Lake at the time the nearby Martin children were not, go to: http://www.blackiowa.org/education/childrens-oral-history-project/stories/ruth-and-ruby-haddix/]

There were few African Americans living permanently in or near Clear Lake before 1980, and there were few Mexican Americans, other than seasonal migrant workers. Those who braved the mono-cultural ethnic landscape of North Central Iowa, however, earned a great deal of money—most of which landed in someone else's eager hands. To cite one example:

Over the first half of the 20th century the much-admired Sam Kennedy family so prominently established on the edge of town had built out of ten acres and a horse a thousand-acre potato-and-carrot farm that was earning over half a million dollars by 1952. The Kennedy family's ascent, however, would have been impossible without migrant (or, during World War II, German prisoner-of-war) labor. Still, their seasonal workers lived in very modest digs.

Hispanic (left) and African-American (top right) migrant workers; German POW laborers (below), 1940s

Nearly every Sunday enroute to church we drove past the long, concrete-block building where Kennedy-employed Mexican workers lived. Lacking a pitched roof, dotted with large square windows and painted robin-egg blue, it looked like a misplaced adobe. At first Mom explained that its inhabitants were seasonal residents, but later it seemed some were enduring interminable prairie winters in its drafty rooms, for even during the coldest months we saw people and cars moving about the compound, despite being tucked away as it was from passersby and shrouded under a canopy of Burr Oak trees. She never offered additional commentary, neither in defense of nor derogatory about those marginalized migrants; she only factually stated, *every* time, "Mexicans live there."

Long before Mexican restaurants opened in Mason City or Clear Lake, my mother's parents accepted an invitation to dine in the home of one of Cerro Gordo County's first Mexican-American families. So, there must have been some interaction between some individual Latinos and Anglos. It seems likely, though, that Grandpa Thrams felt some ambivalence towards individuals or groups different from his family—as suggested by two telling incidents.

Elmer's younger sister, Mom's Aunt Lois, married fellow white-Anglo-Saxon-protestant Clark Pedelty in 1919. In 1949 the couple moved with their three sons to a dairy farm near Haw River in sharply segregated North Carolina. In 1951 Elmer's 17-year-old nephew Russell came to Iowa for a visit—and brought along his Hispanic friend Marco. Mom took an immediate liking to the swarthy, jet-haired guest. After their return to Dixie, Phyllis set off down the lane to post a letter she'd penned to Marco. Grandpa intercepted her—and the letter. "I think you should leave that alone" he told her. At the time, smitten Phyllis didn't understand why. She did discover some years later, however, that handsome Marco and his bride slipped over a state boundary, leaving unpaid rent a goodly distance behind them.

Was Elmer Thrams a "racist"—particularly when it involved whom his daughters might mate? Skin color certainly did not play a role in the mid-1940s when Grandpa unyieldingly dissuaded his oldest daughter, Eleanor, from continuing to court an immigrant neighbor boy. She and Walter Edmund Zuehlke had become "pretty serious" according to her baby sister Phyllis, who later assumed their father's ultimate motive was that "During the war, speaking with a thick German accent wasn't well received." Yet, Elmer was of 100 percent German extraction; it didn't seem to matter that Walter and his brother, Helmut Waldemar, would become naturalized U.S. citizens shortly later, in autumn 1948.

Elmer (left) in publicity shot for Walnut Grove chicken feed, with Helmut Zuehlke and wife Violet, 1950s

As for my dad? Only as of the mid-1980s, after he and Mom had fallen under the pulverizing wheels of the runaway Farm Crisis, did I hear my father speak negatively of groups of people by race—despite having had a grandfather who'd been active in a racist group. By then Dad had come to decry pockets of plotters poised to control first America, then the world by controlling "fuel, food and finances." Before that, though, my parents never looked for scapegoats on whom to dump their bulging bag of burdens.

Instead of condemning people for the color of their skin, Dad judged them for what he assumed was the content of their character. The catch was, in most cases the judged came up, in his eyes, lacking. Much better at understanding floundering horse hooves than the careening course of history, he often mistook the effects of a thing as being its cause. After dessert and coffee, the Thramses' disgruntled sons-in-law groused at each family get-together. Dad adamantly maintained to Uncles Jack, Hank and Thurman that "If the police had only cracked open a few heads" of the students protesting in Mexico City in advance of the 1968 Olympics, "then we could have avoided this whole thing."

anti-war demonstrators in Washington offering flowers to Pentagon guards, 21 October 1967

chapter 73: the rebellion spreads

The "whole thing" over which the four Thrams girls' husbands grumbled for years was a euphemism for dissent and its contemptible cradle, non-conformity. All three of my maternal uncles had served in uniform: Uncle Jack parachuted into, then slugged his way across Europe as the Nazis' bloodied western front collapsed; Uncle Thurman spent much of World War II plying the Pacific aboard various ships; Uncle Hank served in the Marine Corps.

Thurman was a South Carolinian stranded among us peculiar, up-tight Yankees, and Hank a city slicker visiting from Newark. Together, they marched their way through several packs of cigarettes as Uncle Jack—a street-tough orphan from Fresno, in California's Central Valley—sucked on his sweet-smelling pipe. All the while, my father—the only farmer in the troop—railed against this or the other rebellious faction. As a band, the men bad-mouthed "arrogant" students, "uppity" civil rights activists, bra-burning feminists, "filthy" hippies, "queers" (only in passing—and they awkwardly refused to answer my repeatedly questioning "What's that?") and other social malcontents. With a watery Southern drawl which Uncle Thurman refused to shake after living 65 years north of the Mason-Dixon Line, his comments about African Americans seemed tainted. And, Uncle Hank's hefty Jersey accent lent a hard-as-pavement touch to his views on all matters urban and coastal. For prairie dwellers, Dad's downhome tones seemed reassuringly native—more like plain truth.

Uncles Thurman, Jack and Hank with Dad; Mom with Aunts Dorothy, Grandma, Irene and Eleanor, 1974

What my father said always sounded like gospel to me. So, as a teen, I dutifully took up his sword. I once submitted a brazen letter to the Mason City *Globe-Gazette* editor. In it I condemned what Dad—and thus I—saw as the "pampered bad boys and girls" housed at the "expensive," newly-built juvenile detention home across the gravel road from what was then the Cerro Gordo County Farm, not far from our own farm. Like him, I made no allowance for individual circumstances or personal histories. I knew the score *exactly* and was only too pleased to call it.

Dad knew exactly about everything, too—but the problem became, the older I got, the less I could stomach his infallibly airing what he treated like insider information. The longer I lived, the more I hungered to discover my own truth. I chomped at the chance to devour the world and taste all it had to offer, not retreat from it the way—it came to seem to me as I approached manhood—that most of those around me did. When I finally broke free from my father's yoke, I was willing to pay any price, not only to keep my hard-won freedom, but to feed it a steady diet of wild, convention-flouting autonomy.

Still, as a boy, I happily played Dad's patsy, regardless of the price others paid. As self-defeating as it was, my first high-profile victim was one of the persons trying the hardest to open the world for me.

Miss Thompson was the music teacher at Clear Lake's Central School. She seldom shared much about her private life. From what snippets we kids could piece together, it seemed she had been in Southern California as a young woman, caught after Pearl Harbor in the labor vacuum of total mobilization for The War. (At that time all knew which war was meant: There'd never been any other "real" wars; all contenders for the title were only wishful pretenders.) Whatever her role in wartime industry or administration in the Golden State, it must have been a highlight of her existence, as three decades later, back in the American Heartland, she still wore her gold-dyed hair in a Forties cut—combed flat like a monk's cap on the crown of her ever-bobbing head, then encircled with tightly-trained curls

A little bird of woman, "Miss T.'s" slightly-bowed shoulders sat atop a compact torso held up with pencil-like legs, the boney shins of which could be neither fully hidden nor made optically smooth by her opaque, faux-tan hosiery. While truly a livewire, the lady wore conservatively-cut but brightly-colored dress suits that hung loose on her thin frame like bulky drapes. Though not quite stilettos, petite Miss Thompson teetered about on impractically high heels—"the better" she'd call over her shoulder shamelessly, as she dashed on to her next class, "to shake, wiggle and dance about."

Bernice Thompson—photo taken 1942, used on 1960s application to teach music in Clear Lake schools

Despite her frail appearance, our music teacher knew no fear: If she did, she betrayed it by neither word nor deed. Although the lines in them departed from her straight-laced ways, Miss Thompson zealously exposed us to pop-chart hits that in the Iowa that began beyond our playground would have been considered, to say the least, subversive. Hardly understanding the lyrics, we first through sixth graders waded through waves of provocative words and murky sloughs of scandalous images that would have been seen as outrageous, even treasonous if we'd dared drop them at the dinner table.

Oh, Miss Thompson's cleverly disguised brainwashing ploys began innocently enough. At first, she versed us in rather harmless refrains (by four older boys from a place called Liverpool, I think in some place called "Ireland") who sang about the sun coming up:

So far, so good [I thought at the time]: *No problem there—kids' stuff!*

When "they" arrived, there was much noise and flashing of cameras: It seemed like an alien invasion.

When the (were they called?) "Bugs" addressed us as "Little Darlin'" and claimed it'd been a long, icy, lonesome winter I began to take exception:

Wait a minute! [I thought] *Is Miss Thompson directing the lyrics she's chosen at us? Are we her "lil' darlin's?" In any case, it has been a long, cold winter—we're in Iowa—but "lonely?" Since when? How can we be? We're Baby Boomers: kids is runnin' round ev'rywhere!*

When the band repeated that the sun was coming, but announced everything'd be "all right" I thought:

OK, so now the words is gettin' a little silly—even for first graders.

Still, we kept on singin' that it seemed like years since the big ol' sun had been "here," but:

"Years?" We is only six or seven, for heaven's sake! And, we haven't been missin' anything—but now that ya mention it, there are more an' more o' those butter-yellow smiley faces with coal-black oval eyes and half-moon grins poppin' up everywhere: Is there a connection…?

Then came that stupid refrain again, saying the sun was coming…

All right, all right: enough! We git it: arrive already!

When the bob-haired Brits crooned "sun, sun—it's coming" over and over, I gave up:

Oh, brother! You must be kiddin'! We gotta sing this crap, when we could be out fallin' down on the asphalt an' havin' tons more fun knockin' out our front teeth?

When they said that the ice was "slowly melting," under my breath I offered Miss Thompson

I'll melt your ice, Lady! An', ya want "clear?" We have a lake of it—jus' down the hill from here!

Somehow, we hostages of Miss Thompson's no-holds-barred music classes survived the mind-numbing, repeated promises that the sun *was* coming—and that everything was all right. Still, though, we had *no* idea what awaited us next.

"Mike Luick" as a non-comprehending first grader at Clear Lake's Central School, the 1969-70 school year

First soaked in verbal showers of sun, we soon thereafter had to submit ourselves to soggy overdoses of "joy"—and not just a little of it. And that began with:

Jeremiah was a bullfrog, was good friend of mine.

What? You gotta to be jokin'! How could that ever work? I protested. No one answered, so

> *I never understood a single word he said but I helped him drink his wine.*
> *He always had some mighty fine wine.*
> *Singin' joy to the world... all the boys and girls now,*
> *joy to the fishes in the deep blue sea and joy to you and me.*

Where to start with that one? First, as good Methodists, we didn't drink wine: Sour grape juice was Satan's swill. Yep, Dad did keep a few forgotten bottles of low-octane beer stashed away in the cellar for summer haying season, but not many—and certainly never stored above-ground, in plain view or easy reach. As for frogs: I could never understand a single word of theirs, either!

> *And if I were the king of the world, I tell you what I would do.*
> *I'd throw away the cars and the bars in the world and I'd make sweet love to you.*
> *Sing it now: Joy to the world, all the boys and girls,*
> *joy to the fishes in the deep blue sea, joy to you and me.*

hippie bus enroute to an "event;" poster advertising "Krishna consciousness event," 1967

"Throw away the cars?" How'd we get around after that [I asked myself]—tractors? "And the bars?" Fine by me! The one time I snuck a sip of beer when Dad wasn't lookin' it smelled like horse pee, anyways. But, wait: the words "make sweet love to you"—you kiddin' or what? No way!

Now, toothless junk about joy for fish had given way to raw talk of S-E-X:

"Miss Thompson" I protested finally, "you dare too much!"

At that our zealous music teacher barely bobbed her blonde monk's-cap-cut head in my direction, smiled even wider, flashed her teeth even brighter and keep on leading us in

> *Yah know I love the ladies, love to have my fun...*
> *I'm a high night flyer and a rainbow rider...*
> *a straight shootin' son of a gun, I said a straight shootin' son of a gun.*

"High night flyers" and "rainbow riders?" *Huh-h-h?* And "a straight shootin' SON OF A GUN?" *Gosh, I mused, I'd have my mouth washed out with soap if I swore like that back on the farm!*

Still, waving her arms wildly and swinging her scrawny shoulders to an inaudible beat, the melodic evangelist simply cried out with all her puny might

> *Sing it now: Joy to the world, all the boys and girls,*
> *joy to the fishes in the deep blue sea, joy to you and me.*

———

As confused as I was Miss Thompson's rabid performance at school, Dad was even less pleased back home. I wasn't privy to whatever discussions he and Mom might have had behind their closed bedroom door about my increasingly alarming reports of "naughty" music being taught at school, but it couldn't have set well with them. Mom served as both a Sunday-school teacher and ladies' circle officer for years; she and Dad took turns being local 4-H leaders. How should they explain their baby mouthing such filth to the people who populated the tight prairie world in which we moved? "What would the church ladies think?!

In our ancient hymnals "Joy to the world" clearly belonged to Christmas anthems—and while joy was certainly heralded to "*all* the boys and girls" twas definitely *not* to "fishes in the deep blue sea." As a kid I didn't care about the musical orthodoxy of John and his brother Charles Wesley (the melody-minded founders of Methodism two centuries earlier in England and its colonies). I was, though, gittin' pretty sick o' singin' 'bout friendly toads an' blissful amphibians in azure waters. Still, ever eager to please, for the time bein' I jus' kept on...

Most likely, Miss Thompson's encore to the tune about slimy creatures pushed our parents' displeasure to the tipping point. Rumors spread through the Clear Lake School District like grassfire that "This time Miss T. really has gone too far! She's teaching *drug music* to our children!"

And, what did we kids say to that? Not much. By then already pulled along by fanatical Miss T. into the moral fog of the next song, we just thought we were singin' 'bout some magic bridge with strange powers:

> *When you're weary, feeling small,*
> *When tears are in your eyes*
> *I will dry them all*
> *I'm on your side*
> *When times get rough*
> *And friends just can't be found*
> *Like a bridge over troubled water*
> *I will lay me down ...*

Jimi Hendrix performing on Dutch TV, 1967

The luring promise of a friend to wipe away our tears on that dumb bridge aside, our alarmed parents grew increasingly uneasy with the disreputable messengers behind the dubious images Miss Thompson bestowed on us with such innocent fervor. The mystifying music she pedaled arose from bands with weird names unlike any we'd ever heard. We found something bestial about groups boasting names like the Animals, the Beatles, Birds, Turtles, Monkeys, Three Dogs at Night or Buffaloes in Springtime. At least there also were friends of aviation among them: Thomas Jefferson's Airplanes and Starships (in the colonial period— *how*?), Sonics and a lead Zeppelin (but how did it *ever* get off the ground?). True, there were sinful— Flirtations and Temptations—as well as sacred singers: Righteous Brothers, the Creedence Clearwater Revival (dedicated to evangelism—right?), Shangri-Las, Miracles and the Supreme. But, there was also simply the bizarre: Shocking Blue and Electric Prunes, Small Faces, Silver Apples, Pink Floyd, Stooges and Zombies, Steel Wheels and the Troggs. (The Who?) Lovin' Spoonfuls served over Rolling Stones, with Impressions of Kinks in the Velvet Underground—and if you still didn't know, you could consult the law firm Crosby, Stills & Nash or, as a last resort, ask the deli guy round the corner, Simon Garfinkel. Luckily, there were decent family groups out there, too: Mamas and Papas, accompanied to the Beach by Boys or the neighbor kids Peter, Paul an' Mary.

Quaker-raised Joan Baez & Minnesotan Bob Dylan in Washington, 28 August 1963; Janis Joplin

The off-beat names of what Miss Thompson sold us as "right-on" pop-artists notwithstanding, until our parents rescued us from participating in such immorality, we had to keep on singing about a "bridge over troubled water."

And, we kept on seeing those singers' odd names or hearing their evil music—also outside of school and even during summer vacation, *everywhere* we went.

---

chapter 74: hell an' back

In August 1971 our parents loaded pubescent Deb, her blonde-bombshell cheerleader friend Kathy Melhus, David and me into a customized topper bolted onto the back of our two-tone Chevy pickup. They instructed us four kids to "behave" ourselves in the tightly-packed topper. To assure good behavior Dad had removed the windows between our domain and the front cab, where they sat squeezed in together with Grandma Thrams.

As Dad and Mom only indulged us a vacation about every three years, we were filled with high hopes for adventure despite the snug conditions. We were headed for the Big Apple! We kids, however, were in no way prepared for what we would find there.

paving new freeway, 1972; Dad, Deb, me, Dave and Mom with Thrams relatives in New Jersey

Initially, all things new seemed so big, so busy, so exciting! As Eisenhower's interstate system had not yet bulldozed its planned route from Des Moines to the Twin Cities across North Central Iowa's checkerboard fields, we Luick boys had never seen a freeway. Watching Dad navigate two, then four or more lanes both thrilled and terrified us.

Leaving New York's busy highways behind, Uncle Hank and Aunt Dot visited quiet Ashlawn Farm in 1974.

Once we reached Aunt Dorothy's adopted home in Bogota, New Jersey, we wondered if we'd landed on Mars. Everything was *so* foreign. Even our cousins, Craig and Donna, spoke strangely: They called tennis shoes "sneakas" and pop "soda." To top it all off, their dad drove a sleek new car that had seat belts—and, *electric* windows!

Despite stints of having lived in California during The War and in metro-Manhattan for years, "Aunt Dot" remained a Midwest maiden, through and through—even if she didn't always sound like one, having adopted a Jersey lilt. Her husband, however, spoke another language all together, one we Luick kids often understood only after Mom or Dad translated some key word that had sailed past our ears.

Even on a "clear" day in May 1973, the Empire State Building dominated Midtown Manhattan's skyline.

The exotic Bredenbecks happily offered to show us around summer-time Manhattan. Mom and Dad had ventured out East once before, on a low-budget honeymoon eighteen years earlier (during which they first sampled an exotic, cheese-covered round thing called a "pizza"). Now, the whole family shared the experience of peering down into New York's concrete canyons from atop the Empire State Building.

view of Midtown Manhattan from the Empire State Building (left); Port Authority bus terminal from above

Once back at street level, Debbie and Kathy went wild exploring Macy's and other shops around Herald Square. They crazily bought records by the same bands that Miss Thompson had force-fed us little kids back at Central School. When Mom rolled her eyes at the chilling prospect of subsidizing such depravity with our few tourist dollars spent on the hottest vinyl, Aunt Dot rebuked her with "Aw, come on, Phyl—the girls are here only once!"

At that time, 42nd Street west of Times Square was a center for flourishing Big Apple sex and drug trades.

And, "the girls" were lovin' *every* minute of it. Having schlepped their Main Street mentality with them all the way to Broadway, they smiled and offered a warm "Hi!" to everyone we encountered. One Japanese tourist ran up and asked to take their picture; when they asked him why, he excitedly explained "You first peoples I see smile whole time I in New Yawk!"

everyday street-life scenes of Midtown Manhattan, early 1970s

Not everyone they encountered in New York in the early '70s encountered seemed serious or staid. As we roamed Midtown, my sister and her outgoing friend found plenty of other, more approachable Gothamites. And, they tried to befriend nearly each person they met—truly. As a one-time transit cop, Uncle Hank had seen almost every side of humanity. He scowled at them "Hey, you twos can't greet everyone ya meet like ya're back in da beanfields or sompdin'!"

Meanwhile, in a tourist den off of Fifth Avenue, Mom bought the first of what would become way too many stick-on smiley faces. We did not suspect that once we returned to Ashlawn Farm she'd plaster most visible surfaces with those shrill-yellow pests. (Once set loose, they would seem to self-multiply, then spread everywhere on their own.) Irritating little smiley faces, however, were only one of many pop fads or New York treats we first encountered in America's fashion capital; others included "Afro" haircuts, bell-bottoms, hot pants, platform shoes, English muffins, corned beef and crème soda.

Puerto Rican Boy Scout leader with "Afro" hair cut; boy in Brooklyn wearing bell-bottom jeans

Once our little troupe had conquered Midtown, Uncle Hank decided to move our amusing show Downtown. "Come on, yous" he said, calling us all together. "It's time ta see da udda New Yawk."

When our tall host said the word "udda" I froze for a moment and looked around the churning scene at the intersection where we'd gathered. Seeing no cows, I looked up at my parents and siblings ringed around Aunt Dot's towering mate, then quizzed "Hey, you guys: What udder we spos'd ta be seein'?"

Rather than an answer, my family gave me their backs: They'd already started moving in a tight bunch towards a large round building down the long, straight street full of cars, buses, taxis and trucks. From behind, they looked like so many scared ducklings scurrying off atop each other.

With us hayseeds shadowing him, Uncle Hank called out things he said we were passing, but none of it made any sense to me. "Dare's Hen Station" he yelled, but I couldn't see a single chicken. "Hay, we's gonna go into Mr. Addison's Hare Garden now" he then advised as we began to descend almost impassable, cascading stairs—yet, once more, I saw nothing that even resembled a rabbit.

What I did see after we reached the big barn's cellar, however, was a sea of endless faces, of folks pushing past to nowhere partic'lar as far as I could make out. Some had almond eyes, others dark skin: I'd never seen anyone back home with either odd feature. A few men wore faded dishtowels wrapped round their heads; a couple women wore what Mom called "sorry," but I couldn't figure out what she was apologizin' for. The people who fascinated me most, those who I found most exotic, were the countless individuals with chocolate-colored skin.

"Those people wearin' shoe polish?" I sincerely asked our rushing guide when Hank finally stopped in a big cave of a room, where I could squeeze my way through the many torsos and arms in front of me. Tugging on the sleeve of our private guard's slick suit, I wanted to know "Can they wash that stuff off?"

"Sure" he grinned, "wit' enough hot soap an' wadder, an' a brush wit' stiff-enough bristles."

Aunt Dot, standing next to her "boy from Hackensack, New Joisey," rolled her eyes and wagged her bouffant-bearing head. A staccato scolding of "Oh, Hank, now *stop* that!" fell over her frowning lips.

For once, though, I felt content to forgo any further explanation to my endless queries, as the immense crowd around us had captured my attention. Staring at all the different types of people, the likes of which didn't exist back in North Central Iowa, I looked up, following their upward gaze. I found it transfixed on a big, glowing board of light. At that moment, in that most surrealist space I'd ever seen, I realized that all around us, throughout this gigantic cavern, there was only either a great darkness or a great light. But, the light was greater.

Amtrak ticket window (left) and ever-crowded waiting area in New York's Pennsylvania Station, 1974

My childish fascination, however, suddenly faded when I heard Hank shout "Ova dare" and saw him point towards a busy counter behind a window of thick glass, "ova dare yous can buy tickets for New Yawk or even back ta Chicago if yous want. Dat winda ova dare, dat's da new Hamtack winda, for da natz'nal train comp'ny dat opened last May." We all looked at the Amtrak ticket window in unison, then hummed a chorus of uncomprehending, awe. "It'll take a body all da way ta Sam Fran Crisco if yous want" Hank beamed, "an' ya can even pick from tree roots."

Before I could ask Mom or Dad "Who are Sam an' Fran with Crisco?" the white-lettered words and numbers printed on black-plastic cards, hung on rings on a big board began to flutter, sending half of the crowd scattering in all directions. (They looked like the pigeons in our barnyard back home after Dave shot a BB gun in their direction: The panicking birds would fly off to the safety of the silo, flapping madly, like feathered puppets yanked heavenward from above.)

"Come on" Hank ordered, "da real circus is waitin' downstairs."

As the rest of our scared little band silently filed behind him, then stepped onto moving stairs—a sensation I'd seen only once, at Younkers Department Store in Des Moines—I overheard Mom ask her brother-in-law "Hank, you really think it's safe to take the subway?"

"Sure" he shrugged, "yous gotta show dem kids da real world before dey go back ta da melon patch—don't ya?"

Phyllis' hollow, defeated "Ya, I s'pose we do" lacked any trace of true convincement.

escalator connecting subterranean trains with ground-level access; 1970s New York subway scenes

As the sinking steps carried us deeper, ever deeper into dark tunnels beneath the chaotic scene above, I felt stunned. I'd never seen holes in the ground so big, so loud or so stinky.

When we reached the grimy platform bordering a rail bed laced with litter, Dad informed me that my eyes were "the size of Kennedy half-dollars." As I looked to Deb and Dave, however, their ashen faces betrayed not a thing. Even usually chatty Kathy remained speechless.

waiting for the subway at 86th Street Station, with the "hovering Jesus" in front of right iron column

Nothing made sense in this netherworld that Uncle Hank told us we "*had* ta see." Barely able to hear his monologue about where we were and why, I stopped listening. My gaze drifted across the tracks. Just as I thought I'd seen humanity in all its possible forms upstairs in that big cave with the great light, I noticed a man who looked like Jesus but was wearing a black hat and glasses, standing motionless in front of an iron column. His droopy locks of hair fell in front of each ear and white tassels swung from within his buttoned, knee-length coat. *"Why is Jesus wearing a winter coat in August?"* I wondered—but before my busy little mind could pursue that stray-thought thread, a train thundered into the far end of the tunnel. It shrieked to a deafening stop. At that moment—having just spied Jesus on the platform opposite us—I was sure we'd landed in hell and Jesus was hovering nearby, disguised, waiting to swoop over and save us. Surely, Satan dwelled in just such a place—hot and clanking, filled with stench.

changing trains at 14th Street Station

Then, the train's double doors slid open, Uncle Hank reflexively looked up and down the platform (he did not take out the holstered pistol he'd shown us earlier, strapped under his left arm, tucked inside his suit) and shoved us Iowans into the filling car. "Go stand in dat corner" he commanded. Just as we did so, the doors slammed shut with a dull *THUD!* Then, the train lurched into motion.

commuters riding the graffiti-covered New York subway of the early 1970s

With that, our foray into Hades' headquarters came to an end—or at least so we thought.

As we Iowa bumpkins rode in petrified silence beneath the concrete canyons of New Yawk, I made not a sound but my eyes grazed on everything around me. For a time, they nibbled on the pretty, chocolate-dipped woman sitting near the door. Then, they wandered off to chew awhile on the earnest-eyed, balding businessmen digesting endless rivers of crowded print on awkward, unruly newspapers.

Just as I remembered to breathe again, Uncle Hank yelled the length of the car "OK, so we's gettin' out now—at Green Witch's Village." As the subway screeched to a stop, he warned "Watch out for weirdoes!" I wondered if that was a brand of East Coast corn chips; if so, I wanted ta try some real soon.

Once our eyes adjusted to the bright-if-smog-shrouded sunlight above ground, Hank waved in the direction of a rusty sign and said something about "drag queens an' queers"—but I already was studying a nearby deli counter, hoping to spy a can of that tasty crème-soda stuff we'd first tried the day before.

"Come on" he called over his shoulder, "I'll show ya sompdin' ya don't see ev'ry day back in Mayberry."

For too long, we trundled behind our fearless leader, clinging close for fear of the disaster which awaited any of us who might be so foolish as to lose sight of our little army of gawking intruders. As handsome Hank strode ahead of our moving little clump of chumps his pilot's sunglasses coolly mirrored the bell-bottomed young men who sauntered towards us in recurring waves. They smiled sheepishly at Hank or Dad or both, then shuffled on by with sly grins stuck on their mustachioed faces. Some wore shoes with soles as thick as the shoes themselves; most wore bright, tight shirts like few men would have dared wear back on the prairie at that time. All of them seemed to know a naughty secret.

Stone Wall Inn and Hudson-River scene in Greenwich "Gayville" Village

At one point, we stopped at a corner to wait for a light. Although Mom had been pressing Dave and me tight to her side, somehow two of these men (oddly, they all looked like they came from the same family and had the same barber) were standing directly in front of me, between me and Mom's fluttering fingers, trying to grasp mine. As she shrieked "Michael, get up here *right now*—an' I don't mean maybe!" I could only see the clasped hands of the two big boys. I faintly heard Mom repeat "I said..." but was busy tracking the tangy scent of hot pizzas wafting by from somewhere I couldn't see.

When the light turned green and we all stepped forward into the street en masse, I asked my mother "Why was those two men back there holdin' hands?"

For a moment, Phyllis looked down at my puzzled little face and said nothing. Then, she softly replied "Because—because they like each other—" to which Hank finished her brush-off reply with "—a *lot*!"

Then, just as swiftly as we'd come above ground and landed in this village full of green witches, we dove down the littered narrow stairs and boarded the next southbound subway train.

———

At Manhattan's southern tip, we gladly emerged from all that ringing darkness and jostled our way among the huddled masses yearning for ferry tickets to Lady Liberty. Once again, multitudes of strange people surrounded us. Trapped in their cramped midst, we baked in the sweltering summer heat.

When the women and children in our pack finally fled Battery Park's sizzling sun for the shade of a tree away from the swamped ticket window, a pigeon dropped a juicy do-do bomb down the entire length of Aunt Dot's slacks leg. At that exact, dirty moment, Dad and Uncle Hank ran up, triumphantly waving tickets for a Liberty-bound ferry.

We viewed the tip of Manhattan from a ferry crossing New York Harbor.

After we inched our way up to Lady's crown, then descended, surviving the crushing lines in both directions, we rode the packed ferry back to Manhattan. As the groaning vessel putt-putt-puttered its way across the bay, Aunt Dot pointed to a clump of weedy trees behind broken-down chain-link fences. "Hank's folks passed through there when they came from Germ'ny before the war, when they came through Ellis Island." I'd never heard of the place. All we could see was a ruined ghost town, striped by long white streaks of runny seagull shit.

Once we returned to solid ground we quickly forgot the eerie island as Uncle Hank and Aunt Dot resumed our downtown tour. We walked the length of white-marbled Wall Street, then viewed the hallowed box pew where George Washington sat when he served as the first president of the U.S. in the new country's first capital. Upon leaving Trinity Church, we unknowingly departed the throngs treading the standard sightseeing route, as Uncle Hank—a privileged detective for the Port Authority of the City of New York—had a surprise for us.

Aided by a flash of Hank's badge, we took a shortcut through construction-site barricades. Our family's hero-for-the-day shepherded us into a caged elevator where each of us received a hardhat. Then, up we went! Up and up—and up; higher and still higher; further, ever further—until we reached the top of the unfinished World Trade Center's South Tower.

As the last floors consisted of mostly wall-less steel-beam frames, we had to lean into the stout wind in order to stay upright. Unlike us kids, my mother did not find the feat amusing. Literally scared stiff, Mom clasped my little hand so tight that by the time we descended it had turned ruby red.

Landfill created while excavating World Trade Center grew Manhattan.

The South Tower had no walls when we were there, and a Hudson River oil spill crept past Lady Liberty.

It was the highest above-ground point we flatlanders had ever reached. We glimpsed far below us a megalopolis that both fascinated and repulsed us—one we hardly understood. As we soon were to discover, however, inspecting the top of the world's then-tallest building without the luxury of walls to keep us there wouldn't cause our only belly-flip-flop that day.

At the beginning of the Seventies, New York City remained in the throes of postwar white-flight. Devastated by a shrinking economy coupled with broken municipal politics, all five boroughs were skidding—fast. A plain-clothes cop, despite the real and readily available danger involved, Mom's six-foot-two brother-in-law didn't hesitate to give his guests from Iowa up-close views of Gotham's grim underbelly. Of course, that dare-devil tour included a locked-car-door drive through Harlem—and that in his shiny, white-wall-tired, football-field-sized look-at-me-then-git-outta-the-way Electra.

In the 1970s, such opulent excess hardly spawned a second thought.

———

Still charred and scarred from recent riots, once-affluent Harlem resembled a Grand Dame ungracefully grown old. She'd become bedraggled and sported a black eye. Boarded-up windows, gushing fire hydrants, abandoned lots and, ugliest of all, the shells of torched houses full of garbage filled our eyes with desolation. Down-and-out men, both ancient and tragically young, sat around with vacant stares and hollow bellies. Teenage mothers towed several small ones from nowhere to anywhere. Boys in ill-fitting hand-me-downs stopped to flip off and curse Uncle Hank's opulent, dark-tinted Buick Electra.

All such scenes were unlike any we'd ever seen back home, in Iowa.

Abandoned or burning houses and wall-to-wall graffiti became norms.

Just as I thought we'd landed in hell again, I strangely recalled Miss Thompson's leading us in singing:

> *When you're down and out*
> *When you're on the street*
> *When evening falls so hard*
> *I will comfort you*

As we rode around for hours, Uncle Hank ducked down this street to show us yet another sorrowful sight, then turned that corner to reveal one more shocking side of life in a ghetto slum. As the late-summer sun sank, he brushed aside Aunt Dot's "fretting out loud" that we leave Harlem before darkness fell.

Then, as he slowly drove us past a low-rise housing project, our detective-cum-guide shouted out (as if finally securing a piece of long-sought evidence) "See dose people carryin' away dat toilet bowl, dose light fixtures an' dat door?" We all turned as one and stared, blankly, as a heavily-loaded procession of some half-dozen Harlemites headed haltingly down the steamy sidewalk. "Know what dey're doin'?" Uncle Hank quizzed us. Of course, we didn't. "I'll tell ya. Dey're stripping dose new units dare. Of everything dey can carry 'way. Ta sell. Most likely for a few bucks. For drugs." Then, he turned the car around sharply and headed the Buick Electra for the George Washington Bridge—and "back ta Jersey.".

Crammed in the rear seat of that lumbering land yacht, scrunched between other prairie greenhorns frozen with disbelief and shock, I felt sick. Then, inside my dizzy little head, I heard faint refrains of:

For ghetto children, tough street life was the only world they ever knew.

> *I'll take your part*
> *When darkness comes*
> *And pain is all around*
> *Like a bridge over troubled water*
> *I will lay me down*

By that point we felt pain all right—endless streams of it. How could we not feel stunned by the unfathomable, and for us inexplicable, suffering we'd just witnessed? We came from another planet, one unimaginable for New Yorkers. In our world, for nightly entertainment folks listened in on party telephone lines to catch the neighborhood news and local dramas buzzing back and forth above the quiet, abiding prairie. Ours was a place where Dad would take a Mason jar into the grove and strip out our one remaining cow while she grazed undisturbed, then return to the house and set the still-warm milk on the table. Where, if a ewe died or rejected her newborns during lambing season, motherless lambs received a rare dispensation to be in the dark basement, in a blanket-lined cardboard box, tucked tight up against the furnace—an exception to an otherwise strict ban on animals in our home.

George Washington Bridge tied suburban refuges to Manhattan Island

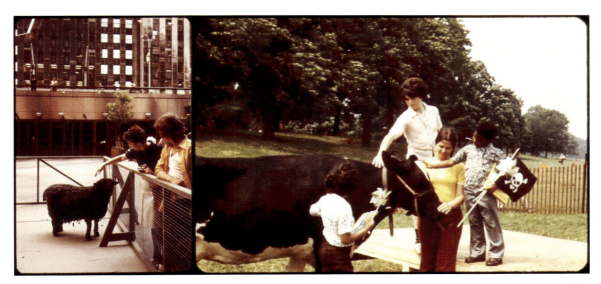

When we Iowa school kids read in My Weekly Reader *that some New York children thought butter came from daisies, we thought they were dumb, even crazy. Many had never* seen *farm animals; we knew them by name.*

In New York, we felt as if we had fallen out of the sky, dropped in from an implausible land where harvest crews still rotated between each other's farms, where double-seated outhouses outnumbered two-stall garages, where for fun we went on lengthy, well-attended trail-rides atop sure-footed, uncomplaining horses, then perused endless potluck tables. The biggest "big city" I'd ever seen had 200,000 souls; here, there seemed to be that many crammed into some high-rise buildings.

Big-city kids found horses a novelty; I counted them among my friends.

Most of our social coordinates centered around family get-togethers, Fourth of July parades followed by picnics and fireworks, the North Iowa Fair, autumnal quilting bees and winter card parties, Christmas pageants or "box-social" fundraisers held in one-room schoolhouses, and rowdy shivarees thrown for newly wedded neighbors. We *never* thought of setting out for church without first polishing our black-leather shoes or perfecting the tight knots in our thin suit ties, and Mom wore freshly bleached white gloves while listening to Reverend Usher's long-winded sermons. Our world had neat, straight lines, and we wore them well.

We belonged in Mason City, not Gotham City—and, we could never belong to it. With our quaint ways and simple pleasures, our slow, down-on-the-farm days and modest treasures, we had dropped in from not just another planet, but another galaxy. We stuck out amidst the millions of New Yorkers buzzing all around us—and that dissonance sat uneasy in our souls.

As brawny Uncle Hank mercifully evacuated us from Hades, he sped us over the Hudson. We visiting, last Victorians felt numb, unable to say anything as we crossed that "bridge over troubled water."

For my part, eight-year-old Mike Luick had understood little of what we had seen in just one, ordinary day in the Big Apple. I knew only that I wanted to "lay me down" to sleep—as soon as possible.

Leaving Manhattan behind truly felt like a welcome escape from hell.

chapter 75: revolution from within

Our family completed our grand East-Coast tour as our parents had planned it: We called on relatives in Mount Holly, New Jersey, and poked about the shadowy slave quarters at George Washington's plantation at Mount Vernon, Virginia. And, for a long day we bopped about the nation's capital—during which farmer Bud careened our makeshift mobile home through D.C.'s busy boulevards, sending us four kids in the back flying through the air, along with weightless boxes of cereal and heavy jars of watered-down juice. Still, we survived it all to return to the Land of Us.

After we had encountered that radical clash of cultures in New York, something in us, in me, would never be the same. Yes, once back in our safe, self-affirming universe in Iowa, Dad continued to cultivate his healthy crop of rigid preconceptions about how human beings, how all creation ticked, and Mom renewed her battle to shelter us children and herself from an encroaching world. Still, we'd sampled a mysterious realm beyond our prairie paradise; its seductive aftertaste would long linger on my hungry lips. It'd be only a matter of time—

For the moment, though, Mom continued going through the motions. Leaving Mason City's bejeweled, 1920s Park Theater after a Saturday matinee showing of Disney's *The Aristocats*, she spied a group of long-haired, jean-clad youth listlessly throwing around Frisbees across the street. She pushed me faster in the direction of our new, white-and-gold Pontiac Catalina down the street, herding me away from "the hippies overtaking Central Park." What she didn't expect, however, was the rebellion brewing at home.

my sister's future husband (left, now deceased) Gerry Wass, Debbie, our twin cousins Cindy & Steve Floyd, and Cindy's future husband, Greg Knowles, "groovin' out" on the front porch at Ashlawn Farm, early 1970s

My older sister, Debra Lynn, was no Sixties radical. Yes, less than a year and a half before our trip to New York City, on a sunny Wednesday morning, 22 April 1970, she had joined some twenty million other Americans in observing the first Earth Day. The brainchild of a U.S. senator from Wisconsin, it was celebrated at the time for its support from both Republicans and Democrats, middle-class and poor, urban and rural Americans. Credited with the creation of the Environmental Protection Agency as well as acts to protect air, water and endangered species, it enjoyed genuinely broad appeal. On that brisk morning, my otherwise mostly apolitical sister and her best buddy, Janine Astrup, pedaled to class from the Astrups' farm on the edge of the nearby hamlet of Burchinal. Although Clear Lake High was less than an hour's ride away, opting to bike rather than bus to school was unheard of among rural people then. To this day, Deb doesn't waste many words about their symbolic gesture, but the act spoke volumes.

Like much of what was seen as "counter culture" in the Sixties and early Seventies, my big-sister's "protest" consisted more of passing fashion than lasting politicization. True, in her upstairs bedroom my sister casually displayed for her friends the latest album releases she could coax Mom to buy or procure herself on the thinnest of budgets: the Beatles' *Abbey Road*, Cat Stevens' *Teaser & the Firecat*, the Velvet Underground's *Loaded* and, of course, Simon and Garfunkel's *Bridge over Troubled Water*.

And, like the candy-pink-and-lime-green paisley sack dress she wore in our 1968 church-directory family portrait (with matching candy-pink, pointy-toed ballerina shoes), Deb had a penchant for sewing super-short outfits as 4-H projects, which clearly displeased Mom. ("Oh, what *will* the other mothers think?") More embarrassing than Deb's immodest hemlines was her readiness to socialize with other teenage girls clad in either mini- or maxi-skirts, accompanied by young men with rumpled hair that dared dangle as low as their collars.

Beyond her daring tastes in music, wardrobe and friends, however, my sister remained securely anchored in the conservative soil of Middle America.

Cousin Cindy Floyd (left) with my sister, showing off then-current "grooviest" fashion; Jack Hunt, Dorothy (Thrams) with Donna & Hank Bredenbeck, Cindy Floyd holding me, Eleanor (Thrams) Hunt, Irene (Thrams) & Thurman Floyd, my brother, Grandma Thrams, Craig Bredenbeck, my father, sister & mother, and Mom's Aunt Bernice (Reid) Thrams; Dave & Deb open Christmas presents, wearing the most recent early-'70s attire.

It was our parents' religion, however, not their politics, against which we children most radically rebelled. While in the late Sixties a chaotic, sexy cultural fringe in chiefly coastal cities stridently tugged the country to the left, as of the early Seventies a less photogenic, intentionally un-sexy counter revolution in the American Heartland silently dragged the U.S. to the right. My siblings—long used to dealing with emotional stress by submitting to a dominant fatherly figure—opted to join the vanguard of social retrenchment. I, on the other hand, took a road less traveled.

Greg Knowles, Cindy Floyd and her twin, Stephen

The later Reagan Revolution, to which the American Heartland's religious realignment of the 1970s lent its blessing (orchestrated by a so-called Moral Majority), however, remained for us what Germans call *Zukunftsmusik*—"music of the future," something that has yet to happen but at present is unreal. Still stranded in the bad-hair Seventies, we Luick-Thrams offspring had things more immediate than theology with which to busy ourselves. We wrestled with creeping moral debauchery, much of which reached our prairie backwater via transistor radio, black-and-white television or the local record shop.

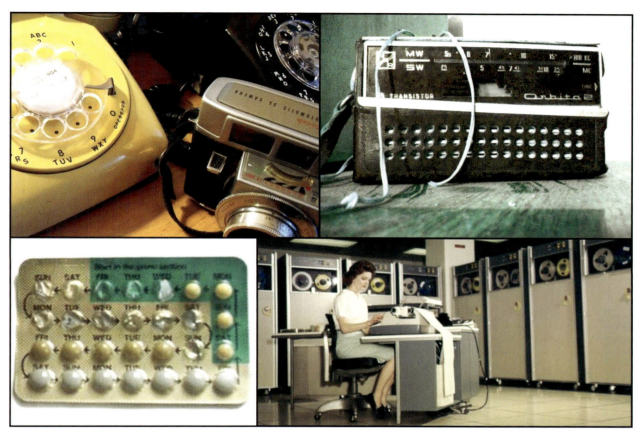

technology from another age and world: telephones, camera, transistor radio, "the pill" and a computer

When the first discotheque in Mason City threatened to open in the mid-'70s in what had been a spacious but failed Piggly Wiggly supermarket, David asked Mom why she so adamantly opposed the new joint. "It'll promote illicit morals" she answered with cold confidence. Perhaps Phyllis had, indeed, absorbed a little tacit knowledge while we were in New York. Had she gathered from her cop brother-in-law that, after the gay-male revolt at Greenwich Village's Stonewall Inn in June 1969 led to lifting the ban on same-gender dancing in public, "discos" were sprouting up across downtown Manhattan as fast and furiously as bitchy drag queens show up at a shoe sale?

Whatever what really hid behind her high-minded objections, Mom's *Angst* reflected her biography.

———

As a child of the Great Depression, Phyllis had grown up with radio, but the "wireless"—as Grandma Thrams sometimes referred to it— had been a different creature in its heyday. Unable to part with it years later, when I was a kid our family still had a console-encased specimen gathering dust in the attic above Ashlawn Farm's storied garage. Bulky, commanding and infinitely impressive, it wasn't just the thing's look that made that early radio's defining difference: It was its content—and lack of portability.

In my mother's youth, clothing and fashion made political and cultural statements, too—as seen in a Works Progress Administration poster for modern-dance concerts held in Los Angeles, July 1937 to January 1939.

1920s ad for console radios; 1930s Rural Electrification Administration promo photo, "Little girl by radio"

When our parents were children, after days of working outdoors, their families spent evenings parked in front of the radio. They sprawled out on the floor (at least in warm weather, in those pre-central-heating days) or sofa, playing cards or with toys. While the Luicks' listening tastes went unrecorded, Bicentennial-era interviews revealed that the Thramses sat around their radio at night listening to the likes of *Fibber McGee and Molly*, George Burns and Gracie Allen, Edgar Bergen with his ventriloquist dummy "Charlie McCarthy," and Lucky Strike's *Hit Parade*. Phyllis especially liked *Jet's Adventures*, with its vivid tales of a pioneer boy headed west with his family on the Oregon Trail—not unlike those Grandma Thrams used to tell of her own grandparents' epic trek west in 1851. (Erma relayed such epic tales to little Phyllis who, in turn, as a young mother, passed them on to eager Mike).

A stationary, centrally-located radio, however, determined to a great degree the behavior of its openly-watched listeners. It also forced those present to negotiate (or submit to) the broadcasting content desired by the group (or dictated by parents). Besides the fact that our Depression-era grandparents would have been hard put to afford such an expensive luxury even if it had existed then, the arrival of transistor radio in 1954 (the year before Debbie was born) meant that we kids were exposed to cultural content (and, indirectly, social values) that either we chose or, more often, simply allowed ourselves to be fed by sales-driven stations.

David's bunk was below mine, and there were many nights I struggled to fall asleep as my big brother listened to "his" radio under the blankets. Down the hall, Deb dozed off most nights with hers still blaring the latest hits. This is, until her batteries ran out, forcing her to earn battery bucks via stray babysitting gigs or by cleaning house for my neighbor-friend Dwight's ancient, help-dependent grandparents, the "old Furleighs."

But, consoles housed not only radios in the first half of the 20th century: The first television set I can remember in our home sat in a mahogany box. Dainty doors with nickel-plated-ring handles concealed the screen when not in use. Every couple years, as TV technology evolved, Dad and Mom replaced each soon-outdated generation of glass-screen tubes with an ever-larger model. Not long before David graduated from high school in 1976, our family graduated to a color set. The subject matter, though, not the clarity or shade of the screen, toppled the last Victorian mores then still prevalent on the prairie.

For years this, my favorite TV series, showed a world away from mine—but maybe that was the lure!

When I got home from school each day, I watched *Bart's Clubhouse*, a cartoon-based show for kids produced by KGLO in Mason City. Almost all of the other available television fare served, however, reflected East or West Coast tastes and sensibilities rather than local ones.

At the time, we received only CBS, ABC and, if the southerly winds from Minnesota were right, NBC. All three network channels peddled programming showing, for us, foreign fantasy worlds—oddballs shipwrecked in the South Pacific (*Gilligan's Island*), families with too many or too many smug kids (*The Brady Bunch*, *Partridge Family*), grouches (*All in the Family*, *The Jeffersons*, *Maude*, *Sanford and Son*), detectives in palm-lined climes (*Hawaii Five-O*, *Columbo*, *Mannix*) or concrete-canyoned New York (*McCloud*, *Kojak*), doctors, cowboys, sheriffs, genies and bewitches—and myriad others. Often airing social issues we in the Heartland could only understand in the abstract if at all, we smiled at their most slapstick antics or cheered when they got the buy guys (which they always did), but the unfamiliar settings and situations more often than not left us confused and disengaged.

About the only series with which we could consistently identify were *The Waltons* and *Little House on the Prairie*, but especially the latter became so altered from its inspiring origins to fit canned television-studio formulas that we shook our heads and eventually turned the dial to other channels.

Unflappable Walter "Iron Pants" Cronkite seemed to fear nothing—even reporting from Vietnam's jungles.

More than fictional characters doing amusing or adventurous things, however, it was real people doing serious or dangerous things that touched us most profoundly. Besides watching the weighty likes of Walter Cronkite reel off the daily "body count" from Vietnam, we watched as our nation began to unravel among the wilting palms of Southeast Asia, as a social revolution bust apart the quiet consensus which had seemed to reign before the bullets flew and bombs fell. We watched as first Martin Luther King and later Bobby Kennedy bled, then cities across the country burned. We witnessed Kennedy's casket crawl across a quiet continent, crowds lining the route, stiff and numb, often crying face-in-hands. We stared with disbelief as students occupied college halls and suburban homemakers marched for "ERA," the much-maligned "Equal Rights Amendment" that failed to pass but pissed off macho-male America as it roamed from statehouse to statehouse, begging in vain for ratification. We watched smiling Anita Bryant sing sunshiny jingles about orange juice, only to get a pie in her puss in Des Moines as she decried "the homosexuals taking over America." All this, brought to us by the makers of Corporate American Television.

———

Television, portable radio, and records brought us children of the Sixties and Seventies distractions and dynamics that our parents rarely succeeded in blocking. All attempts to censor such influences merely made them more attractive. I had no reason to think my teenage siblings ever used drugs stronger than alcohol (or even smoked cigarettes more than a one-time dare), but the fact that we knew such things existed "out there" (as were clothes that scarcely clothed, or no-holds-barred dance floors pulsating with calls to "deviant" behavior) was enough to render the Old Order defenseless. That buyable parallel reality held great sway: a few beats of "decadent" music and, POOF!, it all imploded.

While my grandparents had had old-fashion consoles that housed radios and the earliest models of TVs, my parents invested in a "mod" console around 1970. Deb snuck her vinyls onto the turntable when Mom wasn't around or had let her guard slip, but mostly it was Phyllis' albums that boomed from this big box: Iowa-born Andy Williams, Ed Ames, Burt Bacharach, Pat Boone, Dinah Shore, Dionne Warwick and the like. If I was well-behaved (which didn't happen that often) or ill-at-home (when I had pneumonia for weeks in 5th grade) then I got to listen to my favorites: Burl Ives, Mary Poppins, The Sound of Music...

Cousin Cindy Floyd took as her husband Greg Knowles (here with baby Ben). Greg's love of music, especially folk and blues during a turbulent era, made him suspect for my father. He and Cindy didn't attend Woodstock, but they did go to regional live-music performances—for some a "political act." At the time attending a university in Missouri, Cindy's twin, Steve, wanted to follow the masses of young people to Woodstock, but changed his mind when NMSC staff threatened there'd be "consequences;" if he'd gone, he would have missed a test and thus failed a class, resulting in losing a coveted college deferment from the draft. Steve was one of millions of men avoiding it.

The popular music of the Sixties departed from the stilted tones of the inane Fifties tunes that preceded it. Transistor radios radically altered Western civilization as the new, portable pop music morphed into a private-public forum. And, my Iowa farm family bobbed along in the wake of that sea change even if at the time we had little clue about the societal tectonic plates shifting around us.

Many people—fans as well as detractors—assumed much of the music already then defining the era was composed by musicians on drugs or had cloaked references to drug use. If we did not understand all references, subconsciously we sensed deeper meanings in lyrics like "Lucy in the Sky with Diamonds" or

*Like a bridge over troubled water
I will ease your mind …*

—and our minds needed easing! Shedding a centuries'-old social order was stressful business! Despite (or because of) the music's origins, millions of Americans turned such music on—and many of them were "turned on" by "hippie musicals" like *Hair*, *Godspell* or *Jesus Christ Superstar*. To Mom's chagrin, Deb and Dave could recite entire verses from such "offensive" lyrics.

Ironically, my sister and brother would later espouse social conservatism along with newly found fundamentalist Christianity. But, as young adults they seemed to find little time to conserve the material culture from which we came. Debbie happily sewed for hours on chalk-marked pieces of fabric she'd turn into hot pants or cool jump suits, but she and her neighborhood girlfriends had no use for their grandmothers' quilting needles or their quiet, accompanying "piecing chat." Maturing David could appreciate a handsome horse, but a steed's appeal paled at the speed at which his new cobalt-blue Nova coupe could whisk him away from Dad's long reach and toxic tongue. But, me? I spent hours sorting quilting scraps, all the while listening to Grandma recite endless stories of "our people."

For years, starting when I was little, Grandma Thrams had me sit next to her and sort through scraps of clothes or linens reaching back to the 1930s, pick out 28 colorful, patterned diamonds, then skewer them on straight pins. Over the following years, she pieced together a quilt that everyone admired and speculated for whom she'd invest so much fine work. Finally, when I was in high school, she presented me with her masterwork, a "Garden of Stars."

At the time, the era's pop music left me cold. I was too young, too immature, too inexperienced and thus too reactive to understand or appreciate it. In spite of Miss Thompson's noblest efforts, I hadn't the faintest idea what to make of magic dragons named "Puff," houses called "Rising Sun" or hotels in California one could never leave; of Herb and Rosemary on time, or some girl with flowers in her hair, at a fair, with green sleeves! I was driven mad by silly wailing about people in yellow submarines, men with tambourines, songs sung blue, black birds waiting a moment to be free, singin' birds an' croakin' toads, black ink on white pages, words of wisdom and dust in the wind when we'd been told there should've been *answers* blowin' in that wind!

Clearly, the confusing, discordant times, they *were* a changin'—but I was content to let it be, ta jus' let it all be!

Feeling overwhelmed by content I couldn't understand, my after-school reports to Dad and Mom about "upsetting" music lessons grew louder and more frequent. Joined with similar complaints my classmates aired in their homes, Central's never-smiling principal, Oren Holstad, apparently received enough phone calls to one day finally summon Miss T. to his office.

Clear Lake's Central School, on the "hill" where I learned to be a reader with Fun with Dick and Jane; *1980*

The crescendo of objections to her pop-music selections likely was the last straw for pitiable Miss Thompson. She must have been fed up with what seemed to be ungrateful bumpkins. Did she inform her smug accusers that Three Dog Night songwriter Hoyt Axton originally wrote "Jeremiah was a *prophet*" but "no one liked that" according to one band member in a later interview? Did she even know the song had biblical origins? Would it have even mattered to our shouting, indignant, finger-wagging Midwestern parents, had Miss T. known that and told it to them?

We tortured children finally received a reprieve from times of trouble and beasts of burden, from suns said to be coming up but never pulling it off, scary forests echoing with laughter and dark desert highways. After Miss Thompson was seen "upstairs" storming out of bald Mr. Holstad's windowless office, her lessons in music appreciation changed abruptly. Miss T.'s fuming boss must have demanded immediate spiritual reform, for overnight an entire crowd of invisible-yet-disruptive interlopers simply vanished. We never again would suffer the likes of Jude, Jojo or Rocket Man. Mother Mary, Suzanne and Piano Man were gone for good, too. No longer dished up endless servings of bullfrog, a dog named "Boo" or horse with no name, we could chew on the task at hand: learning "real" music.

For seemly safe materials she might slip past the community's self-appointed censors, clever Miss Thompson turned to the realm of hymns—albeit revised ones. Even I happily crooned:

> *Morning has broken, like the first morning*
> *Blackbird has spoken, like the first bird*
> *Praise for the singing, praise for the morning*
> *Praise for the springing fresh from the word*
>
> *Sweet the rain's new fall, sunlit from heaven*
> *Like the first dewfall, on the first grass*
> *Praise for the sweetness of the wet garden*
> *Sprung in completeness where his feet pass*

Mine is the sunlight, mine is the morning
Born of the one light, Eden saw play
Praise with elation, praise every morning
God's recreation of the new day

---

chapter 76: war comes home

After surviving too many lessons with embattled Miss T., I'd grown so tired of The Whole Thing that already as a pre-teen I hungered for spiritual sustenance. I needed a metaphysical "bridge over troubled water" which might calm my flailing mind. Music, however, would not be my refuge. While Deb and Dave smuggled it into our prairie fortress via transistor radio or eight-track tape, I found (in contrast to Deb and Dave's later-chosen paths) the first cues for my adolescent rebellion against religion *in* religion, but from far outside the Christian mainstream on which we Luick-Thrams kids had been weaned.

One wintry Saturday night while Dad and Mom attended a neighborhood card party, I watched a film on television that set my merciless questioning into unstoppable motion. It was an exotic story set in India, about a quiet boy on the crowded Ganges, confronted by a tragic death—and the reincarnation of the deceased as a noisy cricket kept in a tiny cage on a sunny balcony. Way outside any frame of reference I might have inherited, I went to Sunday school the next morning and waited for a chance to ask the teacher (Mrs. Rosenthal, the quiet but respected wife of the owner of the Corner Drug Store, the apothecary on Main Street that still boasts a functioning soda fountain) about what I'd seen.

"As Christians. We don't believe. In reincarnation" the startled woman explained in rough segments. She showed as little expression as possible while she tried to control a rather rowdy mob of my peers.

"Why not?" I demanded.

Clearly vexed, she did not answer me but turned to the others and ordered "Open your Sunday-school books to the part about Jesus calming the waters. You can see there that—"

Methodist church, where I (3rd from left) went to summer Bible camp to learn how to be a Mensch*; 1968*

After class Mrs. Rosenthal hurried down the hall and brought my blasphemous behavior to the attention of her nearest fellow Sunday-school teacher—my mother! On the tense ride back to Ashlawn Farm, as the news of my heresy soaked in, Mom stared straight ahead and, after a few more moments of punishing silence, muttered "Michael—you think too much."

In the North Central Iowa of the late '60s and early '70s, it didn't take much to earn this label of shame. There was a war going on: Questioning what was going on behind the scenes—on the battlefield or in the cornfields—made many Middle Americans uncomfortable, if not hostile. The U.S.'s direct involvement in Vietnam arched from the arrival in what was then French Indochina of its first shipment of funds, military advisors and napalm in fall 1950, to the departure from Saigon of the last helicopter evacuating embassy personnel and a few lucky Vietnamese collaborators in spring 1975. For the most part, especially early on in the war, the public happily remained oblivious to its government's actions in Southeast Asia. By 1968—when over half a million American draftees were on the ground—such willful ignorance could scarcely be sustained. Still, millions of sleep-walking compatriots only unwillingly shed their selective vision; with their naiveté, they often also shed all civic faith.

protesting the Vietnam War in Washington, D.C., (left) and Wichita, Kansas—both photos, 1967

Born in the middle of that quarter century of extended U.S. military engagement in Southeast Asia, I was not yet a teen when that project ended. My experience of it, and of my family's experience of it, remains more in the realm of sensual than intellectual perceptions. Above all, what remains most vivid to me are the aggregate *feelings* I had arising from a childhood on the tense, tumultuous homefront, rather than any *thoughts* I had. I remember most viscerally, for example, the following:

We often drove to Mason City to visit Mom's oldest sister, Aunt Eleanor, and her one-time-boxer husband, Uncle Jack. Jack liked to drink, then verbally spar with all who might banter back. On the way, our steamy-windowed Rambler passed house after postwar, cookie-cutter house with little, blue-starred service flags hanging in front windows all along Sunny Circle, until we reached the Hunts' yellow ranch-style home. Now and then we'd spy a flag with two stars—silent signs of two family members torn away as fodder in the swelling ranks of the armed forces. Sometimes, we'd see a gold star indicating a fallen son—but then quickly drive on, without comment.

After we pulled into the Hunts' short drive and headed for the warm, relative-packed house, one of the first questions we asked our hosts was "Have you gotten any news from Terry?"

Deb with cousin Cindy Floyd (late 1950s) in front of Eleanor (Thrams) and Jack Hunt home in Mason City

After confirming that their tall, handsome son was alive and reportedly well, our solidly-built auntie would then step back and offer "Come on in, folks. It's a cold world out there!"

One time, as we slipped over the threshold and into the Hunts' toasty house, Aunt Eleanor announced "We got a letter and a package yesterday." Her face showed relief laced with a touch of pride as she held the door open for the last of us to come in. "His ship's in Greece right now—and he sent these lovely ancient Greek urns!" A redhead with help, she made a sweeping motion with a delicate, finely-ringed hand towards the curvaceous, black-and-beige-painted pottery lined up along the mantel of their colonial-style fake fireplace.

"Don't get so excited, El" Uncle Jack bellowed between his pipe-biting dentures. "Those are jus' a buncha replicas!"

"Oh, *I* know that" she sniped back. Her irascible husband, as always, sat in his worn La-Z-Boy in front of the blaring television, amidst a haze of swirling, sweet-smelling smoke.

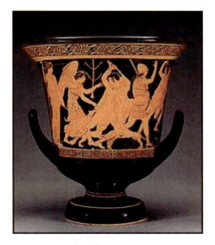

sample of a Grecian urn

Thurman Floyd (white shirt) with all Thrams-Falcon grandsons but one: me, Dave, Terry and Steve, 1969

At some point Dad and Uncle Jack (sometimes with Uncles Thurman and, if the Bredenbecks happened to be visiting from exotic Jersey, Hank) invariably would slide into animated discussions about "Nam." While they rarely aired opinions that countered the gang's consensus, the men's voices did rise on occasion until exploding in thunderous outrage, as if their collective manhood were being attacked.

Upon hearing their clamor, we kids would come racing upstairs from the basement. We had been romping in the mountains of clothes piled up on the clammy basement floor, under the Hunts' laundry chute. (We played next to Terry's unused weight set and bench—dank and dusty, abandoned and lonely since he left for…) Like finely-tuned barometers, we could tell instantly upon entering the living room if we had to be quiet yet or not, for at some point every evening, at every indoor family get-together, an anxious hush would descend upon the room as iconic newscasters like Missouri-born Walter Cronkite or D.C.-native Roger Mudd solemnly announced the day's casualties, the "body count" in Vietnam. At times scenes of soiled, limp bodies being lifted into trucks or helicopters, or of carnage left by blood-spattered panic under towering palm trees, underscored the gravitas of the moment.

After seeing such scenes we kids drifted off—back to the basement to sink beneath laundry waiting to be washed, to Aunt Eleanor's peaceful pink bedroom to hide under her cherry-stained four-poster bed, opposite her glass-topped dressing table covered with myriad prescription drugs, or outside to the knotty apple tree at the bottom of the slope behind the noisy house, to sit on its tender

fighting the Vietnam War on the ground and from the air, 1965

branches and watch angry freight trains barrel by on tracks that stretched off to, then vanished over a foreign horizon. In our busy heads, however, bombs continued to fall through bottomless skies, smoke from napalm-ignited flames continued to rise towards a heaven that refused to intervene, and the jungle continued to crawl with gun-toting Viet Cong.

For a couple of years it was the same, always the same. We arrived at the Hunts' Levittown-on-the-Prairie home; at some point the screaming—of both the middle-aged sofa-soldiers and those in muddy uniforms, flashing across the evening news—would commence. Then, we kids slinked off to find some quiet, safe solitude. Oddly, the whole scene seemed to be an adult-male-dominated drama. If we said anything at all, we children and our mothers spoke only in soft, short sentences. "Anyone want any more ham before I put it in the fridge?" Aunt Eleanor might ask faintly through the doorway between the refugee-filled kitchen and the war-torn living room. Otherwise, we women and children hovered around the dining table, for we dared not be sucked into the televised combat unfolding in the next room. If we did, it could have dramatic consequences.

Operation Linebacker II began on my 10th birthday, 18 December 1972.

Despite our most delicate tip-toeing, a much more personal "war" often raged at home.

Once, I had a chronic cough. Kindly Doc Draper Long—who'd delivered me one bracing, wintry Iowa Tuesday morn at 8:06—had not yet diagnosed my malady as pneumonia. Mom coaxed me to swallow pills she had to relieve congested lungs. When after several attempts I still hadn't swallowed them, Aunt Eleanor—a receptionist at Mason City's Park Clinic—opened her sizeable bag of consulting-room tricks. Between them, the two sisters tried drowning the pills with chocolate milk, placing them on spoons-full of pudding or honey, wrapping them in bread—every stunt they could imagine. By then, I was coughing wildly as I tried to wash the pills down with fizzy cola.

All of a sudden I felt Dad yank my head back by the hair. He beat me in the throat and shrieked "Swallow the god-damned pills, damn it!" He shook my head and throttled my gasping throat until I, somehow, got the pills down. Today still a "choker" and living with a chronic disease, every time I chew my morning cocktail of assorted pills I think of Dad—and The Conflict waged at home.

It would have been one thing, to have absorbed blows from Dad's fists and feet, to have borne his beatings, the sting of rubber hoses against my calves, the shower of gravel that fell upon me as I raced away, having accidentally stepped on the tail of our Golden Retriever bitch, shy Sally, as I came out the back door one day. All that I could have taken. What left the deepest, most damning scars, though, were the verbal assaults, the constant, droning messages:

> "You're stupid an' lazy, fat an' ugly!"
> "You'll never amount to anything!"
> "You're not worth the air you breathe!"

Worst of all were the threats that Dad would "tear off [my] arms and beat [me] over [my] brainless head" or that he "could just kill [me]." The idea that the very man who was supposed to protect and guide me might, at any rageful moment, become my murderer shook me to my core. Living in such a way felt like being under constant assault—not unlike the war we watched going on in "Nam."

———

chapter 77: we all unravel

Compared to less fortunate Luick-Thrams family members, I came away from those violence-shattered days unscathed. The immeasurably worse psycho-trauma that Danny Jones, Dad's older sister's oldest son, experienced in the Vietnam-era Marine Corps would follow him for years until, fed by other, inner fires, it devoured his civilian life, too. Spent and alone, he parked at Saylorville Dam's Mile Long Bridge, north of Des Moines, one fed-up Saturday and ended it all with a shotgun blast to the head.

In December 1971 the Luick-Thrams clan went through the motions of celebrating Christmas, even as its eldest male offspring returned to us briefly from war, changed and tense. As cousin Danny Jones (right) posed with our Gramma Luick, his increasingly weird and aggressive behavior wasn't obvious.

Cousin Terry Hunt (below right, next to his maternal aunt, my mother), sat woolly-faced and soaked in cheap beer—for teetotalling Methodists a real if ignored scandal. We sent clean-cut boys to war: We got back rough-acting young men, toughened by slogging through a living hell and marked for life.

Other North Central Iowa boys, who went into the war less pre-damaged than already troubled Danny had, however, also returned from it forever changed, even if mostly emotionally well and physically intact. Curly-haired, bespectacled Mark Nagel, for one—a neighbor down the road—spent part of the war stationed in Germany. He left our peaceable cornfields a bright, eager boy, but came back deeply affected and permanently altered, if not nakedly jaded. Ironically, it would be *his* absence that later led to *my* later alienation from the very American Heartland he and the others allegedly had been sent to defend.

With her only child no longer home, Mark's mother, Maxine—a WAC in World War II—sold my mother his complete World Book encyclopedia set. Debbie and David occasionally used the hardcover books for homework, but I paged through each well-illustrated volume repeatedly, for years, poring over each article and harvesting as much knowledge as I could. A handful of the articles—"Farms," "Colonial Life," "Pioneers," "Presidents," "Dress"—especially captured my imagination.

young Marine waiting to land in "Nam," August 1965

I was mesmerized, though, by the article about Germany, which I re-read to the point of memorizing whole sentences. Although published in the 1950s, the section about the then-recent Second World War was noticeably meager. The article's other sections were factual but mostly favorable. The several photos showed scenes of postwar West Berlin, as well as classic views of the Rhein, Neuschwanstein and the like. The glowing tales Mark told of Germany when we celebrated his sound return and, soon thereafter, his marriage to a girl from the Dutch-American enclave of Pella, Iowa, only fed my dream of someday seeing that compelling Teutonic country.

For the time being, though, there was both a Cold as well as a hot war to survive. Years later I would become a campus activist in Ronald Reagan's America of the early '80s—a career that had its unintentional inception in Miss Reader's first-grade class. One wintry day in late '69, instead of sending us to don our snow suits for recess, the nervy young teacher announced "Children, this morning, rather than going outside to play, we're going to spend recess indoors." We looked at each other uncertainly, for nothing short of a Soviet nuclear attack would have deterred us from braving any weather in order to enjoy the towering swings, rickety teeter-totters and gigantic slides that awaited us outside.

"Instead" the striking brunette continued, pulling a bulky tape recorder and clunky spools of crackling audio tape from behind her desk, "we're going to learn a song." Stepping to the board with a fresh piece of chalk in hand, she added "That I'm going to record."

We looked at her in puzzled silence.

"Then send to a friend." She peered at her uncomprehending charges, looking hopefully for cooperative—or at least non-resistant—responses. "Who's leaving for a *very* long time."

The room remained stonily still.

medic treats Marine's wounds during operations in Huế, June 1968

"Alone."

More silence.

"To a place very, *very* far away."

We, her otherwise devoted first-graders, remained unsold. We found what she was proposing, the very idea, unimaginable. *Nothing* could warrant foregoing recess.

Until, that is, she added "But, it's a surprise. You may never, *ever* tell *anyone* what we've done"—at which point we yelled "yippee-ee-ee!" and jumped up and down.

Having won us over with a hint of the forbidden, at first stiffly, then hurriedly Miss Reader began writing on the blackboard. In big, straight letters she wrote the words

"ALL MY BAGS ARE PACKED"

in the middle of the chalk-dusted blackboard.

Perhaps Miss Reader foresaw the unhappy fate that would befall her older veteran colleague, Miss Thompson, a couple years later. Or, more likely, the intelligent yet unseasoned educator simply read the tenor of the politically charged times. In any case, she repeatedly reminded us "Now, this is *our* little project. It stays *here*." She needn't have drilled us so emphatically for despite how some of the adults around us acted, most children are not as ignorant as assumed. We sensed that there was more behind what our teacher said, for at the end of a verse or two we saw her eyes mist up. She couldn't fully hide her heart from us on that hushed, secret-shrouded morning. Yes, we were young—but on to her.

Having written out the tune's lyrics at the front of the room and read them aloud several times, Miss Reader then had her makeshift children's choir stand in a semi-circle around the waiting recorder. On her signal, as she set the wobbly audio-tape spools grinding into motion, we began to softly sing:

> *All my bags are packed, I'm ready to go,*
> *standing here outside your door,*
> *I hate to wake you up to say good-bye.*

As we grew more confident, our initial timidity evaporated. We then fairly belted out

> *But the dawn is breaking, it's early morn,*
> *the taxi's waiting, he's blowing his horn.*

As Miss Reader's mouthed the words, she cued us that we should continue, but mournfully, with:

> *Already I'm so lonesome I could die.*

Several times we repeated the refrain that brought tears to our dear teacher's eyes:

> *So kiss me and smile for me,*
> *tell me that you'll wait for me,*
> *hold me like you'll never let me go*

Where was her "friend" going? Where cousins Terry and Danny, and Mark Nagel were?

Christmas at Ashlawn Farm, 1971: Jack Hunt (left), Thurman Floyd, Bud Luick, Willard & Bernice (Reid) Thrams, Cathy (Colleran) & Charlie Ferraro, and me with Terry Hunt, assembling my Sopwith Camel toy

cover to box containing my prized Snoopy fighter-pilot toy kit

Where *was* that, exactly? Who were the people my cousins and Mark—and, now, Miss Reader's friend—would play with there? I knew I didn't know a thing. But, I kept on singing:

> 'Cause I'm leaving on a jet plane,
> don't know when I'll be back again.
> Oh, babe, I hate to go.

Why were the adults around us doing such dumb things—especially things that didn't make *them* happy? They told us we should "behave" and "play well with others"—but *they* didn't!

> There's so many times I've let you down,
> so many times I've played around,
> I tell you now they don't mean a thing.

Whatever they were up to, our parents and teachers; our always-scowling principal Mr. Holstad and our neighbors; the people in the big, peach-colored brick church where we spent hours every Sunday; the folks in the shops and offices, at cattle auctions and ice-cream socials... *all* the adults seemed to say one thing, then do another.

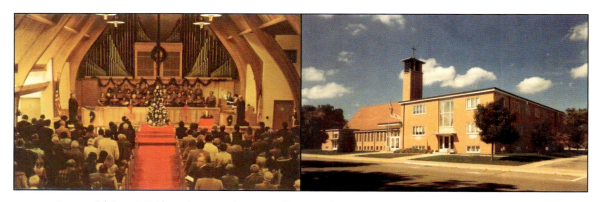

internal (circa 1980) and external images (late '80s) of Clear Lake United Methodist Church

Stupidest of all, they kept making each other mad or, worse, sad. Even when they spoke of "love" there was, at some point, almost always unbearable pain. We didn't get it. But, at least the man in the song *did* promise:

> *Every place I go I'll think of you,*
> *every song I sing I'll sing for you,*
> *when I come back,*
> *I'll bring your wedding ring*

"Is Miss Reader gonna git in trouble for this?" I whispered to a classmate as we pleaded, ever louder:

> *So kiss me and smile for me,*
> *tell me that you'll wait for me,*
> *hold me like you'll never let me go.*
> *'Cause I'm leaving on a jet plane,*
> *don't know when I'll be back again.*
> *Oh, babe, I hate to go.*

There was just so much I could *not* understand:

Why were taxis waiting, honking their horns? Why were young men boarding jet planes—and why didn't they know when they'd be back again? If they "hated" to go, *why* didn't they stay?

And, why were there bombs falling all the time? Why were black-haired children running down roads with their flesh on fire, screaming as scorched skin fell from their quivering limbs? Why did thatched villages lay flattened and smoldering, with old women in round rice hats wailing, rocking back and forth on crouched hinds while American boys in dirty uniforms, carrying unwieldy weapons, trampled about in the background? Why did mute, bloodthirsty Cong comb the jungle? Would they come to Iowa and kill us? Oh, why, but *why* did they hate us *so* much?

women and children massacred by U.S. troops at My Lai, March 1968

Why were my uncles and Dad always angry at students and women without brassieres, people with darker skin or folks they oddly called "queer?" Why were people we saw on TV—white and black, young, old, rich or poor—lining the streets as hearses draped with star-spangled banners passed slowly by? Who fired the shots that made so many people cry?

And, why was Dad always kicking the pigs and slapping the cows and hitting the horses? Why, I wondered, was he *always* hating *me*? Why didn't Mom stop him—or Grandma or Gramma, or Deb or Dave? Why did even fearless Miss Thompson refuse stop my Daddy?

And, *why* couldn't I get pills down or my hopes up, that things would ever change?

Anyway,

> *Now the time has come to leave you,*
> *one more time let me kiss you,*
> *then close your eyes, I'll be on my way.*
> *Dream about the days to come when*
> *I won't have to leave alone,*
> *about the times I won't have to say:*
> *kiss me and smile for me,*
> *tell me that you'll wait for me,*
> *hold me like you'll never let me go.*
> *'Cause I'm leaving on a jet plane,*
> *don't know when I'll be back again.*
> *Oh, babe, I hate to go.*
> *I'm leaving on a jet plane,*
> *don't know when I'll be back again.*
> *Oh, babe, I hate to go.*

———

postscript: war's long shadows

Wars change everything.

Marines entering one of Saddam Hussein's palaces during the capture of Baghdad, April 2003; wounded soldiers being evacuated by plane to Ramstein Air Base in Germany, February 2007; U.S. Army personnel abusing Iraqi detainees at the Abu Ghraib prison in 2003—having written on one's hip "I'm a rapeist" [sic]

They always have—typically, most of all the very thing their instigators initially purport to want to protect, preserve or extend. War's unforeseen consequences often lead to self-sabotage—for example:

The British crown wanted to preserve its North American colonies in the face of growing calls for autonomy by ascending local elites. Through heavy-handed arbitrariness, however, by the time the war against the American "insurgents" ended, George III had alienated the third of the colonial population that reported itself to be "neutral" or "undecided" at the rebellion's onset. (The staunchly Loyalist third fled to British-held Caribbean islands, to Canada or even to the Mother Country.) Thus, instead of securing the flourishing colonies as a permanent flank to Britain, its monarch chased them off.

Stamp Act notice, 1765; romanticized image of New Yorkers pulling down King George III's statue in 1776

In 1914 the crowns of Europe scrambled to maintain power in the face of increasingly industrialized and, later, militarized competitors—yet hubris, incompetence and raw bad luck led to the fall of centuries-old royal houses: Germany's Hohenzollerns, Austria's Habsburgs, Russia's Romanovs and Turkey's Ottoman. The subsequent political vacuum in their absence facilitated the rise of extremists of all sorts—like the Nazis.

In 1939 Hitler and his lock-step supporters sought to buttress what they dreamt of becoming a "Thousand-Year Empire" by subjugating most of Europe—and, if possible, other parts of the world—under Nazi rule. But, deluded by calcified group think and betrayed by their own over-reach, instead of an unchallenged global ruler, Hitler's demonic ambitions and self-centered follies resulted in Germany's decimation, complete devastation, division and half-century-long occupation by Allied victors.

American soldiers interrogating suspected Viet Cong, December 1968

For over a quarter century, the U.S. government led its people in waging both covert and overt war against Vietnam—purportedly to stop a "Red Threat" from overturning America's established order. Ironically, it was its own populace's increasingly eroded faith in the war and in the U.S. government itself that fueled a cultural revolution unmatched by any shifts before or since, that overturned the country's increasingly reactionary order from within.

More recently, two members of the Bush clan waged two wars with Iraq in order to secure a pacific Mideast. Today… well, you know the results.

I grew up in a country at war—as most Americans alive today also have. Even on the remote Iowa prairies, my family personally felt the effects of waging war. And, we carry war's indelible wounds still today. Our veteran cousins returned to the Iowa prairies forever altered or as ticking time bombs that have since ignited, leaving gun-shot-riddled corpses. But we civilians, too, live lives unimagined before our sheltered world imploded.

For us more shattering than all the bombs dropped, all the stone-age villages torched, all the bodies shredded or rendered lifeless on both sides of that protracted struggle, the culture we knew going into the war fragmented and morphed by the war's end. In the process, we morphed, too—as a people.

Eisenhower and newly-elected Kennedy, White House, December 1960

That process—born of and recurrently bathed in deep-reaching conflict—not only caused great changes, but was itself fanned by change: The resulting search for stability claimed many victims. While at the beginning of the '60s the reins of power laid squarely in Eisenhower's hands, they didn't stay there: "Ike" passed them—ruefully—to Kennedy, then they fell to the assassinated President's vice-president, Johnson, who in turn surrendered them, in effect, to Nixon. This transfer of power from a Midwest Victorian to the first Oval Office occupant born in the twentieth century marked a sea change of values, attitudes, goals and strategies to reach those goals.

While factions within the entrenched elite that rules *over* the country vied for who'd control its top offices, we living out *in* the country endured our own inter-generational tussle over power and ways of living. Whereas Grandpa and Grandma Thrams had stewarded Ashlawn Farm in ways that could have continued for centuries with little external input or lasting harm to the prairie's rich loam soil, Dad—pulling complacent, colluding Mom behind—sang a different tune, in petro-soaked, debt-ladened tones.

Phyllis in wagon, behind tractor driven by brother-in-law Jack Hunt; her father, Elmer Thrams, stands in the foreground: circa 1945

As his nephews and neighbors were dropping Agent Orange on faraway jungles, Dad was dropping toxic chemicals—derived from war-related research—on nearby fields. Just as the U.S. Army thought it could use bombs and bullets to steer an entire people's beliefs and allegiances, or gunfire to force the Vietnamese to surrender "insurgents" among them, my father and millions of other American farmers thought they could steer Earth's innate-but-finite ability to sustain life, to force it to surrender ever-greater crop yields in the name of "We're gonna feed the world!"

Yes, by the 1960s the United States possessed the technological ability to completely defoliate millions of acres of jungle, but did we stop to wonder if doing so was wise, moral or even effective? Similarly, by my father's generation, American farmers had the tactical knowledge to steer nature, too, but lacked the wisdom to understand the unforeseen consequences of such brute force, such as over-production. The war against nature that my father and his peers waged took us to places they never intended; and, the trip changed the travelers. Surely, our menfolk meant to secure a better living for us all but, in the end, the industrialization of agriculture wrought the demise of agrarian life in the United States for all but the few mega-farmers left today.

Dad (on top of combine), an unknown hired hand and Grandpa, 1960; Grandpa Thrams (below) reaping wheat at Ashlawn Farm, circa 1920

Although he very likely wouldn't have called it that, my maternal grandfather practiced an art of farming aimed at sustainability, a balance of input verses output that assured that my family not only could survive, but thrive. My father, in contrast, put his complete faith in a mechanized, petroleum-dependent agribusiness model that stressed surplus at any price. In the process of industrializing farming, he and his contemporaries "modernized" everything their mode of farming touched: They straightened streams, removed groves in order to stretch rows, made buildings larger and generic, bred animals for optimal meat, milk or egg production, and even altered grains' genes. In the end, such frenzied mechanization and unswerving standardization eroded not only the soil beneath us, but the world all around us. It accelerated the uglification of the planet and, with it, the spiritual impoverization of us all. And, it happened *so* breathtakingly swiftly. (How long will we need to restore even *a fraction* of what we've lost? But, we must: to continue such developments of the past half century will assure our collective doom.)

Phyllis in front of Thrams family's home, early 1940s; Phyllis (Thrams) Luick at Ashlawn Farm, circa 2000

These processes—devolution wrapped as revolution—didn't occur in isolation but in tandem with larger national, later even worldwide developments. In the America of my youth, the shrinking diversity, vitality and intricacy of rural culture—of the crops and animals raised, the architecture practiced, the rich oral, aural or visual cultural traditions maintained, the bonds that linked us to each other and a shared fate—took place as almost every urban center in the country also became less diverse, less vital, less intricate.

As Ashlawn Farm went from raising up to a dozen kinds of crops in Grandpa and Grandma's day to—under Dad's reign—two, at most four, the range of plant and animal life common on other farms across first the Western, then the industrializing world, also shrunk in number and variation. At the same time, livestock increasingly spent their lives from birth to slaughter indoors, never knowing a day in fresh air or sunshine. And, fruit and vegetables went from being juicy, colorful and pungent to anything but. The very staff of life—fresh, nutritious food—along with things that make life worth living like variety, vivacity and intimacy became flat, stale and empty: Life itself has become a shadow of its former self.

Like an ocean reflected in a drop of rain, these decades-long, global processes are mirrored in the story of my simple Iowa farm folk—over the course of the 54 years my parents knew each other and, by extension, the 52 years that I've been trailing their short sojourns on a fast-changing planet. Dad and Mom's half-century of marriage, alone, witnessed vast changes, both for them and, moreover, the country which they never chose but always knew as theirs. Like their parents, my father and mother came of age during the so-called American Century, that era book-ended by wars with planetary reach—the Spanish-American and the two-part Gulf War. After youths spent in material poverty and rural free-fall, they spent their young adulthoods in an era of unmatched economic expansion and wealth. As they reached retirement, however, they also watched—often sobered, if not horrified—as the nation which once filled them with so much promise and pride, devolved before their eyes and threatened to implode.

When my parents married, they undoubtedly did so with excitement and wonderful plans for the future. Today, seeing both their daily struggles and accomplishments as small cars in a long train, I trust they tried their best to live and prosper. I also know they both suffered frustrations that often were outside their control—as well as endured limitations that not always were—and reacted accordingly. Did my father know and understand he was channeling his own father in his actions toward us, his children? Perhaps. If he did, but knew no other way to act or felt powerless to weave one, his inability to change likely increased his frustration.

Today we so casually bandy about labels like "PTSD," "anger control management" and all kinds of things our parents did not even know they did not know, but with how much success do we make changes in our own lives? Despite all the endless hours of therapy and navel watching, how well do we who have come after them understand and learn from our shared past, so that we make free choices rather than simply being swept along with the tide created around us—in large part, before we arrived on the scene?

As a little boy, of course, I understood none of this myself. I only knew what I saw, heard and felt—and even that I often questioned. It was the things I sensed but could not see—the scary, recurring dreams, or the chills in my spine as Grampa Luick floated across the floor while I played on cool, slick linoleum—which unsettled me most.

An omen? My folks' wedding picture came from the developer with the Luick side of the newly-united couple tinged with a dull, dark shadow.

I also did not know then that my imperfect parents each brought with them to their union at eighteen some decades if not centuries worth of inherited burdens with them—along with genuine familial triumphs. How could I have imagined then, as a boy, that it was not only the things that had happened to my parents' people in generations past that steered their behavior we kids so closely watched, but things that had *not*: the mother-daughter bonds that Gramma Luick never knew; the teaching career she dreamt of and saved for but never had; the loving, faithful husband she at some point realized she lacked...

No, I did not understand such things that defined my early world—till now.

Section 2:
Donald & Charlotte (Juhl) Luick

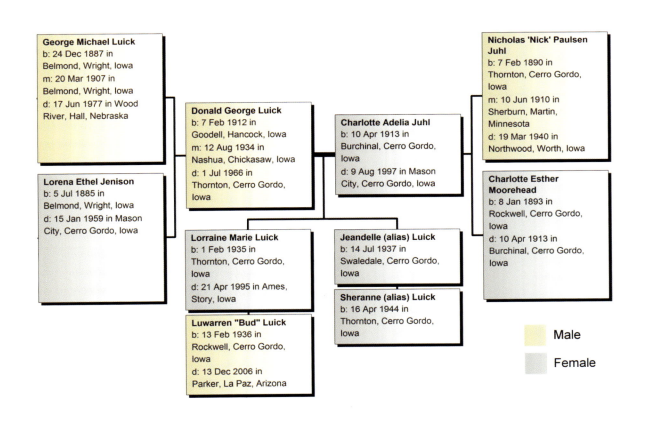

Donald George Luick's nuclear family

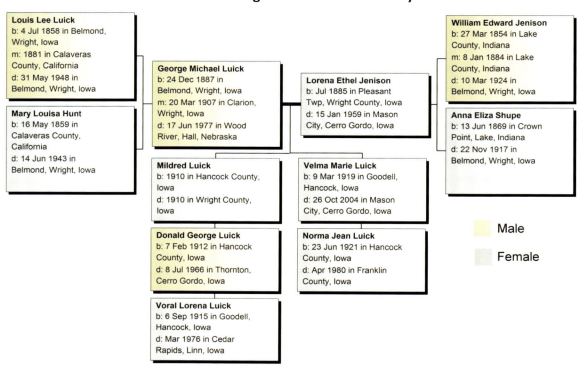

Charlotte Adelia Juhl's nuclear family

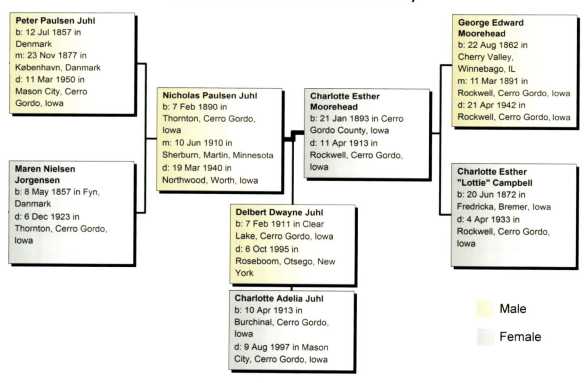

Donald George and Charlotte Adelia (Juhl) Luick

born:	7 February 1912	10 April 1913
where:	Goodell, Iowa/USA	Burchinal, Iowa/USA
married:	12 August 1934	where: Little Brown Church, Nashua, Iowa/USA
died:	8 July 1966	9 August 1997
where:	Thornton, Iowa/USA	Mason City, Iowa/USA

At first glance, the photograph below appears to present a rather happy picture. The viewer can easily imagine several instant narratives that, based on appearances, might fit it well:

- The two individuals are happily partnered, having spent many, blissful years together.
- The corsage-wearing couple is celebrating a happy occasion; or
- The sure-handed photographer devoted all his skill the day he shot this scene and, as the Fates would have it, caught these two in a relaxed, cheery moment of shared satisfaction.

So, which of those three possible narratives is true?

Donald and Charlotte (Juhl) Luick, taken 15 August 1964 in Spirit Lake, Iowa

The answer? Not a *one* of them!

In truth, though:

Yes, Donald Luick and Charlotte Juhl *did* lead a shared life for over 31 years—but "bliss" hardly accurately describes a union that, over time, became increasingly contempt-laced and loveless.

The photo—or, rather, "photos"—were taken on the occasion of the "necessary" marriage on 15 August 1964 of their youngest daughter, Sheranne, to a man (at the time the lovebirds met, a gas-station attendant in Spirit Lake, Iowa) of whom they did not approve. *And:*

The scene was not only posed, but this montage actually consists of two images: Cobbled together pre-Photoshop, if one looks closely, Charlotte's face is much less focused than Donald's. Despite this flaw, Gramma Luick had her and her recently-deceased mate's faces taken from two wedding scenes and manually squeezed into a shared portrait. She had it mass-produced, then distributed it, in thin metal frames, to her four children and, in wallet-sized format, to her 15 grandchildren and, likely, dozens of other relatives as presents for Christmas 1966, over two years after the photos were shot.

What relationship narrative was our paternal grandmother desperately trying to tape together, less than six months after the death of the husband she, at times, seemed to some to despise—and, *why?*

Whenever I think too long, too deeply about my father's family, I suddenly feel like an immense, black locomotive has just barreled through my psyche. It leaves me, like some ludicrous Bugs Bunny cartoon figure, whirling helplessly in its wake as that mighty engine thunders on, stubbornly oblivious to any destruction it's left behind. There I remain, like a pathetic tar baby covered in emotional gunk, abandoned and vulnerable. No matter how hard I might try to kick or moan my way out of it, I cannot wake my way out of this dark, soul-crushing nightmare.

———

chapter 56: the Big Thud

With accelerating discoveries in space, astronomers tell us ever more assuredly that the universe began with one primal, all-determining "Big Bang." A value-neutral occurrence, it resulted in the creation of swirling quasars and shimmering stars, flaring comets, iridescent nebulae, a plethora of planets and myriad moons. Our vast cosmos effortlessly accommodates spiral arms and galactic halos, meteor showers and solar winds... a multitude of gigantic forms revealing a complex universe—one that also includes little-loved, much-maligned "black holes." Space scientists add that a defining basis of all of the cosmos' contents is energy—not "good" or "bad" per se, but rather either primarily "creative" *or* principally "destructive."

Charlotte (Juhl) Luick's essentially unhappy earthly existence—parallel to universal dynamics but on a human level—was determined, in contrast, by a "Big Thud." Like the very cosmos that bestowed her Life and in it found animate sentience, Charlotte's character was a full palette of colors, often opposite deep voids. Her ensuing behavior ran the whole spectrum—ranging from pained private moments to unwanted public hours. Her allotted time on the planet was marked by heart-warming Light forever wrestling with bone-chilling darkness. Tragic in itself, her mostly silent suffering sadly lives on invisibly in her descendants' lives, still tainting those who have not yet faced its toxic legacy.

As amazing—and singularly unfair—as it might seem, one primal event at the time of her birth fundamentally influenced the flow of the rest of Charlotte's ill-fortuned life. No one alive today is fully familiar with all of the disastrous details surrounding it, but several of her offspring have heard varied, confusingly contradicting accounts of her path's sad start. For one, more than half a century after the Big Thud, Gramma Luick told my sister and me that her father, Nicholas Paulsen Juhl, had pushed her mother down the stairs the day after their second child (and only daughter) was born. Each time she recounted the story (which was often, as if she, herself, *needed* to hear it again), she delivered it with such compelling theatrics that I felt as if I could feel the weight of her mother's weakened, ashen-white body fall upon the floor—*THUD!*

When Nick Juhl worked as a clerk in this station, he housed his young family in a frame cottage behind it.

Problem is, however, she told Deb's and my cousin Barbara—the oldest surviving of her seventeen grandchildren—that that son of Danish immigrants had punched Gramma's mother in the stomach and thus sent his wife backwards down the basement stairs; after she hit her head on the floor, she never woke up. One telling has Nick being in an alcoholic rage as he stormed about their small frame house—tucked out of sight behind the Farmers' Cooperative Elevator—while another suggests a sober domestic struggle between the mysterious man and his attractive young wife. A station clerk at the St. Paul and Kansas City Short Line Railroad depot in Burchinal, Iowa at the time, Nick seemed to have few friends or supporters—especially among his in-laws. (Nick did not know that the parents of his future grandson's later father-in-law, Elmer Thrams, owned Ashlawn Farm, only a short three miles [4.8 KM] due north of Burchinal. Even if he had, it would not have helped him ameliorate his—and thus also our—sad fate.)

In actuality, however, as far as anyone in the family now knows or can report with any authority, no other person was present when the reported incident took place. Other, that is, than the mewling newborn, who later said she was born so prematurely small "They wrapped me in cotton wadding, placed me in a shoebox and left me to incubate on the open door of the cookstove."

The "facts" closest to what actually happened *might* be those alluded to in public records from the time—even in the florid obituary written for Gramma's mother, presumably by someone close to her, upon the "Death of Mrs. M.T. Juhl," per its telling headline.

> With the unfolding of a newer and brighter life, nature with a smile that is a harbinger of the unfolding and expansion of the joys and sweetness of renewed vigor and vitality, the spirit of a young life falls into decay in the early morning of womanhood. On April 11th at the quiet hour of two o'clock in the morning the spirit of the life of Lottie Esther Moorehead Juhl fled to its maker and eternal home.
>
> She was born Jan. 8, 1893, the daughter of Mr. and Mrs. Geo. E. Moorehead of Mt. Vernon [Township]. On June 1st, 1910, she was united in marriage to M. T. Juhl. Two children were born to this union, a little boy 2 years old and a small baby 2 days old. The funeral services were held at Burchinal Sunday, the pastor of the [Methodist Episcopal] church officiating.
>
> The flower offerings were many and beautiful, including remembrances from friends in Illinois. At one o'clock she was laid to rest in the Mt. Vernon cemetery.
>
> The little babe will be cared for by his grandmother, Mrs. Moorehead, and a sister of Mr. Juhl will provide a home for the little boy.

Young Lottie's funeral took place in this simple church, where I attended summer church camp as a boy.

A taste of Dickensian mores in place on the prairies at the time, the faded obituary suffers many maladies and outright mistakes. "Nicholas Paulsen"—or "N.P."—somehow got recorded for eternity (twice!) as "M.T." Juhl. More heart wrenching, however, is the forever-negating incorrect citation: little "Lottie"—the last "Charlotte" in three successive so-named generations of women in Gramma's maternal lineage—was erroneously listed as a being *a boy!*

Perhaps, though, the convoluted, difficult-to-read opening paragraph of the obituary was a fitting omen of the convoluted, difficult-to-live childhood that "little [boy] babe" was to endure at the hands of "his" grandmother—and, plausibly, grandfather. In any event, tiny Charlotte was taken from a father who she claimed "didn't want [her]" to be raised by her dead mother's aging parents. What began as a—hopefully unintended—primal loss swiftly became a long-term sentence for a guiltless little girl who had no say in the pending résumé the Fates handed her.

George (left) & "Big Lottie" (Campbell) Moorehead, "Little Lottie" as a hen-pecked girl, her aunt Nellie (Moorehead), uncle Glen & cousin Maynard Raymond Gardner, who died a short time later; spring 1918

Charlotte Adelia Juhl (later "Luick") lost her mother, Charlotte Esther (Moorehead) Juhl, on the newborn's second day. Her grandmother, Charlotte Esther (Campbell) Moorhead, however, was decidedly not an ideal replacement for the infant's deceased mother. The two surviving females—a half-orphaned baby and her half-lame granny—would take turns mourning the loss of the one's mother, the other's daughter. The latter would wade through the waves of grief that haunt an adult mother who's lost an offspring—in this case a child who had left teenagehood only three months before she lost what all assumed would be a long, rewarding life. The former—the dependent babe who someday, far off in her fragile future, would become my Gramma Luick—would bear the loss of a mother who she never knew. First, though, for two tortured decades the increasingly disabled grandmother and maturing granddaughter would both share and vie for a grieving process denied open, emotional form.

mourning "Big Lottie" holding half-orphaned "Little Lottie" Juhl, 1913

Instead, most of "Young Lottie's" immediate survivors seemed stuck in a shocked cult of death. When Gramma—the "Little Lottie" of the trio who shared one forename, if not one destiny—died in 1997, we found several versions of large, mounted and once-framed photos consisting of a montage of a small, diamond-shaped cut-out of Young Lottie's lovely face set inside a pictured wreath of burial flowers. Such morbid memorabilia was not the Mooreheads' one-time response to death: In the same drawer that had sheltered the first images, we found a large, cardboard-backed photo of Gramma's grandfather, George Moorehead, lying in a casket in 1943 surrounded by all manner of flowers in vases, bundles and garlands. And, nearby lay another photograph of relatives or friends conversing, graveside, immediately prior to the lowering of his casket into the cold ground.

While such mementos of the deceased were common at the end of the Victorian era, that Gramma's relatively small collection of family photos should contain so many and such large relics of the dead, for so long, stood out. Perhaps keeping such vestiges of lost ancestors was a way for her to help keep her memories of them alive. The people pictured were, for better or worse, among the only semblance of family she'd had.

Even if she was the only person willing to raise the baby, Charlotte Esther (Campbell) Moorhead—"Big Lottie" to the family—was not a healthy woman. As photographs in coming chapters will show, from a bride whose groom was said to be able to join his two thumbs and index fingers together around her tightly-corseted waist, to a lumbering hulk of a woman who Gramma Luick claimed had to be buried in a piano case "she was so fat," she flipped from petite to obese within a few years. Stricken with "dropsy"—today's "edema," a swelling of body tissue through the abnormal accumulation of fluid under the skin—she labored simply to walk across the room or, even more strenuous, the barnyard. By the time her second youngest daughter died, Big Lottie needed fulltime care. That, she found in Little Lottie.

Claude Miller (left), Jennie (Moorehead) Fuller, Cora (Moorehead) Miller, George Moorehead, Glen Gardner, Little Lottie & Big Lottie: child with big doll is June Fuller, likely 1920; Big Lottie crossing the barnyard, 1920s

As soon as she was big enough to handle a broom, rather than ride a stick horse through the house like other children, infant Charlotte pushed a sweeper around the Moorehead home. While Big Lottie barked orders from her sagging chair, as a girl Gramma turned the family's beds and burned their meals, washed their dishes, scrubbed Grandma's droopy drawers and scoured Grandpa's stiff collars, carried in the coal and took out the night pot, stoked the stoves and baked the bread, topped the kerosene in the lamps, mopped the bottom of the zinc bath tub on Saturday nights, gathered still-warm eggs and scattered flies from cooling pies. While others her age played, she toiled. Her missing childhood would later mar her complete adulthood—and we, her children and grandchildren, had to endure the fallout.

Gramma once told granddaughter Barbara that she "began working at age four." Charlotte's youngest daughter, Sheranne, wrote in March 2014 that her mother

> washed dishes in the local café since she was eight years old. She often laughed when she recalled that she had to stand on a chair to reach the dishes in the bottom of the tubs. She saved all her money for college as she wanted to go to teachers college and get her teaching certificate.

Gramma told me that in high school she "took a job in a dry-goods store on Rockwell's Main Street for a dime an hour" and cleaned houses for neighbors. Despite any tales or incongruous details, it's clear that even if not well trained to cook sophisticated meals (which we tasted X times), not shown how to sew beyond rudimentary repairs (as

Little Lottie caring for her own little one, circa 1915

we saw in her slapdash attempts to fix torn clothes), nor versed in how to most efficiently manage domestic affairs (she put up with cooking on a cob-and-coal-fired stove until 1959 and washing laundry in a steep-staired cellar, using a hand-cranked wringer and a big wooden fork to stir wet clothes, until 1973), "Little Lottie" worked a lot, extremely hard, for a very long time.

ads from Belmond newspapers; butcher shop in Rockwell, 1920s

One time, after I'd returned from attending boys' school in Yorkshire for a year and was studying history at Iowa State, I sat in the back of the folks' new, baby-blue Buick, crammed in between Gramma and a steamed-up window. It was a winter night. We were barreling over the dark, frozen prairie on the way to dinner at my sister Deb's and her husband Gerry's home. Having been active with the Campaign for Nuclear Disarmament back in Britain and then against resurgent militarism when I returned to Reagan's America, I cockily asked my parents and Gramma why they hadn't actively resisted or at least openly rejected Joe McCarthy's "hysterical" anti-communist witch hunt or the "almost-lethal" nuclear arms race in the 1950s—to which Charlotte caustically replied "'Cause we was too busy *workin'*!"

———

chapter 57: children of BOOM!

Gramma was five years old when the First World War ended in November 1918. From that point on, for almost her entire school career, she grew up—conscious of it or not—in an emerging global power. Maybe less so in quiet Rockwell, Iowa, but across America as a whole, the Roaring Twenties were exceptionally eventful and truly exciting. An unapologetic cheerleader for naked business interests, President "Cool Cal" Coolidge focused on facilitating the fortunes of commerce. Despite the conservative national political climate, however, the country danced through a decade dedicated to consumption and "making whoopee." For the duration of the 1920s, Americans largely distracted themselves with the pursuit of making money—*loads* of it.

Besides flinging the country down a road of new—albeit exaggerated, unsustainable—power and wealth, the recent war had slapped lingering Victorian ideals in the face. In the process, it shattered earlier visions of simple morality and innocence. Yanked from the Heartland and plopped down in the midst of battlefield brutality, many Midwest soldiers returned from the war confused by the disturbing contrasts between cozy, small-town life in rural America and the atrocities they'd witnessed in the trenches. In Europe green Iowa farm boys had danced with jaded women uninhibited by Puritanical prudery, who dressed colorfully, wore makeup and smoked cigarettes. And, African-American men among the Doughboys had become celebrities in a France not yet made racist by the influx of former African and Arab subjects. Correspondents eagerly sent home word of that world larger than the limited and limiting realm of church socials, the Masonic Temple and a wire-leg stool at the local soda fountain.

World War I soldiers parading through Belmond, before 1920; Henry Luick's fellow Iowa Dough Boys

During the wartime labor shortage, America's women for the first time had deserted the nation's hearths and henhouses to fill what previously had been male positions. While Victorian ladies had indulged their long, flowing hair hours per week with careful combing, washing and wrapping, modern, mobilized girls could no longer afford the luxury of pampering their hair like they had before America joined the war against the Hun. Now, as they trundled off every morning to tend machines in factories, drive trams through the streets or guide early tractors across the fields, they donned trousers or at least formless smocks instead of fine dresses, and simply left their corsets in the closet and massive hats at home. For the first time, American women tasted autonomy—and, as of 1920, exercised a Constitutionally-guaranteed right to vote. In short, during Gramma's shanghaied childhood a de facto cultural revolution erupted in the midst of the New World's unsuspecting population—and altered the lives of everyone, even busy Little Lottie.

young Belmond women wearing latest fashions, early 1910s; Charlotte Juhl "Moorehead," late 1920s

Injected with new enthusiasm for personal advancement—career and otherwise—and a stable home front after the war, the U.S. economy boomed during the Twenties. In addition to supplying European reconstruction efforts and drawing vast interest from wartime loans, business expanded further through the selling of stocks and bonds. Confident in the prosperity of the times, seemingly everyone invested in the stock market. Not only oil barons and steel magnates, but Parson Smith and Farmer Brown all scraped together their expendable funds and bought as many shares as they could. From 1918 to 1929

Dow Jones Industrial Average highs shot from 89.07 to 381.17. Big corporations bought out smaller companies, farms consolidated as the rural population shrank from fifty-three to forty-three percent of the total population between 1910 and 1930, and increasing numbers of young people flocked to colleges and universities as higher education became synonymous with "making it." Indeed, from appearances at least, it seemed in the heady United States of the Roaring Twenties, that "happy days [were] here to stay."

Lottie with her Louise Brooks bangs and maternal cousin, Arlene Gardner, fishing in Minnesota, 1930

In a climate where fatherly President Warren Harding had promised "normalcy" following the 1918 armistice, then stoic Calvin Coolidge matter-of-factly proclaimed that "the business of America is business," differing social values dueled with each other. While Rotary infected Main Street with community and mercantile boosterism, Hollywood advertised a world of glamour, of unleashed, sexy men snubbing social roles to individually pursue fame and fortune, and of women casually smoking cigarettes and flaunting short hemlines. Ma and Pa may have piously touted prohibition, hard work and familial fidelity back in everyone's hometown, but Junior and Sis off at college carried pocket and hip flasks, went driving in fast cars and necked at illicit parties. Bootleg booze, jazz and "wild" dancing seemed to many as proof of degeneracy.

Yet for most Americans—those not toasted in tongue-wagging *New Yorker* columns or roasted in finger-pointing radio broadcasts—a quiet conformity characterized 1920s daily life. If a noisy minority commandeered the attention of the nation's nascent mass media, the majority of mainstream Midwesterners continued to reside in the self-contained, benighted world of the American Heartland. Thus, my future paternal grandmother remained contentedly embedded in that rural, Middle American mainstream—too "busy workin'" to notice larger events exploding all around her.

Kruggel Hardware store on Rockwell's Main Street, one of the stores Little Lottie could have worked at

Of course, clever Charlotte couldn't have encapsulated herself completely from the wider world. In her graduation photo taken in 1930 she boasted the shiny-black bangs and bobbed side curls made all the rage by Louise Brooks, the Cherryvale, Kansas, girl who Charlestoned her way from New York via London to Berlin and back. The photo doesn't show enough of Gramma's frock to be firmly indicative, nor do we know how "Flapper" her meager budget or Moorehead-family mores at the time allowed her to dare to dress, but later photos taken between 1934 and 1940 show a pretty Charlotte, visibly well-aware of the nation's latest tastes in ladies' fashion.

my grandmother, Charlotte Adelia Juhl, circa 1931

And, it wasn't from nowhere that this skilled scholar of Latin saw in a college education a ticket out of servitude. Was she, too, reading the liberating lines of 1920s' bestselling authors such as F. Scott Fitzgerald, Ernest Hemingway, Sinclair Lewis, Zane Grey, Rafael Sabatini, Edith Wharton or Thornton Wilder? In an era of increasing leisure time, the list of magazines marketed in America mushroomed in the Twenties. Madison Avenue advertising agencies and pioneers in the emerging field of psychology turned from government-underwritten wartime posts spinning propaganda and integrated newly tested techniques into mass-communication and impression management; this led to an explosion in popular media. Did industrious Little Lottie find time to plow through *Better Homes & Gardens*, *Good Housekeeping*, *Home Arts* or *Ladies' Home Journal*? Did she skim *Life* or let her eyes meander in *Maclean's*, *McCall's*, *McClure's* or *Movie Weekly*? Did her mind travel through *National Geographic*, *Radio Digest*, *Reader's Digest* or *Time*? Did she dream of womanly beauty like in *Vanity Fair* or *Vogue*?

Whatever she might have been reading—or not—in those untelevised, not-yet-digitalized days, by the time she reached high school, Little Lottie was plotting to bolt from a barking, disabled grandmother who had both saved and enslaved her. Through part-time labor outside the Moorehead home, she had saved money—all of which she then lost within a matter of moments, through no fault of her own. With the bank foreclosures that followed Wall Street's Crash in fall 1929—some eighteen months before she was to graduate as valedictorian of Rockwell High's Class of '31—hard-luck Charlotte watched helplessly as her dream to outsmart child servitude by going to college and becoming a teacher collapsed.

———

chapter 58: casualties of BUST!

In spring 1931, while Charlotte Adelia Juhl was combing down her bangs and toning up her valedictory speech, two school districts due west of Rockwell, in Thornton, Donald George Luick was also preparing for high school graduation—by livin' it up off the farm while he still could.

my paternal grandfather's graduation announcement and ring; Donald with his car, circa 1930

Looking like Sinclair Lewis' young Elmer Gantry, Donald wore striped suits and slicked-back hair, drove a fast car and lost himself in what youth scene southwest Cerro Gordo County had to offer. A happy attender of bands and dances, he also served as a member of the Thornton High baseball team and of the school-play cast. And, he could never get enough of roller skating—round and round, looking at the girls, the boys… the coy smiles. Young Donald, however, hadn't always lived so carefree. Like Rockwell's valedictorian, he had to venture into the world of work very early—but unlike her, not because of the death of a mother, rather the deaths of millions.

my grandfather (top photo) second from left and (bottom) far left; Thornton's school (center), late 1920s

In 1913, a year after Donald's birth on a farm near Goodell, his father, George, had moved the fledgling family 33 miles (55 kilometers) to the southeast to live in Hampton—a day's drive with a team-drawn wagon or an hour's sprint by horseless carriage in good weather and on decent roads. After only two years of working as a mechanic in one of Wright County's first auto garages, however, the elder Luick took his expecting wife and boy child back to Hancock County to farm. Why? Was it, at least in part, a proactive move in view of the war clouds already raining down on the Old World?

Donald as a boy in Hampton, 1915; his father and mother on parapet

Perhaps the income from the car garage was too inadequate or the call of the cornfields too alluring, for Great-Grampa George swiftly uprooted his growing brood and settled it back on the old farm. No matter what the ostensible reasons for the abrupt career change, the transfer of the family's bread-earning and bed-making assured two significant consequences: George and his wife, Lorena (Jenison) Luick, would increasingly profit from the commodities boom caused by the worsening war then spreading over Central Europe. And, by having more children, George would be unattractive to local draft boards; by engaging in agriculture—one of the Federally-coordinated War Industries Board's three pillars—he also would become untouchable.

Donald Luick's undated report card from Twin Lake Township #1 rural school near Goodell, circa 1919

Problem was, with so many young North Central Iowa men leaving to work in war-related factories in the cities or, later, to fight in the trenches of Europe, George and Lorena could not find, let alone afford hired farm hands. So, they turned to two little ones—Donald's. Only five years old when the U.S. belatedly joined the First World War, Donald found himself perched upon the seat of the horse-drawn cultivator even though he couldn't reach the pedals. The day Donald's father sold his son to the adult work world he pressed him into a chain gang based merely on blood and stole whatever scant childhood my grandfather had ever known. While his peers who came from more-fully-financed farms likely had more time to catch crawdads in the pasture crick or hammer together goat carts out of battered boards, little Donald had to stock America's "arsenal of democracy" by fortifying its granary of foodstuffs—one cornrow at a time.

my grandfather back on the farm, circa 1917; his father, George, and mother, Lorena, in background

It would be the same seductive commodities boom of the Teens that would lead to many farmers' bust in the Twenties. Uncle Sam had encouraged overproduction to meet wartime demand for foodstuffs; the resulting glut after the armistice skewed the balance between existing supplies and tapering consumption, leading prices to collapse. Having risked enormous debt to mechanize their farms during the war, with the end of price controls and decreasing postwar farm income, farmers faced skyrocketing rates of loan defaults and, consequently, foreclosures. While urban parts of the country roared right through the 1920s, rural America limped along.

Until dark days settled upon the United States with the stock market crash of fall 1929, though, Donald—and his then-unknown future wife, Charlotte—had little reason to believe their post-high-school lives could be anything *but* rosy. Every day, in every direction they looked, in my paternal grandparents' pre-Crash youth in the Land of Opportunity they saw ordinary people achieve extraordinary feats. With more money flowing through more fingers—and thus more people devoting more time to leisure than ever before—their fellow Americans hit harder (Babe Ruth), flew further (Charles Lindbergh), looked sexier (Rudolph Valentino), sang jazzier (Al Jolson), trumpeted louder (Louis Armstrong) and massacred more bootlegging competition (Al Capone) than ever before. It seemed, in the heady Twenties, that individuals' abilities—as well as their potentials—were virtually infinite. Having grown up the previous eleven years witnessing ever-greater waves of fortune and fame on America's national scene, they could not have foreseen the misery that was to come. But, come it did.

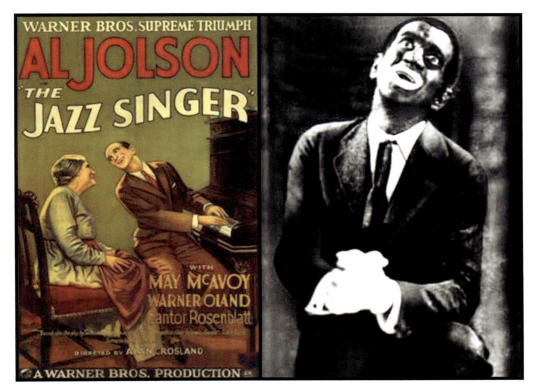

Born Asa Yoelson and a Jew in Lithuania, "Al Jolson" became famous in "black face" and was a '20s star.

When stocks collapsed in late October 1929, rural America fell on its face—and the rest of the country fell with it. After modest regains in stocks in 1930, by spring 1931 any rallying on Wall Street couldn't compensate for general economic conditions that by then were almost all in sharp decline. Between 1929 and 1933 the nation's Gross Domestic Product declined by 46%; by 1933 one-quarter of the nation's banks had failed. Under such chaotic, uncertain conditions, unemployment grew so quickly and so severely that by 1933 twelve million Americans—25% of the workforce—were without a job. In pockets across the country, one of three people had no work. In such a job climate even promising young valedictorians could sing only unemployment blues. So, both of my father's parents left high school with few job prospects and even less hope; Little Buddy would begin Life under dark shadows.

During the Great Depression, millions of dejected American men lived apart from families and friends.

As he would tell his future son some twenty years later, Donald dismissed college as being "for playboys." Like "Bud" after him and generations of Luick men before him, he turned to farming with his father as a default means of feeding himself. For her part, a few miles away, Charlotte's own post-high-school "career" took an unexpected turn that eventually would bring her to meld her fate to Donald's.

Per the subsequent obituary that appeared in Cerro Gordo's County's daily newspaper already on Tuesday afternoon, 4 April 1933, Charlotte's grandmother,

> Mrs. George Moorehead, about 63 years of age, died this morning at Rockwell at 6 o'clock. She had been in poor health for a long time. Funeral arrangements have not been announced. Mrs. Moorehead is survived by her husband and children: Mrs. Jennie Fuller, Mrs. Cora Miller and George [Jr.], all of Clear Lake, Mrs. Della True of Thornton, Mrs. Nellie Gardner [corrected] of Pine River, Minn., and Charlotte Moorehead at home. She was a member of the Methodist church. Mr. and Mrs. Moorehead were pioneer residents here.

"Big Lottie" perched on the edge of a porch, while "Little Lottie" (right) carries her cousin, June Fuller

122

As she had been just days after her birth, Charlotte #3 was once again misidentified—this time as one of her "children" although she was the deceased woman's granddaughter. Just six days before she would leave teenagehood behind, six days before her twentieth birthday, "Little Lottie"—still legally a "Juhl" despite the family's silently assigning her their own surname—suddenly found herself a free woman. Although she would continue to keep house for her grandfather until her eventual marriage, the obligation she felt to care daily for a woman for whom she felt deep ambivalence had—in a quiet, early-morning spring moment—evaporated. "Free," however, did not necessarily mean "easy."

———

chapter 59: best option imaginable

In her high school years Charlotte had visited maternal relatives in Minnesota, but had that trip included a stop in the contiguous cities of Minneapolis and Saint Paul? If it did, had she had the courage to explore either of the two downtowns from their darker sides? At the beginning of what would be a decade-long Depression, looking for a viable future, did Charlotte know that thousands, tens of thousands of other young women as well as men of all ages from rural Iowa, Wisconsin and the Dakotas were joining their peers from Minnesota in scrounging for viable employment in the Twin Cities? Was she aware that following her classmates there (or to Des Moines, Chicago, Kansas City, Denver, etc.) likely would entail hardship—made even harder by the lack of tangible, accessible support?

Desperate unemployed Americans flooded employment offices in search of work, despite grim odds.

Almost thirteen years older than Charlotte but born in Murray, in the heart of hardscrabble Southern Iowa, Meridel Wharton found herself in Minneapolis at the beginning of the Great Depression. Hard-up and resourceless, she was one of the multitudes seeking a job. A struggling political activist and by then a writer known as "Meridel Le Sueur," while sitting in the women's section of the city's "free employment bureau" in January 1932 she wrote about the fate awaiting farm and small-town girls who had drifted to the Big City in search of work and bread*:

We have been sitting here now for hours. We sit here every day, waiting for a job. There are no jobs. Most of us have had no breakfast. We sit looking at the floor. No one dares think of the coming winter. There are only a few more days of summer. Everyone is anxious to get work to lay up something for that long siege of bitter cold. But, there is no work; sitting in the room we all know it. That is why we don't talk much. We look at the floor dreading to see that knowledge in each other's eyes. There is a kind of humiliation in it. We look away from each other. We look at the floor. It's too terrible to see this animal terror in each other's eyes. So we sit hour after hour, day after day, waiting for a job to come in. There are many women for a single job. There are girls, too, fresh from the country. Some are made brazen too soon by the city. There is a great exodus of girls from the farms into the city now. Thousands of farms have been vacated completely in [the Upper Midwest]. The girls are trying to get work. The prettier ones can get jobs in the stores when there are any, or waiting on tables, but these jobs are only for the attractive and the adroit; the others, the real peasants, have a more difficult time.*

Meridel Le Sueur, 1930s

*This text has been adapted for use here.

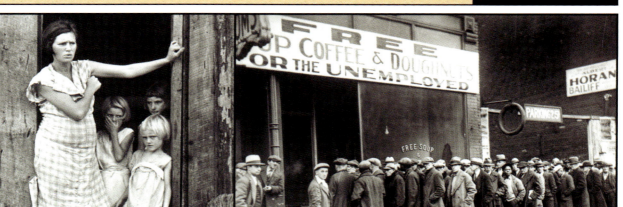

Especially single women—with children or not—struggled to survive the hard times, even as men queued for food. As the Great Depression ground on, many women found the First Lady a role model. Some of Eleanor Roosevelt's quotes became classics: "You have to accept whatever comes and the only important thing is that you meet it with courage and with the best that you have to give" or "No one can make you feel inferior without your consent."

As she looked around, surveying adult-world options available to her, Charlotte well knew how limited they were. Yes, by then American women had been allowed to vote for thirteen years, but they continued to be disenfranchised in most other ways. Single woman still had great difficulty in owning land or other capital, in buying insurance or legal services, and in competing for university slots, academic appointments or professional positions. Even if they managed to secure a white-collar job, woman almost universally earned significantly less for the same work as their male counterparts.

In short, Charlotte's list of viable options wasn't long. So, she did what billions of women had done for thousands of years: She tied her fate to a man she found attractive and snappily judged as suitable. In mating with Donald Luick, however, she'd later find she had competition.

———

Gramma always remained non-committal when I asked her—repeatedly—how she and Grampa met. She'd stir her hands loosely in the air and, with a lowered voice, murmur something about "a dance" and "meeting afterwards."

In contrast to the norms of her parents' and grandparents' youthful days, Charlotte's post-Victorian, postwar generation rejected the protective presence of a chaperone. Thus, unlike her most immediate ancestors, she found herself alone in a mobile, closed space that belonged to a would-be lover. By 1929 over half of American families owned cars—already then referred to as "brothels on wheels." Like so many millions of his compatriots, dapper Donald Luick dashed about not in his folks' horse and buggy, but on his own four wheels.

Was their quick connection "love" or more infatuation—or, even less than that? Did Donald or Charlotte really wish to spend the rest of their lives with the other? In any case, the two soon discovered they had contracted the same condition that had plagued Charlotte's mother (who gave birth to her brother Delbert less than eight months after marrying Nick Juhl—whose birthday was the same as Donald's), as well as, years later, their oldest and youngest daughters—and, likely, Charlotte's chemistry-savvy Aunt Della, who married at sixteen… and uncountable other girls and young women.

If their post-dance date led to Charlotte rolling her career dice across a steamy seat during sudden passion, she wouldn't have been the first woman to do so. Had she spoken about it openly, however, she would have been among the first of her generation to be so brave. But, in any event, unannounced and unaccompanied other than by a married friend of the impromptu groom's, the two married.

Donald and Charlotte snuck away to the Little Brown Church to marry quickly—as did thousands.

On Sunday, 12 August 1934, Donald and Charlotte drove 100 miles, round trip, due east of Thornton and Rockwell, to the site of thousands of other "spontaneous" unions near the banks of the Little Cedar River. There, at 1 o'clock in the afternoon, they joined their fates forever—and set mine, too.

Only afterwards did they join Donald's parents and, later, reportedly some six dozen well-wishers to publically mark the occasion—as noted in two local newspaper notices published a few days later and compiled here into an expanded account, under the headline of one of them:

Couple Married at Little Brown Church

Donald Luick of Thornton and Charlotte Juhl of Rockwell were married at the Little Brown church near Nashua. The Rev. William Kent performed the ceremony with Mr. and Mrs. Will Nelson of Thornton as the only attendants.

The groom is a young farmer, now working with his father. He is a graduate of Thornton's class of 1931 and is well and favorably known. The bride has grown to womanhood in this vicinity and has been keeping house for her grandfather. One of Rockwell's finest young women, she is well qualified to preside over the home they expect to establish on a farm in the spring on the George Moorehead farm 7 miles northeast of Thornton.

A wedding supper was served at the home of the bridegroom's parents, Mr. and Mrs. George Luick. About 75 friends and relatives assembled afterward for an informal reception. The young couple left for Pine River, Minn., where they will spend several days visiting and enjoying the fishing.

The Tribune joins the many friends of Mr. and Mrs. Luick in wishing for them happiness and prosperity.

"Happiness and prosperity"—indeed.

the newlyweds with "15-week-early" baby Lorraine at rented Moorehead farm; below, a rent check

chapter 60: life's no holiday

It might have been easy to get married, but Donald and Charlotte would find it much harder to get settled, to build a fulfilling life together, farming. By the spring graduation ceremonies of 1931, when Donald could fully turn his focus from math to milk cows, from chemistry to corn and from Shakespeare to swine, the agricultural sector of the American economy had collapsed. Having had as good as no organized help from faraway Washington for more than a decade, the thoughts of even the most cautious, the most staunchly conservative of farmers in America's Heartland began to drift leftwards. Radicals, however, are not born; they are cultivated in soil where the center cannot hold, where the coping mechanisms and survival tactics of more moderate times no longer work.

As my yet-to-be grandfather, upon leaving boyhood and seeking an adult life, chose to look for his future well-being on the farm rather than one off it, the gamut of possible strategies seemed best placed not on his own, unseasoned shoulders, but on those of more mature men caught in similarly distressed straits. While the rest of the society seemed to careen under the constant whirl of the conflicted, confusing times, like other men of the rural Midwest in the 1930s Donald attempted to simply remain standing.

George Michael Luick (center) as part of threshing-ring crew, mid-1930s

Young and impressionable, he would witness the down-home rebellion of the Farmers' Holiday in the mid-Thirties—a dramatic, if mostly useless uprising that would color his worldview for the rest of his life.

Donald (center, with zippered shirt) & George Luick (right) with threshing-ring crew

Fresh out of high school, as he struggled to start a farm of his own Donald shared the same fate as most farmers at the time—a curse reflected in a popular, anonymous ditty they circulated:

Farmers say that corn and hay
    Don't pay them for their time.
        That oats and rye don't get them by
            And the cows don't earn a dime;

That all that's high is what they buy
    Or have to have from town,
        And even rain don't show a gain
            For it pulls the prices down.

The Solons beef of farm-relief
    To get the farmers' votes,
        While Wall Street stands with clutching hands
            To get their corn and oats.

They bought the dirt and lost their shirt,
    And the banks have called them in.
        But, just the same, you'll find them game.
            Next year they'll try again.

Forced to rely on their own resources, America's Depression-era farm folk had no choice but to be self-reliant.

In response to such stubborn, not readily remediable conditions, men like Donald—especially young, angry men—tagged their hopes for relief from their and their families' daily misery on powerful, larger-than-life figures. And, they invested their most ardent hopes on those men's larger-than-life polemics or larger-than-life promises. Two such men would come to clash over theory as well as practice, over each one's proposed remedies to abate a lingering farm crisis that predated the Great Depression. In the process, they would inspire or incite millions of American farmers—and shake the nation.

One Depression-era farm crisis star was Milo Reno. Born to a farm family in Southeastern Iowa's Wapello County in 1866, he attended first a local Quaker school, then the Friends college in Oskaloosa. While his mother appealed to her seventh son (the twelfth of thirteen children) to become a minister, Milo wanted to become a farmer despite his genuine passion for theology. Marrying, then watching two of his three children die before reaching adulthood, he took up political activism and championed agricultural reform. In his view bankers and "capitalists" were about the business of converting America's agrarian stock into a modern peasantry.

At the end of World War I, Reno joined the recently organized Iowa Farmers' Union; after only three years' membership he became its president in 1921. In that position he supported especially those farm-relief bills proposing federal farm-price support and protection for domestic farm prices by attempting to maintain price levels that existed before the recent global conflagration. After "Cool Cal" vetoed Congressionally-approved relief four times between 1924 and '28, Reno opposed the Republican Party with an almost biblical conviction. Desperate to thwart Iowa-born Quaker Herbert Hoover's 1932 presidential re-election efforts, he worked closely with his fellow farmboy from Southern Iowa, Henry Agard Wallace. Twenty-two years younger than Reno, the would-be New Deal Democrat came from a prominent pioneer family and published the weighty *Wallace's Farmer* magazine: The man had power.

Problem was, for Wallace's tastes the likes of Milo Reno were too radical. Whereas Reno sought grassroots action such as collective bargaining and guaranteed, centrally set commodity prices, cautious Wallace proposed a government-orchestrated, supply-versus-demand-driven Agricultural Adjustment Act (AAA). The AAA would pay farmers to not grow crops and to not produce dairy produce such as milk and butter, up to a total of a third of previous production levels. To fund his intensely controversial and initially fiercely opposed plan, Wallace proposed that the Federal government tax farm-product-processing companies. The AAA sought

fellow Iowa agrarians Milo Reno (left) and Henry Wallace, 1930s

> a reduction in food production, which would, through a controlled shortage of food, raise the price for any given food item through supply and demand. [...] In order to decrease food production, the AAA would pay farmers not to farm and the money would go to the landowners. The landowners were expected to share this money with the tenant farmers. [...] Reno and Floyd Olson, the Governor of Minnesota, insisted on compulsory production control and price-fixing, with a guaranteed cost of production. Wallace argued against the idea as it would mean licensing every ploughed field in the country. Reno accused Wallace of "betraying the farmer" [and of being an "ignoramus"].

At a time when too many insolvent farmers were found hanging from their barn rafters or with fatal, self-inflicted shotgun wounds, such matters meant life or death for millions of farm folk—then some forty percent of the U.S. population. Such gravity called for swift and decisive action—but which? According to a later biographer of the once-influential Secretary of Agriculture and one of Franklin Delano Roosevelt's most visible cabinet members,

> Wallace was uncomfortable with populist insurrection. He thought Reno's notion of a farm strike was ill conceived at best, but he understood well the anger and frustration behind it.

At least for the short term, though, the tenor of the times bestowed more visible support for the pitches of a fiery radical rather than the policies of a measured member of the ruling classes. Reno seized his chance and at one point headed a column of some three thousand rebellious farmers that marched on the Iowa statehouse in Des Moines. There, Reno proclaimed a list of complaints and threatened to call a nationwide farm strike if the farmers' list of demands was not satisfied.

farm folk walking along a paved highway, carrying their belongings

Already in October 1932 Reno and his followers had declared a tax and mortgage-payment moratorium that quickly developed into a strike against farm mortgage foreclosures. The *New York Times* reported that the Farmers' Holiday Association (FHA) leader in Nebraska swore that

> If we don't get beneficial service from the Legislature 200,000 of us are coming to Lincoln and we'll tear the new State Capitol Building to pieces.

To defuse the mounting strife the governor of nearby North Dakota, William Langer, halted foreclosures and even mobilized his state's militia.

For the inherently conservative Midwest, some of the strikers' strident actions seemed tantamount to naked warfare: According to one agricultural historian, they "dumped kerosene in cream, broke churns, and dynamited dairies and cheese factories." As early as 1931, despairing Iowa farmers had been fighting

> the impact of the Great Depression. In Logan 500 farmers joined forces outside the courthouse to prevent the sale of Ernest Ganzhorn's farm. At Storm Lake, rope-swinging farmers came close to hanging a lawyer conducting a foreclosure.

Tragedy became a daily occurrence during the Great Depression—as in Grafton, northeast of Mason City.

Even the relatively apolitical act of veterinarians testing dairy herds for the devastating scourge of tuberculosis led to a so-called Iowa Cow War. After an estimated one thousand men had traveled in special trains in vain to lobby the Legislature in Des Moines to make such tests optional, farmers began to take matters into their own hands. Thereafter, in southeast Iowa,

> Veterinarians attempting to test cattle were increasingly met by large groups of farmers mobilized to obstruct the tests. They were subjected to minor levels of violence, such as thrown eggs or mud, and kicks from farm wives.

Rural women and children were not spared the misery of the times.

First providing vets with law officers as escorts, after sixty-five lawmen couldn't get two animal testers past 400 obstructing farmers, in late September 1931 Governor Dan Turner declared martial law and sent thirty-one Iowa National Guard units to the Tipton area to enforce testing. Two of the revolt's leaders were sentenced to three years in the Iowa State Penitentiary near Fort Madison.

In such a radicalized, explosive political climate, Milo Reno emerged as the leader of the swelling Heartland rebellion by calling into being the Farmers' Holiday Association. With the slogan "Let's call a Farmer's Holiday, a Holiday let's hold. We'll eat our wheat and ham and eggs, and let them eat their gold" he bid farmers to withhold farm products from the market to strike for higher prices. In response, pickets blockaded the roads near several Iowa cities and stopped trucks taking farm produce to market.

A rousing orator, natural showman and cunning strategist, Milo Reno's impassioned pleas moved farmers to

> refuse to ship food into Sioux City [Iowa] for thirty days or until such time as they got the "cost of production." Farmers blocked highways with logs and spiked telegraph poles, smashed windshields and headlights, and punctured tires with their pitchforks. When authorities in Council Bluffs [Iowa] arrested fifty-five pickets, one thousand angry farmers threatened to storm the jail, and the pickets were released on bail. In Nebraska, where farmers carried placards reading "Be Pickets or Peasants," strikers halted a freight train and took off a carload of cattle.

FDR-appointed Secretary of Agriculture Henry Wallace met with the president only four days after Roosevelt's inauguration on 4 March 1933. Wallace argued that Roosevelt must expand the current special congressional session to address the farm crisis as well as the cascade of bank closures reverberating across the country. In response Roosevelt summoned farm leaders to an "emergency conference" in Washington and Wallace told the country on national radio that

> Today, in this country, men are fighting to save their homes. That is not just a figure of speech. That is a brutal fact, a bitter commentary on agriculture's twelve years' struggle. [...] Emergency action is imperative.

Wallace—and the East-Coast-Establishment president for whom he worked—accurately judged

The sense of urgency was hardly theoretical. A true crisis was at hand. Across the Corn Belt, rebellion was being expressed in ever more violent terms. In the first two months of 1933, there were at least seventy-six instances in fifteen states of so-called penny auctions, in which mobs of farmers gathered at foreclosure sales and intimidated legitimate bidders into silence. One penny auction in Nebraska drew an

Jeandelle, Lorraine & Bud in their barnyard gateway, late 1930s

astounding crowd of two thousand farmers. In Wisconsin farmers bent on stopping a farm sale were confronted by deputies armed with tear gas and machine guns. A lawyer representing the New York Life Insurance Company was dragged from the courthouse in Le Mars, Iowa, and the sheriff who tried to help him was roughed up by a mob.

forced auction on a foreclosed farm in Iowa, 1933

On 27th April at Le Mars in Plymouth County, a mob of six hundred farmers marched on the local courthouse. A spokesman for the group asked the judge to promise that he would not sign any more foreclosure orders. Judge Charles C. Bradley said he had much sympathy for the farmers who had lost their property, but that he did not make the laws. The men did not like this answer and dragged Bradley out of his courtroom and took him to a crossroads outside of town, where his trousers were removed and he was threatened with [presumably genital] mutilation. A noose was pulled tight around his neck, and the mob demanded that the strangling judge promise no further foreclosures. The sixty-year old Bradley bravely replied: "I will do the fair thing to all men to the best of my knowledge." Bradley was just about to be hanged when he was saved by a local newspaper editor who had just arrived in his car.

As newspapers across the nation featured the events unfolding across Middle America, the sense of spreading chaos even screamed from the front page of the faraway *New York Times*. Iowa Governor Clyde Herring declared martial law and ordered troops to the turbulent town. Contrite Reno pretended that the Farmers' Holiday Association had nothing to do with the most sensational of an ever-more-jarring parade of intensifying incidents, but the arrest of the Plymouth County Farmers Holiday Association president along with 85 other men taken into custody after the latest courtroom drama belied Reno's claims.

Generally, as desperate farmers succumbed to drastic action, support for the wider Association swiftly shrank—and a triumphant, now seemingly moderate Henry Wallace watched his program waltz through Congress and become the country's official plan to combat more than a decade of hard times down on the farm.

Lorena (Jenison) & George (standing), Donald & little "Buddy" Luick on the Luick farm, late 1930s

In the midst of so much unrest, did Donald, his also-politically-keen father George or the many fellow farmers among the wider Luick clan join the Farmers' Holiday? As the unprecedented actions taking place all around them literally affected their bread and butter, the men certainly knew about and kept abreast of the explosive strikes—but did they participate in them? Any recorded support on their part does not survive, but Donald's third daughter, Sheranne, holds that her father "was an avid newspaper reader, kept up on current events and was active with several farm organizations. A [National Farmers Organization] member sign stood at the end of the driveway for years." And, at the auction held at the Luick farm after Donald's sudden death, "THE N.F.O. LADIES" served lunch that autumnal day in 1966.

scenes of America's infamous "Dustbowl:" Childress County, Texas, 1938 (left) & in South Dakota, 1936

Although my paternal grandfather died of a heart attack before my father and his cohorts dragged a provocative float down Clear Lake's Main Street one Fourth of July to back collective bargaining, it is known that Donald attended early NFO organizational meetings and advanced its purported goals: Soon after Donald died, the North Central Iowa chapter of the state NFO presented Gramma with a clock in honor of Grampa's activism. And, as we shall see, Donald's father, my Great-Grampa George, had a history of supporting radical movements on behalf of "the little guy."

---

chapter 61: wracked by darkness

The 1932 national elections had swept out the old, ineffective guard that had dominated the Federal government since Harding's election in 1920 and whisked in a fresh army of New Dealers. After a dozen years of disconnected, *laissez-faire* policies, fairness-minded men like Donald welcomed an activist program in Washington—among other reasons, having married eighteen months after Franklin Delano Roosevelt took oath as the 32nd president of the United States, the man who would become my paternal grandfather almost thirty years later was expecting his first child. So, he only too happily left national politics to national figures—at least for the time being.

Lorraine with baby-brother Bud, summer 1936 (top left); the two in winter clothes, early 1937 (right);
Jeandelle, Lorraine & Bud sitting on back step of their family's farmhouse near Thornton, late 1930s

Charlotte gave birth to baby Lorraine—said to have arrived "15 weeks early"—on 1 February 1935. A little more than twelve months later, on 13 February 1936, Donald and Charlotte had their next child—Luwarren, my father (nicked "Bud" as a toddler)—followed by Jeandelle on 14 July 1937. Their last child, Sheranne, joined the family on 16 April 1944.

It would be the mostly serial births of their children that would forever change the rest of the young couple's shared life. It would be those very little ones who'd eventually grow up and, in turn, profoundly impact the lives of their unsuspecting parents. Curiously, it would be the oldest and the youngest of the four children who'd present Donald and Charlotte with the most "trouble"—and it would be the middle two who'd carry around with them the most resentment-fueled anger.

Lorraine, Bud and Jeandelle Luick, circa 1940; kindergartner Sheranne Luick, late 1940s

What strikes a family historian most as she or he dives deeper and deeper into the generations-long traces of one's own life are the patterns that emerge, the most sobering of which are traits, behaviors or choices in one's own persona or résumé recognized in the lives of those who have lived before you but who also, you realize, live on *through* you. The Big Thud resounded "at the quiet hour of two o'clock in the morning [when] the spirit" of a twenty-year-old beauty—stranded in an obscure, now-almost-vanished hamlet in the middle of a vast, silent prairie—"fled to its maker and eternal home." That it should resonate so loudly, so long, seems incredible. Still, the wider Luick-Juhl clan was forever marked by that primal emotional black hole—one that proved to be expressly dark, dense and destructive. And, it *always* sucked us in.

Is there any empirical evidence to carry this theory that unresolved patterns of dysfunctional familial behavior repeatedly resurface—with deadly results—unless the patterns become conscious and confronted? Examples from the Luick lineage are plentiful, but to cite merely the most cogent:

"Young Lottie," circa 1910: Her life was so short, but left such long shadows.

Donald and my father, Luwarren, were the only sons of four children in each of their families. February babies, both were five years old when their country joined in a global war that brought with it such demand for foodstuffs that each boy had to take to the fields to help his labor-short parents put bread on otherwise bare tables—even though neither could reach the pedals of the machinery which his father ordered him to operate. (Note: I was five when my father inexplicably withdrew almost all demonstrations of affection or kindness.) Both were the sole (male) "farmhands" working too closely with stressed fathers who'd gotten a reprieve from serving in the U.S. Army for being occupied in a "war-essential industry." In the process, both were subjected to marring emotional as well as physical abuse—which they passed on to their sons... who... ?

Thirteen years old during the United States' much-celebrated Bicentennial, as a teenager I interviewed all the relatives I could coax to let me record their most vivid family-related stories. I used those novice interviews as parts of larger family-history projects at Clear Lake's junior, then senior high schools, the results of which I hand-published in six illustrated, black-ringed booklets. Two of them won first place at local- and state-contest levels, thereby awarding me two expense-paid trips to Washington, DC, to compete at National History Day, 1980 and 1981.

my forced-farm-worker father with his father and tractor, circa 1940

When I cornered Aunt Lorraine and, finally, Gramma Luick to conduct separate interviews with them, their recollections of Donald's treatment of "Buddy" left me stunned, if not surprised:

"It was terrible" Aunt Lorraine recounted. "Your Grampa Luick used ta throw things at yer dad—he'd yell so loud an' hurl stuff with such a force that the wallsa the barn wud shake," my dad's attractive but hardship-plagued older sister confided. (I didn't have to imagine the scene: my brother and I had *lived* it, too many times.) "I felt sorry for 'im—I honestly did. We three girls always had alotta work ta do in the house an' garden an' chicken coop, but nothin' like yer dad."

Bud with feeder calves and Ring, the Luick family's Collie, late 1940s

Normally one to play poker with her words, Gramma Luick confirmed without so much as a blink that "Donald had ta work hard ta farm all that ground an' feed all those cattle when your dad was a boy, Mike. So, when Bud was little he had ta work outside like a man. Sometimes" she nodded slowly, hesitantly agreeing with her own assessment, "your grampa drove him a bit hard." She thought a moment, then added softly, as if betraying a secret, "Well, Donald drove Bud hard all right—*real* hard."

―――

Violent anger, though, was not the only drug of choice Luick men used to numb other, for them more threatening emotions such as fear, longing, disappointment or sadness. Sex was another popular medication—but that emotional anesthesia wasn't used by only the menfolk of the clan: Luick women could use sex as both a tool and refuge, too. The problem for its female users was it often led to two other destructive patterns: teen or unplanned pregnancy and poverty. Half of Donald and Charlotte's offspring fell into this trap—and neither found a way to ever fully escape it.

Henry Luick (far left) and other Belmond-area boys, some perhaps brothers; Sherrane (Luick) Joyns, 1982

―――

chapter 62: a grinding poverty

In fall 1950—at the age of 15—Lorraine Luick met with a 20-year-old former high school basketball star, Bob Jones, from nearby Swaledale. With his wavy ebony hair, charismatic eyes and towering, athletic physical presence, he fascinated her—to her core. When they discovered after they met up that their compelling attraction to each other had led them to conceive a child together, they eventually married even though enlistee Bob was about to transfer to Colorado Springs' Fort Carson. A month after they married—and with Bob now in the Rockies—Lorraine gave birth to a son the expecting newlyweds already had named "Micky." He died thirty hours later, having been born blue due to the umbilical cord being tied around his neck.

Donald Luick (behind gate) and Bob Jones in barn doorway, mid-1950s

Although she had few of her own resources or job skills with which to launch a self-reliant adult life, Lorraine had dropped out of her sophomore year of high school, left her parental house, followed her new husband—unaccompanied, by cross-country bus—and found shelter in a small apartment in a large off-base house. With the birth of that doomed baby, Bob and Lorraine had launched a family that eventually would have nine children—seven of whom Lorraine raised alone after Bob left her in July 1966, the day after Donald's funeral. With each additional child Lorraine's relationship with the rest of the Luick family shifted and irrevocably changed—to the point that all of its members struggled with the ensuing poverty of a daughter and sister raising so many children on her own, with almost no money nor steady employment.

Despite their difficulty with knowing how to share Lorraine's immense physical as well as fiscal burden, her parents and siblings kept on loving her, and it would be *that* conflict that provided a central quandary for the rest of the family. Lorraine's parents had loudly protested her sudden marriage to Bob yet Charlotte, for one, continued to feel exceptionally bonded to her first child. Years later Gramma Luick told Barbara—her oldest surviving grandchild, who by then was an adult—that, at a time when long-distance telephone calls were expensive and thus rare, "The night your mother lost Micky, I sat in a chair an' rocked the whole night and could not go back to sleep. I could feel that something wasn't right at the hospital: I didn't know what it was, but I could just *feel* it."

On 31 October 1952 Lorraine gave birth to a second baby. In December she brought Barbara to Iowa by train when the infant was six weeks old. Riding in an unheated car, the child developed pneumonia. Thornton's Doc Ward gave Lorraine black-licorice-flavored medicine to put in formula for Barbara—who to this day can't bear the taste of black licorice. At first, the two girls—the 17-year-old mother and her weeks-old babe—lived with Donald and Charlotte. It was there that our Gramma Luick first showed her grandmotherly instinct, per Barbara's experience:

> She'd sit up all night, holding me, making sure I could breathe although I had pneumonia. She was determined that her oldest daughter wouldn't go through again what Mom had already gone through with Micky—the loss of a baby. Gramma refused to let me die; she insisted that I'd live—and she was going to do everything she could to make that happen. Given all that she'd been through, Gramma was a survivor—somehow, despite all the odds. Growing up, I would experience, again and again, how Gramma would hold things together, how she'd patch the sinking ship we all were in. It wasn't a very fancy ship, but Charlotte helped keep it afloat.

Bob & Lorraine (Luick) Jones with Charlotte & Ring

As Barbara had no winter coat to wear when she left for college in 1971, Gramma loaned her hers. It's unknown if the chicken coop Bob rebuilt into a home for his family was this one, but it likely was similar.

Less than a year later, after Bob returned from military service, the former farmboy soon rebuilt a nearby chicken coop for his young family to live in. Then, after living a short time in a little house next to Swaledale's town park, Bob renovated an empty, two-floored school building into a home for a family that would grow by one new member almost every second year for the next dozen years. Had he chosen such a large space so as to accommodate what he envisioned to be an endlessly ever-bigger family? When asked once about having so many children, my mother overheard Bob answer "Those kids are gonna be there for me in my rockin'-chair years."

Bob Jones in the Luick farmhouse kitchen, 1950s

Between juggling building projects and burping new babies, Bob took odd jobs to try to earn any money he could: He delivered newspapers, drove a school bus and worked as a school janitor; for "pocket money" he even dug graves at the Swaledale cemetery with my father. Still, whatever Bob earned, at home there was never enough dough to put sufficient bread on the table to still hungry little tummies, let alone adequately clothe, educate or entertain the couple's increasing collection of kids.

Even though funds were tight, however, Bob somehow always found enough small change to smoke long chains of cigarettes and polish off bottle after bottle of cheap beer—or to have his shirts dry cleaned and pressed for when he "went out." And, out he went! Lorraine, meanwhile, seemed to simply ignore Bob's sloppily-hid womanizing and affairs.

Unexpectedly, it was changes in Iowa's liquor laws—and its citizens' shifting mores about alcohol consumption—that aided and abetted Bob's quest to have a life separate from his family. The state legislature approved liquor by the drink in 1963—and no sooner was the ink of the declaration dry than individuals and businesses around Iowa began featuring booze as the centerpiece of larger entertainment offerings, some of which were already extant, some new.

Swedish singer Östen Warnerbring; Globe-Gazette ad about Sahara Club's opening, October 1962

In late October 1962 Bob's maternal aunt, Dena Kramer Riggins, and her co-owning husband, Robert, had opened the Sahara Supper Club. It quickly became an area landmark along Highway 65, then the sole paved artery between Mason City and the next county seat to the south, Hampton. When they learned that they'd be able to sell liquor by the drink, they hired Dena's handsome nephew to tend its extensive bar. Initial reports from his first night serving demon rum seemed positive, as seen in a *Globe-Gazette* review of liquor sales on Monday, 8 July 1963:

In the early 1960s, entertainers still maintained a veneer of decency, if not wholesomeness: Dinah Shore with Keith Thibodeaux (left corner) and Desi Arnaz, Jr.; American Bandstand host Dick Clark (below), 1963.

Few things in Bob's young-adult life seemed to flow totally hitch-free. Already on 28 August of that same summer, for example, the *Globe* revealed that he soon found himself at the center of a legal powder keg—only to be announced cleared in a subsequent article run on 17 September.

APPEARING THIS WEEK AT

The Sahara Supper Club

TWO HEADLINERS
DINK FREEMAN
and
JERI JORDAN

DINK FREEMAN

One of the funniest comedians in show business—Funny in any language when he tells his rib-tickling stories in over 10 dialects.

JERI JORDAN

Glamorous blonde singing star of national fame. Jeri has appeared on the Bob Hope, Jimmy Durante and Arthur Godfrey TV shows.

August 27, 28 and 29
First Show at 8:45 P.M.

NO COVER CHARGE
$1.00 Minimum Towards Beverages

SAHARA SUPPER CLUB
Highway 65
Sheffield, Iowa

Hearing set on liquor charge

DES MOINES — Charges that the Sahara Supper Club of Sheffield violated the state liquor law are to be heard Friday at 10 a.m. by the Iowa Liquor Control Commission. The commission said state liquor agent Frank Meskimen of Cedar Falls reported buying a drink at the club after the 1 a.m. weekday closing time.

SPECIAL ATTRACTION
SATURDAY NIGHT
Aug. 29

Free Dancing
To The
Fine Music Of
DENNY And The FABULOUS DYNAMICS

At The
SAHARA SUPPER CLUB
Sheffield, Iowa

No Cover   No Minimum

Denny And The Fabulous Dynamics Have Recently Appeared With Del Shannon, The Everly Brothers And Jan & Dean

---

Owners of Sahara Club are cleared

DES MOINES (UPI)—Operators of the Sahara Supper Club, Sheffield, were cleared of a liquor law violation charge Tuesday.

The charge was brought by Frank Meskimen, Cedar Falls, a member of the commission's enforcement staff, who contended he was sold a drink at the supper club after 1 a.m. Meskimen also testified that the bartender at the supper club mixed two drinks after making the sale to the state agent.

Robert Riggins, operator of the club, denied at the hearing that any drinks had ever been sold after hours at the club. His bartender, Robert Jones, testified that on the night Meskimen visited the club the last drink was mixed at 12:57 a.m. After Meskimen consumed the beverage "in a single gulp," he asked for another and was told, "nope it's too late."

"MR. AND MRS. VERSATILITY"
JOANIE and DON LARSON
Appearing In Person At The
Sahara Supper Club
SHEFFIELD, IOWA
NO MINIMUM — NO COVER

"BROADWAY A LA CARTE"
SOPHISTICATED SUBTLEY —
UPROARIOUS HILARITY!

These Two Delightful Broadway Stars of TV, Radio and Recording Fame Have Appeared In Numerous Big New York Show Tunes!
Singing All the Big New York Successes
Tues., Wed., Thurs., Oct. 15 - 16 - 17
First Show at 7:30 P.M.
Be Sure To See This Sparkling Vocal Duo. Loaded with Laughs . . . They will Captivate You with Their Stylized Impression of Musical Humor and Fast Moving Fun — Bright and Bouncy.

Our Halloween Treat For Our Wonderful Customers
Coming — Oct. 29 - 30 - 31
In Person — The Ink Spots

For Reservations: Phone 5-3761 — Sheffield, Iowa
No Cover   No Minimum

Globe articles about the Sahara's alleged liquor violations appeared next to ads for coming attractions.

Amidst all the tumult at his new job, Bob drifted further and further from the family he had helped create. His and Lorraine's second-oldest daughter, Peggy, later recalled her father having an apartment in nearby Sheffield for at least part of his stint at the Sahara. While Barbara could not remember that, she did have the impression that

> When Dad finally moved out of our house, for the last time, some of us kids saw his nice mobile home in Clear Lake. When we went inside I had the feeling that he had had it for some time; it seemed to be fully furnished and, well, "his."

Tonight Show *bandleader Skitch Henderson (left), Johnny Carson & Ed McMahon on New Year's Eve, 1962; (back row) Danny Joe, Barbara Lee, (front) Thomas Rae & Peggy Anne Jones, late 1950s*

While still married to Lorraine, wherever Bob was staying overnight when he wasn't where my aunt and their children were, it seemed he wasn't always alone, for sometimes he'd return to the family with lipstick on his collar or perfume in his hair.

Even if it might have seemed contradictory to what was going on behind closed doors, almost every Sunday Bob and Lorraine sent their growing roster of children through the local Methodist church's doors, even as they, themselves, stayed home. "Guilt" Barbara now holds, "kept Mom from going to church other than at Christmas and Easter—but, she was committed to sending us." According to her oldest daughter, Lorraine's motives had social as well as religious roots:

> By getting pregnant so young and out of wedlock, Mom carried with her immense guilt. She wanted to atone for that guilt—so, among other things, she made a kind of vow of poverty. She took the biblical phrase "blessed are the poor in spirit" literally, as a way into heaven. The resulting destitution, though, led to depression and only reinforced her underlying sense of unworthiness.

Despite the destructive influence of religiously spurred guilt, Lorraine clung to her faith:

> She'd open the Bible for signs—and speak about the dangers of cults, which she said were "of the devil." She'd warn us "Don't let the devil get ahold of you!" I had the feeling, later, that she knew something about, and was terrified by, cults around the Midwest that abused children. Anyway, she hinted at some connection to hidden forces that led to abused children.

Lorraine felt challenged by her first surviving child, "Barbie," even as a little girl. At times having prophetic, awake-state dreams she felt were confirmed soon thereafter by lucid moments of *déjà vu*, Barbara (whose name means "foreign" in Greek) would tell her parents of such experiences—which Bob dismissed with "You're crazy!" and Lorraine labeled "the work of the devil" so "pay them no attention."

Whether or not the shadowy child-abusing cults or dreaded demonic influences my aunt Lorraine believed in were real, the signs of abject poverty that hung like heavy, gloomy drapes all around her and her swelling brood indubitably were. When I was a child, we would visit the Joneses' home from time to time. The moment we stepped over the worn, splintery threshold, a jumble of threadbare furniture atop thin, third-hand rugs silently greeted us. What tatty curtains there were had varying lengths and rarely fully covered their assigned windows—which often lacked screens or storms, or were broken. The kitchen cupboards and rickety fridge always seemed sparsely filled; the chrome-legged '50s-era table sat mostly empty, surrounded by a hodgepodge of pastel vinyl-covered chairs, often torn and shedding billowing cotton stuffing. Usually, in whatever domicile Aunt Lorraine was sheltering her poorly clothed children at any given time, the invariably old, rundown house lacked a functioning phone or steady heat.

"Every year, though," Barbara later recalled ironically, "we did have frozen pipes."

Barbara at graduation, 1971 (left), and her wedding, 23 August 1975: Terry, Danny, groom Tom & bride, Lorraine, Jeannette, John, Peggy, Tom

Every time Lorraine went to the hospital to deliver another child, Gramma Luick stayed at the Jones home until the children's mother returned; during the day my mother helped her. "By the time they left" Barbara remembers, "they'd have washed the laundry, bought groceries, cooked and cleaned till the entire house—from top to bottom—was immaculately spick and span."

Lorraine did her best to keep it that way but, invariably, within a short time all her efforts went begging. Whatever her shortcomings as a chaos cop, however, according to Barbara her mom was a true wizard at gathering boxes of clothing that thrift shops couldn't sell. Lorraine's youngest sister, Sheranne, would tag along on such successful gleaning quests—amazed how a cost-minded single-parent of seven could "go to Goodwill to get old coats and bathrobes and jeans, then cut them down to fit the kids." Sheranne also recounted the low-budget tactics Lorraine employed to be sure that Christmas didn't go without being duly celebrated in her struggling family's cash-strapped household:

> She'd buy old dishes and paint birds or other scenes on them. She was skilled at sewing so she'd make clothes or pillow cases. She'd make little gifts and decorate them by hand. She was real good at that.

For their part, Lorraine's parents assisted her as much as their conflicted consciences would let them. Each year at Christmas Grampa Luick lined up us grandchildren in their living room, based on age and height—which always placed Barbara at the front of the queue. Whether it was a cloaked way of both helping as well as indoctrinating the Jones kids to save along with the rest of their grandchildren, or it was an annual

Lorraine in a happy, contented moment, with pieced pillow, mid-1980s

holiday manifestation of post-Depression fiscal values they would have chosen to make visible anyway, once we'd taken our spots in commanded formation, Donald would go from child to child and hand her or him a silver dollar. "If you hold on to this" he'd promise us, "it'll grow and be worth a *lot* of money some day."

That yearly award felt for Barbara like being presented with

> a chunk of gold—the problem for me always being "How do I hold on to this when we don't have anything to eat?" Inevitably, one by one, each one of us Jones kids would spend that silver dollar on one thing or another.

Children do not perceive the politics of presents—but adults certainly do. A half century later my now-adult sister still vividly remembers when "Grampa gave David a pair of cowboy boots once [around the time of my birth] and I was *so* angry because he didn't give *me* a thing!"

When I asked "Why'd he give Dave cowboy boots, Deb—for some special occasion, or as a reward?" she answered, humorously but audibly still stinging, "Jus' *'cause!*"

Our mother confirmed the contentious event but also registered her displeasure, decades later, over "Donald's playing favorites—which [Phyllis] never approved of." At the time, she cringed at her father-in-law's unapologetic indulgence of my brother in plain view of the Jones boys, who barely had tennis shoes, let alone stylish Western boots.

Grampa's "favorite" (and sole) daughter-in-law also wasn't pleased when he gave Dave a lip full of snuff to suck on, as well as let my sister try his chewing tobacco—and she "almost puked! It looked better than it tasted" Debbie remembered long after.

Dave & Deb, 1966; baby Dave & Mom, pregnant Jeandelle, late 1950s

Even after Grampa Luick died, Gramma continued to show their grandchildren the importance she ascribed money by enclosing with each card she'd send us at special occasions a crisp, mint-fresh $5 bill that she had specially requested at the busy counter at Thornton's First State Bank. Even as she was dying of two kinds of cancer at Ashlawn Farm in summer 1997, she quietly confided to Barbara "I haven't been able to take care of sending cards lately." After her briefly visiting granddaughter told her not to worry, Charlotte fretted anyway "I don't know who'll take over sending out all my cards—"

Even if Gramma Luick's annual, cash-stuffed birthday, Christmas, Easter and other cards someday would stop appearing in our mailboxes, she wasn't the only one in the family over the years, seeing to it that the Joneses didn't go hungry, naked or without operable wheels. Dad would roll his eyes over the latest news of "Guess what Lorraine's done now!" relayed by Gramma or Jeandelle or Sherranne, and I always wondered why Dad's older sister ever stopped to call on us when each time she dared to do so, as she never got away without at least one patronizing scolding from her bossy baby brother. Still, Bud never failed to help her—with cash or in-kind. More times than I could count, we'd be out in the farmyard working when Dad would spot Aunt Lorraine's latest automotive acquisition sputter into the end of our driveway, then murmur to anyone willing to listen to his tired vitriol "Well, I wonder what she wants *this* time?"

Still, rarely did Dad not stop what we were doing to change a tire or top the oil, tune her motor or replace a muffler for Lorraine—who without fail was constantly cheery, always appreciative and forever optimistic that the next day, the next hour, the next moment would hold something special. Despite the serial trials that Aunt Lorraine always seemed to draw to her and her brood, I can't remember her complaining or shoving blame onto someone else for her burdensome lot. I found her goodwill contagious and liked having her around. As I got older and began to write myself—fancying both my present and imagined future to resemble that of my TV hero John-Boy Walton—I enjoyed comparing literary techniques with Lorraine, who for a time would show up at Ashlawn Farm with a camera hung around her neck and a reporter's notepad held ever-ready in her hand. "Who knows when a good idea might pop up?" she'd explain when Dad dismissed what he assumed would be another of his errant sister's come-and-go "career kicks."

baby Bud (left) and his year-older sister, Lorraine, summer 1937

Whether it was his or her idea, Dad's brotherly assistance didn't always consist of charity. Sometimes the whole, noisy Jones tribe would arrive riding a sagging chassis, come to help their Luick kin bale hay or walk soybeans—both of which were seasonal jobs that unavoidably felt like being handed scratchy, sultry sentences. Sometimes we shook our way atop shuddering flat racks across the clod-covered hayfield, then stacked prickly-ended bales in our barn's airless haymow. At others, we made our way through what felt like razor-edged soybean plants, hacking out weeds with dull machetes. At all times, we kids prayed for swift deliverance from such miserable penance.

Once they'd proven themselves morally worthy, Dad would reward the Jones boys' atonement-through-toil with half a butchered beef—while we Luick kids didn't get as much as a quiet "thanks" or "good job!" Along with brown-paper sacks full of frozen meat, Lorraine typically would also depart our place with a tank of gas, a gallon of milk or a peck of freshly-picked green peas for her family. And, Mom always had a just-read copy of *Better Homes and Gardens*, *Redbook* or such to send home with her sister-in-law for a later leisurely read.

For her part, Barbara thought the seemingly endless hours of "walkin' beans" to be particularly unpleasant. Years later, she remembered

> how oppressive I found those miles after miles of corn and bean fields. Our parents' thinking—and that of the community around us—seemed to resemble those long, straight rows. I just wanted to get away from all those rows and rows and rows of corn and beans. I knew there was a world "out there" beyond all that—but "for now" I had to slug my way through it.

invitation to, and Barbara Jones as guestbook attendant at, our aunt Sheranne's wedding, August 1964

The oldest child in a household marked by material poverty but, worse, burdened by unspoken, unnamed dynamics that swirled on in guarded darkness, Barbara had the feeling of

> living in an invisible fog—that inside our house there was one reality, but outside there was this totally different reality. I found it very strange to go through a door and be the same person, but be expected to act in totally different ways. Outside the house, I felt this pressure to do well, to represent my family in the best light—to show that we came from good stock. I often felt that I was the one who had to "play parent" if the real ones weren't going to.

As long as she can remember, Barbara has sought answers—as well as ways out of situations she found insufferable—through education:

> When I was about two years old I had a potty chair with a little brown bear on the back and would sit on that and "read" those Little Golden Books to seek answers that would help to solve my parents' problems: That was my passionate mission. Mom would call me to dinner, but I just would *not* leave those books, so she or Dad would have to carry me, still sitting on that potty chair, to the table so I would eat with them.

Proving her ken with materials a little more challenging than reading Little Golden Books, Barbara would go on to graduate in the top ten percent of Sheffield-Chapin High's graduating class of 1971. Combined with one based on exemplary merit, the needs-based scholarship awarded to her made it possible for Barbara to pack up her few belongings a few months later and move to Cedar Falls to attend the University of Northern Iowa, the alma mater of her mother's Aunt Velma. There, she majored first in Interior Design, then after moving to Ames with Tom—her engineering-student, soon-to-be husband—to study at Iowa State University in Family Environment, as she

> wanted to show the world "We weren't junk!" I wanted to create a different view of my family. I also wanted to design beautiful spaces and, later, ones where families could live comfortably together. I wanted to take what I'd come from and "make it all right."

As the first person in the Luick-Juhl lineage to study at a university, Barbara gave her mother reason to be proud. Perhaps it was a glowing sense of pride that led Lorraine to drive Barbara back to UNI at the end of the first weekend that her daughter spent at home after her first term had started. Along the way, however, Barbara was to learn something she hadn't expected. Lorraine, looking straight to the

Tom and Barbara as newlyweds, 1975; mid-'70s interior design

edge of the prairie's undulating horizon as she slowly chose her words, announced "Your father and I are seeing each other again"—some six years after Bob had left his family, a day after Lorraine had buried her father, dead of a heart attack at age 54.

Barbara just stared at her and thought *"Oh, Mom—that's the* worst *thing you could* ever *do."*

Bob Jones inspecting downed windmill at the Luick farm, mid-1950s

My aunt, indeed, chose to rejoin her one-time high school basketball star, Bob Jones—who by then was dealing tractors in Mason City. With his wavy, salt-and-pepper hair, soulful eyes and powerful-if-battered physical presence, he once again fascinated her—to her core. When they discovered after they met up once more that their still-compelling attraction to each other had led them to conceive yet another baby together, Bob ditched any talk of a shared marital ship, but Lorraine decided to carry the child to term, then surrender it for adoption. Personally aware of the perils of unplanned pregnancies, Gramma supported her, to the point of driving her 37-year-old daughter to the hospital when it came time to deliver what would be a fourth girl out of Lorraine and Bob's nine children. Clever-yet-cautious Barbara sensed already in that disclosure-dominated car ride back to campus that *"This can't end well."*

chapter 63: wading into darkness

Along with multiple little bundles of joy, Robert Lewis Jones had brought to the Luick-Juhl clan his own filled-to-the-brim bag of burdens. With a grandfather who had stowed away from Wales around 1900 on what he thought was a boat headed for Australia, then was forced to tend the cattle on the ship as fare when he was discovered to be aboard, Bob grew up on a farm not far from the Luicks where he, too, was beaten as a boy. Bob's Dutch-born mother, Alfina, and prairie-raised father, Lee, had been neighborhood friends of Donald and Charlotte for years.

Late in Bob's and Lorraine's marriage, Bob's buddy Chuck Olesen—Jeandelle's kindly but career-driven husband—tipped off the hapless chap about a sales job with International Harvester's outlet in Cerro Gordo's county seat. There, the father of seven earned more in a year than he usually had in several, yet still avoided handing Lorraine more than symbolic support for their many children. Upon learning that his older sister had, again, conceived out-of-wedlock with a man who he, too, once had befriended, my father wrote a scornful letter in which he damned his former, philandering brother-in-law. Further, Bud banned Bob Jones from our lives forever.

Ironically, Bob's extra-marital behaviors actually fit well with long-practiced Luick family sexual "boundaries," which effectively were nonexistent. Sexual intimacy outside of marriage with consenting adults, however, was one thing: *What* was going on inside Bob that led him to turn to his own children for sexual contact?

Little Barbara, for one, would pretend to be asleep when her father would stumble home late after a smoke-veiled, alcohol-lubricated night out, enter her darkened room and fondle her. He would quietly finger her genitals, as well as lay his penis on her bare belly. When Barbara stopped pretending to sleep to protest, her

Bob Jones (left) at Chuck Olesen's and Jeandelle Luick's wedding; my father is fourth from left, Sheranne on far right; 12 June 1955

father would verbally abuse her, saying things like "Oh, you're just a girl—get used to it; that's all you're good for." Reflecting on such experiences as an adult, she found that

> The verbal abuse felt more painful and lingered longer than the sexual abuse for a little girl who truly loved her father and wanted to be loved by him. I know now that those words were not true then, but they still hurt.

Years later, when my oldest paternal cousin confronted her mother about Bob's sexually abusing her and, similarly, her brother Danny in places like the janitor's office under the Swaledale school stairs, Lorraine curtly replied "Barb, why dig up old bones?" When Barbara, who by now had set professional interior design aside to become a certified psychiatric nurse, then approached our grandmother about what Barbara had been told had been Donald's earlier sexually abusing Lorraine, Gramma merely answered "Oh, men—they're all just human can openers!"

Belmond-area young adults, circa 1910

Although not directly involved, I once unwittingly walked in on an incestuous occurrence between two members of the extended Luick family. Parallel to but unaware of Barbara's process, she and I each spent years trying to understand the roots of incest in our family, its insidious effects and its spiritually cancerous legacy. For her part, Barbara concluded her adolescent future-mother was "doing everything she could to get out of reach of her father—even if that meant getting pregnant at 15 by my emotionally and physically abusive, alcoholic dad as an excuse to leave her parents' house."

The emotional baggage my cousin inherited from both her self-sabotaging mother and outwardly raging father took Barbara years, decades to sort out. In researching, then writing this book, I often turned to Barbara, both to know how she was dealing with reliving so many painful memories, as well as to invite support for me, dealing with same. One cool, rainy day in Dresden in spring 2014 I picked up the phone and dialed my blood-bonded collaborator in Denver.

"Hi, Barbara! It's me, Michael—in Germany." Before she could answer, the lingering nervousness in me about what all this was doing to her prodded me to add "How's things in the Rockies?"

"Oh" a crackling voice croaked, "we're all well here, really—but the wind-driven pollen's doing a number on my throat. Then, there's the pollution that we have to wade through every day, anyway."

"Sorry to hear that" I offered.

"So, I'm glad you called—but I have to be brief."

"Sure" I deferred, "we don't have to talk long. I just wanted to touch base and—"

"I read the draft chapters you sent, Michael."

"Really? Great!" My hand gripped the phone tighter. "So, what'd ya think?"

A long silence settled upon the line. I shifted my weight from one tense foot to the other, until finally thoughtful Barbara continued.

"You asked what effect publishing our family's stories might have on its various members."

"Yes, that I did" I affirmed.

"Well" Barbara's raspy voice breathed into the receiver, "if you print all this—even if it's all true—in its present form…"

I waited a few seconds, then goaded her with a hissing "Yes-s-s?"

"…I'm thinking how to say this."

(from the right) Marion and Mattie Luick with unidentified girls, 1910s

"OK—take your time" I offered, affecting patience.

"If you print this in its current form, it's gonna hurt a lot of people's feelings—not just in our family, but many who read about it, because everyone'll take away the impression that there was only darkness and drama in our family."

"*And*" I thought to myself, "*that's untrue because—?*"

"Nothing comes from nothing" Barbara pushed on. "We didn't turn out the way we did for no reason: There *must* have been something good in all that."

"Well" I stammered, "I suppose… yeah, sure, but—"

Refusing to entertain my lesser angels, Barbara added "You're a good example: Look at you!"

"*I'd rather not*" I heard my inner demons retort.

"Somehow, you turned out not just 'good' but *great*!"

"Thank you, cousin" I quietly replied.

"No, really" Barbara protested. "I'm not just saying that: Michael, you truly *are* a blessing!"

"You are, too, dear" I replied.

"But then, so are the people we came from" she continued. "There *had* to be something good, there had to be some Light in them, too."

Belmond-area father with three young sons

"Yes, I'm sure, if we looked deep enough—"

"Ya know" Barbara interrupted, "I want to offer you a challenge."

"And what might that be?" I wondered out loud.

"What's in this for you, Michael? At the end of writing all this down, what's this mean to you?"

"*What should I tell her?*" I asked myself. "*My goals in writing—or how the writing process is changing me and how I see not just my whole life, but where I come from, and…*"

"I worked on what happened to me for years" Barbara mused further, "and one time, at a certain point, I sat for three days because I'd given myself the assignment to not leave the chair until I could think of at least one good reason why it 'had' to have been worthwhile to have been born to the parents and families we were: What would have made it worth putting up with all the pain and hardship we endured, just to have learned one simple thing? And, what do you think was that *one* thing?"

I leaned against the window sill as I looked out at the parting rain clouds. Again, as so often, the stubby dome of the rebuilt *Frauenkirche* emerged from the shifting shadows and mist.

"I dunno: What *was* that one thing for you, Barbara?" I asked, absently.

"I suddenly sat up and remembered" she continued, "that when I was two years away from finishing college, I sorely needed a loan. The problem was, the bank refused to give me one, even a year-long loan, without a reliable co-signer. The only person who I knew who might qualify was my dad, so I asked him to do it and, to my surprise, he agreed. We went to the bank and met with the banker—but when the banker explained that I'd have to take another job to help earn the money to repay the $300 I wanted to borrow (it was the mid-Seventies, so that was a lot more money then), I reacted very strongly, because I knew what I wanted and needed to do: I was determined I was going to graduate two years from then—and that was that! More part-time jobs were out of the question, so I stormed out of the bank—and Dad followed me."

As she paused, I cleared my throat, once, quietly, so she'd know I was still right there with her.

"Now, for my father, money meant love—and I knew how exceptionally tight he was with money, so when Dad agreed to co-sign on that loan, to risk losing some of his own savings, I knew what that meant to him. I also knew how much he believed in education, how much he had longed, himself, to attend barber school—and always regretted that he hadn't. His one word of wisdom was 'They can't take education away from you' so education was important. In his willingness to risk, to potentially lose some of that all-important bank account he was always frantically feeding, that symbolized for him a form of self-love, I realized that in that moment he loved me even more than he loved himself—and *that* was unconditional love."

Barbara's already-breaking voice became barely audible; I could hear it tighten as she spoke, her throat fighting to swallow. "There I was, and he was determined that I should get the money I needed"—she stopped, took a deep breath, then persisted—"to live on for my two last years"—I heard Barbara choke down a strangling knot—"even if that meant Dad risking losing his own money."

After I let my cousin's words settle into the depths of the tight space between us, despite the thousands of miles that physically separated us at that moment and our markedly different biographies since each of us left the Iowa cornfields, I thanked her, saying "I guess that story's one of the rays of Light that wanted to be included—made all the more precious by its rarity."

"Yeah" Barbara managed to squeak, "that's it—that's the Light that was there, all along, amidst all the darkness."

Sometimes, in moments like that one, it felt as if Barbara and I had each—through some improbable stroke of grace—found a life raft, some intangible platform that had held us up long enough for us to float out of range of our respective familial vortexes. Somehow, we then slowly started the process of healing hurts that were only partially our own, some of which we sensed were older than we were but did not know how much. We both realized early on that we were able to heal largely because of shifting going on in the culture at the time that allowed us the space and vocabulary for such inner work. Not everyone in our extended family, however, had been so fortunate.

Belmond-area man holding onto back of chair

In our numerous dialogs about the myriad buried subplots of our family's larger drama, we wondered if Sheranne—Donald and Charlotte's "baby girl"—might have had similar motives for fleeing her father's reach as Lorraine had had. As a boy, my mother hinted to me in passing that Gramma had "annulled Sheranne's first marriage." Too young to know what "annulled" meant, when I asked further Mom would only shrug and claim to know no details. Like so much of what took place in too many Luick homes, too much of significance occurred behind closed doors, wrapped in darkness and squirreled away like faded, scratched poker chips for possible, usually underhanded future use.

As with most of the whispered rumors and suggested secrets that pervaded my childhood contact with my paternal clan, Mom's intimation rang true. While researching this book, our cousin, Tony Luick, discovered two newspaper clippings from the winter of 1962-63 confirming this long-concealed event:

SHERANNE LUICK* ASKS ANNULMENT

A petition on file in District Court asks annulment of the marriage of Sheranne Luick and Gary Jack. The suit was brought by the girl's mother, Charlotte Luick. The petition states each party was a minor when the license was issued and the marriage performed in Minnesota Nov. 4 without the consent of either parents. It is alleged in the petition that Gary Jack misrepresented his age as 21 and never intended to live with the plaintiff.

SHERANNE LUICK'S MARRIAGE ANNULLED

In District Court Friday, Judge L. E. Plummer granted Sheranne Luick an annulment of her marriage to Gary Jack. The petition was brought by her mother, Charlotte Luick, who claimed both parties were minors when they were married in Minnesota Nov. 4 In the petition, the Luicks claimed [the accused man] misrepesented [sic] his age as 21 and never intended to live with the plaintiff after the marriage.

Globe-Gazette *court notices, winter 1962-63; *both have been altered to protect privacy of the involved*

When I asked Aunt Sheranne during of our on-going phone interviews about the existence of incest in the family, she swore that she knew nothing of such dynamics existing in the Luick clan. Then, that same day, in an email she sent to Barbara but not to me, she wrote:

> I am very hurt and upset and angry. I just got off the phone with Mike Luick. We talked about many things that he will write in his book. We also spent a long time talking about many things that will NOT be in his book. I learned some news from him today that really upset me and hurt very deep! He talked a lot about his Dad and many things I already knew---about the beatings he gave Mike etc! I witnessed many of them. He also told me that Bud told him that Mom gave me money because I blackmailed her by saying something about family incest. WHAT THE HELL? What is this? There was never any family incest that I was aware of. This is really way too much!! I never blackmailed Mom for anything. I loved my mom---evidently far more than Bud and Jeandelle ever did! Who comforted me when I went through a very painful divorce----MOM---who gave me encouragement many many times when life threw me bad circumstances---MOM---who did I laugh with the most of the family---MOM---I love and miss my mom so much!!! How dare a mentally sick, greedy mind say such a horrible thing about me to his kids and others! I feel horrible---I am so mad and so hurt---when I got done talking to Mike I went to the bathroom and threw up! Right now I need my Mom to hug me and tell me it will all be OK---as she did many times during my life!

In response, Barbara wrote back to our aunt:

> Sorry to hear that you are so hurt, upset and angry!
>
> My cousin, Michael, is writing a book that will include 30+ years of research about our family's history... history that goes back to the 1500s and includes photos, newspaper articles, public documents, drawings, etc.
>
> I do not know anything about the "blackmailing" issue you mentioned, but I do know about the family incest. Mom (your sister, Lorraine) and I discussed her incest by your dad. I asked mom why she never confronted her dad? Mom's response, "Why dig up old bones?" (Those words are Mom's exact quote!)

In other words, keep quiet, say nothing, keep the family secret and it will go away… but, it doesn't… it gets passed on from generation to generation… for Mom then married my father who sexually and physically abused me and his other children. (as well as our mom)

Again, I'm so sorry to hear that you are "very hurt, upset and angry." I truly am! Incest is an ugly family secret that wounds many generations.

Be kind to yourself.

With love… your niece,

Barbara

Louis, Lorraine, Donald & George at the Luick home, likely late 1935

chapter 64: lust's lasting legacies

Incest isn't the only sex-based secret most afflicted families keep for decades. It's also not the only form of sexual contact or behavior that leaves deep marks for generations: To sire a child out of wedlock, especially during an adulterous affair, affects a multitude of people—voluntarily or against their wishes—for the rest of their lives. Sadly, the Luick-Juhl clan learned this truth in one of the hardest ways—for already-traumatized Charlotte, one of the most humiliating and demeaning imaginable. As with almost all larger family tragedies, however, this one, too, had its roots not only in the dreadful dysfunction of one family, but also in that of another's.

Born in 1900 near the shores of Lake Seminole, in the Florida Panhandle town of Sneads, on 9 August 1925, William Jefferson Maloy married a Southern girl who at least at one time caught his searching eye—Mattie Steward, a lil' miss from Hatchechubbee, Alabama. Cited on several documents as a "laborer," he took his bride to Tampa in search of a promising life together.

There, the young couple gave birth to a baby girl, Lynann, on 21 May 1926. By fall 1928, however, "Willie" and Mattie had moved to the booming oil country of North Texas, where they found a simple frame bungalow at 1633 East Stella Street, in a generic neighborhood a mile and a half from downtown Fort Worth, less than a block from the porch-lined corner house occupied by his father, William.

On 7 October of that year the fresh transplants to Texas gave birth to a son, Clarence Edward. Soon after, though, their life together spun out of control, for a little over nine months later Willie slit Mattie's throat, then his own. A compilation of articles that appeared at the time reported in July 1929:

postcard scenes of Tampa, Florida—with train station below, circa 1920

ESTRANGED COUPLE SLAIN IN FORTH WORTH STABBING ORGY

Penitent after he had killed his wife, William Maloy, 28, met death from self-inflicted wounds as he mumbled:
"wish I could die."

Mrs. William Maloy, 21, is dead and her husband died in an infirmary as the result of a stabbing at their residence here today. Infuriated at his failure to effect a reconciliation with his wife, Maloy slashed her fatally with a pocket knife after he had cut his own throat.

Mrs. Maloy, with a gash in the back of her neck, was found dead in the front yard. Her husband was lying nearby with knife wounds. The woman's spinal cord was severed.

Police were of the opinion that Maloy was wounded first, inside the house. His wife is thought to have been stabbed to death after running from inside to the front yard. A knife was found by the side of Maloy.

Maloy returned from Chicago last Sunday, police learned. The Maloys had been separated for six months, he living in Chicago while Mrs. Maloy lived here. Maloy asked his wife to come back to him. He and his wife had been married for four years.

Mrs. Sally Steward, Mrs. Maloy's mother, who witnessed the double killing, said the trouble arose when her daughter told her husband she would not return to him.

This morning the couple quarreled while discussing the matter, and Mrs. Maloy screamed for help. Her mother ran to her aid and clasped her in her arms to protect her just as Maloy stabbed his wife in the back of the neck, severing the spinal column. Mrs. Maloy died at once, but he lived several hours.

Mrs. Steward said that Lynann, the 3-year-old daughter of the couple, pounded her father's back with her hands as he fought to push Mrs. Steward's hands away from her daughter's throat so he could plunge his knife into it.

Inquest verdict that William Maloy stabbed to death his wife and then killed himself yesterday at their home, was returned by Justice of the Peace Faulkner today. Two children, ages 10 months and 3 years survive.

Amidst the chaotic aftermath of the dreadful, deadly drama that had unfolded right in front of her, Sallie Steward cared for the resultant orphans as best she could. At 58, though, she lacked the full health and thus stamina to keep up with heating baby formula and bottles, or disinfecting diapers: Granny was simply too old to play young mommy. And, besides, her live-in boyfriend, soon-to-be husband Jack Nowlin, seemed not too keen on kids.

Willie Maloy's brother then agreed to take the children—but only unwillingly, as a "last-ditch" solution. After they'd weathered stints in Lone Star State orphanages, a moneyed-but-childless couple offered to adopt little Lynann and Clarence, but their paternal aunt, Cora, would have none of it. She brought them to North Iowa—according to an in-family source "because of an inheritance left to them."

Their auntie, however, did not host the siblings long: When she discovered that the policies their parents had invested in their futures could only be paid out upon their reaching 18, she quickly lost interest in them. After a few "lost years" of presumed wandering from station to station, in 1940 the two teens were listed as "lodgers" on the Howard and Ethel Box farm in Wright County. A short three years later, Lynann—by that early summer having just turned 17—found work, as well as at least a daytime home, with my paternal grandparents, Donald George and Charlotte Adelia (Juhl) Luick. The trouble was, she found more than just work among the Luicks.

Lynann Maloy (forename altered), circa 1949

Gramma gave birth to a fourth child, Sheranne, on 16 April 1944. With a garden waiting to be planted, lambs needing tending or chicks incubating night and day... with both laundry and mending piling up, and cows as well as sows dropping babies, too... with three pre-adolescent children plus an ever-working husband needing meals and a cookstove requiring close watch in order to prepare them—plus having a new infant to care for... with clunky cloth diapers washed by hand, then wrung... Charlotte felt overwhelmed. What she didn't imagine, however, was that the girl she and Donald hired as an on-site helper for her would turn into a live-in lover for him.

As a baby born of disruptive dalliances, Lois Jean only later learned about her biological father, when she was in her forties; no one alive and willing to talk about them today knows the exact details: only speculation remains. Lynann could hardly have left the Luick home pregnant with Lois, however, as the math simply fails. Not only did Lynann take up residence and complete her high school career in Thornton, but she gave birth to Lois on 29 March 1946—almost a year after graduation. Perhaps, given the instability and want that she had experienced all her life till then, Lynann was determined to make something of it yet: With the money she and Clarence inherited upon reaching legal age, she used her share of the bequest to attend La James College of Hairstyling and Cosmetology in Mason City (which by happenstance Sheranne later also attended), while Clarence later bought a new car with his.

Considering that Donald and Charlotte's daughter Jeandelle adamantly maintains that Lynann appeared on the Luicks' vulnerable home front by fall 1943, as Gramma became increasingly disabled as she grew heavier with child, an already dense plot thickens. Both Jeandelle and Sheranne hold that Lynann's presence among them ended by fall 1944—with Sheranne noting "When mom found out that Lynann was pregnant, she kicked her butt off our place and told her to never step foot on it, ever again." A pregnancy on Lynann's part in fall 1944, however, would have had to result in the birth of that baby by, say, April 1945. Lois' documented birth at the end of March 1946, though, means that Lynann had to have conceived her during a rendezvous with Donald around the 1st of July 1945.

My paternal grandfather's periodic clandestine meetings with his banished lover regarding the material welfare of their shared progeny through March 1949 suggests Donald knew and interacted with Lynann, in aggregate, from fall 1943 through spring 1949, regardless of how much of that time their relationship included sexual contact. Not only does an indicated pregnancy at the time of Charlotte's ejecting her handsome "helper" by fall 1944 suggest that *that* pregnancy ended in an abortion, a miscarriage, death or adoption: It begs the question if the lovers conceived *two* children. If that thesis is true, then Lois likely resulted from an ongoing and not from a one-time affair. And that, in turn, hints at a romantic, not just a carnal connection between Lynann and Donald.

Lois [Luick] Maloy in Thornton, Iowa, spring 1948

But, what did his teenage mistress mean to Donald—who was fourteen years older than Lynann? Was there love tucked among the lust he felt for her? That will remain forever unknown, although what's certain is that the two kept meeting long after Lynann either was thrown out of the Luick house by an outraged Charlotte or left on her own—at least through July 1945, for nine months later baby Lois came into the world, to an unwed mother. Donald passed Lynann cash to help support the child for most of three years—until she slipped away on 10 April in 1949 (only a coincidence, that it was on Charlotte's 36th birthday?) to the Little Brown Church in the Vale (the same venue as Donald and Charlotte's wedding, fifteen years before). But, what are the chances that Lynann would marry a man with the same forename as the city where her father, two decades earlier, had killed her mother, then himself: "Worth."

Donald Luick with "Little Buddy," summer 1937

"Church in the Wildwood" lyrics as souvenir of the Little Brown Church

And, what did her husband's pubertal sweetheart mean to Charlotte, who years later told granddaughter Barbara "a little part of me just curled up and died" when his illegitimate mating came to light? The most apparent consequences of Donald's betrayal of matrimonial monogamy for him appear to have been more material (vis-à-vis child support) and immediate (by the time of his parents' married-life drama some three years later, he showed no qualms in supporting his father George's self-serving actions), with few lingering visible effects. My grandmother, on the other hand, seemed to have never really recovered: The real damages and bottomless pain she carried until her dying hour were both public and external, as well as private and internal.

Farmers on the wide, open prairie have the luxury of being able to exist largely independently from surrounding communities for long periods. Still, we never lived fully separate from the society around us. While Donald's days typically unfolded on the farm or off-farm in livestock-auction barns, farm-equipment dealerships or other places populated mostly with his peers, his wife's work-world necessarily involved trips into town. Every time Charlotte left the farm to buy bread or gas, to pay a bill, stop by the bank or order a service, she felt in her chest that everyone in Thornton (or Swaledale or Rockwell or…) took note of her presence among them. And, with few exceptions, she assumed those populating her small world held a mum or, worse, whispered opinion about this or that Latest Luick-Family Scandal—which we only too often adeptly supplied. She knew, too, that the party-line phone her family used was an open forum.

Sometimes the neighbors she encountered past the end of the Luicks' long, buffering driveway included Lynann, occasionally accompanied by her and Donald's baby girl or, later, the family which Lynann married into and thereupon adopted her daughter. Once, for example, Gramma was in Mabbs' and came around a corner blinded by grocery shelves, only to bump her unruly shopping cart into Lynann and her new mother-in-law,

Mabb's grocery occupied a former bank on Thornton's Main Street; Sheranne and Charlotte in a dry-goods store in North Central Iowa

Esther—who promptly shoved little Lois in the opposite direction and distracted her from any heated or revealing words that might be exchanged. This policy of deliberate public avoidance by both parties, however, didn't stop Lynann, back home, from referring to Charlotte in front of her impressionable offspring as "that old bag."

Even worse than the open secret that hung round Charlotte's ankles and wrists like unrelenting weights every time she dared wade her way down Main Street were the private doubts and sense of rejection that plagued her. What could she expect from—or suspect of—the man to whom she remained legally bound and on whom she depended for her very livelihood? What, if anything, did he still feel for her? Had there been other women before Lynann; would there be more after her? If she tried to hide them at all, the nagging distrust and persistent misgivings were palpable by all but the least sensitive or observant. Her Jacobsen nieces and future daughter-in-law Phyllis reported decades later—respectively—that "We never saw Uncle Donald and Aunt Charlotte being physically next to each other or affectionate in any way," and

> She never had anything good to say about him. It was as if she hated him intensely, but never uttered a word to show it. I think, by the end of her life, she hated men in general—and it stemmed mostly from her feeling that her father, Nick Juhl, didn't want her. Even Bud, who took such good care of her as she was dying—she didn't seem to hold him in very high regard, either.

The ancient Roman lyric poet Horace warned "For the sins of your fathers you, though guiltless, must suffer." Similarly, in Shakespeare's *Merchant of Venice* the English bard claimed that "The sins of the father are to be laid upon the children." In this multi-family drama that took place on the Iowa prairie, at least, their words rang true:

One Sunday morning in the early '50s a pickup barreled into the Luicks' yard, then screeched to a gravel-spitting stop. A livid neighbor jumped out and aimed his rifle at Ring, the family's beloved Collie. As Donald and little Sheranne ran toward him, shouting that it wasn't so—that Ring had spent the night shut in the barn—Pete screamed that the dog had ravaged his flock of sheep in the early hours and thus had to die. Before they could reach the man, with a *BANG!* his gun took down the innocent sheepdog.

Sheranne with Ring and puppy on Luick farm; Ring alone, late 1940s

"I never understood why he had to do that" Sheranne says still today. "Pete returned a couple days later an' said he'd since found out it had been another dog—but he never apologized an' I hated him for what he had done." Taking a deep breath, Sheranne quietly noted "When he died years later Ma said 'It's good, so.' An' Esther—she was a grumpy ol' thing! I *never* liked her."

Clearly, when Worth married Lynann and adopted Lois, his entire family accepted the two newcomers as their own—as well as the open conflict with the Luicks. During phone interviews in early 2014 my mother, Phyllis—not yet aware of her former father-in-law's connection to Pete and Esther's adopted granddaughter, Lois [Luick] Maloy—wondered "Why was Esther *always* so unfriendly to me? I was new in Thornton and could never figure out what she had against me." When I revealed the truth about the connections between the drama's main actors, Mom realized, too, that Donald and Lynann's relationship had cast lasting shadows.

Perhaps the part of the entire affair that pained Charlotte most was that which was the least visible. Since early childhood Gramma had believed the narrative—self-imposed or spun by and absorbed from the grudge-carrying Mooreheads around her—that her father, Nick Juhl, "did not want [her]" so only took her brother, Delbert, to live with him and, eventually, his new wife and half-dozen daughters. Just as she, legally, was a "Juhl" but in fact was known as a "Moorehead," when Lynann married Worth (wait for it!) *Juhl*—Nick's oldest brother Nels' grandson—Donald's illegitimate daughter, a "Luick" in fact, became legally a "Juhl." Thus, by pure coincidence wedded with a tainted fate, Charlotte's husband's bastard child became at three years of age what Charlotte had always longed to be—a "Juhl"—but her entire life had been cruelly denied.

Charlotte Juhl, June Fuller in window, circa 1920

---

chapter 65: setting records straight

As a boy, I grew up on a lonely prairie crowded with moaning ghosts. I felt the presence of people and events all around me. They waved frantically, trying to flag my attention even though my eyes could not visually see them. They desperately pleaded for my pity, even if my ears could not audibly hear their woe. No matter where I went or what I did, those sad, yearning figures followed me like sticky shadows. Even in my sleep they regularly begged to be noticed.

As I would learn when I later ventured out into the wider world, unlike millions, tens or even hundreds of millions of moderns, I had grown up closely surrounded by family—perhaps, by "too much" family. For half a century I have tried to sort out which of my ample encumbrances come from others indelibly linked to me, versus what troubles belong solely to me, arising from the choices I have made over the course of a richly varied life. Having felt little lasting happiness among the people who populated my father's childhood and, later, adulthood, I have spent years, decades trying to free myself from the inherited shackles of unresolved trespasses. Now, I'm about the meticulous work of carving out more space in my jam-packed soul for genuine joy.

Having come not into a blank world of my own invention, but rather having found myself in a pre-existing, burdened one born out of the trials, errors *and* periodic triumphs of those who passed Life on to me, my task has been to sort through the baggage left over from my people's various journeys across continents and through time. That process, though, by its very nature could never be done alone, as a solo project. To find true freedom, to create real and durable relief from the weight of what has preceded me—us!—I've sought allies.

To wrestle out of the grip of what's now mostly invisible but has left long shadows we cannot merely wish away, I've sought liberation not only for my Self: I have long offered others a boost or even a nudge—as unconditionally as I could—in wriggling their Selves loose from our shared afflictions. While trying to respect others' sovereignty, I've sought to shed Light where they, too, might have been stuck in stubborn, suffocating darkness.

My commitment to "publishing truth" led me on 15 April 2014—aka "Tax Day" in the U.S., a national day of reckoning outstanding sums and settling old bills—to pick up the phone and dial a number cousin Tony had found for Lois [Luick] Juhl, whose existence and birthright in my family I'd only learned of days before. With a slightly trembling hand, I clenched the receiver and waited as a muffled ring echoed between my home in Southeast Germany and hers in Southeast Iowa.

When I heard a cautious "Hello?" I forced myself to speak, despite my throat being tight and dry.

"Hello-o-o!" I heard her take an exasperated breath. "Who's there?" the older, high-pitched female voice demanded.

"Hi, Lois. This is Michael Luick-Thrams, calling from Dresden. In Germany."

"Who did you say you are?"

"Michael... LUICK... Thrams" I repeated. Before she could say anything I blurted out—curtly yet clearly, cutting off each word from the tip of my tongue so that she could not *not* understand me—"I. Am. Call-ing. You. A-bout. My. Grand. Fa-ther: Don-ald... LU-ICK."

Silence.

I waited.

Then, finally, the faceless voice drilled "Who gave you this number?"

"Our cousin Tony Luick, in Florida—but that's not so important. Rather, I'd—"

"*Why* are *you* calling *me*?"

"Well" I punted, "because records indicate that your mother, Lynann Maloy, knew my grandfather, Donald, especially well, and—"

"That was years ago..." and so it went. Until, that is, after another pregnant pause, Lois mumbled under her breath "I *thought* this call'd come one day."

Having cleared that hurdle, the jump from public pretenses to private truths didn't take long.

For the next two and a half hours my newly discovered aunt tried on how it felt to have a nephew, one who she didn't even know she had until a few minutes before but now was telling her all about "our" family.

my grandfather, Donald George Luick, circa 1931

Lois' initial reticence steadily collapsed in the face of a decades-old hunger to know. Whereas at first I steered, she soon took over the conversation. "What's *your* name again?" Then, before my answer barely had passed my lips, she asked "And, what's the names of my brothers and sisters? Where do they live—and what do they do? Do they have children? What are *their* names?"

At that point, I poured myself a glass of Shiraz filled to the brim and pulled the padded foot stool to the front of the winged living-room chair. We continued to volley questions and answers back and forth. I sat down and put my feet up: I was settled in for a long haul.

"Oh, my father!" Lois suddenly shouted, as if remembering something she wanted to say. I feared she was going to curse the man who'd afforded her birth—"illegitimately" as some chose to see it—but what she wanted to know was, "Who *was* he?"

"DAHN-ald" I pronounced that ancient Gaelic name for "ruler of the world" as exaggeratedly as I could. "As I told you before, his name was Donald Lu—"

"No, no," she almost snapped. "I know his *name*: What was *he* like?"

"Sorry?" I asked, as I cleared my throat.

"What did he *do*?"

"*Ah-h-h*... he farmed—near Thornton."

"I mean, what did he *enjoy*—what were his pastimes?"

"Well, he liked to roller skate" I began feebly, then, searching, added "He played on the Thornton High baseball team, played saxophone in the school band and was in his class play—"

Donald (right) with Thornton High School baseball team, circa 1930

"Oh, rea-a-ally" Lois cooed, as if I'd just announced that during his lifetime the man had discovered a cure for polio or how to split the atom.

"Yes, and as an adult, Grampa was an avid newspaper reader and liked to attend public gatherings, especially those of farm-related organiza—"

"Yes, yes—but, how'd he *look*?"

"Well, I have a photo of him as a young man, near the end of high school, with his hair slicked back under a huge ol' hat, standing on a porch—"

As Lois interrupted me once again, this time with "Okay, but..."

I took a breath and waited for the inevitable: "was my father h-a-a-andso-o-ome?"

"Yes, I'd say so."

"*Hum-m-m,*" I thought to myself, "*how do I put the painful truth behind a good-looking Luick's beguiling, woman-winning smile and the consequences of the seeds it and he sowed?*"

"You see, though" I stalled, "that was part of the problem." I took another, deeper breath, then dropped my voice and asked without any packaging "Look, Lois, do you want to know only the pretty, lovely things about your father and his people—or do you also want to know the not-so-nice things?"

"Oh, I wanna know it *all*!" she replied. The anticipation in her voice was not unlike that of a child on Christmas morn.

When she asked about the earthly figure my paternal grandfather had cut, it gave me an idea. While I continued fielding her barrage of questions, I emailed Lois an assortment of photos of Luicks *and* Juhls (given that she and I are twice related—once by blood

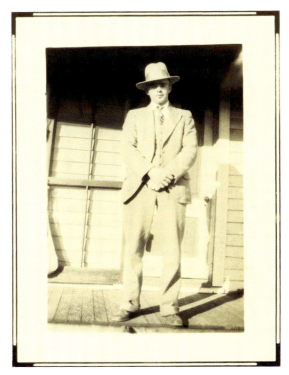

Donald George Luick on porch, late 1920s

through my grandfather, the other by marriage through my grandmother).

"See that little boy, Lois—the one third from the left in that crowd in front of the porch?"

(back row) Lorena (Jenison), Donald & George Luick; Seymour & William "Joe" Jenison; Myrtle (Jenison) & Curtis Luick; (middle row) Madge, Emma (Arends) & Nora Jenison, Lulu (Schmalle) Jenison, Anna (Shupe) with Mona & William Jenison; (front) Marie & Cyril Jenison, Leslie Luick, Leonna Jenison, Myrle Luick & Faye Jenison; likely at the Jenison home on a farm in Pleasant Township, Wright County, winter 1912-13

"Which one?" my newly found kin asked, as I heard a computer keyboard clack with commands.

"The man holding him is Donald's father, George Michael Luick, and the woman on the far left is Grampa's mother, Lorena Eth—"

"Is he the little one, wearing the white hat?"

"*Ah-h-h...* actually, that's a white *cap* he's wearing, but, yeah—that's the one." I smiled to myself and beamed with growing satisfaction. "So, do you see the little boy?"

"Yes-s-s."

"That little boy's Donald; *that's* your father" I announced.

Silence.

Then, like a soft echo, Lois repeated my words, not as a question, but as if she wanted to see how it felt to finally be able to factually affirm it: "That's *my* father."

More silence.

"Yes—that's him" I nodded, even though my "new" auntie (and, concurrently, cousin) couldn't see me. "That's Donald Luick."

Once Lois had a photo, an image, a face instead of the tired old fantasy she'd carried around for the better part of seven decades, it took a moment for her to recalibrate the narrative she'd recited for years. Much of that tale had been fed to her by Lynann, and by Charlotte's cousin and Lynann's in-laws, Pete Juhl and his wife Esther... by staid Cerro Gordo County Lutheran churches, by 1950s romantic films... by Lucy and Ricky, by Ward and June—and of course, *Father Knows Best*... by girlie magazines and boy behavior, by pop songs and pulp fiction, by the scuffed-up baggage of an entire culture, and by her own unfulfilled longings.

Then, we reached the unavoidable question: "Do you wish to meet your two remaining, biological Luick half-sisters?"

my grandfather's illegitimate daughter, Lois, late '40s

Lois' voice dropped in both tone and volume. "I have to think about that." As she admitted her ambivalence, images of Donald and Ward, of June and Lynann (with Charlotte close behind), of stiff poodle skirts and relaxed picnics flashed through my mind.

"I can understand—and it doesn't really affect me" I said. "That decision's up to you, Lois. It's your life, not mine. I'll support your decision, no matter what you do."

After a few seconds of uncertainty, she confessed "The idea frightens me a bit."

"What frightens you about the idea of meeting your siblings, Lois—that they might reject you?"

"Yes" she responded reflexively. "Yes, that's it. I'm afraid." She continued haltingly, "They—, they might— reject— me."

After so many years of naked lies and cloaked hints, of wondering and wanting, of looking for love and longing for belonging, this was the moment when Lois—the personality, the biography behind the voice on the other, distant end of a weak phone connection—bumped against the truth of who she is and how she got where she is. She tried to square the startling data about her father with who she, herself, had always been and with the sireless world she had occupied up until now. She also had to reimagine who she might yet become, having been handed these new blueprints and scripts.

At first I imagined it was I who offered Lois this treasure trove, this nomads' cache of accumulated family heritage. The longer we spoke, though, *she* began to edify *me*. It surprised me, for one, to learn that Worth (who'd married Lynann when her daughter was three years old) had been sold to Lois as her father, complete with a faked birth certificate that cited him as a gas-truck driver. And, it shocked me to learn that Worth had told his and Lynann's other, half-dozen children that Lois "wasn't [his]" before anyone told *her* that. Only in her fourth decade of life did Lois hear from her word-mincing mother "Well, Worth isn't *yours*."

Of all the things I learned during that lengthy and tender exchange, the last revelations remained with me the longest. Finally told "Worth isn't yours," Lois could confirm what she'd suspected for some time. Interestingly, her mother had hinted about "a man named Luick" and fed her newspaper clippings (like my aunt Lorraine's obituary and about her subsequent funeral) or other documents to tease her appetite to know more. She would talk for a while, then take to her feet, walk around the room in ever-tighter circles, then just as suddenly sit back down and resume speaking vaguely about things Lois hardly understood, let alone could integrate into wider contexts.

Lynann's approach reminded me of my interviews with trauma or loss victims who would reveal the most intimate or shocking of details, at great depth—then suddenly snap "But don't put that in your book!" *Why* would an interviewee, who knew the eager man sitting opposite them (or hanging on the other end of a telephone line) was shifting through years of shared familial slag searching for "flesh" to put on the skeletons of those who've come before, spill the most potentially compromising information—then, in a second, back away from it? Why do convicted criminals, who sat weeks, months in crowded court rooms, insisting that they were innocent, years later freely confess their crimes? Why do nations brave enough to engage in truth-and-reconciliation trials find more than enough perpetrators to fill years' worth of public scrutiny?

A second, mystifying dynamic I repeatedly recognize in adults like Lois—whose childhood world had been so fluid and intrinsically, even if incomprehensibly incomplete—was this unshakeable drive to find a real and lasting sense of belonging. It grows stronger with age, as we inch ever closer to own approaching mortality. We homo sapiens seem to be wired to require a sense of place, as well as at least one consistent person (if not a set of same) to afford us a grounded sense of "self." Only to the degree that our understandings of our own personhood are securely anchored in something larger and longer than our small selves, can we stand and weather whatever Life might throw our way. Problem is, we often don't feel up to the task.

Although this photo was taken in the 1930s or early '40s, my childhood memories of the farmhouse my great- and grandfather Thrams built at Ashlawn Farm center around this scene exactly as captured in a photo taken well before my time. Even today, just seeing this humble house pacifies me like little else—instantly and at my core.

After a full day had passed, I called my newly acquainted aunt again to ask "How ya doing with all this, Lois? Are you all right?"

My paternal grandfather's fifth child had existed all my life, yet I'd only known her less than twenty-four hours.

"Oh, I'm *so* glad you called" she said without offering a salutation in return.

"Really?" I responded. I assumed she meant now, a second time—by coincidence on the 70th anniversary of Sheranne's birth, ostensibly the reason for Lynann's landing in the middle of the unsuspecting Luicks in the first place.

"Oh, *yes*, I am."

"Why's that? I mean, I'm very pleased that you're glad I called and everything, but I was simply afraid that it'd all be—"

"No, no" she interrupted, "before you called *yesterday* I felt like I was floating, like I didn't know where or to whom I belonged." She took a breath, then declared "Now, that's all changed."

As Lois and I felt our way into our second extended conversation in as many days, she explained that when her step-father and Lois' mother would fight, Worth used to bark at Lynann "You and your daughter can just leave." She had other clues, too, that he wasn't her biological father.

Appalled by the scenario's brutality, I asked Lois how she dealt with this topic all those years.

"I didn't" she shot back. "I just ignored it—or, at least, tried. When my half-sister Ann attempted to get me to talk about my roots, I brushed her off and told our siblings 'You tell her to mind her own business or I'll tell her off' 'cause I just wasn't ready to deal with it. It was all just too much."

"What changed? I mean, 'cause we're certainly talkin' tons about it now!"

As I said this, I noticed out the kitchen window that the snail-paced clouds that had hung behind the squatty, sand-colored dome of the resurrected *Frauenkirche* were parting—and bright sunshine was trying to break through.

"Well, it didn't go away. There was always this part of me, in the back of my mind, that wondered and wanted to know. I didn't want to hurt my folks, though—as if my digging for my real roots might hurt them. So, I just didn't."

"Okay" I sighed, "but you don't seem overly resistant to me or my message now."

"First Worth died, and then my mother. With them gone—and you know, I just had to know for myself: 'Who am I—*really*?' I wanted to finally find the other half of myself. I wanted, after all that's happened, over all these years, to know the truth."

———

Dresden's rebuilt Frauenkirche (Church of our Lady)

chapter 66: a fluid truth

My father's mother, to put it generously, had a fluid sense of "truth." My noticing naked, confounding discrepancies between what the woman told me and what I either knew or later discovered to be real, began early in Charlotte's and my relationship. Already when she gave me that mid-sized, dime-store globe at a Christmas gathering at Sheranne's—who was living in Northwest Iowa's Pocahontas County with her husband, Wayne, then a 7-Up truck driver—did our on-going duel over personal integrity begin in earnest.

"Oh, Gramma" I begged as I handed her the sphere I'd just unwrapped, "won't you show me where our people came from?"

Lorraine (left), Sheranne (Shelley Joyns on floor), Gramma, me, Jeandelle & John Jones, Christmas 1971

Normally, Charlotte didn't miss a beat before rattling off her oft-sung chorus of "We're Scotch-Irish, English, Welsh, German, Dutch and Dane!" This time, however, she looked at me, clearly pondering a sellable excuse. Dead silence hung in the air uncomfortably long, until I finally prodded "Well?"

"Ya know, Mike" she postured, visibly uneasy, "this globe's too small to show towns the size like the ones our…"

"Okay—so, how about showing me what *countries* they came from, then?"

That task appealed to her better, but Gramma's identifying individual European countries on the crammed orb became a project in itself—until, arriving late as she never failed to do, Aunt Lorraine and her many children suddenly burst onto the scene. She promised to help us locate obscure, distant lands just as soon as the Jones kids had taken off the multi-layers of clothes which their mother cocooned them in before leaving Rockwell on a two-hour ride in a car without a working heater. Lorraine's method of bundling her children enough to survive frostbite in the unheated car left them arriving at Sheranne's place near Albert City resembling slowly-thawing snow people.

Meanwhile, Gramma's grumpy look betrayed her lack of excitement over the prospect of having to sustain a farce *she'd* spun: She moved about like a spider trapped in its own, unyielding web.

Ann (Kew) Moorehead in Rockwell; circa 1915

In her long-winded list of our ancestors' national origins, Gramma Luick always cited first those of ours—above all, those of *hers*—who hailed from the British Isles. "Gramma Moorehead was born a 'Kew' and she was *very* English" she would tell engrossed little Mike.

"Wo-o-ow" I swooned in response, standing at her knees, the elbows of my bent arms planted squarely on her lap and my hands holding up my cocked little head, "rea-a-ally, Gramma?"

"Oh, yes" she'd assert for the umpteenth time. "Gramma Kew always ate dry toast and sipped black tea every day for breakfast"—just like herself—"and she'd sit in her ol' rocker an' read the worn Bible she always kept nearby." (Again, just like herself.)

When I asked if her list of "our people's" ethnicities included those of the Thramses, she'd tsk a bit, as if unhappy to acknowledge Mom's family's existence, then barely audibly admit "Yeah-h-h."

Given her detested father's Scandinavian roots, Charlotte always reeled off "Dane" as if that little Nordic nation were an "also-ran"—with the Dutch an afterthought acknowledged only for genealogical accuracy. And, "the Germanic hordes" she'd mention at times? As she carried not a drop of Teutonic blood in her diminutive body, their appearance on Gramma's list of our familial origins only occurred as if belonging in an "honorable mention" category, a concession to her dead husband's ancestors, who she half-heartedly referred to as "those Germans Donald came from."

Those folks interested me the most—for Charlotte a detectable slight and clear displeasure. Luckily for Gramma I didn't yet know that her very name comes from "Charles," a French form of the Germanic male name "Karl," which means "free man" and from where we also derive the feminine variations "Caroline" and "Carla" in English. If I had, I surely would have happily told her what I had learned—or that "Adelia" comes from the German name "Adelheid" and means "nobility," or that…

I had the feeling, over and over, that if she could, my father's mother would just as soon have snapped her fingers and done away with any trace of the for-her-problematic Germanic blood in her husband's lineage—but, that wasn't an option. As it was, though, Charlotte relished each occasion to emphasize her line's touted Englishness, for example, by zestily rolling the "R's" in "Ballywalte*r-r-r*, County Down, I*r-r-r*eland" every time she reminded me her great-grandfather John James Moorehead was Celtic. Then, she'd add daintily "And, Gramma Kew—she came from Thist-le-ton in Lin-coln-shire, in ol' Eng-land, and..."

"Yeah, Gramma—but where'd the *Luicks* come from?" I wanted to know.

Seeing she'd already lost the battle, one time Charlotte conceded the fight with a sigh and rashly answered "*U-u-uh*, they came from 'Luick,' Germany."

"You mean there's a town with our last name?" I pushed her to confirm as my mind soared on the back of such an exciting revelation.

"Well, it... *um-m-m*... it's more a village, really."

"Where is it, exactly, Gramma?"

"I'm not sure" she said, then turned to my mother—"Phyl, ya got any more tea over there?"

Velma, Donald, Jean & Voral Luick; circa 1923

Not so easily brushed off, the next time Gramma visited Ashlawn Farm I ambushed her at the door, waving in her face one of the Nagels' fire-truck-red, hardcover World Book volumes—the one containing all things in the universe beginning with "G."

"Gramma" I assaulted her without so much as a greeting, "look! I found a map o' Germany!"

Unable to wiggle out of the trap she'd set herself, Charlotte sat down next to me and pretended to quickly scour the gray-purple-and-cranberry-coded map of the Luicks' Germanic homeland.

"No, I don't see it here" she begged off within a millisecond of having even sniffed the bait.

"Maybe it's listed in the legend" I suggested, at which point Gramma flew down the column of foreign, unpronounceable names with her pointy index finger, hardly even noticing the words as she went. "Nope—not here, either" she said *Blitz*-fast and feigning disappointment.

"How can that be?" I demanded.

"Now that I think of it" she offered, leaning back in her chair, "I remember hearing that the spelling of the name changed after the war—"

"Oh, I have it" I called out, studying the map's list of towns as if it were a holy grail. "Is it named 'Lübeck' now? Maybe it used to be called 'Luick' and they added—"

"No, that's not it" Gramma attempted to lure me away from a patent, moreover provable

Gramma set to blow out birthday candles, April 1977

untruth. "Lubbock's an old, old town" the erstwhile valedictorian informed me. "That's not it."

"That's too bad—it has a great, big ol' city gate" I reported glumly, pointing hungrily to the nearby black-and-white photo of that Hanseatic city's double-towered Medieval entrance. "It'd be neat to see what's behind that old wall. Hey, Gramma, we could go to Europe someday and see it for ourselves!"

Charlotte only peered off into the room, quietly looking for something—like an escape hatch.

"Wait!" I soon called out, shifting through the "L"-named towns like a down-and-out digger panning desperately for gold, "maybe it's called 'Lich' now... or maybe—"

"No, no" Gramma countered, holding up her shriveled little hand, palm-to-the-front as if she were Superman, trying to stop a runaway train, "that's not it, either, Mike."

Opening the book further, I pushed down its arching pages, as if by flattening them I might discover that somewhere in Germany a village with the proud name of "Luick" had simply fallen into the crack.

"Maybe" I scrambled, trying so hard to find "us" on the map, "maybe it's called 'Lucka' or—"

"—or, maybe it's now in Poland" my father's petite mother bluffed.

"Whaddaya mean 'now in Poland'?" I protested, my most ardent hopes now utterly deflated.

"Well, the borders changed after the war, too..." and so it'd go on, each of the half dozen or so times I tried to pry the semblance of a satisfying answer out of squirming Gramma. Little did she or I suspect, but one day I'd find out the truth— myself, digging about in the land of the Luicks.

what generations depended on to learn about the world around them

———

I didn't know then that the fudge-the-details-and-mask-the-truth gene I inherited through my father's groin came in the same gunk-covered package as the can't-keep-the-pants-up-or-the-dress-down-so-can't-keep-them-legs-closed gene that would cause so much fun as well as so much suffering for generations of Luicks. I also didn't imagine, as an innocent child, was, that in the Luick family the control of information—and its sinister attendant, the keeping of secrets—were the primary, unchallenged strategies to establish and maintain power.

Any sweetness in my character likely has come from my mother's family, while any savvy has mostly come from my father's. Whereas the Thramses with whom I grew up were relatively open, forthright and consistent, in contrast—as a group and as a norm—the Luicks could be closed, indirect and maddeningly changeable. Just like the favorite tricks of Württemberg's controlling king whom the Luicks had fled when Heinrich and his brothers bolted out of Swabia back in 1833, in America they cultivated an intra-familial culture where who knew and acted upon what was closely monitored. Challengers would be sabotaged from within to frustrate all threats of any substance to centralized power. As in any self-perpetuating tyranny, all decisions flowed not from those immediate and affected, but rather via a central, alpha figure. Any power "sharing" was done through subterfuge; any decisions of consequence were made not through consensus but through decree. In such a self-consuming, abuse-prone system, one can never know what's really happening, for to know is to be able to act sovereignly—and sovereignty on the part of anyone but The Sovereign is seen as treason. It is not tolerated.

Belmond-area couple

The Luick-Juhl family—no democracy, but rather a traumatized ring ruled by tyranny—functioned per a silent code. There was no transparency, for transparency would have exposed the real lines of power and how shallow (and thus vulnerable) they truly were. That anomalies like Barbara and me—the oldest surviving Jones child and the youngest Luick kid—might come along and begin poking holes in that culture of denial-based darkness by naming things as they really were, was not part of the system.

By our very questioning we were demanding transparency: That earned us the shameful "You think too much!" label. We wanted to know the actual, underlying forces at work, so that we could both act and re-act effectively: That earned us a "You're crazy!" dismissal. We didn't want to waste our time and energy unproductively on projects based on untrue, untenable or even non-existent factors: That was seen as disloyal. We refused to suffer very long looking for German villages named "Luick" when, in fact, there weren't any; we did not want relatives to touch us in places too intimate for relationships where we could feel safe and healthy; we wanted to be seen, heard and respected for who we were in the deepest parts of our souls: That was all "too much."

We wanted to live with dignity and integrity: That put us directly at odds with the lying, the abuse and the insidious dynamics that dominated too much of what lay in the center of all that connected us, one to another. The pervasive dissonance between what was said and what took place, between what was taught and what was acted out, between what was meant and what was felt—that created conflicting yet hidden dynamics which were always present, in every moment, behind everything one could see. There are light years of distance between real causes and their lasting effects, between foundations and facades—and that is why my contact with the Luicks has always left me feeling so intensely confused and helpless.

John Hansen presenting a clock in honor of deceased Donald's NFO work, 1966

I consistently have the feeling when I'm among my father's people that there's something in the room that isn't being revealed or named, yet is all-powerful and, ultimately, destructive rather than creative. Charlotte and Donald's surviving offspring seem forever stuck struggling in a cult of death instead of thriving in an atmosphere of enlivening love. It is the emotional black holes so prevalent in the ever-shifting Luick-Juhl cosmos that devour so much Light—leaving what's left fractured and frail.

―――

postscript: series of surprises

In summer 2014, my boyfriend Christian and I spent a month in the Upper Midwest. Among other things, we took my mother on a road trip and did some long-over-due family-closet house cleaning.

As we drove the hour and a half from her sister's, Aunt Irene's house in Knoxville, to our destination in Southeast Iowa, Mom and I talked quietly about the meaning of meeting her dead husband's previously unknown half-sister, my half-aunt Lois [Luick] Juhl. We both reported jittery stomachs. My mind raced, my palms grew clammy.

me with Lois, the paternal half-aunt I didn't know I had, August 2014

We arrived to find Lois hardly mobile. She had hurt her right leg several times over the recent months—in fact, she first fell soon after I'd called her in April. After the initial stiff and halting pleasantries, we all warmed to the idea that the stranger sitting across from each of us was kin by blood as well as by marriage, and soon agreed that "going to lunch would be lovely."

As we sat over applewood-smoked, ripped-pork sandwiches, our increasing comfort with each other led Lois, Mom and me to free associate.

"What'd you say my middle sister's name is?" Lois asked me unexpectedly.

"Jeandelle" I confirmed, having supplied her with the same information exactly five months earlier, when I called on Tax Day 2014, from Dresden.

"*Hum-m-m*" Lois Jean pondered, "now just *why* would my mother give me the same middle name as Donald's second daughter, 'Jean'?"

"Good question" I echoed.

"And I married a 'Donald' myself, you know" Lois winked.

"Well" I spun my thoughts aloud, "that was a common name for a man then. Charlotte's half-sister, Jan's mother Cleo, also married a 'Donald,' as did—"

"But doesn't that strike you odd?" Lois insisted.

"I dunno" Mom piped in, "John Jones—that'd be your sister Lorraine's youngest son—married a 'Lorraine' and, by then, that pretty name wasn't at all common for girls of her generation."

"Ya" I nodded, "an' cousin Barbara reported that the folks in Missouri who adopted her youngest sister gave the baby the same middle name as her long-deceased oldest brother, Micky—and they simply could have had *no* idea that it was 'Lynn,' so I mean—"

"Oh, really?" Phyllis piped up. "That's Debbie's middle name, too—'Lynn' is."

"Okay, well, if we wanna play that game, Great-great-grampa Louis Luick had the middle name 'Lee' just like Barbara and me. Look, all these recurring 'coincidences' are certainly fascinating stuff, but—" I shrugged as I refereed a sidebar that threatened to quickly become a self-contained novel. "We could sit here all day an' list off repeating names in familial lineages—like, jus' how statistically unlikely is it that Lois' mother, Lynann, would marry a man with the unusual name of 'Worth,' the same name as the city where her father slashed her mother's and his own throat? But" I shrugged again, "what's it all mean?"

Then, completely out of context, Lois announced "You know what, Phyllis: I've met you before."

"Oh, really?" Mom replied, visibly taken aback. "But, I can't recall having ever met you, Lois."

"Indeed" Dad's illegitimate sister explained, "I was visiting Gramma and Grampa Juhl on their farm west of Thornton one time—I was often at their place for longer stays—when you and your husband came by."

I tried not to smile at the irony of my newly discovered aunt calling her brother "your husband."

The only reply Mom could muster was a genuinely incredulous "You don't say."

"Yes, I was about nine years old, but I vividly remember him asking me, very directly, what I wanted to do when I grew up—and you didn't say much, but I remember you, all the same."

Speechless, Phyllis peered at me as if begging for a rescuing intervention.

"Well" I mused, "Dad had to have known who you were and pondered what might come of you, his little sister." Mom didn't look convinced. "I mean, otherwise would you pose a little girl you never met before such a pointed question, unless you felt some sort of vested interest in her?"

Thawing a bit and coming back to life, Mom wondered "But why would we have visited the Juhls? We knew they were distant relatives through Charlotte's long-lost father, but—"

"I can tell you why" Lois ventured. "Michael said you and Bud farmed west of Thornton when you were freshly married—"

"Yes, that's right."

"—and you would have toured that farm before committing to rent it, right?"

"Yeah" Mom nodded and shrugged, "I s'pose we would have."

"Then tell me, was the house you folks rented dark red—maybe built of dark-red brick?"

Thus began Lois' detailed description of the '20s farmhouse and outbuildings that my parents had rented from Doc and Norma Voetberg as of June 1955. Accurately drawing with her finger on the Formica tabletop in front of her the entire farmstead as seen from above, Lois confirmed that as algebraically improbable as it might be, out of the hundreds of farms that then surrounded Thornton, Iowa, my parents rented the one Lois' adoptive grandparents, Charlotte's father's nephew and his wife, Peter and Esther Juhl, had until then occupied—and where Lynann had likely lived, again perhaps as a live-in helper, upon leaving Donald and Charlotte's employ. And where, later, during uncountable visits to her adoptive grandparents, little Lois used to play on the front porch—the very same spot where, only a short time later, Lois' biological father would read the latest news...

Mom & Grampa Luick on "that" porch, mid-1950s; the house as seen from road, after my family moved in

At that moment, sitting in a sandwich shop hundreds of miles away from Thornton and decades later, we were all mindful, once again, of how interwoven all our lives—our very fates—really are.

———

PART II b
Warriors without Wars

Section 3:
George & Lorena (Jenison) Luick family

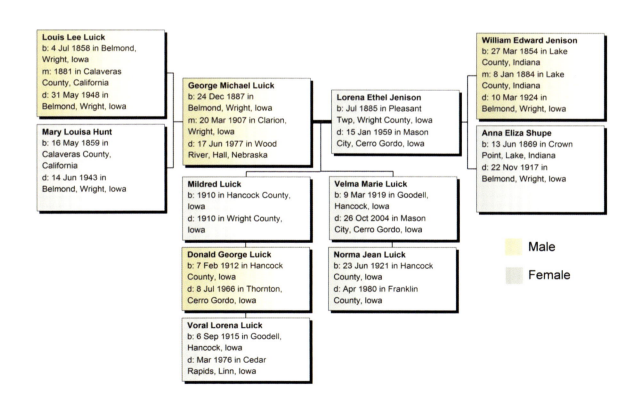

George Michael Luick's nuclear family

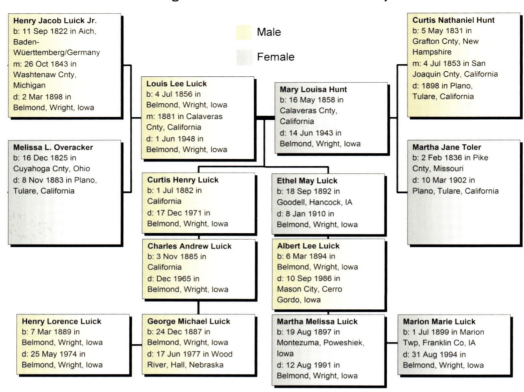

Lorena Ethel Jenison's nuclear family

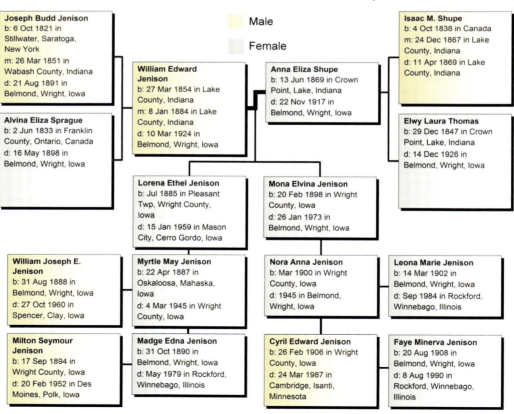

George Michael and Lorena Ethel (Jenison) Luick

born:	24 December [1886 or] 1887	5 July 1885
where:	[likely] Belmond, Iowa/USA	Belmond, Iowa/USA
married:	20 March 1907	where: Jenison family home, Clarion, Iowa/USA
died:	17 June 1977	15 January 1959
where:	Grand Island, Nebraska/USA	Mason City, Iowa/USA

We know so many conflicting facts about a man who left such contradictory legacies: alleged spousal "cruelty" as well as documented wife abandonment; anti-immigrant activism as a young father, then, as an older man, marrying an immigrant's daughter with a pronounced Danish accent. And, then, there's that messy matter of his stint as an amateur terrorist… all of which hangs in the air contra exclusively warm, positive memories almost all relatives have of personal encounters with him in his later years.

Perhaps it's fitting that what's said to be Great-Grampa George's baby picture consists of *two* figures—a rare specimen of twin-exposure images of one and the same baby, at the same sitting, simply rearranged atop a footstool and the same set of repositioned cushions between shots. An apt finishing touch, even the numbers scratched along the top of the negative now appear in reverse for the rest of time, stretching like a banner over two completely contrasting expressions of one and the same child.

photo said to be of George Michael Luick, born in 1886 or 1887

Regardless of any moral ambiguity I might feel towards them, as a historian I regularly have to wade through conflicting biographical data about my chosen subjects. I'm not sure—for starters—where or even when my paternal great-grandfather, George Michael Luick, was born. Gramma Luick (citing credibility-challenged Charlotte as a source alone should set off alarm bells) swore he was born in Calaveras County, California, yet Federal as well as State of Iowa documents show him as having been born in the Hawkeye State, even as his older siblings were enumerated on census forms as hailing from "Calif." Although all citations agree that his birth had been on Christmas Eve, some—like his obituary, presumably written by family—record the year as "1886" while others, such as the U.S. Department of

Social Security, say "1887." Some accounts insist that George's parents brought their growing family "to Iowa from California by train in 1888" but, then…

———

chapter 50: two in one

Despite George's embodying what Goethe's Faust warned of as "two souls in one breast," all disinterested sources document that the man who'd one day be my paternal grandfather's father grew up amidst a large-yet-fluid roster of household members at the end of the 19th century, on a string of rented farms near assorted, small prairie towns with peculiar names: Iowa Falls, Hickory Grove, Latimer, Goodell, Meservey and the Luick-family-founded bastion of Belmond. Deeply embedded in a closely-knit extended family with nine children (including [half-?]sister Leora), George married Lorena Ethel Jenison on Wednesday, 20 March 1907. Theirs was a double wedding shared with his four-years-older brother, Curtis Henry, and her two-years-younger sister, Myrtle May.

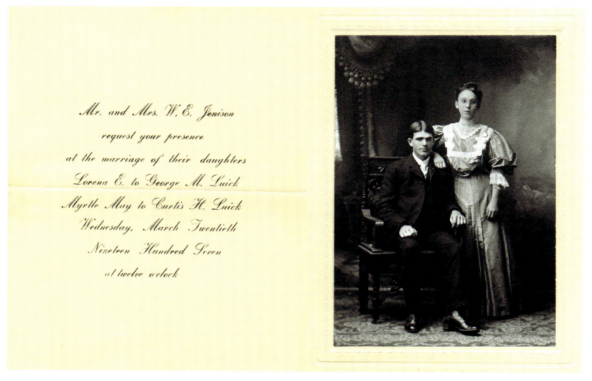

George Michael and Lorena Ethel (Jenison) Luick's wedding invitation and picture, winter 1906-07

For the times and place they lived, newly-wedded George and "Rena" were unusual in that the bride was a year (or two; see above) and a half older than the groom, and that they bore their first surviving child only after half a decade of marriage. (Their first child, Mildred, was born in 1910 and died that same year of unrecorded causes.) It was while farming in Twin Lake Township, west of Goodell, that they had a son, Donald George, in the winter of 1912—on 7 February. The number of then-expensive photographs that the couple took or had taken of their son, their first child, suggests excitement and pride in having finally been able to begin a family five years after having married.

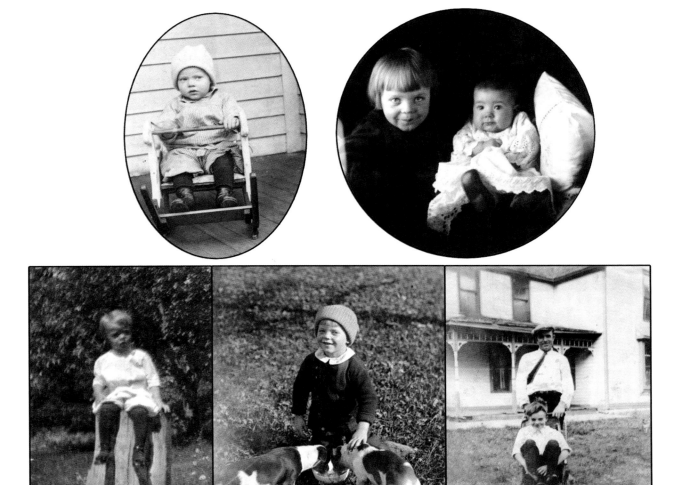

scenes from Donald Luick's early life: (top left) Donald, likely spring 1913; (top right) with sister Voral, winter 1915-16; (bottom) George by himself, with puppies, and with his father, George, circa 1922

For at least part of his youth, George had grown up on a farm near Goodell—but one of the numerous stations in his parents' shell-game-like serial moves around mid-continent North Central Iowa upon coming from California's Mediterranean Central Valley in the late 1880s. In turn, he and his wife chose the town as a base during the geographically fluid first years of their married life. Goodell, then, served as the childhood hometown of both my paternal great- and grandfather. It colored their characters for the rest of their lives, even as they helped shape its later fate.

Never a settlement of substantial size or significance, Goodell's résumé nonetheless mirrors thousands of comparable communities across Anglo North America, where hundreds of thousands, where literally millions of Americans' and Canadians' families also sojourned on their way to today.

Founded in 1884 and named after John Goodell, a financial backer of the railroad that literally put the planned railway stop on the map, it arose on some of the last land in North Central Iowa to be settled. (Years later, Donald told my father that as a boy he "helped make hay on the last patch of native prairie, east of Goodell, north of Meservey.") An earlier town, Amsterdam, had tried to take hold a few dozen rods' distance away, but with the announcement of the railroad's final route its residents picked up and moved their houses westward exactly one mile (1.6 kilometer) to the new town site, thus abandoning their by-passed one. When Amsterdam's post office also shifted to newly-founded Goodell, that officially recognized transfer relegated the dissolving hamlet to eternal obscurity.

Amsterdam's string of misfortunes, however, didn't deprive nascent Goodell of having a few of its own. On the Fourth of July 1888, for example, a devastating cyclone tore through the young town, killing little Willie Stockwell, an infant son of early settlers. Vern Schluter, a later Avery Township trustee, wrote that "The pioneers were not discouraged, and they rebuilt their homes." The same would not be true thirty-one years later, however, when in December 1919 a fire "destroyed the entire north side of the Main Street business block and many of the businesses burned out did not rebuild."

The 17 December 1919 edition of Belmond's *Herald-Press* ran an article under the headline "Goodell Nearly Wiped Out by Fire." Illustrating in nuanced detail the casual intimacy that bound townsfolk to each other in such a small, mutually dependent community, it surveyed the scope of the fire's impact:

> Goodell suffered fires last week which destroyed fully half of the business part of town. Some ten or eleven buildings along the north side of the business street were burned to the ground, leaving standing only the bank building and the lumber office of the business buildings on that side of the street. The first fire started Tuesday evening about seven or eight o'clock. The *Goodell Globe* says of that fire:

> "Goodell has suffered the most disastrous fire in her existence. While all were going on peaceably about their business Tuesday evening someone smelled smoke and upon investigation it was found to be issuing from the rooms over the Goldberg Market and Grocery. These rooms are occupied by Mr. Goldberg and family, but Mr. Goldberg was away in Minnesota, and Mrs. Goldberg was at a neighbor's home and the boys were in the store. Someone quickly ran up stairs and the smoke was seen to be thickest in a bedroom in the northeast corner of the building. From all appearances at that time it was burning quite lively between the ceiling and the rafters so an ax was secured and a hole knocked in the ceiling. Such was the case. The fire had already made great headway and before a minute had passed the flames had broken through the roof. A crowd had collected by that time with pails secured from the hardware store and with small chemical fire extinguishers from all over the town. These fire extinguishers were used without having any appreciable effect at all upon the flames. There is a well situated at the northwest corner of the Goldberg building and two men were on the pump and water was brought up the stairs as fast as it could be pumped from the well and poured on the fire, which by then covered a considerable

portion of the roof. There was very little wind at the time, but little was needed to spread the fire along the row of frame buildings that lined the north side of Main Street. By the time the Goldberg building was enveloped by flames, the Wilson harness shop on the east was on fire. Mr. Wilson had been branching out from the harness business and had quite a stock of automobile tires, oils and accessories and these oils of course served to make the fire burn faster. A considerable portion of Mr. Wilson's stock of shoes and automobile accessories was carried out, but was piled and strewn around in such shape as to be practically worthless. He also lived alone in a room in his building and his bedding and clothing were completely destroyed.

"Men had taken their stations on the roof of the Cashman furniture store at the outbreak of the fire and for a time it looked as if the fire would not spread to the buildings on the west but when the Goldberg building began to collapse, after the fifty-gallon tank of ammonia which they used in their coaling plant had exploded, the side of the furniture store next to the fire became so hot that firefighters could not remain there and it was soon enveloped in the fire shroud. Miss Cashman had a large stock of caskets and as many of them were saved as could be and the hearse was run to a point of safety. The second story of the Cashman building was occupied by the I.O.O.F. lodge and most of their records and paraphernalia were destroyed. In a short time, the post office building next to the furniture store was burning, but not until postmaster McNutt, with the aid of a number of volunteer workers, had had sufficient time to move the mail and records and his stock of school supplies, etc., into the street. Mr. and Mrs. Robt. McNutt lived in the dwelling rooms over the post office and their household effects and clothes were also brought down before the fire reached them.

"But, we are neglecting the other side of the fire where we should perhaps be most vitally interested. The *Globe* was located in the old State Savings Bank building next to the Wilson harness shop. This old building had ordinary siding covered with tin and several were of the opinion that this tin covering would sufficiently protect the building that the fire could be checked there, but it was a vain hope for if anything, this building caught quicker than any of the others. The tin became so hot that it shriveled up and then the walls seemed to be covered in flames almost instantly. The *Globe* equipment was all so heavy or had such a tendency to disintegrate that it could not be moved and the equipment, with the exception of the Webster International, was completely destroyed. We have this 'editor's friend' around which to build a new plant. Mrs. Ed Martin had her household furniture in the rooms over the *Globe*. Her furniture was almost new and was brought down in fairly good shape.

"T.O. Letch owned the building next to the *Globe* office, of which he occupied the lower floor with his feed store and shoe repair business. His stock was un-insured and a special effort was made to get his stuff out. $1200 worth of feed was carried out and piled in the street. There will be some loss of course due to the handling, but he will not come out so badly as if the feed had burned; also it would have made the fire much harder to check, as the ground feed always has a tendency to smolder for a long time. Mr. and Mrs. F. L. Stockwell and three small children resided in the rooms over the feed store. Their stuff was practically all brought down but was in bad condition, as the fire was getting pretty close when the last of their furniture was brought down, consequently it was handled hurriedly and quite roughly.

"The last building to burn was the telephone office and at the same time the home of Mr. and Mrs. W.O. Butterfield, which they had occupied for a number of years. Their goods and the telephone company's property including the switchboard were practically all destroyed, and but little insurance was carried. The fire was perhaps a little harder on the Butterfields than the rest, for they are both well along in years and have had their home in the same location for a good many years, and it is not so easy for people of their age to settle amidst strange surroundings and start a new home as it is for the younger people.

"The lot between the Butterfield home and the hardware store was vacant and as soon as it was found that the fire could not be stopped short of there, all efforts were centered at this point and by heroic work the fire was stopped at that point. Water was poured constantly upon the wall and roof of the hardware building and long timbers were brought and placed against the telephone office and as soon as it had burned so as to weaken it, these poles were managed and the burning building pushed so as to the west into the space which had already been burned and thus the ravaging flames were checked.

"We will not attempt to estimate the loss. It is too great. Thousands of dollars' worth of property was destroyed, five families were left homeless in the mid-winter and the merchants that saved a part of their stocks haven't a roof to put it under. We can't even use the time worn expression 'blackened ruin' for no ruins were left. Everything was destroyed except an occasional heating stove or some other iron article. The people of Goodell, with one exception which several have mentioned to us, were absolutely unselfish, taking in the people that lost their homes and offering their already over-crowded buildings to any sufferer from the fire. And these people are grateful."

Before the Great Fire of 1919—the aftermath, if not the actual burning, of which George, Lorena and their son Donald, my Grampa Luick, would have witnessed—Goodell's downtown constituted a vital thoroughfare. There, both individuals and families made as well as lost entire livelihoods. Among others:

> Ole Sandberg operated an early blacksmith shop and continued in business for over 50 years. Henry Mayor had the first furniture store and undertaking parlor. He later sold out to Ed and Eliza Cashman [who also bought the grain elevator]. John Lasher had the livery barn and B.F. Porter the harness shop. A.J. Bauman started the bank in 1892. He also built one of the first business buildings in Meservey [7.5 miles/12 km to the east] and was the first in Goodell to own an automobile. Goodell for a time had a weekly newspaper, *The Globe*, and a movie theatre, "The Star."

Goodell didn't have only a shining cinema "Star;" it also had dark-skinned local celebrities. Vern said:

> No story of the township would be complete without mentioning James and Lorinda Preston, a Negro couple who lived on the farm [near] the bridge over the Iowa River to this day known as "Nigger Bridge." The Prestons were born in slavery in Tennessee and moved to Missouri with their master while they were children. When James and Lorinda married, their master gave them their freedom for a wedding present and helped them get out of Missouri into Iowa. They lived in Avery Township many years. Mrs. Preston died in 1886 and is buried in the Amsterdam cemetery[.] Jim was much in great demand at pioneer dances as he was a master of the violin.

What did my great-grampa George Michael Luick, growing up as a boy in rural Avery Township, adjoining Goodell, think of his family's African-American neighbors? Or, of the local supporters of "radical" ideas such as women casting votes? According to one of its own trustees, Vern, "The township has always been strongly Republican in politics. In the days before woman sufferage [sic], the Democrat party in the township consisted of seven non-conformists who dared to defy the GOP elephant."

Regardless of any non-white or non-conformist neighbors they might have had, George and Lorena later thought Goodell an auspicious place near which to live. Still, despite any satisfaction he derived from being a new father in what seemed an agreeable locale, soon after Donald's birth George wasted no time in beginning what became a series of moves and new occupations.

Voral (on pony) and Donald Luick, with family dog in the background, circa 1922

In 1913 George took his wife and baby boy to Hampton, where the twenty-something young man worked as one of the first auto mechanics in Franklin County's seat. The $400 income he reported on the 1915 State of Iowa census ($9,321.96 in adjusted 2014 dollars) comprised a disappointing sum for a beginning father hoping to better provide for a growing family. Perhaps for more than purely financial reasons, George came to the quick conclusion—having just started the precision-demanding job the previous year—that, in the long run, it would be heaps more gainful (or at least bearable) after all, turning hay on an old farm, than turning bolts on a new Ford.

Rockwell Auto Company garage with I.O.O.F. hall upstairs, 1920s; ads from Belmond newspapers

In any event, already by the time little Voral Lorena joined the family on 6 September 1915, George—whose very name means "farmer" or "earthworker" in Greek—had taken his growing brood back to the farm near Goodell, where the family spent America's stint fighting the first of what would be two global wars. Though assured a deferment by the local draft board as a 30-year-old father of two and, moreover, an exemption as a farmer occupied in a "war-essential industry," George dutifully registered for the draft on 5 June 1918. The resultant registration card described him as having "Medium" height and build, with "Blue" eyes and "D[ark]. Brown" hair.

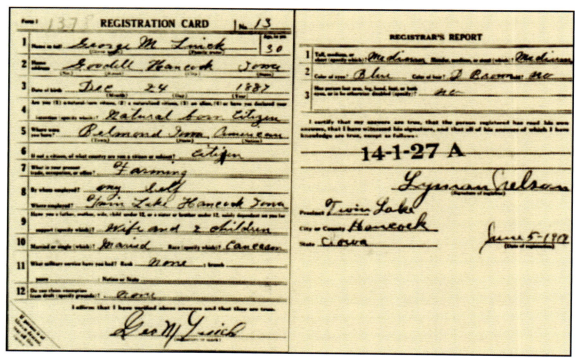

Hunkered down on the farm, soon the father of four and in any case a "war-essential" farmer, my great-grandfather, George Michael Luick, was set to weather any crisis, natural or human made.

Who could have foretold, at that point, that he'd help brew a social Molotov just a few years later?

chapter 51: the dutiful bigot

Was it out of an overriding sense of personal onus that Great-Grampa George went through the motions of registering for a world war in which he well knew he'd never fight? If so, might this same, misplaced yoke of self-appointed "duty" led him in the mid-1920s to become active in the re-emergent Ku Klux Klan? And, to place the genuine drive behind his most burning social convictions in the hands of opportunistic charlatans? In any case, such characters were clearly willing, without hesitation, to bastardize American history to excuse outrageous behavior. In George's readiness to use terror to realize ugly, ultimately untenable aims, however, he wasn't alone. At the same time, his hopes to swiftly reshape society apparently outreached his ability to discern the difference between might and right, between social Darwinism and civic integrity.

images of early Klan history: 1868 cartoon (right), circulated in the South to intimidate Northerners

The Klan of my middle-aged paternal great-grandfather was the second of three incarnations of a monstrous movement that has plagued American society for a century and a half. The first wave hit the post-Civil War South as frustrated, largely disenfranchised whites paraded about in outlandish, intentionally frightening costumes as they attempted to intimidate African-American (or other minority) neighbors from claiming civil and economic rights that had been confirmed theirs in the course of a devastating war between the free-labor, industrializing North and slave-labor, plantation-based South. Members of the so-called "Hooded Order" believed in the infallibility of "Anglo-Saxon" authority, and in the use of force to create a racist social order per their warped, self-serving worldview.

The second wave arose amidst the social fragmentation left by the horrific, game-changing First World

Ku Klux Klan members march through Washington, D.C., 1928

War. Adopting the robes, masks and conical hats of their earlier role models, the "new Klan" added frightful nighttime cross burnings to their repertoire of intimidating stunts meant to advance regressive social strategies. Arising in an era of anti-immigrant backlash, the Klan of the turbulent Twenties hawked "One-Hundred Percent Americanism" and harked back to the nativism of a fading 19th century. Ironically, while claiming to be political heirs of 18th-century British colonial revolutionaries, the second Klan (founded in Atlanta in 1915) used the modern business systems of commercial franchising and pyramid marketing, which rewarded street-level organizers with much of its initiation fees and commissions from costume charges. The Klan's registration agents, so-called Kleagles, pocketed forty-percent of the $10 joining fee—including that from "American Krusaders," foreign-born Protestant recruits. In an era that promoted individual advancement via careerism, several million answered the call to join the Klan—in particular, outside the KKK's traditional Southern cradle: in the urban as well as rural Midwest, in the West and even as far as the Northern Great Plains of Saskatchewan.

Perversely, the revised KKK preached a "purification" of politics—including better enforcement of recently-enacted Prohibition—and strict morality. Touting what it called "white supremacy," the Klan claimed to protect "womanhood" but used those two cloaks of righteousness to abuse African-American men. The Klan said it supported "clean living" and decried

> dope, bootlegging, graft, night clubs and road houses, violation of the Sabbath, unfair business dealings, sex, [extra] marital 'goings-on,' and scandalous behavior.

Appealing exclusively to white Protestants, it railed against the perceived "threats" of the Catholic Church—the religious anchor of recent Italian and Polish immigrants—and Jews, especially those newly arrived from Eastern Europe. While some local groups took part in attacks on private homes across the nation, the most physically violent incidents took place in the Klan's spiritual homeland, the Deep South.

sheet music popular in the U.S. in mid-1920s; 1926 cartoon advocating expelling Catholics from America

Still, the Upper Midwest endured its share of local brushes with Klan terror. Those flare ups of hooded force—exhibited to muffle public discussion and stifle dissent—were sporadic, but pronounced. In a pamphlet published in January 1922, future American Civil Liberties Union chair Albert de Silver wrote of an incident that occurred in late summer 1921, when a

> group of rowdies first described as American Legion men [...] tore Mrs. Ida Crouch-Hazlett from a Socialist platform in Mason City, Iowa, last month, and drove her out of town[. They] were quoted by the United Press correspondent as saying that "they preferred to be known as the Ku Klux Klan;" and the *Kansas City Post* frankly describes the Klan in that part of the world as an anti- Nonpartisan League organization.

The first female candidate for U.S. Congress from Colorado and a former Prohibition Party member, Chicago-born Crouch-Hazlett had come to Mason City to address a public gathering. Before she could speak, however, self-identified Klansmen kidnapped her and took her some ten miles into the countryside, at night, and left her there, alone. A one-time elocution teacher, longtime journalist and suffrage campaigner, according to one source "This experience did not break Crouch-Hazlett's commitment, but it did nonetheless coincide with an end to her tenure as a Socialist Party organizer."

Once they had shown that they could successfully block open debate, North Central Iowa's emboldened Klan members hungrily searched for their next highly-visible publicity coup. They found one in the death of William Cook, a 51-year-old brick mason at one of Mason City's cement plants, the first of which had opened only some eighteen years earlier but already had attracted a relatively high number of African-American workers to work and live in the area, along with immigrants from Greece, the Balkans and other parts of Southern or Eastern Europe. Some of Mason City's residents found its recent, exponential growth more and faster than they could deal with: From 1910 to 1925 the population doubled, to about 22,500 inhabitants.

Postville (Iowa) Herald *article of 10 April 1924 detailing Klan rally George Luick attended in Mason City*

Apparently having chosen Cook as one of their own and to make him an embodied martyr for their amorphous cause, on that rainy April day

> [as] many as 4000 people attended [and watched as] 600 Klansmen paraded down Federal Ave. toward the Fair Grounds, and the newspaper reported claims that up to 200 Mason Citians were klansmen. A volunteer [has found] a MN klan tabloid [titled *The Minnesota Fiery Cross*] that shows a klan funeral in MC with the robed participants marching in a cross formation with the coffin from the MacCauley Funeral Home to Elmwood [Cemetery]. That was in 1924...

...and the Klan's masked, volunteer foot soldier championing its racist cause in lily-white Goodell—duty-driven George Luick—was on hand! According to two of my father's surviving cousins—the two youngest of Donald's sister, Velma's three children—as a girl their mother

> went into the barn once and found Grampa's white robe and hood. Lorena had been furious that he went on that march to the fairgrounds that time! She was very English—very proper and proud: Everything had to be in order, to be correct and just right. [George's daughter Velma] said that when she was young, Grampa would be gone some nights—away at some Klan meetings.

Ku Klux Klan members attending a parade in 1922

The hamlet of Goodell lies six miles (nine km) due north of Belmond. In the event of a civil emergency—say, strife spawned by disillusioned suffragettes, or an armed takeover by bootleg-swilling, jazz-addicted, dark-skinned polyamorist Papists—with good weather and decent roads, George could have been in the Luick stronghold on the Iowa River in a quarter hour, easy. If he barreled his Tin Lizzie o'er Nigger Bridge, then tore open-throttle across the endangered prairie, even in a cool ten minutes. One had to prepare for such contingencies, after all: Dutiful, "real-American" citizens had best rally up group action *before* such unpredictable events took place.

An article that appeared in the Belmond *Independent* on 26 October 1922 confirms Velma's later, hushed revelations, that there were local meetings of a then-ascendant Klan:

The tenor of the cited articles run in northern Iowa at the time conveys a concealed but clear concern about the welfare of the writers' hometowns. The second of the two hints at underlying local power struggles: It was "business men" and "other parties" who were targeted by such harassment—oddly, with some being warned, beforehand, they'd be getting "severe advice" (aka "threats"?). To what degree was Wright County's Klan activity a question of class? Clearly, based on his income as well as his deficient level of formal education, careworn George Luick belonged to anything but the local elite.

While individuals of all classes are drawn to fringe movements such as the Klan, Nazism, Islamic fundamentalism, etc., in 1920s America especially white, Protestant men among the Midwest's disenfranchised rural population provided the muscle behind the Klan blossoming outside of Dixie. Certainly, directly following World War I's cessation, farmers as a group sank into hard times even as urban America boomed for most of the immediate post-war decade. They were, then, a receptive audience for extremists' promises of a restructured social order in short order.

Ku Klux Klan Organized Here?

Rumors Of Business Man Receiving Letter Signed By Famous Initials.

MAY BE JUST A JOKE

The town has been running over the past week with reports of one of the business men receiving a letter recently, containing some severe advice and signed by the "K. K. K." Other parties also received such a communication, this paper understands, of a similar nature, and one or two others are reported as expecting to be favored (?) with letters. On top of these stories, the Independent has been told by a citizen of the community that several nights at 11 to 11:30 several auto loads of men in large cars have passed his place going toward the grove, and around 1 to 2 in the morning they returned. Pipe dreams? Many at least have been expecting to hear of the Ku Klux Klan organizing in Belmond. It is reported that one is being formed at Clarion also.

Cross burnings arose on Stone Mountain on Thanksgiving, 1915

In an era when austerity marked life down on the farm, the theatrics of the Klan appealed to many, as they offered distraction from otherwise often dull, defeating days. Already in 1932, social historian Frederick Louis Allen critiqued the Klan for its

> white robe and hood, its flaming cross, its secrecy, and the preposterous vocabulary of its ritual [which] could be made the vehicle for all that infantile love of hocus-pocus and mummery, that lust for secret adventure, which survives in the adult whose lot is cast in drab places.

Typically, men from the lowest social echelons lack adequate education, despite any other personal strengths or other resources they might possess. I personally knew George Michael Luick to be a gentle, jolly, contented man. It's undebatable, though, that all his life he remained poorly educated. The 1920 Federal census indicated he'd completed the tenth grade (his wife, Lorena, the twelfth), but a note he once penned to his granddaughter Lorraine, then twelve years old and likely in Thornton's public school's seventh grade, belied sub-standard written-English skills:

April 27 1947
Benkelman Neb

Dear Grandauter, Well Lorrain i think i better anser some of thoes nice letters of yours How are you i am OK i supose you are gowing to school every day I am working every day douing carpender work I am starting Monday east of town to build a ketchen on a house and porck i have another man that is woiking with me I give hem 1.00 dollar fer hour. i get 1.35 and one meal I furnish the tules I have got a 100. worth of them Will i supose your daddy is bizy in the field I supose it keeps you and Buddy bezy with churs Tell the Folks hello fore me you grand daddy

When I contemplate how such a sweet man could be so foolish as to invest his time and energy, his highest hopes and lowliest brute actions in such a clearly reactionary, fear-driven project, it helps to see Great-Grampa in fuller context. A man of too little empowering education and from a family content to do with less rather than dare to aim for more, he attached his dreams for a better life and a more decent community to a hate-spewing terrorist movement. Clearly, he saw in the swiftly growing Klan a way out, a boost up. The problem was, at whose expense? *Not* his!

teen brothers Curtis, Henry & George Luick; D.C. Stephenson, Indiana's KKK Grand Dragon, 1922

As with my paternal great-grandfather's son's and grandson's later NFO activities, after a short-lived intensity, George's KKK involvement thankfully withered and died on a frail vine. The demise of the Klan's second wave occurred as swiftly as had its ascent. Internal power struggles, criminal behavior by leaders—such as that featured in a 1926 trial in which Indiana's Grand Dragon was convicted of raping and beating a woman, who then took her own life—and organized external opposition led a collapse in membership. It dropped to about thirty thousand in 1930, before fading away altogether in the 1940s. At its peak in the mid-'20s, the second Klan claimed 4-5 million members—an improbable (but if true, incredible) 15% of the U.S.' white-male Protestant population. A homespun fraternal organization, while it thrived it offered a blustering vent to disillusioned recent U.S.-Army discharges, renegade law officers, boot-strap business men and would-be entrepreneurs, middling social climbers and Southern sharecroppers, as well as Midwest tenant farmers—including "renters" in North Iowa.

Voral (left), Velma & Jean Luick with "Loretta," 1930

Federal and state censuses confirm George Michael and Lorena Ethel Jenison Luick as "renting" farmers by 1910, through to at least 1930. Although struggling to make ends meet like many of their farming neighbors at the time, the 1920 and 1925 censuses also note the arrival in the Luick-Jenison home of two additional daughters—Velma Marie on 9 March 1919 and Norma Jean on 23 June 1921. While at first glance the 1925 census appears harmless, that of 1930 quietly portended a "situation" that would impact all members of both involved families for the rest of their lives.

———

chapter 52: a lasting love

Born in the winter of 1897 to Danish immigrants who'd arrived in *"Amerika"* less than a decade before, Olga Hansen didn't have an easy early life—even if her forename in Old Norse did mean "holy" or "blessed." As she tried to graft her Nordic family onto the rolling, inhospitable short-grass plains of Central Nebraska, her mother, Ane B. Hansen, navigated hers and her children's lives through a series of trials. Surviving hardships that might have meant the end of less hearty souls, by 1910 the 48-year-old "widowed" mother had a farm mortgage to service and seven children—ages 20 to as young as nine—to feed, all on her own.

By their marriage on 22 August 1917, Olga somehow had hitched herself to the family of fellow first-generation-American Frederick Christensen and moved in with him, his Danish-born father, Emil, and Swedish-born mother, Marika, on the family's farm among the Danish-American fold settled around Thornton, Iowa. By 1925 "Fred" and Olga (educated till the 8th and 7th grades, respectively) headed their own household and, by 1930, had two children—Martin, 9, and baby Deloris. *Where* in Cerro Gordo County's Pleasant Valley Township they had chosen to farm would prove less life-changing than *next to whom*. According to the 1930 national nose-count, across the fence from Fred, Olga and kids lived an unhappily married man with a wandering eye and a watchful wife—the fetching and, apparently, footloose father of four, George Luick.

Bud & Lorraine Luick, Olga (Hansen) Christensen's daughter Doris & a cousin, Voral & Jean Luick, Olga's kin, Velma Luick; circa 1938

And... *so-o-o*, what happened *next*?

Nobody alive today really knows for sure—but what we *do* know is that by 1940 Fred took Olga and their youngsters away from that farm abutting George and Rena's. Whether their farm's owners now had other plans, or the Christensens had found a better place at a better deal—or if perhaps Fred thought moving his wife into Grimes, just across the township line away from what had become an increasingly "Unpleasant" Valley for the thick-accented couple, might restore their marital bliss... no none knows. In any event, they took up residence in a white clapboard farmhouse with coal-black shutters just south of Thornton, on the edge of the part of town called "Sunny Side," along the ruler-straight, paved-flat trunk road leading to Latimer.

About the same time, Olga's would-be suitor, George, also left the farm he and his long-time mate had been renting. By 1940 half of their children, Donald and Voral, had married and were heading households of their own, and Velma was away attending Iowa State Teachers College in Cedar Falls. Thus, my paternal great-grandparents sold their livestock and equipment, moved teenage Jean with them to a modest house in Thornton and, with the proceeds from farm liquidation, bought a black-and-yellow bus—the first in the school district. Years later Velma—who in 1946 interrupted a ten-year teaching career first at a country school, then at one in Thornton, to marry a returning local-boy soldier, Hans Peter Jacobsen—recalled "It was a big thing [and] quite a deal!" In earlier days horse-drawn panel wagons or large, bulky automobiles were used to transport rural pupils to school. Graduating to a purpose-built school bus, the parents of his patrons paid self-employed George every month for their children to ride his bus and the school district also gave him periodic payments. Somehow, now facing the end of their working lives, for most of the strife-torn Forties "Mr. and Mrs. Geo. Luick" got by (at least, for the while) and got along—at least, for appearance's sake.

Jean, Donald, Velma & Voral; Lorena (Jenison) & George Luick, 1940s

At some point, however—at the latest around the end of the Second World War—the itch that has unsettled many a Luick man also, and irreversibly, afflicted George. And, any discontent on George's side with his marriage to the erstwhile Miss Jenison likely arose, at least in part, in how the two treated each other. For her part, decades later her daughter-in-law Charlotte and oldest grandson, my father Bud, used adjectives or phrases like "stiff," "cold," "bossy" and "devil in a dress" to describe Lorena.

Whatever words might have more accurately described George and Lorena's rapport, other, less subjective sources offer telling hints. As in the rural Upper Midwest of the mid-20th century divorce was relatively rare and socially scorned, the terse announcement appearing in Mason City's *Globe-Gazette* on 10 September 1947 spoke volumes:

> Rena E. Luick divorced George M. Luick on grounds of cruelty. She is given title to the household furniture and real estate located in Thornton. Granted by default.

Even if the public notice of George's literal walk-away abandonment of his wife of forty years betrayed few details, his most immediate descendants would carry them for decades. His daughter Velma's three children vividly

my paternal great-grandmother, Lorena, on her own, late 1950s

192

recalled the desertion's chronology, years later:

> Grampa would always accompany Gramma to go grocery shopping on Main Street; he'd go to the tavern, have a drink and chat with the boys, then go pick her up at Mabbs' and carry the groceries home. One day, though, Gramma paid for the groceries and waited for Grampa to return… and waited, and waited some more… until she finally just walked home—where she found a note on the table. That was it: He was simply gone—for good. He never came back.

George and Lorena's youngest daughter, Jean, rushed after her father to beg him to return—but he refused. It seems he did see Lorena again in their lifetimes—once, during which he handed her a $100 bill. A foreshadow of a family scandal to come, said to involve $80,000 of Charlotte's savings, Jean would ask to borrow money from chronically cash-strapped George for years, yet all sources claim that he left Lorena "destitute," to die of "a broken heart." Laid to eternal rest only after her casket had been put in the family's home for a private viewing, Lorena seemed to never recover from what she maintained had been her (reportedly) henpecked mate's totally unexpected departure.

Ytzen's Skelly station, on Thornton's busiest intersection, early 1950s

Did Lorena truly have "absolutely no inkling" of underlying marital discord or duplicity in the last years of her married life, as she claimed till the day she died? George's courting Olga hardly could have been a hasty or—in tiny, life-in-a-fish-tank Thornton—private matter: When he was pumping gas at Ytzen's Skelly station as an after-school job in high school, Lorena's grandson, Don Jacobsen—for one—heard from his boss that when his grandfather, George, also had worked for Murl years earlier,

> George'd go buy ice cream on his break, walk down the back alleys and meet up with Olga for a spell—when he knew Fred Christensen wouldn't be around.

What led George, by then 60 or 61, and Olga, 50, to leave their spouses of, collectively, seven decades? With Jean by then working as a telephone operator at Thornton's small switchboard and Deloris finishing high school, neither had children still at home. Sheranne claims that, according to her mother Charlotte, "Fred had been beating Olga"—while my mother says of Lorena that her grandmother-in-law was "not a happy person. You never see a photo where that woman's smiling." Third-hand talk and intra-familial twiddle-twaddle aside, within a year George had married Olga in a private ceremony in Grand Island, Nebraska. Then, as his grandfather Henry had done some 80 years before him, he high-tailed it with a neighbor's wife to hide in Missouri.

*soda jerk at work
serving ice cream,
December 1936*

George Luick and Olga (Hansen) Christensen around the time that they married, mid-1940s

"Bud's grampa rarely visited Iowa after that" my mother maintains,

> like he just wanted all that behind him. His daughters didn't seem keen on his having left Lorena, but Donald and Charlotte visited him often, as if Donald was all right with his father having left his mother.

Apparently, my father also had few qualms with his grandfather's choosing to spend the rest of his long life with his second wife. Having trekked to South Dakota in August 1952 with Phyllis to visit her relatives, over the long Thanksgiving weekend just months later that same year, my future father took his new girlfriend "on a rushed road trip to visit Grampa and Olga in the Ozarks."

Great-Grampa George playing hillbilly and Olga posing with young Phyllis in Missouri, 1950s

Then still a teenager, Phyllis later reported feeling immediately well among the Luicks living in Missouri's Ozark hill country.

———

The very name "Ozarks"—likely a linguistic corruption of the French abbreviation *aux Arcs*, or "of the arches"—evokes in me a kind of spell. My mind immediately swims in images of knotty woods carpeting gentle hills. I effortlessly can "see" trout hovering in sun-dappled pools below limestone bluffs lining meandering streams. Long before I'd ever physically toured the place, my parents' mere mention of "the Ozarks" sent a thrilling bolt of bottomless curiosity through me.

From my folks' stories of paying visits to my father's family's patriarch and his last love, who by their retirement age lived there on modest means, as a boy I absorbed tales of slow summer days, of licking ice cream cones in the diner George and Olga opened between a busy bowling alley and skating rink.

George (upper-left) doing dishes in the home (upper-right) he and Olga shared in the Ozarks of Central Missouri; George bowling a round (lower-left) and helping Olga (lower right) take lunch-counter orders

Having failed to successfully harvest big enough yields from their first "retirement" cash crop as would-be chicken farmers, they'd retrenched and opened a lunch counter to cater to Lebanon, Missouri's growing leisure crowd that, as paved roads in the rural Show-Me State improved and multiplied, ventured out of the cities. As Dad and Mom described it, their hosts' existence there was a relaxed later life among harmless-if-rough Hillbillies and happy tourists who happened to get hungry bowling a few frames or rollin' round the rink.

Dave (left), Dad, Olga, Jeandelle, Dennis & Doug Olesen, George & Deb; Deb, George, Olga & Dave; 1950s

My grandparents, too, found time to set aside crops and chores in Iowa long enough to linger in Lebanon. About six years old when her grandfather and his second wife started a new, shared life in Central Missouri, Sheranne liked those seasonal social calls to George and Olga. She especially enjoyed hanging round the loud bowling alley or lively skating rink along either side of the diner. Donald did not, however, let his deeply disappointed little girl skate on "Negro Night," the weekly pre-integration Thursday evening dedicated to the rink's use by African-Americans who came by the carload from Fort Leonard Wood, the U.S. Army base a long hour's drive east on Route 66.

"Grampa George" in a parking lot in the Ozarks; Sheranne with George in Central Missouri, circa 1950

No matter how they spent their time in the Ozarks, the Luicks—Donald and Charlotte, as well as Bud and Phyllis—never failed to return to Iowa with glowing reports of "the good life" enjoyed there by Grampa and his new mate. In their previous lives, though, neither had been so happy.

———

chapter 53: a "queer duck"

George was married to Olga for thirty visibly-contented years—and knew her for half a century.

Still, whether our mutual sentiments were kept cordial-but-cool from her side or ours, among George's family she never rose in our esteem to earn an epitaph any worthier than "Grampa's second wife." As far as I can document, soon after he died our family had little contact with the woman who clearly had meant so much, for so long, to the beloved head of our clan. When she went to live with her son Martin in Acton, near Los Angeles, after our (great-)grandfather's death, then died, too, her passing warranted hardly a mention among us, George's descendants.

When we were younger, however, we took more—and more exact—notice of "Grampa's strange-talkin' sweetheart." We quipped that her pronounced "accent's as strong as her Dane-brewed coffee" and pretended to be interested as we followed her through their cramped retirement-center

George and Olga on an outing in the Ozarks, 1950s

apartment and Olga proudly reeled off dozens of names she'd given her hundreds of dolls of all shapes, styles, sizes and colors—but mostly small-child-sized.

We thought it curious how meagerly-furnished their home was, yet Olga was always buying fine cloth and trim, flashy accessories and chic shoes with which to "doll up [her] little ones." We noted that she always found the funds to add to her over-spilling collection of dainty tea cups, saucers, salt-and-pepper sets, silver spoons with miniature porcelain emblems of U.S. states, trimmed thimbles and… yet she quipped with misplaced pride that she "cooked simple" for Grampa and herself.

When Olga went to buy groceries for us guests, she'd bring home plastic bags full of marked-down chicken wings. My malcontented parents would then drive off-campus from Grand Island's Golden Age Towers complex to buy what Mom called "real meat." When she returned and discovered that Olga secretly had bought a "big angel-food cake and hid it at the back, on top the cupboard to later take to 'her' family," Phyllis felt sharply offended.

The sting of that perceived slight would linger decades—as would my teenaged brother David's feeling "creeped out" by Olga's "odd hobby of paging through the *TV Guide* or *Ladies' Home Journal* and writing in fantasy names on pictures of people in ads or articles even though she had no idea who they

Gary Luick's sister Mary and father Albert; Albert's brother George, with Olga; Gary's mother, Ava, and sister Madonna: The doll was a gift to Ava, but its name went unrecorded; in Nebraska, early 1960s

were." For years after our short sojourn in their home in summer 1974, in a high voice Dave would quack in quick succession "queer duck, queer duck!"—a demeaning imitation of her pet name for folks exotic Olga, herself, found odd.

Professed "good Christians," we only tolerated and—cowardly, behind her back—mocked a person about whom we, in truth, knew almost nothing. Even as I, a know-nothing kid and ungrateful guest, traipsed through her home, she seemed to us to be a "dotty old woman." How humbling I find it now, exactly forty years later, to discover credible reasons why Olga collected "little ones," then showered them with rich clothes and surrounded them with thin china or shiny silverware.

Could it be that bestowing highfalutin' names to her well-behaved dolls, or to pretty people in glossy magazines, was a way of populating an inner world that little resembled the vulgar, ugly one she'd survived as a scared, scarred little girl with a foreign name, stranded in an enclave of "outsiders" in the heart of America? Her battered mother's wrenching autobiographical account that Tony Luick unearthed during genealogical diggings would support such a plausible-but-pathetic explanation—as seen in excerpts from her extensive narrative:

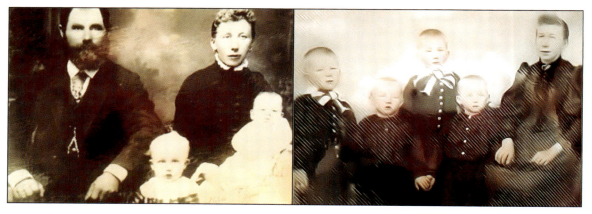

Ane B. Hansen with her first husband, Mads Nielson, 1891; Ane as a widowed mother of four sons she had with Mads—from the left: Jens, Engward, Nels & Louis, circa 1896 (both photos as found on-line)

ANE B. HANSEN left Denmark, Europe — March 8, 1888. My home was Grimstrup, North Jutland and I came to Dannebrog in the last week of March 1888. I worked [there] that summer til school started. Then I left and came to Nysted to work for Pastor Skovgaard who had a church and a high school there. Pastor Skovgaard had many high school boys that lived with him so I had my hands full up every morning making many pancakes for breakfast until all of the boys had been fed. At one time we had 25 of them.

In the evening when all was done around 8:00 Pastor Skovgaard would come and we would all sit around while he read to us before he ate. Then I would get coffee for everyone and as soon as we were done we would stand up and sing beautiful Christian songs that I had never heard before but I still remember. Then it came May 1 and high school ended. I had a wonderful time. I loved the delightful songs and when the boys left school I cried for I missed those wonderful voices of the young boys but I still remember the songs of Jesus. I loved Jesus and I believe that He has been with me wherever I have gone.

So after they had gone and school was out I didn't have any job. I had a good friend I thought I would marry some day. But my neighbor Mrs. Anderson who liked me said she hoped that maybe I would marry her brother who was coming to visit her from Australia. She hoped that he would not go back to Australia. She said he had quite a bit of money and could buy whatever farm he wanted. He did have plenty of money and I came over in the summertime and became acquainted with Nielsen. I thought he was okay and could be a good man to marry and I liked him and could have a home with him so we got married on May 4, 1889.

We lived together until December 4, 1894, when he died of cancer. It was hard for me. There I was with 4 small boys, 4-3-2-1 years old. And so they came and took the farm from me. I stood there with the 4 small children and didn't have anything. I didn't even have enough money to pay for the funeral and other expenses. As there was no will, I could not sell anything until I had received permission or gotten the thing resolved up in St. Paul, so I went there many times to get it fixed so I could sell something, but it took over a year before I could.

But my friends were good to me. They gave me money and groceries and flour and clothes for the children and coal and wood. I had 7 sacks of flour so we had plenty. We didn't suffer but I had to work and do chores all winter. I had an old lady, Mrs. Fissor, to come and stay with the children. I had to go to town one time a month to get groceries and mail. That was hard on me but I was strong and that helped, and Jesus was with me and therefore I could do what I had to do. I did a man's work all winter and when Spring came I had 7 cows that had calved which I milked.

I separated the milk and cream and churned butter every other day. When I went to town I took the butter with me. I had to go before it was warm so it wouldn't melt, but I had to leave my little boys alone at home. But in the 2nd year the creamery man came and got my cream and I was certainly glad for that. It spared me a lot of work. I learned a great deal of English from him. When my husband died, I couldn't speak one word of English and my neighbors were English so it was hard on me to stay there alone, but many of my friends from Nysted came and saw me.

In the 2nd year that I was alone the papers were finally fixed so that I could sell some properties, so I sold some of my pigs and got a little buggy. It was easier for me than a lumber-wagon. But now I needed to have one of my horses broken in to pull the wagon and I needed someone to help me, but that went well. I had a man from Dannebrog who farmed for me that 1st summer I farmed the place. I gave him ½ of the crop. He used horse machinery and lived there during the time when there was work. During the other times I was alone with my boys.

But the man that had my horse and worked with him, the horse was hurt in the foot and could not be used, so I had to do something for I didn't have any other horses. So I wrote to him in Nysted to see if he would loan me a horse. He said he would and that I could use it the whole summer. It would not cost me anything but I had to go get it. There was no time to waste so my hired man stayed with my children that night so I could go early the next morning to Nysted to get the horse. I went across the land, I took off my shoes and stockings because the shoes hurt, but sometimes my feet were so full of stickers that when I came to the river I put my shoes and stockings back on. I had to figure a different way to get to Nysted but had to do it quickly. I needed the horse and the man who was loaning it

to me was very good to me, and his wife made me stay over that night until the next morning and then had him take me back to Dannebrog with the horse, although I still had 6 miles to walk from Dannebrog with the horse. I had it all summer and it didn't cost me anything. The hired man was glad because he could work again.

Then I married again. I needed a person to help me move into the farm that I had bought. Jens Stenholdt

came to the Dannebrog hotel. He was on his way to Denver to see an uncle. But when I told him that I needed someone to help me move he came out to see me, and I said I would give him $10 if he would help me move. That was all right with him. That was in Nov. 1896, but after Christmas in January 1897 I married him. The time that he was with me until we were married he was very good to me and my boys, giving them little presents and many other things and they were glad with him.

But after we were married I had not lived with him many weeks until I found out that I had gotten the wrong man because he was very mean to my boys. He hit them in the head and kicked them around. He made them water 12 cows and 5 horses. He made Jens pump the water to them even though he was only 6 years old. He just could not do that much work, so this man that I married hit him in the head until blood flowed. When I came out and took him away from the pump and stopped the blood then I told him that he had better not hit the boys in the head because that was very dangerous. But he said that they were bad boys. I tried to keep him away from them.

He kept them from school. Louis was hit in the head until he couldn't hear in one ear. Niels was hit and took him out in the snowstorm with a bare head and caused some problems. He laid in bed all summer at age 12. Stenholdt wouldn't allow the Dr. to come. So a neighbor, Loren Freeze, took the boys to the Dr.

Stenholdt said that he would not tolerate any crying when Olga was born. When she was 2 years old she got pneumonia and he said it was my fault. I prayed to Jesus that he would save her. Stenholdt came in and saw me praying. He came to the bed and said "Such a mother you are, you have a spot in your eye, you are a devil, etc." Then he hit me in the head until I was unconscious. He hit a chair on the floor and broke it to pieces. Pete was in the kitchen and Stenholdt took him and threw him up in the air. He flipped him up and got plaster in his eyes and broke a light.

One time after supper was over and I was sitting by the stove with Pete, the dog went into one of the rooms and wet on the floor. I asked Stenholdt to dry it up. So he did without saying a word. It made him mad and he cussed at me and rubbed my face in it.

I was anxious for the boys to go to work as soon as possible so they could not have to stay at home. When Louis was 14 years old, Stenholdt told him if he would stay home that summer he would give him good pay. After working hard, on Sunday, he told Louis to feed the pigs. Louis hadn't a Sunday off so he wanted it off. It made Stenholdt mad, he jerked him out of the house and didn't pay him for all summer. While I was milking Stenholdt threw a tantrum and it scared all the cows out. I couldn't get them back in to milk them. The cows were scared of Stenholdt.

One Sunday we had company and after supper the boys were told to put the separator together. Stenholdt told them not to, that I should put it together and milk the cows and if I didn't he would feed the milk to the pigs and he did. He gave the cream to the pigs also, so we had no butter etc. to put on bread for school. During the days we didn't have anything he went in and ate at a restaurant so he plenty. Before we were married he waited on me hand and foot.

I helped in the fields and when we came home, he rested but I had to fix lunch and take care of Lydia. Then he was ready to work again. I was afraid of him, so I did what he wanted. If I didn't he hit me. He abused me until I was black and blue on my breasts. He took the eggs and sold them. Some he put in the grainery [sic] and put a lock on the door. Pete went to get grain for the cows and when he got in there he found a box full of eggs. He told me then I knew where the eggs were. When I went to the store I had to buy on credit. He pocketed the money.

One day after being in St. Paul, I came just before dark and Olga came out and wanted to tell me something. At the same time Stenholdt came and looked mad, so I told Olga not to say anything. He was coming out with a shotgun, acting as though he was going to shoot me.

Now all my troubles are ended after 12 years. I thank Jesus I now have it good. He leads me where I have to go and has been with me and my children.

I am 84 years old when writing this.

———

As if bloody head injuries, deaf ears and denial of urgent medical treatment weren't dramatic enough, with the appearance of a shotgun on the scene, the account Olga's mother recorded of their family's terrific experiences with Jens Stenholdt comes to an abrupt stop. The vague—but deliberately devout—information on the next line promptly implies that soon after that frightful moment an unexpected resolution of the conflict took place—maybe one of the five sons finally had enough of their (step-)father's cruel abuse, grabbed the gun from him and did away with the monstrous man... or, perhaps, Jens Stenholdt died soon thereafter of natural causes.

The 1910 Federal census for Hall County, Nebraska, however, suggests a very different story. In one entry either Ane categorized herself to the census taker as a "widow" or that person assumed same on their own. Whereas only Ane's and Jens Stenholdt's two (of later three) children appeared on the 1900 census—likely reflecting Ane's stated wish to get her four oldest boys off-farm as laborers and thus out of her livid second husband's reach—after his "death" all seven children again were listed in 1910 as dwelling in one shared household, headed by her.

"Clean an' easy"—right? No, *not* so fast!

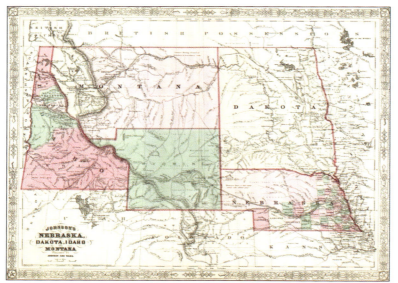

A "Jens Stenholdt" (apparently also born with the surname "Hansen") appears in the same census, perhaps taken later the same summer, and marked as "divorced," residing elsewhere. His and Ane's son Peter appears under his father's entry, too—but is marked not as "10" years old as on his mother's entry, but "11" and thus indicating that he had observed, in the meantime, a birthday since a census taker had cornered his mother and siblings for an official headcount.

While it seems to have been acceptable in 1910 for a man to admit to being "divorced," for a woman that label constituted a social kiss-of-death. Was it was easier for Ane, then, to risk being exposed as a liar than to confess to being a divorcee?

finally together, in the end and 'til the end: Olga an' George

In any event, the disturbing narrative left by her mother documents that Olga, Great-Grampa George's late-in-life great love, personally knew not only the horrors of living in a violent home, but that divorce did exist as a possible remedy—apparently even after thirty years of marriage.

———

chapter 54: exorcising old demons

By creating idealized "little ones" to substitute for the less-than-ideal family she had inherited as a girl, was elderly Olga perhaps trying to "recast the past"—a common adult-life response among children who've experienced trauma? If she were, she was not alone. Not only did Great-Grampa George's second wife unconsciously do that; so did, it seems, his only son.

In 1979 and '80 a Swiss psychologist of Polish-Jewish origins, Alice Miller, published two meticulous and convincing groundbreakers, *Das Drama des begabten Kindes* and *Am Anfang war Erziehung*. When the English-language editions, *Drama of the Gifted Child* and *For Your Own Good*, appeared, they caused sensations in- and outside academia and psychology. In the latter, she credibly argued that traumatized children typically become adults who recreate conditions reflecting, directly or indirectly, those in place at the time they experienced long-reaching distress. They then reflexively attempt to resolve or "remove" the stressor—in most cases, sub- or unconsciously.

The most dramatic example Miller offered of this dynamic was that of Adolf Hitler.

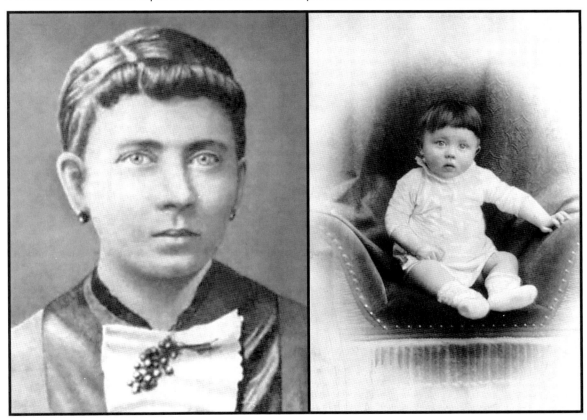

Klara Hitler and her son, Adolf, circa 1890

First as a child with rumored Jewish ancestry and illegitimate birth, then as a young adult with displaced disappointment and rage over a failed art career, after the devastating First World War a deep-seated sense of betrayal and humiliation traumatized the man further. The imperial power he'd grown up in gone, he could not accept the new order. Per Miller, Hitler spent the rest of his life striking out at others—in particular groups of "stressors" he held accountable for his own, unresolved issues.

A second, more recent example might be what some psychologists—both degreed and dime-store—claim was George W. Bush's desire to "settle a score" with Saddam Hussein, who remained in power even after his father, George H.W. Bush, supposedly united most of the world behind an effort to contain a dictator whom the U.S. previously had supported.

We need not look to infamous figures in 20th–century world history, however, for case studies in "past recasting." Between their marriage in 1934, when they began farming on Charlotte's grandparents' place northwest of Swaledale, and when they finally settled on the Harkens farm southeast of Thornton in 1950, my father's family moved, on average, every three years. As Dad's uncooperative sister, Jeandelle, pointed out during the one interview she grudgingly granted me, multiple moves were not atypical for non-land-owning Midwest farmers at the time. The truth of her comment, however, does not diminish the emotional toll which so frequently disturbed the homelife of those affected. Moving an entire farming operation so often required massive effort, with lingering impact. Those recurring disruptions left marks not only on the children, but on their stressed parents.

George, Donald, David and Bud Luick, 1959

fall aerial view of George and Lorena (Jenison) Luick farm, 1930s

Donald, for one, may have had a covert, unconscious agenda. He was made to move about so much as a boy, then roamed for the first sixteen years of his own farming career. According to his youngest ("legitimate") daughter, Sheranne, "Dad always talked about going back to where George and Rena had lived the longest—about buying that place an' fixin' it all up right." And, that's just what he did—with or without his wife Charlotte's support.

My own parents had already sold most of Ashlawn Farm when, in 2002, they auctioned off what remained of the land, equipment, tools, extra furniture and household furnishings, etc. Then, they pretended to "retire" to a modest-but-comfortable, single-story brick house in Mason City (coincidentally built in the year of my birth). Their "retirement," however, did not in the least reflect being "retired." The two were on constant call: Besides various civic and secular duties they carried out outside their own four walls, within them they were always altering those very walls.

First, it went without saying that every room "needed" to be painted anew or livened up with wall paper. As soon as they crossed that mammoth task off their foot-long to-do list, they hired a Mennonite joiner from nearby Mitchell County's Amish community to come and, over many months, completely renovate the kitchen. When that was done, they "had" to wholly rebuild the basement, removing old walls or erecting new ones, installing a "useable" bathroom and a storage space, etc. ad infinitum. And, of course, in their Iowa-farmer eyes, the "poor" garden wasn't serviceable in the condition they found it, so Dad "had" to remove the top couple feet of soil in most of the beds, haul in fertile loam from countryside fencerows in soft-sided buckets, then…

In the midst of this frenetic, prolonged process, I repeatedly wondered (but only once dared to ask) *why* my parents found it *so* crucial to keep *so* busy. What would have happened—or *not* happened— had they simply spent some time, at least briefly, upon concluding their entire lives spent busy on a farm and done, oh, *n-o-t-h-i-n-g*? It did seem, as Mom whole-heartily maintains, our parents grew closer in the last years before Dad dropped dead one night, as the two aged "snowbirds" from Iowa sat in their cozy camper, on the quietly-lapping shores of Lake Havasu, in the middle of the dark Arizona desert. Still, did at least one of them feel the need to stay busy, lest in a state of repose one might think—or, worse, *feel*—"too much for [their] own good?"

Such a theory is plausible, because the indications for it being so are plentiful. Sheranne, the last of their four children to leave the familial home Donald and Charlotte shared for over thirty taxing years, recalls a continual routine of work at her parents' place, varied only by the gradual shifting of seasons or overnight variations in market prices. Her oldest niece, Barbara, remembers that our

> Grampa was always busy. When I used to go spend weekends with Gramma, he'd always come into the house, sit down for a break, say little, page through the paper, finish his coffee and roll, then get up again and go outside to keep working. The whole time, he hardly spoke—and he certainly didn't have time to play or even talk with us grandkids. He always had "things to do."

Charlotte totting groceries and mowing the farmhouse yard; the car the Luicks bought new in early 1966

As I've said elsewhere, my brother and sister can't recall the actual sound of our grandfather's voice—nor can I. Despite being only three-and-a-half when Donald dropped dead—at 54, from a heart attack, one summer evening, eating an ice cream cone with Gramma, her half-sister Cleo and Cleo's husband Don, on Thornton's Main Street, having hayed the whole day and been "rewarded" for all that hard work with a freshly-baked peach pie from my mother—I do remember that whenever our wordless head of family passed through the room, a cold, lingering chill literally went down my little spine.

(He couldn't have been completely void of warmth: Gramma later reported that after he died their snippy Shetland Collie, Tammy, would sit all day at the end of the driveway, waiting for Donald to return—"only coming back to the house at night, after dark, with her tail between her legs.")

Happily, however, humans vary: While conceding that the man seldom spoke ("He didn't *have* to open his mouth; Charlotte's was runnin' all the time!") Mom liked her father-in-law and felt comfortable in his presence. Yes, she had asked my dad, Bud, early in their marriage, about the nuanced rumors she got whiff of soon after moving to Doc and Norma Voetbergs' farm just west of Thornton, concerning "Donald and some hired girl." Her young husband, however, only tersely recited "If you can't say anything good about somebody, then don't say anything at all." That was that—end of story.

A foreshadowing of the post-mortem photo that Gramma later had surgically rigged to present the hollow appearance of a happy couple, Charlotte refused to help Donald when his attention finally, after a decade devoted to completely transforming George and Lorena's old place, went from fixing up the outbuildings to replacing the outhouse with a new, indoor bathroom for the remodeled farmhouse. "So, he asked me to go with him" Phyllis related once,

Charlotte putting away groceries from Mabb's into her 1940s fridge

to pick out a new tub and tiles for the bathroom he was going to build in what had been a downstairs bedroom. Charlotte absolutely would *not* go with him, in public, and do it—so he and I went to the lumber yard and looked at material samples. I did go with her, though, to Sheffield once, to pick out wall paper and cupboards for the kitchen. There was a nice home-furnishing store there then; upstairs they had lovely things to choose from. Each time the woman would lay out something that Gramma liked, Charlotte would ask how much it cost—then, when she found out, have to say it was more than she had to spend. Still, the woman kept pulling out these really pretty samples—but time after time, Charlotte would get all excited, only to find that the money Donald had allotted her wouldn't be enough. Finally, getting exasperated, the woman huffed "Mrs. Luick, you know what your problem is? You have champagne taste on a beer budget!"

Donald's remodeling the dwelling—where Charlotte still, till about 1960, prepared hot meals on a wood-and-coal-burning cookstove and washed laundry in a simple tub, then fed them through a rubber-roller wringer—came in time for Sheranne's long-planned graduation reception in spring 1962. It came, though, only *after* completing all other building projects outside, which were myriad. Among others, Donald and (until Dad married and moved away in 1954) his son Bud—with help hired only for tasks requiring trained hands—toppled the windmill and replaced it with a power pole and automatic night light, tore down the old hog and chicken houses, poured an extended concrete-lined feeding floor for fattening beef, modernized the big barn and constructed one specialized for farrowing pigs, built new machine sheds and a garage, erected fences, felled aging trees and supplanted them with newly-planted windbreaks around the buildings and along the gravel lane...

summer aerial view of Donald and Charlotte (Juhl) Luick farm,

A curious thing about this whole renovation frenzy is that there remain founded doubts about Donald's true motivations. In interviews with my mother, Phyllis claims that while Donald and Charlotte happily helped her and Bud start farming on the Voetberg place, my parents' taking over Dad's folks' farm "was never the plan." As for when the young couple, apparently abruptly, moved to Ashlawn Farm in the winter of 1962-63, Mom has stated "the break with living near Bud's folks, first outside Thornton and then towards Swaledale, had nothing to do with them."

Then, to complicate the story, my aunt Sheranne has asserted that

> over the Fourth weekend, when we visited them just before Dad died in '66, [then-husband] Wayne and I were there, visiting the folks, and I was so happy, 'cause they said that we should take over the farm—but then, a couple days later, Dad was dead an' all that talk led ta nothin'.

Sheranne's tale, however, hardly holds up. Wayne had been a gas-station attendant when they met, then soon conceived my future cousin, by which point they decided to marry even though my grandparents did not approve of Sheranne's would-be husband. (They hadn't approved of her earlier choice of a husband, Gary Jack, either—but Gramma simply had that union legally annulled.) After the perfunctory wedding ceremony, my cowboy-boots-and-tight-jeans wearing Uncle Wayne drifted

front of Sheranne's wedding invitation; getting her hair set at home

between managing a farm near Spirit Lake and driving trucks out of Albert City. Since the young couple lacked significant assets of any kind, Grampa and Gramma would have had to finance completely setting them up in a cash-crop agricultural system that already by the mid-1960s had become capital-intensive. And, in any event, Mad Jeandelle would have raised an unbearable stink, had her parents funded her baby sister's family's future—but that displeasing story, sadly, will resurface later.

If Donald wasn't driving my dad and the rest of the family so hard to completely renovate the farm that his parents had farmed for most of a decade when he was a lad, in order to hand it over in top form to one of his and Charlotte's own offspring, then why all that work and expense? Was all that exhausting effort, say, part of a well-deliberated, long-term investment? Was he "banking" on it?

Or, rather than out of a conscious attempt to proactively script the future, did Donald's tireless dedication arise more out of an unconscious drive to rescript the past?

I assume the latter.

———

chapter 55: visiting vanished worlds

While Donald and Charlotte slaved to remake George and Lorena's old farm back in North Central Iowa, down in South Central Missouri George and Olga played with how to enjoy their retirement most, on the least amount of money. An eternal "fiddler," George found his and Olga's quiet, jack-of-all-trades existence in the hardscrabble, do-it-yourself Missouri hill country agreeable. He collected junked bicycles, cobbled together re-useable parts, then sold or simply gave away the recycled two-wheelers; her knack for cooking found profitable expression behind the lunch counter. My mother, who saw them in tandem for over 25 years, said the two were "good together." As an adult, Sheranne wrote

Olga and George at Golden Age Village, early 1970s

I loved Olga---she was so nice to me and a very sweet person.... I dearly loved this lady and really looked forward to seeing her each year. She was much nicer than Grandma [Lorena Jenison] Luick was to me! [...] Grandpa and Olga were a very sweet, loving couple!

At some point, though, even sojourns in "paradise" end. Unable to fully care for themselves any longer, by the early '70s the two left Lebanon to be near Olga's daughter, Deloris, and friends in that flat, dry land her people knew so well and where Olga had begun Life—in ruler-flat Central Nebraska.

Eventually finding an affordable home not too far from Deloris, in a single-story unit on the edge of the Golden Age Towers' campus in Grand Island, George and Olga kept more than active enough to keep them moving. Each outfitted with a three-wheeled bicycle, they glided around the complex with great glee at being so mobile, so old. More than just buzzing about Golden Age, my elderly great-grandfather cleaned a nearby bowling alley for pocket money and, for the fun of it, played "sidewalk superintendent" at the construction site of a local Lutheran hospital.

Eli-brand windmill next to a farm pond in a pasture south of Nebraska City, Nebraska

George and Olga showing off their three-wheel bikes; article about George "overseeing" construction site

We singularly enjoyed our time spent with Great-Grampa George and Olga that summer of '74, on our way home from a rushed trip through the wilds of Wyoming. During the too-few, full-packed days we spent with them, especially Olga proudly showed us around prosperous Grand Island. As they took us to admire expanding Lutheran Hospital, on the way we drove through a well-manicured and tree-lined new park on the edge of the growing community, and marveled at a foreign phenomenon for us farm folk from Iowa—an enclosed mall.

For my part, I particularly enjoyed the outings we made to two nearby museums. The first, the Stuhr Museum of the Prairie Pioneer, had opened only about six years before Grampa and his locally-born second wife guided their wide-eyed guests through the first open-air museum I'd ever experienced. For a country kid like me, who'd only twice left the prairie in my first dozen years, it was like briefly visiting a new, tantalizing world. Designed by Edward Durell Stone—the architect of the John F. Kennedy Center for the Performing Arts and the National Geographic Society buildings in Washington, DC— the big, moat-encircled main building seemed like a shimmering, white-stone palace worthy more to be showcased in the center of our national capital city than relegated to the outskirts of some sprawling town

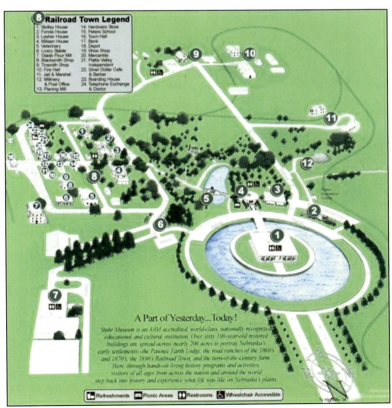

on the Great Plains. Still, its marble floors, twin spiral staircases and four gurgling indoor fountains implanted in our excited little group a hushed reverence that would accompany us through the entire tour.

Although our hosts had been to the Stuhr Museum and our next destination of Harold Warp's Pioneer Village countless times, they beamed as they excitedly competed for our attention—reciting each of their animated narrations about some interesting artifact as if showing us something from one of the numerous homes or farms they'd occupied in their collective course of about 165 years of living. They told almost all of the historical notes or details they offered their attentive audience in first-person, relating larger national or global events through the prism of their own, wise eyes. Sitting in the darkened theater, for example, watching the introductory film narrated by Grand Island's native-son actor, Henry Fonda, Olga whispered

> His peoples came to dis county da same yar as my mudder—in aid'een hundret an' aidy'aid! Da Fondas, dey came fon Upstayt Nu Yorq, but my mudder—see came fon Danmark, don't ya know? Ya-a-a, da Fondas—dey vas here, vhen ve vas.

cover of John Steinbeck's Pulitzer-winning novel, Grapes of Wrath; *Henry Fonda (center) starred in the film*

My paternal great-grandfather and his later-years companion seemed most at home as our curious band later inspected the 1890s rural homestead, complete with a patch o' prairie grass, white-washed one-room schoolhouse and jade-green-trimmed Danish-Lutheran country church, built the same year that Olga's persevering mother, Ane, and the venerable Fondas found their way to Central Nebraska. In each room we entered I listened entranced as Great-Grampa served up rolling commentary about the here-tangible traces of a slice of time he and Olga personally had lived.

Both children of pioneers, all their long lives they had been about the business of sinking roots in the deep prairie loam of the Upper Midwest—and in the process made a nest for the rest of us. Theirs was a swiftly-passing world that we, their progeny, later would inhabit, however briefly, before it all began to quickly fall apart, then slowly sink away forever.

George Michael Luick feeding hogs, picking corn and moving harvested corn, likely in Southern Missouri, late 1940s

Hanging on to every word as the two held forth about never-to-be-repeated experiences of which we, their descendants, could only imagine or dream, I felt transported to another time and another place. In their heart-felt stories I began to find visible, albeit fading proof of a past I didn't know I had.

As I followed them through that unique moment and space, I found in George and Olga's tales the roots of my own existence. What I could not have fathomed at that point, however, was how transitory it all was—the farms our people had worked so hard to carve out of the fertile prairie, the people we'd both encountered and become in the process, the troubles we'd endured and the treasures we'd found… the personalities we thought we were and the individual biographies we believed belonged solely to "us" yet later would discover were largely borrowed from and built upon the efforts of those who had preceded us.

postscript: dark, indelible hues

The moment the Greyhound pulled out of downtown Chicago's bumper-riding-bumper bus terminal and merged into traffic on the freeway headed for Iowa City, he turned and asked me—head cocked and eye wary—"What *you* doin' sittin' in the back o' the bus? Ain't ya a lil' too white ta be sittin' back here?"

For the next several hours Joseph and I chatted animatedly about life, the universe and, well, *almost* everything. Strikingly handsome and clearly bright, the thirty-something man had dropped out of some South Side Chicago ghetto school long before his sharp mind could earn a degree—or a better future.

African-American boy in Cincinnati, Ohio, early 1940s

As we each talked about our families, I did not mention that mine had fought the Pequot War of 1636 against a local tribe in Massachusetts, or that my colonist ancestor Robert Jennison had helped ship some 800 of the captured Native-American men off to slavery in the Caribbean.

As Joseph wasn't Native American, I didn't feel morally obligated to share that distressing tidbit from my family's past. And, as I had no idea at the time that my beloved Great-Grampa George had been in the Ku Klux Klan in the 1920s, I didn't feel addressed when, at one point, Joseph looked at me and said out of context "You know, your people owe my people."

"Sorry" I retorted, "but you're barking up the wrong leg. My people might be lily-white but they've also been working the North American soil for 350 years—and that without a single slave" I reeled off proudly. "The peasant stock I hail from, my friend, would *never* have even thought of owning a slave."

Oh—knowing what I know now—if only that were true!

———

As a young father, my great-grandfather George Michael Luick (whose own grandfather had fled Swabia as a boy with his refugee father and family) watched as economic as well as political refugees from Europe landed on Iowa's then-booming prairie. Jews fleeing Czarists pogroms became merchants and within a generation successful business people or professionals. Destitute Greeks and Serbs, Poles, Italians and other minorities found work in Upper-Midwest meat-packing or cement plants, in tractor or automobile factories, etc. And, during World War I, some half a million African-American laborers fled the Jim-Crow South for comparatively lucrative wages in the urban, industrialized North. They were, even if at times unwittingly, replacing white workers serving as soldiers on the front.

As those white soldiers began returning home from the battlefields of Europe in early 1919, they expected to return to jobs they now found filled by cheaper, in part Southern, labor. Along with female workers expected to go back to tending hearth and towing trailing hemlines, African-American workers were considered treasonous interlopers by white men. In such a climate, the competition to earn living wages swiftly grew fierce and politicized. Tension between various ethnic groups, social classes and races mounted as month by month conditions became increasingly drastic. With little recourse in a deregulated labor market, Americans began to fight Americans of different skin color over jobs. With wartime price controls just dropped, inflation soared, as did unemployment. Millions across the country struggled to keep their families, farms or businesses solvent; frustrated, they looked for scapegoats.

white militia vs. black Chicagoan, 1919

By mid-year, pronounced social friction over jobs morphed into physical violence over racial politics—in what National Association for the Advancement of Colored People (NAACP) field secretary James Weldon Johnson coined the "Red Summer." The allusion referred to a common fear among whites that returning black soldiers would bring with them the "communist virus." In a private conversation in March 1919, President Wilson worried that "the American Negro returning from abroad would be our greatest medium in conveying bolshevism to America."

Indeed, the increasing conflict involved not only competition for jobs in post-war America, but over ideas how Americans should live together. NAACP leader W.E.B. Du Bois wrote in that organization's monthly magazine that African-American men who'd also been demobilized from the U.S. Army

> return from the slavery of uniform which the world's madness demanded us to don to the freedom of civil garb. We stand again to look American squarely in the face and call a spade a spade. We sing: This country of ours, despite all its better souls have done and dreamed, is yet a shameful land[.] We return. We return from fighting. We return fighting.

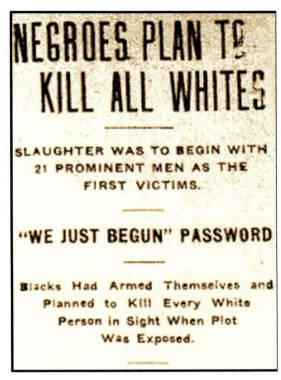

inciteful headline from the Gazette, *Elaine, Arkansas, 3 October 1919*

And, a fight it was—in the end resulting in scores dead, hundreds injured and millions in property damage. From May to September 1919 race riots erupted in over three dozen cities. In most instances, whites attacked African Americans; in some, blacks returned the aggression. The greatest losses were in places like Elaine, Arkansas, and in Chicago, where white neighbors went "nigger huntin'," lawless rampages during which they destroyed hundreds of their black neighbors' homes and businesses. The mayhem and destruction began innocently—when a black youth, Eugene Williams, swam into a South Side beach along Lake Michigan normally reserved for whites, and then was stoned and drowned. The incident ended only after 38 people laid dead (23 blacks, 15 whites) and over five hundred injured.

gangs of South-Side Chicago white men and boys "nigger huntin'," late July 1919

As the rural Midwest had few if any non-white minorities until the 1980s (I was 12 before I met an Afro- or Hispano-American), the Klan that flourished briefly in the 1920s in my people's homeland rarely mentioned or bothered the few Afro-Americans in our midst. Instead, the wrath of the disenfranchised white underclass largely was fueled by anti-Catholic (so, anti-Irish, -Italian or -Polish immigrants), anti-Jewish and anti-business-class (those with money or means). With, however, one tragic exception.

In late summer 1919 accumulating anti-black resentments boiled over when Agnes Loebeck—a German-American teen living in South Omaha—accused a 40-year-old stockyard worker, Will Brown, of molesting her. Two days later a crowd of between five and ten thousand angry, largely working-class whites gathered outside the Douglas County courthouse and demanded the sheriff hand over the accused man.

By the time the smoke cleared the next day, Omaha's mayor had barely survived after being hanged himself from a downtown lamp post while trying to protect Will Brown from the seething throng, and the courthouse lay in charred ruins.

rioters scaling the south side of Omaha's Douglas County

original captions: "Red Cross Women in their Qtrs;" "Wreakage in Judge Sears Office, Sept. 28, 1919"

The governor of Nebraska called out 1,500 state militia to guard against further rioting, and the nation expressed shock over the chaotic destruction wrought by runaway fear bred with blind hate.

Fourteen-year-old Henry Fonda watched the riot from his father's printing-office window, across the street from the courthouse. Years later the Oscar-winning actor recalled

> It was the most horrendous sight I'd ever seen... We locked the plant, went downstairs, and drove home in silence. My hands were wet and there were tears in my eyes. All I could think of was that young black man dangling at the end of a rope.

At least two of Fonda's later films included scenes of lynchings. He said that the one he witnessed in Omaha as a boy stayed with him his entire life.

Grand Island native Henry Fonda as a young man

But, what had happened to Will Brown? The overwhelmed police, who had retreated to the roof with him and other inmates from the burning jail below, surrendered him in hopes of saving their own lives.

Even Brown's fellow black inmates eagerly thrust him forwards in order to placate the advancing mob. As he screamed "I am innocent, I never did it; my God I am innocent" the white horde dragged the helpless man down the jammed staircase to the street, where they beat him unconscious. According to one local (here edited) account,

> His clothes were torn off by the time he reached the building's doors. He was dragged to a nearby lamp pole, where a rope was placed around his neck. Brown was hoisted in the air, his body spinning. He was riddled with bullets. His body was then brought down, tied behind a car and towed through the town. At a main intersection his body was burned with fuel taken from nearby lamps and fire truck lanterns. Later, pieces of the rope used to lynch the man were sold for 10 cents each. Finally, Brown's charred body was dragged through the city's streets.

original caption:
"Will Brown, Victim of Mob's Wrath"

original caption: "Burning of Brown's Body, Riot of Sept. 28, 1919"

And, my namesake, George Michael Luick? While my great-grandfather most likely was not on-hand during one of the darkest moments of Midwest history, he surely heard of the drama that unfolded across the Missouri River in Nebraska, Iowa's neighbor to the west. If so, his reaction went unrecorded. But, his clandestine activities at the time worsened an already tense and frequently hysterical regional social climate. A product of the era and culture in which he lived, he made choices that, along with those of others, led to tragic consequences—and indelible shame.

All humans live in a specific and unique era; each of us is affected by the era in which we live, even as each of us helps co-create that era: An era is the sum of its parts—including our individual parts. To understand how my beloved Great-Grampa George could have been active in the Ku Klux Klan, I have to know what happened to or around him that made him think such involvement was necessary—or acceptable. That's why I look at the times in which he lived—times that included violent, recurring hate, a hate that still casts shadows over us.

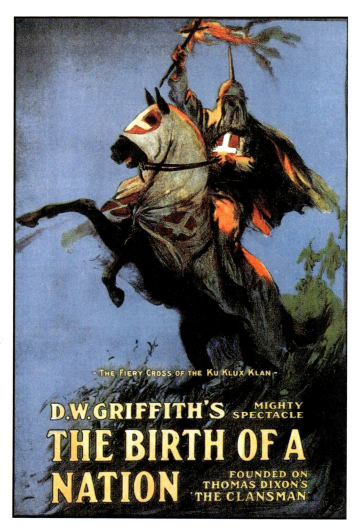

1915 poster advertising Birth of a Nation, *a silent film widely cited to have revived the Ku Klux Klan*

As I search today for clues to how my kind-hearted, quiet old Great-Grampa could have been part of such a horrific legacy, I am mindful that monstrous events and historical moments don't come out of nowhere. The conducive soil needed for seeds of hate to not only survive but thrive needs time and cultivation. Without them, they cannot carry such self-destructive energies into each new day. In George Michael Luick's case, the farm he struggled to save after the post-WWI commodities-price collapse laid only a few miles from what locals then referred to as Nigger Bridge, even though the freed slaves from Missouri who once had found a safe haven near there had long died or moved away. Nonetheless, as a boy George absorbed intolerant, hate-laced attitudes from the culture around him. Sheet music on sale at the time cheered "We are All Loyal Klansmen," while pamphlets advocated chasing Irish Catholics into the sea. Such banal influences might seem diffuse, even miniscule at times, but as an inflammable whole they can kill. History has shown this too many times, in too many places, with too many devastating results.

When will enough of us learn this lesson, so that such travesties might cease to reoccur?

PART III a
Children of Pioneers

Section 4:
Nick & Lottie (Moorehead) Juhl family

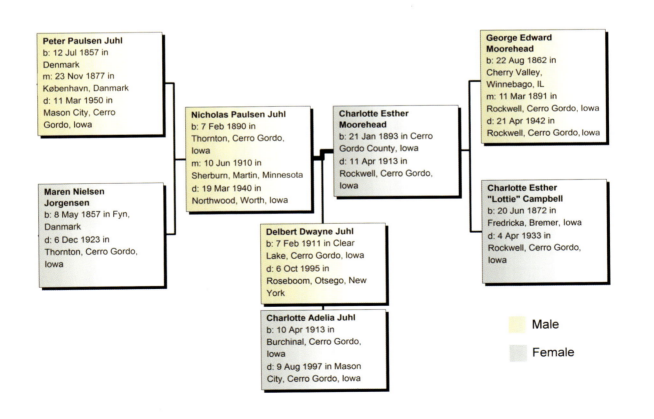

Nicholas Paulsen Juhl's nuclear family

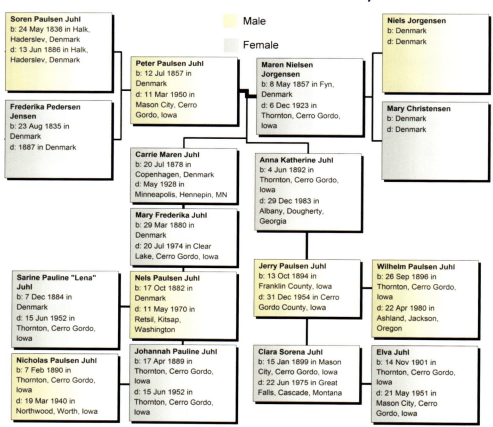

Charlotte Esther "Lottie" Moorehead's nuclear family

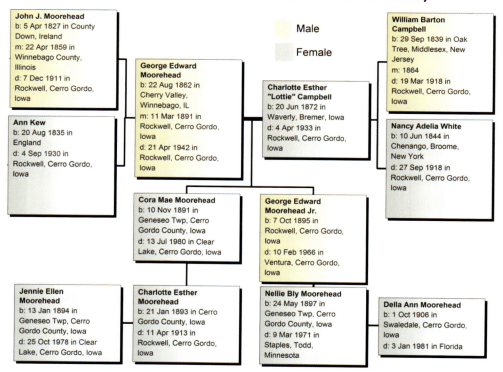

Nicholas Paulsen and "Lottie" Esther (Moorehead) Juhl

born:	7 December 1890	8 January 1893
where:	Sheffield, Iowa/U.S.A.	Rockwell, Iowa/U.S.A.
married:	10 June 1910	**where:** Sherburn, Minnesota/U.S.A.
died:	19 March 1940	10 April 1913
where:	Northwood, Iowa/U.S.A.	Burchinal, Iowa/U.S.A.

Perversely, the man in our family-photo collection whom I most physically resemble is the man about whom we know the least. And, until recently, the only photo our family possessed of him as an adult showed Nicholas Paulsen Juhl not with his first wife—my father's maternal grandmother—but with the woman with whom "Nick" replaced her after, reportedly, having forced the labor which then, supposedly, led to my Gramma Luick's mother's early death.

As for the middle of the three "Charlottes" in my father's immediate maternal lineage, the sole photo we have of "Young Lottie" shows her inseparably nestled between two of the sturdy women who ruled her small-town clan.

"Big Lottie" (Campbell) Moorhead, her daughter "Young Lottie" (Moorehead) Juhl, "Young Lottie's" grandmother Nancy Adelia (White) Campbell and "Young Lottie's" son, Delbert Dwayne Juhl; 1911

Despite all efforts, until now the only documented knowledge we have found of the enigmatic man who sired my paternal grandmother comes from three stray newspaper clippings—two about him, one about his brother, Jerry—and "journal notes" hand-written by Nick and Bertha's eldest daughter, Cleo, for her eldest granddaughter.

Similarly, with her closest kin now all deceased, the most detailed glimpse into the pre-marital family life of Nick's first bride, Charlotte Esther Moorehead, comes from the heart-tearing story of her youngest sister, Della—and, tragically, her ill-fated babies.

Nick and Lottie did not sojourn long on planet Earth: When each left it, he was forty-nine, she but twenty. Having spent so little time here among us, they left less than a handful of recorded traces. All of the information—thus, really inferences—we have suggests that at least these Juhl and Moorehead progenies were not "taking" to the American Heartland as their pioneer parents might have hoped when they arrived in North Central Iowa and tried to graft their nascent families onto the open prairie. Based on the self-destructive behavior of at least two of the four Juhl brothers and, parallel to them, Lottie's kid sister's eventually consuming her own flesh and blood, we have credible, convincing reason to suspect that while their parents had toiled to sink roots into the rich Iowa loam, these offspring of the early settlers failed to find satisfying lives in the New Canaan of their hope-driven forebears.

Nick and Jerry's, Lottie and Della's parents had come—respectively—from post-feudal Denmark and from Illinois and New Jersey, looking for space and place, but the endless Iowa skies were not enough for some pioneers' children. Their parents sought the bounty of freshly-broken sod, but the subsequent mountains of golden grain worth millions were not enough. Those who came to the American Midwest wished to secure common creature comforts, but the material wealth they were able to amass there in a dizzyingly short time, which the next generation took for granted, surpassed the finest luxuries the richest Medieval kings ever could have imagined. They came from the hungry Danish hinterland or the evermore-crowded American East, longing to work, to prove with hardened muscles that their brains were supple enough not only to survive but thrive on the harsh frontier. For their children such autonomy and self-reliance was too much. The parents hungered for freedom; the children tripped, then perished under it.

---

chapter 46: an endless treadmill

Nick's mother, Maren "Mary" (Nielsen Jørgensen) Juhl, came from the wind-swept Baltic island of Fyn to even windier Iowa in the 1880s. There, she and her husband, Peter Juhl, eventually bought a farm tucked within the Danish enclave that had formed around Thornton, and raised a large family. One of eleven children, Nick's often got lost in the sea of shrill voices that competed to be heard in a herd of thirteen. By the time he reached adulthood, then, he would have known his share of stress and frustrations—as well as remedies to relieve them, healthy or not. According to Gramma Luick "like many men of Danish descent," Nick took to drinking long before he landed the station-agent job at the small train depot in Burchinal, a dusty railroad stop halfway between Thornton and Cerro Gordo County's seat, Mason City.

My paternal grandmother also always went on, during her recurring recital of what a wretched man her father was, to accuse him (depending on the day and the degree to which she could recall which version of the story she peddled to us the previous telling) of either punching Charlotte's mother in the stomach and thus setting her into premature labor, pushing his weakened wife down the stairs so that she broke her neck and died instantly—or both.

The problem with tapping Gramma Luick as a source of information was, what bits she selectively provided usually entailed a fingerful of truth, but were badly mangled and editorialized as they passed through a head full of wild, vengeful nonsense. She was two days old when her mother died: Every sad song that "Little Lottie" ever sang about her despised father—or, for that matter, her deified mother—was composed by another, by someone with a subjective viewpoint if not agenda.

Charlotte "Little Lottie" Juhl "Moorehead" with her cousin, June Fuller, early 1920s in Rockwell, Iowa

Stripped of emotion-fueled conjecture, the only confirmable facts at hand are few:

- Nicholas Paulsen Juhl was born on 7 February 1890 (the same day as his future daughter Charlotte's future husband, Donald's, birthday) on a farm near Thornton, Iowa—the second son and fourth child of eleven children born to recent Danish immigrants Peter Paulsen and Maren "Mary" (Nielsen Jørgensen) Juhl.
- On Friday, 10 June 1910, Nick married Rockwell-born Charlotte "Young Lottie" Esther Moorehead in Sherburn, Minnesota. She was the daughter of George and "Big Lottie" (Campbell) Moorehead.
- Eight months later, on 7 February 1911, the couple gave birth to a son, Delbert Dwayne Juhl.
- On 10 April 1913 the couple gave birth to a daughter, Charlotte Adelia Juhl, in Burchinal, Iowa; within the next two days, her mother was dead. Nick kept Delbert—just over two years old—with him; his dead wife's parents, George Edward and Charlotte Esther (Campbell) Moorehead, took the newborn baby girl directly after her mother's funeral to live with them in Rockwell, Iowa, where they raised her to adulthood.
- On 12 April 1917 Nick married Rockwell-born Bertha Mae Hadsall of Mason City, Iowa—two days before her 24th birthday, and four months and ten days before the birth of their daughter, Cleo Marian, who later wrote as an adult that "[Bertha's] mother fell down a flight of stairs in an unfamiliar house, during a heavy rainstorm at night, and died instantly when I was about 3."
- The 1920 Federal census shows Nick and Bertha as renting farmers about 24 miles (38 KM) north of the Iowa border near Waltham, Mower County, Minnesota, with three children: Delbert (8), Cleo ("2 [years]-8/12") and Edna (1). Cleo wrote years later that Nick had worked there as a "hired man to a farmer whose name was Kimball. My Mom always spoke kindly of him and of his wife."
- The 1930 Federal census shows the couple as renting farmers in Lime Creek Township, just north of Mason City, Iowa, with three additional children: Hazel (7), Helen (6) and Esther ("9/12" months).
- By 1940 Nick had fathered—as far as records show—eight children, seven of whom were girls. He raised all of them with Bertha (Hadsall) Juhl, except for my grandmother, Charlotte (Juhl) Luick.

Bertha (Hadsall) and Nick Juhl's wedding picture, April 1917

Between 1920 and 1933 Nick had dragged his ever-growing, mostly-female family with him to live on at least three different farms—and that during one of agriculture's most difficult times in American history. Nick and Bertha's oldest daughter, Cleo, later wrote that her parents were

> hard-working, busy, usually tired. They cared for us always in decent, honorable ways, but were not demonstrative of affection. [Still, Nick] had a jolly jingle he sang to us in Danish when he was in a relaxed mood, and Mom would sing to us, too.

How often a father of a growing family in a shrinking economy could find himself in "a relaxed mood" remains unclear, but as Cleo's notes attest, not all was dire in the depressed Thirties:

> With 5 younger sisters there was always someone to play with or take care of. We moved from farm to farm so often that it contributed to a lack of Sunday school or church connections. We played simple outdoor games—hide and seek, leap frog, pump-pump-pull away, and ante-over a small building with a soft ball; snow angels, fox and goose on a big snow-pie ring; a simple tree swing from a piece of old hay-rope and a board or tire seat, etc. I liked to be outside. Being on a farm, we had cats and dogs (and kittens and puppies) and horses, chickens, and my Mom liked to have geese. (Have you ever held a new, fluffy, green-gray gosling right close under your nose? Also, we had some great feather beds to sleep on as a result of saving the choice feathers when the geese were prepared for eating.)

> My Mom's sister Mary and my Dad's brother Jerry each had girls of about the same age as my sister Edna and I. Company for Sunday dinner and fun hours together are good memories from the years we lived close enough together to see them quite often[.] Aunt Mary had 2 daughters the ages of my sister Edna and me. They lived in Mason City and when my folks farmed around Rockwell and Mason City we spent lots of week-end time together in the country. When we lived in [that] area one of summer's high-lights was going to Clear Lake for July 4.

Despite all low- or no-budget ways to let children be childlike, Cleo's parents could not change the fact that the rural America of her youth had fallen on such protracted misery. With so many mouths to feed on top of struggling to make farming pay during hard times, it hardly could have been a surprise when on Tuesday, 21 February 1933, a notice in the *Globe-Gazette* announced a

Closing Sale for Nick Juhl to be held Saturday

The closing out sale of Nick P. Juhl is scheduled to be held on the place known as the old Kjerland farm, 2 miles east and 2 miles south of Northwood, Saturday, Feb. 25, commencing at 1 p.m. Seventy-seven head of livestock will be sold at auction, including 7 head of work horses, 33 head of Holstein cattle, and 37 head of hogs. Mr. Juhl also wishes to dispose of 125 chickens, 10 bushels of yellow seed corn and a full line of farm machinery. C. L. Bolender will serve as clerk and the auctioneer will be Ora Bayless.

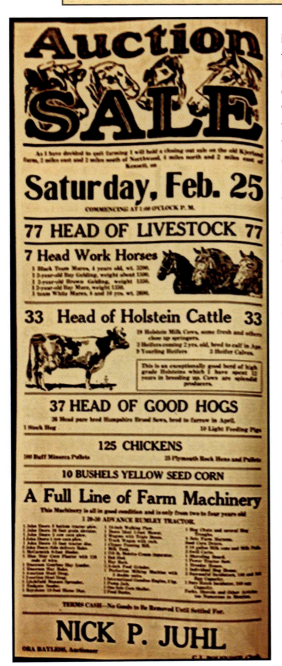

It couldn't have been easy to be a man, to be a father in an era when men—especially men with families—were to know everything, to be able to do anything... to be held responsible for all things. That, in a time when at least every fourth, if not every third would-be working adult wasn't. That, in a time when Wall Street tycoons crawled through office windows to reach sidewalks far below—flying... when Big City professionals took to selling apples on small street corners, when in the South not just dirt-poor African-American children ate the red soil... when Americans begged "brothers" they didn't know for a measly dime. It couldn't have been easy to be Nick, in America, in the Great Depression, with six young girls, a wife and impatient bills. He found himself with no one to turn to, no one to take over the literal reins in an agrarian line of work which couldn't even feed the family much less pay the rent no matter how hard he slogged from sun up to sun down but how it could all end other than in tragedy some sad day.

In times of hunger, the least of these eat the Earth.

If that weren't enough, in the middle of it all Nick lost his fifth-oldest daughter, Esther Pauline. Born on 29 July 1929, the girl had a history of suffering seizures—so bad that her oldest sister Cleo would recall her "on the floor under the table, having epileptic-like fits." On 19 April 1935 five-year-old Esther died during an attack. It distressed her already-fraught parents greatly, who still had a family of seven to somehow squeeze through merciless poverty. (Bertha once told Cleo regarding her and Nick's early married life, "Every time I saw overalls on the end of the bed, I got pregnant with another child.") The Great Depression, however, did not care what had come before; like a messianic Great Leveler in some biblical trial, it tested all for righteousness.

"The times truly were very difficult, and with all those girls" Nick and Bertha's first-born, Cleo, would tell her daughter, Janet Gullickson Dahlby, years later. In turn, Janet recounted

> when there were guests around, [Nick] could be the proudest father of the greatest daughters in the world—but as soon as the family was among itself again, then it was 'You better get out there an' get to work!" The family was so poor, that [daughter Cleo later] said that when they butchered hogs they "used everything but the squeal." As for the drinking, there was this idea, "Dad wasn't a lifelong alcoholic, but he drank when times were bad." He'd visit a tavern for a few more drinks than would've been good for him—and he knew it. Nick would go to the tavern, drink, then he'd leave his truck parked outside and walk home from the tavern, 'cause he'd had too much to drink. It was on one of those nights…

Gramma Luick told me, growin' up, "Nick was drunk and walkin' down the middle of a road on New Year's Eve and got run over by a car." Then again, Gramma told me *a lot* of "things" as I was growin' up. Oddly, it seems that in 1940 New Year's Eve came on 19 March that year, as documented by banner headlines in Worth County's largest newspaper:

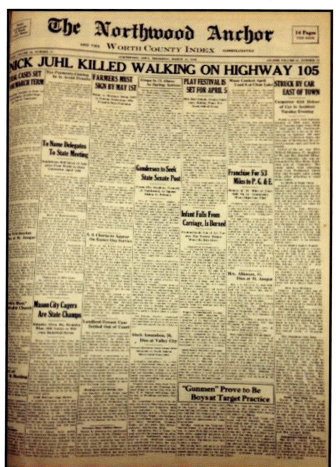

A few days later, on 23 March, the *Northwood Anchor* announced:

> Funeral services for Nick P. Juhl, 49, were held Friday afternoon at the First Baptist church.
>
> Mr. Juhl, a Northwood trucker, was instantly killed last Tuesday night on highway 105 one mile east of Northwood when struck by a car driven by Miss Mildred Ellingson, 17, of Carpenter. He was walking eastward from town and the car was traveling from Northwood toward Carpenter.
>
> He was married to Charlotte Moorehead of Clear Lake in 1910 and she preceded him in death on April 11, 1913. Two children were born to them, Delbert Juhl, now of Rockwell, and Mrs. Donald Luick, of Thornton. In 1917 he married Miss Bertha Hatsall [sic] of Mason City, who survives him. Six daughters were born to them, Mrs. Donald Gullickson, Northwood; Edna, Hazel, Helen and Phyllis, living at home in Northwood; and Esther, who died on April 19, 1935.
>
> Also surviving are his aged father, Peter Juhl, Clear Lake; six sisters, Mrs. Harry Welker, Clear Lake; Mrs. Soren Nielsen, Thornton; Mrs. Kirk Rader, in South Dakota; Mrs. Jack Malloy, Albany, Ga.; Mrs. Albert Rhein, Great Falls, Mont.; Mrs. Mervin Jensen, Clear Lake; and two brothers, Willie P. Juhl, San Jose, Cal., and Jerry P. Juhl, Manly.

Bizarre but true: At least once, George Luick (top far right) appeared in drag with other rural men.

Was alcohol really the drug of choice that Great-Grampa Nick used to numb out that with which he couldn't cope? Or, possibly, was it the religion of the holy-rollin' Baptists? Food? Rapid-fire sex, maybe—or sniffin' glue? Was he forgetting, even if only for a while, the unrelenting bills and hungry tummies at home by going out on the town… smoking, gambling, shooting loud guns at hollow targets… incessantly gossiping at some buzzing Main Street dive? Did he drive fast cars or jump out of bi-planes? Did he shoplift, make obscene anonymous calls… or wear women's panties, neck with the church organist (male or female)? Did he play the stock market or send naïve young men to war? Did he push skinny punks down back alleys or threaten bookish boys wearing thick glasses with bodily harm? What was the kick that Nick kept as a short-notice salve—some substance or process that took him, at least for a while, away from his suffering Self?

Gramma said it was alcohol that Nick used to anesthetize what he couldn't organize—as does his granddaughter, Janet. Was it, really? *Only* that? Then again, does it matter?

What matters more, to me at least, than *what* or even *why* he used, was *who* he forced to "co-pay" when he used. The man had not yet turned fifty when he was hit by a Miss Mildred Ellingson of Carpenter, a now-traumatized teenage girl from a pint-sized settlement on the Iowa prairie. Maybe a half-century of Life had been enough for him—but what about the half-dozen dependents he left behind, who now were without a head to earn their bread? What about the people whom his choices affected, especially those whose fates he was deciding, even if without their input? Did he ask them what his drinking meant to them, how it affected them and their daily lives—the tense, uneasy hours they spent in his presence or, worse, in his still-smelling absence? Did he care?

Hazel (left), Edna, Bertha (Hadsall), Phyllis, Cleo & Helen Juhl, circa 1942 in Northwood

I once lived with Pete, an alcoholic roommate from Rock Rapids, in the northwest corner of Iowa, not far from the highest geological point in our beloved Hawkeye State—a feedlot! Pete was a sweet guy—the most likeable on the planet that you could ever imagine—but he *never* paid his rent as my roomie on time. Each month he'd tell me, repeatedly and so soulfully, how very sorry he was—but, well, his step-daddy was gonna cable him some money to the Des Moines Western Union office, and… well, then… some other personal calamity would occur, which had nothing to do with me, but it was the all-consuming focus of his ruined life at that moment—at least, until the next drinkin' binge. I believed him—at least, *wanted* to believe him—cause I *liked* Pete.

And Nick—whose very name, ironically, means "victory of the people" in Greek—was he the same? What lies—that he *truly*, honestly, "so-help-[him]-god" believed—did he tell cross Bertha? The same ones he'd told Young Lottie… before he hit her in the gut… or pushed her to her death down the bumpy stairs… or neither? Did the lies change, depending on how many glasses or, more likely, bottles he'd just emptied? Was that where the dollars flowed, the money for corn for the cows or shoes for the girls? Was his self-absorbed drive to buy "just one more" bottle, glass or sip what kept him from seeing that he was torturing the very ones he professed to loved most? From seeing that he literally was pissing away, a bottle or beer mug at a time, the only Life he really knew, for sure, that he'd ever have the chance to live? Or, maybe *that* was the reason—that he couldn't bear the thought of so much wealth, of such an intense trip as to really occupy Life, to live it fully, so he chose a cheaper, easier, more manageable trip: booze.

If so, Nick wasn't alone—not in his time nor in his emotionally-repressed Danish-American immigrant family; not in the culture; not in the Western World. Maybe Gramma Luick was half right, for on New Year's Eve 1954, two months after his 60th birthday, Nick's younger brother,

Delbert (back row, left) & Arvilla (Fellsman) Juhl; (middle row) Marjorie, Robert & Paul; (front row) June & Betty; mid-1940s: It is unknown why Paul and June appear to have black eyes.

JERRY JUHL FOUND DEAD AT FARM HOME

The body of Jerry Juhl, 60, was found late Friday afternoon at his farm home on Route 3, Clear Lake, when his wife returned from work. Coroner R. E. Smiley reported Juhl had committed suicide with a shotgun, having left a note for his wife.

Juhl had been restricted in the use of his car, due to recent charges of driving while intoxicated, and to have [sic] been despondent.

He was born Oct. 13, 1894, in Franklin County near Thornton, son of Mr. and Mrs. Peter Juhl. He spent his childhood on a farm near Thornton and attended the Clear Lake schools. For a number of years he farmed in the Clear Lake vicinity.

He was married to Dorothy Ball and they established their home on a farm near Northwood. She preceded him in death. He was later married to Lois Shroyer at Nashua, Aug. 24, 1925. They moved to Mason City in 1942 and had lived in this vicinity since that time. For the past two years he had been employed by the Midwest Roofing Co.

Surviving are his wife, a daughter, Lola Mae Ackerman, Madison, Wis.; two sons, Pvt. Richard Juhl, Marsh AFB, Riverside, Calif., and Airman 1/c Robert Juhl, Davis Monthon AFB, Tucson, Ariz., and two daughters, Doris Nagel, Mason City, and Vale Low, Emmons, Minn.

Four stepchildren also survive; Mrs. Walter (Ruth) Bussa, Mason City; Mrs. Clark (Ara) Van Hooser, Kensett; Dean Thompson, Des Moines, and Marion Thompson, Mason City, as well as 12 grandchildren, three sisters and a brother. He was preceded in death by two brothers and three sisters.

Especially when compared to those of today, one of the first things a historian notices about traditional obituaries are the ubiquitous long lists at the end noting "surviving" F-A-M-I-L-Y members. Of course, "surviving" can mean at least two things: 1.) to have lived longer *than* the deceased, or 2.) to have lived longer *despite* the deceased—i.e., "She survived his drunkenness."

All psycho-babble aside, the modern researcher gets a clue as to how central a role the institution of family played in American life before the cultural revolution of the 1960s, with its individualistic focus and "me"-driven agenda. In the lengthy notice of Nick's burial only the first two sentences busy themselves with explaining the cause of the man's death; the entire remainder focuses on his connections to two dozen others, living or also dead. More than half of the account of Nick's younger brother, Jerry, says nothing about the dead man, but rather about those related to the hapless chap. Even though written in the less-transient first half of America's 20th century, the Juhl brothers' relations had—within only two generations of their clan's founders having swapped Denmark for Iowa—spread out across the young nation, reaching points as disparate as San Jose and Georgia, Tucson and Great Falls, Montana. Likely, however, most still saw Iowa as "the old home place."

In these endless public recitals of to whom the dead as well as the living "belonged," we see how fundamentally one's standing in rural or small-town American society depended on her or his performance in and relationship with one's family. For our pre-postwar-born ancestors and their kin, one soared or crashed and burned in local society largely to the degree that one's own family also thrived or ailed. For the people from whom I descended, one's clan's standing in the wider community inseparably equated, to a great degree, one's own sense of success or shame.

(back row) Cleo, Hazel, Helen & Edna;
Bertha (Hadsall) & Phyllis Juhl; 1950s

---

chapter 47: fouling crowded nests

My sister, Debra Lynn, is eight years older than I. Yes, she left our parents' home when I was only ten and a half years old. The decade we spent living under the same roof, though, left deep imprints on the person I became. We were raised by the same two mortals, attended the same school and church (often taught by the same teachers, using the same Dick-and-Jane readers, outdated pre-War maps and duck-and-cover films), played with some of the same toys and read some of the same books, interacted with the same extended relatives and myriad neighbors or family friends. Inside us, then, flash similar strands of thoughts or emotional impulses, flame many of the same public passions, and flow genetic codes that only our brother also carries. Even though we waged an intractable, unwinnable cold war for more than thirty years over religion and social politics, her life after we no longer lived together has mattered to and affected me until the present day.

My sister, Deb, & I examine a photo, July 2014, in Mom's Iowa home. Charlotte (left) & Della; circa 1920

I can't imagine that Gramma Luick could not have had a comparable connection to her mother's youngest sister with whom she grew up in the same home—then, after Della's heinous deeds, acted as if she'd never heard of the woman. In fact, however, she intimately knew Della Ann Moorehead, who was six and a half years older than my paternal grandmother, Charlotte Adelia... legally a "Juhl" but, in fact, raised a "Moorehead."

I also can't imagine that Gramma could sustain such a massive, well-guarded lie so successfully, so long—but she did. Gramma gave all of us, her children as well as her grandchildren, the flawlessly spun, unquestioned impression that she had grown up "an only child" in her grandparents' home. However, like so much the deeply damaged woman sold us, that was a patent lie.

Gramma's maternal grandparents, George and Lottie Moorehead, had taken the newborn half-orphan with them on the long buggy ride home across the lonely prairie after the funeral of their second-oldest daughter, 20-year-old Charlotte Esther (Moorehead) Juhl. That was in April 1913. What happened after the trio arrived in Rockwell? No one I know alive today has the faintest idea.

Charlotte Juhl, George Moorehead & June Fuller in buggy, 1920s; "Little Lottie" as a toddler, summer 1914

Seven years later, though, the 1920 Federal census listed "Charlotte A." erroneously as a "dau., age 6"—directly below the entry "Della Ann, dau., age 13." In effect, then, Della—although the half-orphaned girl's youngest aunt—functioned as Little Lottie's "big sister."

Presumably, Della remained in her parental home until just before she married Lawrence Ivan Hughes on Thursday, 23 August 1923, in Central Iowa. Della was sixteen years old: How did she come to marry, so young, a man so far away from her parents' house in Rockwell?

Nellie Bly Moorehead—Della's older and dead Lottie's younger sister—had married Glen Raymond Gardner on 9 March 1911. Like many Midwest farmers at the time, Glen's father, Robert, hired a series of hands to work on the Gardner place near Maxwell, in Central Iowa's Story County. Perhaps Lawrence had worked for the Gardners at some point. Or, maybe, Della made Lawrence's acquaintance while visiting dark-haired Nellie and her towering husband. Certainly, Della would have spent extended time in Central Iowa in spring 1918.

It was during some of the darkest days, as a ferocious world war ground to an exhausting end in faraway Europe, that the pall of mortality also fell upon the young couple's house. Death descended to the wide, open prairie to snatch away the life of Nellie and Glen's firstborn, their toddling son.

Glen Gardner with son Maynard Raymond, summer 1917; obituary and gravestone for Maynard, 1918

A connection between Della's sister's family through marriage and the Hughes clan in Central Iowa is plausible, given the substantial documentation of obvious closeness between various Moorehead family members. Indicative of how pervasive Della's family of origin was in her life, no matter how far she might roam from them, she had been given the diminutive form of her grandmother's forename, "Adelia," which was also Gramma Luick's middle name and comes from the German for "noble."

(standing) Cora, Jennie, George Jr., Nellie, (seated) "Big Lottie," Della & George; "the folks"—late 1920s

Perhaps, in marrying Lawrence, Della simply exchanged one extended family, the Mooreheads, for another, even more extended one, the Hughes. The 1925 State of Iowa census for Garden Township, Boone County, shows a notably curious living arrangement for the well-raised bride and her groom:

Hughes, Howard, head, age 27, 8th grade education, agriculture - renting
Myrtle, wife, age 21, rural education
Louise, dau, age 1
Lola M, dau, age 1

Lawrence, brother, age 26, 8th grade education, agriculture
Della, sister-in-law, age 18, 10th grade education

Carl, brother, age 23, 9th grade education
Lester, brother, age 19, 10th grade education
Ruth, sister, age 17, 10th grade education
Helen, sister, age 14, 9th grade education
Ralph, brother, age 12, in school
Nora, mother, age 48, divorced, 8th grade education

Della, late 1910s or early 1920s

Chicago and Northwestern Railroad trestle viaduct over the Des Moines River in Boone County, Iowa

So, in the mid-Twenties, while the rest of America boomed, Della bore babies—and apparently lived in a commune some four decades before Beatniks, then hippies made them "in." While multi-generation households were not only common but, moreover, the norm in the pre-WWII United States, what would have been rare, at least in the rural Midwest, would have been the presence of *two* related married couples *and* school-age siblings, *all* living under one matriarch's roof. That four Hughes brothers of majority age still resided at home, with two of them married and one of them with two toddlers, made such a living situation "unique." That the one daughter-in-law was a peer to two of her in-laws—Lester and Ruth—made the setting outright strange.

By the end of that roaring decade, however, such an arrangement must have been too much even for big-family-fan Della, for by the winter of 1928-'29, she and Lawrence occupied a home and farm of their own. An article printed 21 February 1929 in Ames' *Daily Tribune* reported, however, that

> ### Deserted by Spouse, Mother of Three Is Asking for Divorce
>
> Deserted, left without fuel except for corn cobs in the field, with three young children, and about to become a mother again, Mrs. Della Hughes of Nevada township is asking for a divorce from Lawrence Hughes. Mrs. Hughes states that he left her and their three children in a helpless condition on Jan 29 of this year. On that day, he went to Nevada [Iowa] to pay the rent on their farm and never returned. After paying the rent, he would have had about $1,675 left. Mrs. Hughes asks for an attachment on the farm machinery and the custody of their three children, Ivan 4, Bernard 3, and Paul 2, and of the child to be born. The couple were married in May of 1922 at Jefferson.

Alarmed by her baby's marital misery, on Friday, 4 October 1929, Big Lottie Moorehead filed off a less-than-fully-literate letter to Della (below, left, in the collage), counseling her youngest daughter to:

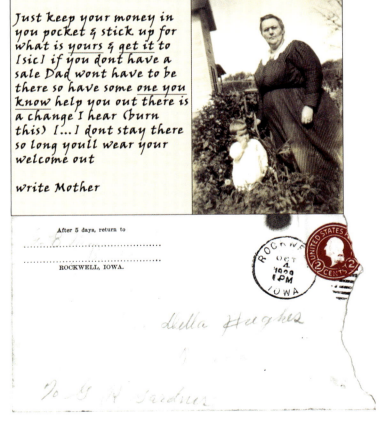

June Fuller in garden with her "Gramma Moorehead," early 1920s

Independent from what actions she took against her runaway husband, less than ten months after Lawrence left her Della had given birth to Beverly Hughes, as well as married 38-year-old Benjamin True, a Missouri-born tenant farmer fifteen years Della's senior. (The couple had married across the state border, in Albert Lea, Minnesota, on Monday, 9 December 1929; for unknown reasons, several Moorehead children went to the North Star State to marry.) By the time of the 1930 census, the patchwork family of five was living no longer in Central Iowa but in Bath Township, in the middle of Cerro Gordo County—a short ride from Della's parents in nearby Rockwell.

Perhaps as a consequence of a court petition, Della's oldest child, five-year-old Ivan George Hughes, was living not with his mother and three younger siblings, but with his 55-year-old grandmother, Nora Sapp Hughes, who by then was residing in Colfax, Iowa.

Grandmother Asks the Custody of Hughes Child

DESERTED BY HUSBAND, MRS. DELLA HUGHES ASKS FOR A DIVORCE

Mrs. Nora E. Hughes of Boone has filed a petition of intervention today asking for the custody of her four and a half year old grandson, Ivan Hughes, when the divorce proceedings involving her son Lawrence Hughes and Della Hughes, his wife, and plaintiff, comes up for hearing in the September term of court.

Mrs. Hughes Sr., says in her petition that she is amply able to care for this child properly and she fears that he may be placed in the home of strangers who may not be able or willing to give him the care which she states she will give without remuneration.

The divorce case of Della Hughes vs. Lawrence Hughes was filed in January, 1929 after the defendant walked away one cold January day leaving the wife and three children without food or fuel, and failed to return. The couple lived on a farm in Nevada township.

Because of this desertion, and the fact that the family were left in poor health and without necessities the wife was granted a writ of attachment upon the personal property on the farm. She asked for a divorce, the custody of the minor children and $2,000 permanent alimony.

Big Lottie holding granddaughter June Fuller; with daughter Jennie, circa 1920

Only two years later, however, the coordinates of a seemingly constantly-changing life shifted yet again. Expecting their first child, Della and Benjamin True transplanted their cobbled-together household once more, this time moving in with his parents, who'd migrated north from Missouri—but not for long, for on 18 December 1932 the *Globe-Gazette* announced

> John W. True, 85, died Sunday night at the home of his son, Benjamin True, who resides on a farm southwest of Clear Lake. Funeral services will be held Tuesday morning, and burial will be made in the Clear Lake cemetery.

Obviously struck with ill fortune—or at least something that made the old folks ill—death revisited the True home less than two months later, for on 12 February 1933 Mason City's "newspaper of record" again reported about loss through death among the ill-starred family:

> Sarah E. True, 71, died Saturday afternoon after a lingering illness. She was brought from her farm home in Union township Saturday morning to Clear Lake for treatment and succumbed several hours later. She was born May 8, 1861 in Cooper County, Mo. Funeral services were held Monday morning, and burial was made at the Clear Lake cemetery. Her husband, John True, died several months ago. She is survived by a son, Benjamin True, with whom she made her home.

Oddly, wherever Della was, it seemed that birth and death were not far away. (Since when is less than two, "several" months—the time between the two deaths?) The same year that her live-in father-in-law "succumbed," Della gave birth to Virgil Benjamin True; then, a year later, to Merle Alfred True.

By fall 1936, Benjamin and Della packed their swelling collection of kids into the family's jalopy and set off up the road. They drove about an hour's distance, to what they assumed would be better fields—almost due north, just across the

South Broadway Avenue in downtown Albert Lea, Minnesota, 1930s

border, in Minnesota. For reasons we do not know but could well have included a nostalgic hope that things might return to how they were during better, less eventful days, they took their revolving roster of charges to rented farms near Albert Lea, where "Ben" had married Della seven years earlier. In September of that same year they fled whatever had not suited them in Iowa, Della gave birth to Ardith Margaret True. By then, two tired adults were in charge of six children.

For two years, the couple tried their unsuccessful hands at farming—first near Oakland, then Grand Meadow. Finally abandoning farming forever, they moved into a worn old clapboard house on the edge of downtown Albert Lea. A month later, Ben rotated out of this eternal cycle of sequential moves—as reported on 22 December 1938 by Albert Lea's *Evening Tribune*:

> **Benj. True of Newton Ave. Passes Away**
> **Death Occurred at Seven o'Clock This Morning at the Naeve Hospital**
>
> This morning about 7 o'clock Benjamin True of South Newton Avenue passed away at Naeve Hospital.
>
> For some time Mr. True has been suffering from a cancerous growth, which caused his death. He was 46 years old.
>
> Besides his wife he leaves six small children: Bernard, 12; Paul, 11; Beverly, 10; Virgil, 6; Merle, 5; and Ardis [sic], 2, all at home. Three of the children are from a former marriage.
>
> Mr. True was born in Clinton, Mo., March 30, 1892, where he grew up to manhood, and remained in this native state until 15 years ago, when he moved to Perry, Iowa.
>
> Dec. 9, 1923, he married Miss Della Moorhead of Rockwell, Iowa. They moved to Minnesota and farmed for two years south of Oakland, and then moved to a place near Grand Meadow, where they stayed a few months before returning to Freeborn County and about a month ago South Newton Ave. in this city.
>
> Owing to Mr. True's failing health he and his family have been in desperate circumstances.
>
> The funeral will take place Saturday, December 24, at 1 o'clock at the Bonnerup Funeral Home on West Clark Street. Rev. H.W. Bondo of the Trinity Lutheran Church will officiate.

A "cancerous growth?" Benjamin's death certificate suggests something a bit more subtle.

STATE OF MINNESOTA
Division of Vital Statistics
CERTIFICATE OF DEATH

1. PLACE OF DEATH
County Freeborn
Township or Village or City Albert Lea
Reg. District No. 24-1 No. in Registration Book 179
(Above numbers to be filled in only by local registrar or his deputy.)
No. Naeve Hospital St., Ward
(If death occurred in a hospital or institution give its NAME instead of street and number)
2. FULL NAME Benjamin Alfred True
(Please PRINT names in capitals)
(2a) Residence, No. 810 Newton St., Ward Albert Lea
(Usual place of abode) (If nonresident give city or town and State)
Length of residence in city or town where death occurred yrs. 1 mos. ds. How long in U. S. if of foreign birth? yrs. mos. ds
3. SEX M
4. COLOR OR RACE white
5. SINGLE, MARRIED, WIDOWED, OR DIVORCED (write the word) married
5a. If married, widowed, or divorced HUSBAND of (or) WIFE of Della True
6. DATE OF BIRTH (month, day, and year) 3-30-1892
7. AGE Years 46 Months 8 Days 22 If LESS than 1 day, hrs. or min.
OCCUPATION
8. Trade, profession, or particular kind of work done, as engineer (type of), miner, sawyer, bookkeeper, etc. Laborer
9. Industry or business in which work was done, as railway, mine, (kind of) saw mill, bank, etc.
10. Date deceased last worked at this occupation (month and year) 11-19-1938
11 Total time (years) spent in this occupation life
12. BIRTHPLACE (city or town) (State or country) Clinton - Mo.
FATHER
13. NAME (Print) John Wesley True
14. BIRTHPLACE (city or town) (State or country) Illinois
MOTHER
15. MAIDEN NAME (Print) Sally Evans
16. BIRTHPLACE (city or town) (State or country) Mo.
17. INFORMANT Mrs Della True
(Address) 810 Newton St.
18 Buried at or Removed to Lakewood Albert Lea Date 12-24-1938 (Cremation—No Yes)
19. UNDERTAKER Jens J. Bonnerup
(Address) Albert Lea Minn
20. Filed Dec. 27, 1938 Mrs Anna E Calhoun dep. Registrar.

21. DATE OF DEATH (month, day, and year) Dec 22 - 1938
22. I HEREBY CERTIFY, That I attended deceased from Dec 6 1938 to Dec. 22 - 1938. I last saw him alive on Dec 21 - 1938 death is said to have occurred on the date stated above, at 8 15 A m.
The PRIMARY UNDERLYING CAUSE of death was
General Peritonitis — Duration 12 da
following Cancer of stomach — 6 mo.
(operated Dec. 6-1938)
Contributory causes of importance in order of onset: — Duration
(1) mod. secondary anemia — ?
(2)
(3)
Did an operation precede death? Yes
If so, state condition for which it was undertaken Prepyloric Cancer of stomach - resection
Date of operation Dec. 6-1938 Was there an autopsy? Yes
23. If death was due to external causes (violence) fill in also the following:
Accident, suicide or homicide? Date of injury 19
Where did injury occur? (Specify city or town, county, and State)
Specify whether injury occurred in industry, in home, or in public place.
Manner of injury
Nature of injury
24. Was disease or injury in any way related to occupation of deceased?
If so, specify.
(Signed) W. P. Freligh M.D.
12-22, 1938 (Address) Albert Lea Minn
Sub-Registrar. Received Dec. 22 1938 Jens J. Bonnerup

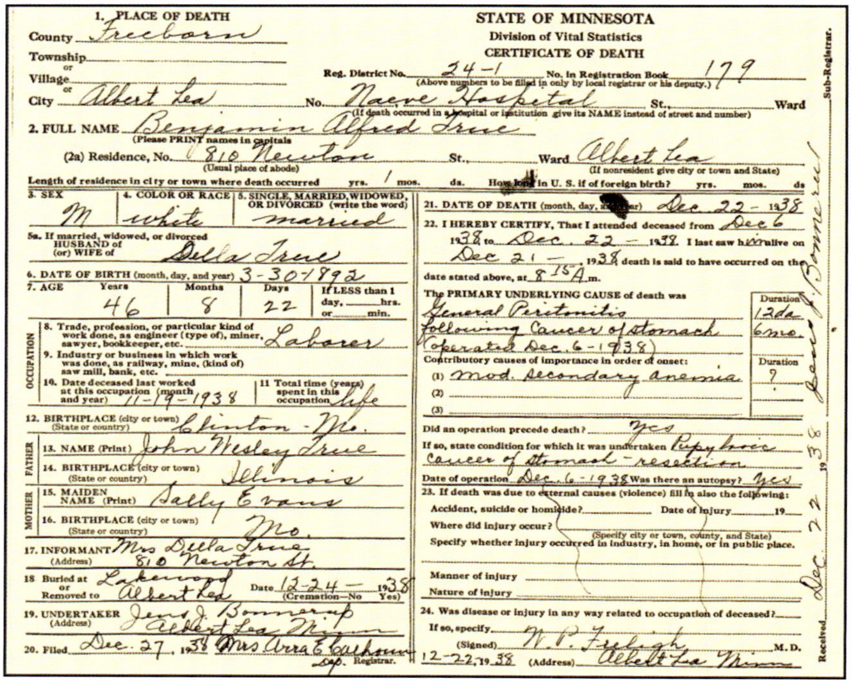

According to one leading medical authority, a common cause of peritonitis is

> an infection that develops directly inside the peritoneum. Doctors refer to this as primary peritonitis. The two major risk factors for primary peritonitis are:
>
> - cirrhosis - scarring of the liver which is often the result of prolonged alcohol misuse
>
> [or]
>
> - peritoneal dialysis - a widely used treatment for people with kidney failure

No documents found in researching this mystery indicate that Della's second husband had suffered recently from kidney failure, leaving the most likely cause of the "general peritonitis" that reportedly killed him to be cirrhosis, a typical result of "prolonged alcohol misuse." Given Benjamin's parents' deaths—especially his mother's, so soon after her husbands'—one might wonder if there may have been other possible origins of his stomach or liver afflictions.

In any event, Benjamin's funeral (on Christmas Eve, no less) marked the end of Della's second marriage—and beginning of her coming first murder.

---

chapter 48: consuming one's own

With Benjamin True gone and done, Della's life in South Central Minnesota lurched on per her own design. According to one source, she

> kept close touch with her former husband [Lawrence Hughes, by that time living in Florida, who] came to see her in Albert Lea, at one time since her second husband's death and that he had lived with her a while until they found that because of their meeting again, another baby was to be born. According to Mrs. True [...] this baby was never born.

This long-distance, high-drama intrigue, though, unfolded against a backdrop of low-brow banality. Since a month before Benjamin's dying, Della had been housing her brood in a dingy, run-down house on Albert Lea's busy main north-south thoroughfare, Newton Avenue, on the edge of busy downtown Albert Lea, for which she paid $12 a month rent—about $165 in 2014 dollars.

Della's niece-cum-kid-sister, Charlotte (Juhl) Luick, later told her daughter Sheranne that unemployed Della "was hangin' out with tough characters all around town; she was smokin' an' drinkin'—a *lot*!" Like another North Central Iowa native, a man named "Nick" just down the road and just across the border at Northwood, Della would find that routinely escaping the distressing distractions around her via addictions was sure to claim, at some point, victims—those least responsible for their parents' poorly-considered choices.

The True Home on South Newton Avenue

This house stands just south of the vacant lot at the southwest corner of South Newton avenue and Second street. It is better known as the old Andrews home.

downtown Albert Lea from the south, during a parade; Freeborn County Courthouse in foreground; 1930s

As so often with private family tragedies, this one, too, unfolded amidst great public sensation. On Friday, 16 October 1942—in the middle of the first fall that the United States was fighting a second world war—Albert Lea's *Evening Tribune* informed its readers on page three that

Ardith True, 6-Year-Old, Dies Thursday
Funeral Sunday at Bonnerup Funeral Home

Ardith Margaret True, the six year old daughter of Mrs. Della True of 810 Newton Avenue, passed away after a brief illness on Thursday.

Ardith was born near Austin on Sept. 24, 1936. She came with her parents to Albert Lea in 1938, and was in the first grade at Ramsey School. Her father, Benjamin A. True, passed away in 1938. She is survived by her mother, four brothers, Vargil [sic], Merle, Paul and Bernard and one sister, Beverly.

Funeral services will be held at the Bonnerup Funeral Home at 3:30 p.m. Sunday, with the Rev. W.G. Holmberg officiating, with interment in Lakewood Cemetery.

Six-Year Old Victim of Mrs. Della True

ARDITH MARGARET TRUE

Interestingly, just as family members typically write obituaries, doctors and other public-health-related officials in turn rely on relatives for information about the ill or recently deceased. Journalists, too, turn to those closest to their subjects as "reliable" sources of "solid" information. In the above serial cases of death, however, one begins to wonder: *Who* told the *Globe* reporter that Benjamin's mother, Sarah, had had a "lingering illness"—and *what*, exactly, needed urgent "treatment" one Saturday morning that resulted, just hours later, in her "succumbing?" And, as for Benjamin himself, whose death certificate revealed he arrived at the hospital suffering from "secondary anemia" (common among alcohol abusers), who told the press—and for that matter, the operating doctor before Benjamin, too, had "succumbed"—it was "cancer" that was causing Della's second husband so much stomach trouble? And now, with little Ardith's passing, who told whom that the girl—once again—had had a "brief illness" that led to *her* "succumbing?"

Regardless of what was really happening behind the scenes, Della's family continued to offer her their support—as cited in the *Globe-Gazette* on 19 October 1942:

> Mr. and Mrs. George Moorehead [Jr. and his sister] Mrs. Claude [Cora] Miller drove to Albert Lea, MN to attend the funeral of their niece, Ardith True, 6, who died at an Albert Lea hospital Thursday. They were accompanied by Mr. and Mrs. Floyd [and Netha, George Jr.'s daughter] Dodd and Mr. and Mrs. Donald [and Charlotte] Luick, cousins. Ardith, who was the daughter of Mrs. Della True, was born at Albert Lea shortly after the family moved there from Union township [in Cerro Gordo Country, Iowa]. Her father, Ben True, died four years ago.

Della's raging-if-sedated misery wouldn't stop with Ardith's involuntary sacrifice, for just over four months later Della's desperation consumed yet another family member—as announced in the *Evening Tribune* on 3 March 1943; the attached photo only appeared three days later, after Truth had prevailed:

Strange Death of Nine Year Old Son of Mrs. True
Merle True Found Dead Near His Bed by Mother

This morning Mrs. Della True, 810 Newton Avenue, was shocked when she stepped into her son Merle's room to find him lying dead by the side of his bed, partly on his back. She ran over to the neighbors and telephoned for a doctor and Coroner Louis Kuchera. Coroner Kuchera is investigating the case and may call for a post examination.

Merle was apparently in good health yesterday. He went to school as usual and played after school last evening. When he went to bed he did not complain. It may be that he fell out of bed, breaking his neck. Besides his mother there are several other children in the family.

Here Is Where Merle Died After Drinking Poison Given by His Mother

Bedroom of Merle True, being investigated by O. C. Nickish and Charles Reiter, of the criminal apprehension bureau of Minnesota. The house is one story and all the family slept downstairs. You will note a second bed in this room.

"Maybe [Merle] fell out of bed, breaking his neck:" *Who* came up with *that* one? At least this time, despite Della's best diversion tactics, someone entrusted to protect the vulnerable stepped in and, even if at first hesitant, called for an investigation. This time, Della couldn't just brush away the curious and publicly responsible. This time, living with all those Hugheses, all those nights of drinking, the revolving lovers, the dropped-dead in-laws, the endless moving from one rented farm to the next rented farm… the food bills and empty purses, smoky bars and borrowed cars all came to a head. Della had to account for herself—and it would be neither easy nor pretty.

CHILDREN OF MRS. DELLA TRUE

Merle to the left is standing with his brother Virgil.

Merle is standing to the right, just back of his sister Ardith, both victims.

Three days later, on the 6th of March, the *Evening Tribune* broke the news to its eager readers in screaming, front-page headlines that the criminal had confessed to her heinous crimes. In numbing, nauseating detail, it recounted everything everyone doesn't want to know:

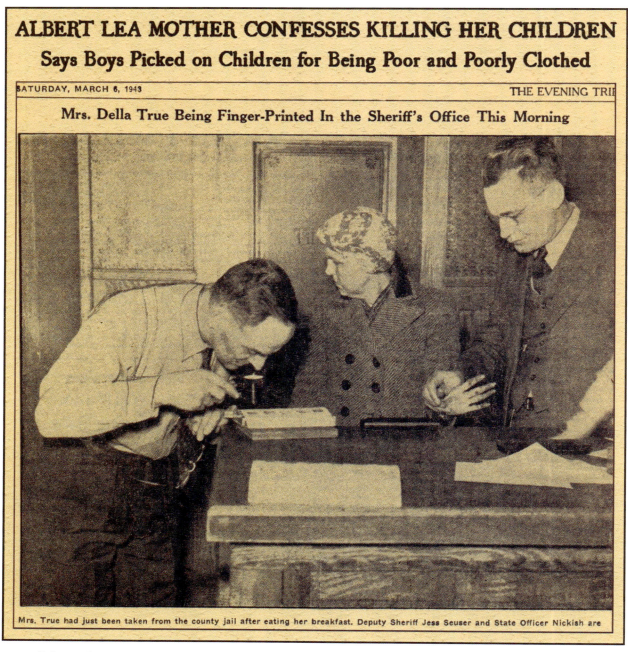

Della's confession did not end the sensation that flashed through spectacle-hungry Albert Lea; it fed it. As soon as the authorities concluded their questioning and got the weary woman a bite to eat, the *Tribune* reporter managed to win access to one of the biggest local news stories in ages. He began his article with the subtitle "Dry-Eyed, Mrs. Della True, Newton Avenue, After Hours of Questioning, Confesses to Sheriff Hjalmar Wulff Tragic Story of How She Deliberately Poisoned Six-Year Old Ardith on the Night of October 14, 1942 and How She Made Way with Nine-Year-Old Merle by Placing Deadly Drug in His Milk." The headlines, however, only hinted at the horrific details to follow:

All Albert Lea was thoroughly stirred this morning when it was learned that Mrs. Della True, 810 Newton Avenue, after long hours of questioning by Sheriff Hjalmer Wulff and two state investigators, had confessed to the killing of two of her children, Ardith and Merle, by giving them poison drugs.

The questioning of Mrs. True started about two o'clock yesterday afternoon in the office at the court house before Sheriff Wulff and two state investigators ... had been called by Sheriff Wulff early yesterday morning after he and County Attorney Sturtz, were thoroughly convinced that the two children had not met natural deaths.

Mrs. True, with no apparent emotion whatsoever, looked at her questioner, eye to eye and stoutly denied that she had anything to do with the death of either Ardith or Merle - and didn't know what had caused their deaths. Not until about 8:30 o'clock in the evening did she admit that she had killed them and that she was ready to tell Mr. Wulff the whole story [then asked] for cigarettes and smoked them as she was questioned.

Sitting by the side of Sheriff Wulff she unfolded the awful story of the double murder. She gave as her excuse for her acts that boys - old enough to know better - kept making fun of her children because they were poor and could not have the things that they enjoyed. Later she gave the same story, told to Mr. Wulff, in the form of a confession, before the officers with Julius Knieval of the district court taking it down in shorthand.

Without showing any signs of remorse she said that she was telling the story without threats to her or under any promise of leniency on the part of her questioners. "It is of my own free will and accord that I tell the whole story." she said. The confession takes up about ten pages of typewritten legal sized paper.

After she had completed her almost unbelievable story, Sheriff Wulff took her over to the jail and she walked across the court house grounds without any help and without any apparent signs of physical weakness or mental agony.

In an interview with a Tribune representative this morning, as she sat in her cell drinking her coffee and eating her breakfast, she again told the story, practically as she had given it to Sheriff Wulff and as related in her final confession.

She stated that boys, who ought to have known better, continually made fun of her children because they were poor and didn't have nice things like they had. "I just couldn't see any way out of it, but to do what I did," she said.

Sitting on her cot in the cell she told the Tribune man how she had made away with Ardith. She said her husband's mother had some drugs in an old trunk in the house that was used for headaches. It was a portion of this drug that she used to kill her daughter, she said. Mrs. True stated that she took about two spoonfuls of the drug - a white powder - and gave it to little Ardith. This was late in the evening on October 14, 1942. She had Ardith wash the powder down with a glass of water. Ardith died in the Naeve hospital on October 15. Death was supposed to have resulted from ulcer perforations of the stomach. At the time of Ardith's death, it is reported, and autopsy was suggested to determine the actual cause of the child's death. Mrs. True insisted that the autopsy be not taken. She stated today that the reason why she didn't want the autopsy was because she knew the real cause of Ardith's death would be revealed.

To the Tribune reporter she also told how she killed Merle. She said about midnight last Tuesday night Merle called from his room that he wanted a drink. This was her chance. She said she took the drug—about a spoonful—and sifted it into a glass of milk and had him drink it. When the reporter asked if the drug she used to kill Merle was some of the white powder that had been in the trunk, she said, "No." She said she got a package of poison—white powder—from a local drug store explaining to the druggist she wanted to kill some rats. She said she used some of this poison for Merle. She said Merle didn't make any sound after he drank her poison milk and that she didn't go in to see what had taken place until after eight o'clock Wednesday morning. She stated she found him on the floor with his clothes on. Merle was dressed just as he was when she gave him that milk. Mrs. True explained that she went to the neighbors before nine o'clock that morning and told of her son's sudden death and then asked that the doctor be called. Not only was the doctor called by the neighbor but Coroner Louis Kuchera was summoned. Dr. Kuchera lost no time in getting to the scene and has been on the job ever since.

In the jail Mrs. True told the Tribune reporter that she was first married to one Lawrence Hughes of Mason City, Iowa [...] and that he deserted her years after, taking one child, a son, Ivon [sic] with him. Three others were born to this first union: Bernard, Paul and Beverly. Virgil, 10, is now the only living one born to the union with Mr. True. She says that Hughes went to Florida and married a Florida girl. They now live at Bellgrade [sic], Florida, where Hughes operates an airplane, used to dust bug poison over orange groves. Hughes, she says, has two children from his second marriage. Mrs. True hesitated saying much about having detailed information of Hughes' second marriage, his children and what he was doing.

Continuing her interview with the Tribune representative, Mrs. True who is 34 years old, said she was formerly Miss Della Moorhead and was born on a farm near Clear Lake, Iowa. Her folks moved to Spring Valley, Minn. and later she lived on a farm near Austin. She came to Albert Lea about 4 1/2 years ago. Her husband, Benjamin A. True died in the Naeve Hospital in 1938 of stomach trouble.

She kept close touch with her former husband. She told County Attorney Sturtz that Hughes came to see her in Albert Lea, one time since her second husband's death and that he had lived with her a while until they found that because of their meeting again, another baby was to be born. According to Mrs. True's story to County Attorney Sturtz, this baby was never born.

Mrs. True also told County Attorney Sturtz that after she had bought the poison from the drug store, for the purpose of killing Merle, she hid it in the cellar of the home. Two or three times she got ready to kill Merle, she says. She would go down, get the bag of poison, and then losing her nerve, she would take the poison back down into the cellar and hide it. Finally on last Tuesday at midnight she said she got the poison and finished the job.

Mrs. True says she has three sisters and one brother living: Mrs. G.R. Gouder [sic] of Pine River, Minn.; Mrs. Herbert Fuller and Mrs. Claude Miller, and George Moorehead [Jr.], all of near Clear Lake, Iowa.

1935 Clear Lake telephone book ad; Mason City funeral home, 1946: photo labeled "casket of Mrs Geer"

After the shards of protracted cascading disaster had finally landed, it was the job of others to pick up the pieces. Coroner Louis Kuchera ordered an inquest at Bonnerup's Funeral Home, for which Freeborn County Attorney William Prescott Sturtz took testimony. The findings included the conclusion that Merle's death had occurred

> between the hour of midnight and 8:00 o'clock a.m. on March 3rd, 1943. His death was caused from poison administered to him by the mouth by one, Della True, mother of said Merle True, which poison was administered between the hour of 11:00 o'clock p.m., and midnight on March 2nd, 1943; we further find that the organs, including the stomach of said Merle True, contained residue of such poison in sufficient quantity to produce death. We further find evidence that said Della True premeditatedly and with intent to kill administered such poison to said Merle True.

Based on university-lab findings, that "death had resulted from strychnine poisoning," district-court judge Norman E. Peterson ordered that Ardith's corpse be exhumed and an autopsy conducted "to see what drug was used to cause her death." In addition, County Attorney Sturtz stated that

> the acts were premeditated and that [Della] will be charged with murder in the first degree [and] that Mrs. True had told him that she had planned the killing of Merle for more than two months, but just couldn't make up her mind to do the deed until last Tuesday. [Furthermore, it would] be necessary to call a special grand jury for this murder case.

As the initial post-disaster cleanup began to produce factual answers, the public started looking for interpretative ones, hoping to find an impossible answer to the question "Why?" tucked throughout this senseless calamity. One undated, anonymous newspaper clipping noted that

> Edgar Naplan, in charge of the Freeborn County welfare office, stated this morning that the True family has been cared for by his office since their coming to Albert Lea. He says they received a cash allowance each month. He states at the time of the death of Ardith his office would have paid for the casket and funeral charges, but that Mrs. True didn't ask for the money. The costs of this funeral were born by Mrs. True in installments. The casket was paid for by one Bernard True in installments.

> Mr. Naplan also stated that his office was in duty bound to pay Merle's funeral expenses but that Mrs. True had not asked for any help. According to reports Mrs. True has spent much of her time in drinking parlors about the city for some time past.

As soon as Mrs. True was arrested and brought to the court house, Deputy Sheriff Carl Lindahl was dispatched to the True home to make a strict search for letters or clues that might throw more light on the case. Mrs. True told Sheriff Wulff and County Attorney Sturtz that when she used the poison for Merle, she threw the rest of the package into the toilet.

Even as far away as Jefferson, Iowa, newspaper editors fed their readers' hunger to know more about the gruesome child-murderer as if she were one of their own. An article in the *Jefferson Bee* that appeared on 23 March 1943 noted that

THREE OLDEST CHILDREN OF MRS. TRUE

Left to right, Bernard, 16; Beverly, 13, and Paul, 15. All are children of Mrs. True's first husband, Lawrence Hughes, who is now married and lives in Florida. When he deserted Mrs. True he took with them their son Ivon. He has two children by his second wife, Ann and Larry. Virgil, the only child left of the second marriage, is 10 years old.

> Mrs. True told the court that she decided to kill the children first and then follow them, because she did not have any desire to live. It is of interest to note that Mrs. True started on her marital career Aug 29, 1923, when she was married here in Jefferson to Lawrence Hughes of Madrid.

Mrs. True was then 16-year-old Della Moorehead of Rockwell, and her husband was 25 years of age. They became the parents of four children and then were divorced in 1929. Her second husband, Benjamin True, died four years ago, and a daughter, Ardith, died Oct 18. The child's death is being investigated.

---

chapter 49: an overdue autopsy

What difference would an investigation have made? An unfathomable familial tragedy had already destroyed the lives of countless people: Merle was dead. As was Ardith. And their father, Benjamin. And his parents, John Wesley and Sarah (Evans) True. Della freely admitted that she'd killed the two children. Did she murder their father, too—the man about whom "someone" told a busy doctor that his stomach maladies came from "a cancer" but could have come from…? Had Della slowly "helped" her in-laws "succumb" to her desire to finally be rid of them—just as she, eventually, longed to be rid of so many mouths to feed in an already filled-to-the-brim household, and thereby also be rid of endless bratty questions to evade or stale Wonder Bread sandwiches sans filling to serve, of hand-me-down clothes that no longer fit or honors to defend when neighborhood boys "who should know better" mocked her kids' poorly-dressed poverty?

Della reportedly told an eager audience that she'd "made way" with Ardith using "headache drugs" in an old trunk left over from her mother-in-law's last suffering days—but the poor woman had been dead just shy of ten years: How had much-moved-about Della been able to drag a trunk full of lethal potions around for a decade, from farmhouse to broken-down farmhouse?

Is it true, that "The poor shall inherit the Earth?" If so, how—and why?

Was one-time Miss Moorehead—who said, by the point she carried out her long-plotted deeds, that she'd lost "any desire to live"—essentially a damaged woman? Had she been that for years—already back in Rockwell, but if not as a child (as my Gramma Luick's "older sister," who in fact was her youngest aunt) then certainly by the time she'd lived in a house in Boone County packed with almost a dozen cramped souls? Is that why her first husband left her—despite obviously feeling *something* for the fertility-plagued woman? Did Lawrence still care for her—enough, almost fifteen years after he walked out the door to "pay the rent" and kept on walking, that he risked his marriage with a Texas filly, Elizabeth Ballou, and their shared family life in Florida, for the sake of driving over several days back to the heart of the American Heartland and shacking up with down-trodden Della long enough (as if in an unwitting prequel to her grandniece Lorraine's similar stunt, four decades later, after also having "finished" with Bob Jones) to create yet another (this time, out-of-wedlock) baby?

On that icy January day in 1929, when he set off to "pay the rent on their farm" but never came back, he must have felt that the mother of his first child was a threat to at least his namesake, for Lawrence Ivan Hughes went to great effort to safeguard Little Ivan with Nana Nora in Colfax, even though he thought himself unable to adequately care for a child who a week and a day before Lawrence deserted Della had blown out four little birthday candles. Getting his son away from distraught Della had seemed important enough to remove the boy from his mother. Was Lawrence's mother's going to court to win custody of Ivan a sign that even her estranged husband thought Della dangerous to life and limb? Was she? Does it matter? What does it change, to know a human being can be born unblemished and unburdened, grow up, become increasingly troubled and tied, then take the lives of her own offspring?

Perhaps a more edifying exercise might be to ponder how far back the roots of Della's demise reached: Where did her training to kill begin? In a crowded farmhouse somewhere in Iowa? Perhaps, it started even earlier, in a frame cottage in Burchinal—tucked out of sight behind the farmers' cooperative grain elevator—"at the quiet hour of two o'clock in the morning [when] the spirit of the life of [Della's older sister] Lottie Esther Moorehead Juhl fled to its maker and eternal home."

Or, did Della's displaced desperation, the rage that ultimately led her to consume two of her own babies, originate with even earlier, unhealed traumas—with her father George's unimaginable losses: first, of all four of his younger sisters within a few weeks during a wave of typhoid that washed across an unprepared prairie in 1885; then, of his lively wife and two babies to pneumonia and tuberculosis—all within a devastating seven months in 1889? If that weren't enough loss through sudden death, between May 1918 and July 1929 the Moorehead clan's patriarch witnessed those of two young grandchildren, Maynard Raymond Gardner (18 months) and June Audrey Fuller (11). Could it be, that Della's sacrificing two of her babies had something (even if only remotely) related to her father's having lost three of his own—two of her half-siblings—as well as a later daughter, my great-grandmother, Young Lottie?

Or, put differently: When did Della's crimes "begin"—and when did they "end," if at all? Did her wrongdoing begin with slipping sleepy-eyed Merle a laced glass of midnight milk? No—clearly not: She'd already handed adorable little Ardith a fatal sip of laced water four and a half months earlier. OK, then: Did Della go astray further back, as she was unable to cope with Benjamin True's parents, then with the man from Missouri himself? Had the freshly-married teen violated "laws of nature" with some of the many members of the Hughes household down some Boone County back road? Just when, exactly, *did* Della first taste the forbidden fruit which forever banned her and her people from Eden's plenty?

Wagon Bridge spanning the Des Moines River in Boone County, Iowa

If you ask "Does it matter?" ask Merle or Ardith. Or Charlotte, who spent the rest of her life acting as if she didn't even know Della's name. Ask my loveable aunt, Lorraine, if she might not have harvested a few helpful hints from her mother's "older sister" for use in her own procreative career—i.e., being the mother of seven then, years later, conceiving another baby with a former husband, out of wedlock.

Where do *any* of our "trespasses" begin—or end? For that matter, where do *we* begin and end? To better comprehend that, one must look at the physical core of a human being, to her or his genetic construction. For centuries, Westerners saw human history—on a macro level, but by extension also in a human lifetime, as a micro form of the same dynamic—as a linear progression, with a specific beginning (when "...God created the Heavens and the Earth") and a foreseeable end: the "Second Coming," "Judgment Day" or some-such millennial end-of-time event. A fitting image of that one-dimensional understanding of Life on Earth, and of an individual human being's limited stint on it, might be "time as a piece of uncooked spaghetti," long, flat and straight, with a definite beginning and a "done-and-over" ending. Modern science, though, no longer supports such a segmented, limited and limiting worldview.

Seeing a here-one-day-gone-the-next scenario of human existence and of our experience of "time" as too limited, the passé "raw spaghetti" image fails to cut the grade. Okay, then—how 'bout *this*? We know (well, at least some of us) that none of us exists alone on the planet, that our individual sojourns on Earth occur parallel to those of others—chinks in an endless chain of lives stretching as far back as we can see and as far into the future as we can imagine. So, what about a "railroad-track" image of existence: two linear, parallel "rails." Also limited and limiting, huh?

bridges of Boone County; stone pier (left photo) holding it all up

One problem with this adapted image, an evolution of the "raw spaghetti" metaphor, includes the real-time fact that every railway has a definite beginning—a locomotive roundhouse, a railway yard or at least a train station—as well as an end: one of those same three places or somewhere else. In the "railroad track" motif at least we've done away with the self-indulgent notion that "each [wo]man is an island, entire of itself" and made allowance for the next part of John Donne's graphic sonnet, that each of us be "a piece of the continent, a part of the main." We still have the pesky problem, though, that tracks aren't dynamic: They can't bend or change; they don't and can't evolve. And, they aren't readily passed from one generation to the next; they aren't open-ended, but bolted down.

Hum-m-m, let's see here—

Seeking to leave behind the flatness and definite-beginning-and-end conundrum of our conceptual pet the "railroad track" as a representation of the human condition, how about if we steal from Nature itself? What if, say, we humans concede our inability to represent Life any better than Life reveals itself under a microscope, and simply rally behind a metaphorical banner featuring a DNA strand? That microscopic speck of coding incubates, transfers and then enables animate sentience itself—a "twisted ladder" that allows Life to climb between generations, to move across time and space... to prevail, *always*. If one's willing, one can "see" this double helix stretching from lifetime to lifetime, from the barely imaginable primordial soup that emerged millennia ago through the current confusion as we humans reach for the stars and, in the process, contemplate leaving the planet which afforded us Life.

Okay? Still with me?

Okay—good!

What I particularly like about a strand of DNA encapsulating a human Life-line, indeed, "time" itself, is that the spiral consists of two "backbones" as frames, bonded by connectors filled with information—"events" waiting to happen, if you will: future carriers' skin, hair and eye color, cheek-bone shapes, suggested height and weight... and predilections for intelligence, abilities and temperament, as well as, regrettably, certain congenital afflictions, perhaps addictions, etc.

Even more than the grooviness of being so richly endowed, able to carry so much in such a compact design, the DNA strand—at least figuratively—has no "beginning" or "end." It is able to modify itself over time, as it's relayed like a warm, supple baton from generation to [re-]generation. While, yes, a specific, isolated strand, squished between two microscope plates, might appear to have "ends," in fact they are OPEN ends!

So, folks—you're hearing it here: It's *all* malleable and, ultimately, changeable! WE are capable of adapting, to setting down old programming that no longer helps our species survive or even blocks our ability to thrive. WE are fully capable of releasing one way of being in order to make room to embrace something new, something better! We can only do that, however, if we first can clearly see, then more fully understand what it is we've been doing—as individuals and as a species. Especially where there have been "injuries"—physical or emotional—we need to recognize them for what they are, then stop replicating and passing them on, unresolved, for those who come after us to carry.

Easy? No. Essential for our species to survive? Without a doubt!

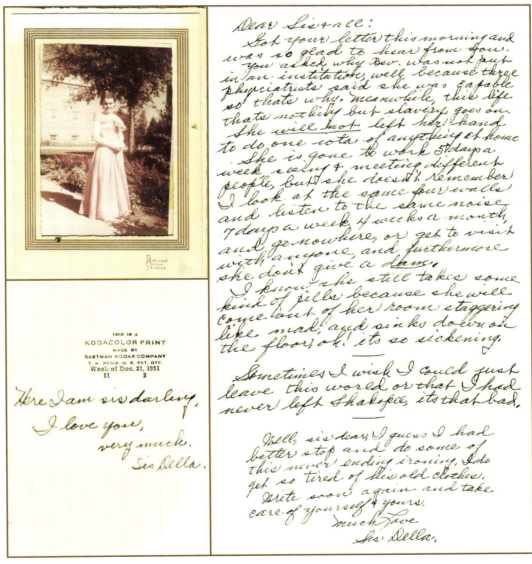

dolled-up Della during a special event held while she was incarcerated in prison, summer 1951; excerpts from a letter Della wrote 16 January 1962 to sister Nellie (Moorehead) Gardner & family

postscript: "This Everlasting Light"

When I was a teen, considering future career options, my father wanted me to be a lawyer.

"You cud argue yer way outta a pit fulla tigers" he'd say.

"But I don't want to study law" I'd reply.

"Then what *do* ya wanna study? Ya gotta be *sompthin'*."

I'd hesitate, steel up for the ironclad disapproval I knew would soon shower down on me, then dare whisper "history."

"*What* do ya wanna do with *history*?" Dad would shout with disbelief wedded with disdain every time we drifted into this displeasing topic. Each time, both of us later left it shaking our heads.

"*What* would I wanna do with *law*?" I would answer, evasively.

My father wanted me to earn a ton of money so I could live on Easy Street; I wanted to learn a lot about life so I could live on deeper levels. His aspiring for me to be a lawyer was primarily enrichment for me while serving others; my aspiring to be a historian was about enriching others while serving self. Ironically, even if they seemed diametric opposites to Dad, the two professions share something key to mastering either discipline. As with an adroit student of law, an advanced scholar of history can cogently argue a case, even in defense of a "guilty" cause, yet remain light of foot intellectually enough to dance to another tune if opposing evidence later presents itself. After careful scrutiny, if even contradictory data proves sound and convincing, she or he can shift moral weight behind a new argument and present it succinctly yet credibly. In short, a skilled lawyer or historian shies from rigid thinking.

One of the many rewards of undertaking this project has been becoming reacquainted with long-lost cousins or even meeting relatives I never knew I had. Of the latter, during research done in tandem, newly-found cousin Tony Luick in Orlando located Steve James Gardner, the grandson of Nellie Moorehead Gardner, "Young Lottie" (Moorehead) Juhl's younger sister. In Minnesota.

Steve Gardner and me following a program about our family, which we gave at the Freeborn County Historical Society, July 2014; cousins June Audrey Fuller and Della Ann Moorehead with Mooreheads' dog, circa 1920

Like me a nephew-removed of hers, years ago Steve began digging into the multiple-murder case that led to our Aunt Della's imprisonment. What he unearthed shook the underlying assumptions upon which I'd based my until-then unchallenged belief that the woman was guilty-as-convicted. As with any serious, grounded detective work—whether to back a lawyer's argument or front a historian's thesis—it widened the realm of possible explanations for the otherwise inexplicable, unconscionable act of a mother murdering offspring. And, it spoke of life beyond as well as before incarceration.

Even before I knew of Steve's existence, I'd gotten glimpses of a story more complex than the headlines hinted. Dad's sister Sheranne spoke of "Beverly comin' ta our place several times—each time with a different, always older man. Yeah" she marveled, "each one was more bizarre than the one before. Anyway, the last was particularly creepy. They was to stay fer a few days—probably on the way back ta Florida from the women's pen up in Shakopee—but then Beverly got sick an' they staid, oh, a week, maybe ten days before Ma finally had enough an' told 'em ta leave. Beverly always acted weird anyway, but the two was smokin', drinkin' an' swearin'—an' that didn't go. So, Ma kicked 'em off the place. They set off south. We never saw Beverly again."

Terry (on horse) & Sherry Hughes, Sheranne Luick, Ella Mae Hughes, Charlotte & Donald Luick, mid-1950s

Sheranne fell silent, then after a reflective moment snapped back to life with "Oh, there *was* one more thing: Beverly's brother, Bob [referred to as "Bernard" by the Albert Lea *Tribune* and accredited with having paid for Ardith's little casket 'in installments' as a dutiful, teenage half-brother], later died in a crop-duster crash. His brother, Paul, married Bob's widow, Ella May, and raised Bob's kids, Terry and Sherry." With that, late-coming Sheranne exhausted all she knew about our kin in the Sunshine State.

That wasn't, though, the end of the story. For one thing, Steve produced a post-prison letter from Della (by then living with Beverly in Florida) to her sister, his great-aunt Jennie (Moorehead) Fuller, and later sent to Nellie, his grandmother. It documents Beverly's being, well let's just say, "unstable."

> Bev still isn't very well, and her disposition is so bad…. She was in the hospital phyciatric [sic] ward for about a month awhile back, something is so wrong with her thinking that I know, and it is so hard to live

with. If it hadn't been for little Elliott, I would have gotten permission for different arrangements for me long ago.

A note on the back of the letter, in Nellie's handwriting, states:

Della's letter to Jennie Jan 1 – 62
She's been there over a year now.

The back of another letter from the same period also betrays Nellie's fears for Della's safety:

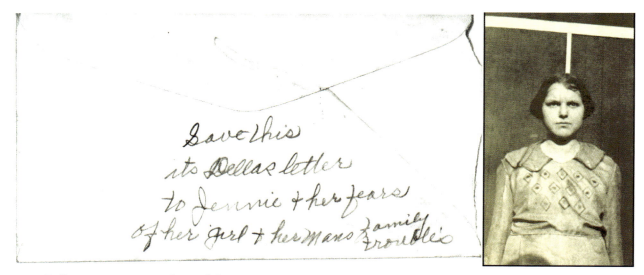

Della as a teenager, in front of the Mooreheads' shed; early 1920s, likely before her marriage at age 16

Certainly, there was more to this story than first appearances might belie. If, for example, as Steve has pointed out, Della had killed two of Beverly's siblings and, now as an adult, Beverly had an eleven-year-old child in the house, why would she allow her recently released convicted-murderer mother to reside with them—often alone with Little Gus? In any case, Beverly's own listlessness, squared with repeated waves of domestic tumult, hardly facilitated her mother's smooth reentry to civilian life.

As Steve waded further into the case, Della's morning-after confession increasingly didn't sit right. "Even in those pre-Miranda days" he explained to me,

> such a tell-all confession, right after having been arrested, was unusual. Her story was so pat yet vague, and so coldly told. It was as if she were trying to draw attention—and culpability—to herself, away from someone else. If so, who—and *why*?

Even more perplexing, in her often self-contradicting formal recantation twelve days later, Della expressly declared Beverly and—astoundingly—Lawrence Hughes (at the time documentably in faraway Florida) innocent of any wrongdoing. That Della tried to lure suspicion away from her teenage daughter and former husband seems odd, as neither Steve nor I have seen a word of anyone suggesting either of the two were involved in the heinous acts.

For clues to this broadening mystery, Steve approached Bill Sturtz, the son of the prosecutor of the case—himself a lawyer. After a disinterested review, Steve received this open-ended reply:

Hi, Steve:

First of all, thanks for sending me all this stuff. It is, indeed, a fascinating bit of local history.

I have some general comments, and some substantive ones. The general ones first.

Almost 70 years have passed. The passage of time has erased a lot from our thoughts and memories.

It is hard to evaluate Della Tarue's honesty, her guile, and her degree of sophistocation, as they were in the atmosphere of the 1940's, in the light of the levels that they exist today.

The interrogation of Della by my father is pure "William P. Sturttz". Ask a series of innocuous questions, to put the subjecxt at ease, before getting down to the nitty gritty. I felt that he put her pretty much at ease, and that it was a pretty good and thorough questioning. Still, there are some questions that I could wish had been asked.

I was in law practice with my father from 1951 to 1969. During those years he certainly appeared to be a most competent lawyer. I "second-chaired" him during a few trials, and I felt that he was quite sharp. By the mid-70's his condition had noticeably deteriorated. He died, in 1980, having suffered for some years with what we now know as Alzheimer's.

I wish that I had taken the opportunity, during his "good years", to have some fireside chats with him about the case. In all those years I do not believe we ever spoke of it.

Substance-wise:

I came away with no greater, or lesser, feelings as to Della's guilt I am still not totally convinced that she was guilty, but it is also hard to believe that she was innocent.

I did not get a feeling that she either had, or was, an accomplice. As I read over the material I did get a vague feeling that I was reading a "prepared story", where some of the questions were not anticipated, and, consequently, the answers were not rehearsed. This would faintly suggest that Della was not the murderer, but that she

And, on the next page:

> and whomever actually was, conspired to create a story. In other words, Della might have been guilty only as an "accessory after the fact".
>
> There is just too much variation between the things as to which she seemed certain, and those things as to which she professed ignorance.
>
> Underneath it all, I think Della emerges as a fairly intelligent woman. Some of her words - and conduct -would suggest otherwise, but I rather thought they were almost in the nature of a "smoke screen". I got the feeling that she was smart enough to know that without her story it might have been quite difficult to get a jury to convict her. ButI still had the uneasy feeling that the story was concocted by a lesser mind than hers. (Or, maybe, even concocted to make it look that way.)
>
> All in all, it seems that we are pretty much left at where we were. There were, I believe, always some faint questions as to her guilt. It seems to me that we have neither reinforced those feelings, nor set them to rest. It is a story which seems to send some shadowy mixed messages and we shall probably never see them resolved.
>
> It would be nice to be able to say that "this much is clear", but it isn't. One inalienable set of fact remain: Daella did confess, voluntarily as far as we can tell; she was convicted; and she served her time. Against that, any feelings that we might entertain to the contrary tend to be just straws in the wind.
>
> But, I do thank you for getting me involved, and interested. I have enjoyed delving into this bit of our community's now forgotten bit of history.
>
> *Bill*

The letter left Steve feeling even more uncomfortable with the assumption that Della committed the murders, solo and both times. In an email to me, he outlined other scenarios:

> Della married very young, and in January 1929, with three children and pregnant with a fourth, her husband Lawrence Hughes abandons the family. She sues for divorce, which is granted, has her baby, Beverly, and marries Benjamin True, all before the year is out. They have three more children of their own.
>
> Benjamin is a farmer, and it appears he's not particularly successful. Then he gets cancer, and the family moves in to town in Albert Lea. His death notice includes the snippet that the family is in dire straits financially. He's buried on Christmas Eve day, and Della is once more alone.
>
> After Lawrence Hughes left Della, he remarried, to a woman in Texas, and by circa 1940 is living in Florida with his new family. It is somewhere around this time that he and Della reconnect. Who knows which of the two reached out to the other, but according to the jailhouse interview with the *Tribune* reporter, they were intimate with each other.
>
> Then, her two youngest children die, first Ardith, then Merle, under strange circumstances. Within a few days, Della "confesses" to their killings. I say "confesses" because there are two confessions. The first is recanted, and in the second she goes out of her way to specifically exclude her daughter Beverly and her

ex-husband, Lawrence, from any responsibility in the deaths. She is convicted, and her remaining children moved to Florida to live with Lawrence and his family.

Two possible portraits of Della and her motivations emerge in my view:

The first, that she believes that Lawrence would take her back if she didn't have the True children in the picture, and thus she in fact commits the murders. This becomes the ostensible reason for her actions and subsequent conviction.

Or, the second, where she has some sort of involvement in their deaths, or at least in a cover-up. We know from letters and other stories from family members that Beverly is mentally ill as an adult, which would likely suggest that she was not well as a young teen. My father and his family believed that Della was, in fact, covering up for Beverly.

What if that's the case? Della could have decided that she needed to keep Beverly out of trouble, and that if she (Della) took the fall, Beverly might get some help. Further, the rest of the children might be able to have a better life if they are living with Lawrence and his family. Can it be that in taking responsibility for the children's deaths, Della is performing an act of love toward the rest?

What complicates drawing a clear conclusion are other, contradictory indications. In July 2014 Steve phoned with Virgil True, Junior, who reported that Della had offered his father "the poisoned drink" but he refused—which if true implicates Della in at least Merle's murder. On the other hand, Beverly's documented mental illness leads at least some family members (as Sherrane says was Charlotte's belief) to still suspect she might have killed Ardith, given the two had different and, at least in terms of their mother's favors, "competing" fathers. As Steve has pointed out, hints of jealousy, of very real sibling rivalry could have fed Beverly wanting to eliminate *her* competition: Whoever took the below photo, for example, seemed not to notice or, apparently, mind that while adorable Ardith got full billing, half of banished-to-the-wings Beverly's face went forgotten.

Della as a baby in Iowa in 1908; Ardith's 3rd birthday in Minnesota, with Beverly, 24 September 1939

So, who *did* kill the two True children, Della or Beverly—or both, perhaps in turns?

Ultimately, as no one privy to the truth has revealed it on-the-record, the rest of us know little of fact but too much that is uncertain about our family's greatest tragedy. What is known, unquestionably, is that Della earned the earliest possible probation for a sentence like she received: After seventeen years of "good behavior" Della Moorehead Hughes True was released from the Minnesota State Reformatory for Women to the custody of her then-adult daughter, Beverly (Hughes) Roberts Lott. On 15 March 1976, at the age of 69, Della married David Herman Jacobson. On 3 January 1981, at the age of 75, she died—and, for unknown reasons, was buried in Calloway County's Hazel Cemetery, in Kentucky. The inscription on her gray tombstone reads:

I AM HOME IN HEAVEN, DEAR, IN THIS EVERLASTING LIGHT.

fog patch in Boone County, where Della once lived in an "early commune" as a young wife and mother

We do know, less factually but visibly nonetheless, what we can *see*. And, what we can see in photos of Della—as well as her ill-of-health mother, Big Lottie—says much about each of them as personalities and about their fates. Beginning with one snapshot—likely taken in the mid-'20s, at some point with the inscription "Happy Days" added later—we see that in all but one of the six known adult images of her, Della either blocks her face from full view or looks away from the camera.

George Moorehead Jr., Della (Moorehead) Hughes, Cora (Moorehead) Miller; Della and husband Lawrence Hughes, with children Bernard & Ivan, likely summer 1927

The one of her sitting on a lawn with Lawrence Hughes is even more stupefying, given that if one looks closely, it appears as if red marks stretch from Della's right eye to her lower chin. Had she been beaten? Or, was she simply suffering a rash? What other explanations might be plausible? At the same time, on the back of the picture, Della wrote in some moment of longing:

"Dear! Do you remember when this was taken? Oh! Lawrence, please dear, let us be like this once more."

face shots of Della Ann (Moorhead) Hughes True, over period from 1927 (far left) through 1951 (far right)

"Nothing comes from nothing," though. Where did Della pick up the idea that she had to evade the eyes of even cameras? Was the clearly clever girl avoiding betraying low self-esteem, impossibly high expectations, or what she thought were naughty impulses?

Perhaps Big Lottie's expressions, as caught on a palette of images over the course of her pained life, reflect a precedent to hide one's face in order to mask one's suffering soul. There's hardly a one where she isn't looking afield or blankly. It seems something burdened her since at least young womanhood. Was it related to what later burdened Della, too? Did that underlying shadow in our family share at least part of the blame for what ultimately claimed two young, guiltless lives—a grandmother's and mother's own flesh and blood?

face shots of Charlotte Esther (Campbell) Moorhead, over period from 1891 (top left) through 1920s

And, what role did their mate and father, the ever-handsome patriarch and community pillar George Moorehead, play—he, who once watched *ten* loved ones die: seven young and vulnerable souls who perished in a matter of mere months as innocent victims of plagues stalking the prairie; and, later, a teenage daughter and two grandchildren? He, whose life was forever marked by disease and death.

face shots of George Edward Moorhead, over a period from 1880 (top left) through 1936 (bottom right); as seen in below scene in Minnesota, fishing with son-in-law Claude and grandson Alvin Miller, mid-1920s

Conclusions

VOLUME I

                Volume I: *Roots of Darkness*

1) from the *persona*: my disrupted granny

                Volume II: *Chasing Restless Roots*

2) about the *populi*: my disappearing people

                Volume III: *Tap Roots Betrayed*

3) for the *polis*: my derailed country

conclusion from the *persona*: my disrupted granny

As the train glided into Stuttgart's torn-up, scaffolding-draped *Hauptbahnhof*, I couldn't help but think back over thirty years to my first arrival in the Swabian capital city—as a green, grasping 19-year-old Iowa farmboy in search of solid roots. As I now was already late to meet waiting cousin Margrit, however, my reverie had to be short-lived: I had a mission to accomplish.

Changing to the *S-Bahn*, the commuter train to Esslingen, I once again felt a hushed reverence, a keen sense of going back to my Luick family's ancient origins. Glimpses of the Mercedes-Benz factories and the Untertürkheim stadium flickered by, then gave way to the steep vineyards lining the crowded, narrow Neckar valley. I realized I was making yet another, umpteenth pilgrimage to the Luicks' *Heimat*, the "homeland" where the emotional gauntlets I had experienced, growing up on that lonely farm in the middle of the North American prairie, really had all began.

Esslingen-am-Neckar, Württemberg, as seen from Eisberg hill, 1835

I had come to Germany, originally, to meet with German relatives and, in their midst, to dig deeper amongst the spiritual soil of our shared Luick blood. Among many other surprises, I discovered that while I could indeed find traces of "us" in them, the fact that my line had left the Old World and ventured into the New changed the people we in our branch had been upon setting off. In turn, it colored all those who came thereafter. The first Luicks to arrive in "*Amerika*" altered the land they found, even as they contributed to casting the vast, complex country yet to emerge. In coming to better know the story of my people, then, I came to more fully understand the country we helped build.

Even if at the time unconsciously, I first went to Esslingen to find patterns in my family's past in order to understand its (and thus my) patterns in our present. And, I found them—a *lot* of 'em: deeply set, mostly reflexive patterns that have long dictated how we have lived—as well as how we have died. As improbable as it might seem, I found some of the most telling clues not in the rich topsoil of the Iowa prairie, but in the musty air of the Luicks' ancient *Heimat* in Swabia.

One example:

The *S-Bahn* had not ground to a complete stop before I popped out of the opening door and dashed across the platform, down the tight steps and across the ageless cobblestones of Esslingen's main shopping street. Fearing making Margrit cross, I risked my neck racing through the Luicks' hometown in the old *Reichstadt*, oblivious to nearly everything and -one around me.

the Stadtkirche (right of two churches in drawing); Eugen, Elisabeth, Margrit & Michael Luick, 1982

Inexplicably, though, as I tore past the open door of the *Stadtkirche*, Esslingen's quiet parish church, I jerked to a stop, backed up three paces, then pivoted and slipped into the darkened entry of that immense Gothic structure. Sure, period images of Luicks past flashed through my mind, but on this unplanned, ill-timed visit, it was something other than the fanciful fact that centuries ago "my" people would have entered this exact same door in search of solace that beckoned my attention.

Leaving my clacking, wheeled travel bag near the front door, I instinctively followed some silent Siren's summoning. I slowly made my way further and further into that sandstone building's dim, cool nave. The myriad sculptures, lavish crosses, carvings, paintings, plaques… none could seduce me to stop: intuitively, I felt that what was luring my inner compass waited for me behind the altar.

Indeed, reaching the ornately-carved choir benches I knew I'd discovered what I did not know I needed to see. These benches were whittled out of massive trees in 1518. I was unsure that I'd ever seen them on one of my many trips to Esslingen, yet felt certain that my Luick ancestors had. And, thus, I wondered what they thought of the nearly life-sized carved busts buttressing the ends of each bench, of the elaborate likenesses of *guten Bürgern*, the leading merchants, guildsmen, priests, soldiers and others who held power in prospering, self-ruled Esslingen half a millennia ago.

What particularly provoked me were the miniature skulls adorning several armrests, scattered amongst the other human or animal heads gracing same. The morbid leftovers from the rampant, premature mortality rates of the late Middle Ages reminded me of things existent yet unseen or not understood. While desperate to make sense of their death-stricken lives, our ancestors knew nothing of germs, of the sources of infections or how to effectively combat them. Stalked by maladies today cured by a jaunt to the local apothecary, those who preceded us fell by the millions in the face of diseases they attributed to a vengeful, score-keeping god. Unable to comprehend the value-neutral nature of bacteria or genes, they ascribed moral judgment to women dying during childbirth, babies born with cleft palates or Downs Syndrome, and to any number of illnesses or physical defects they could not fathom having natural causes. Groping for explanations, they turned to superstition and prejudice rather than science or plausible proof. In the process, they made life a living hell for those already innocently burdened.

Lorraine and Gramma (in front of paint-by-number picture Sheranne made in grade school), at the time Charlotte had breast cancer, 1995; mask worn in 1600s during plagues, with anti-septic herbs in "beak"

Disease and death were not the only things our pre-Enlightenment ancestors saw but did not fully understand. Although they ruled much of the occidental world for over two thousand years as one of the most expansive and, for their time, technologically advanced culture in history, the chariot-borne Romans never figured out a symbol for zero—for nothing. For that, we can thank humble, donkey-bestriding Arab mathematicians. Medieval scribes, in turn, were confined to mostly reading out loud due to lack of spaces or punctuation between written words: a missing concept of space, an allowance for nothing, separated oral from recorded stories. Both examples show that often the thing—or no thing—right in front of us is often the most difficult for us to see. We're too close; we need distance from a thing to get inside and better understand it. And, it seems we need first an empirical experience in order to then have a conceptual experience of a thing, if we are to fully and truly comprehend it.

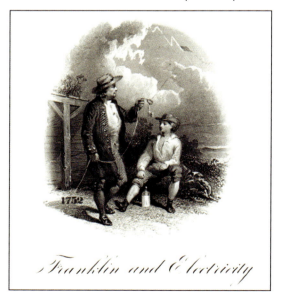

Before Isaac Newton watched apples fall, for example, our ancestors knew nothing of gravity although this planet's pulling force had always anchored them to Earth. And, until ol' Ben Franklin risked his life by flying key-strung kites during lightning storms, electricity pulsated through everything they saw, yet for most of hominins' millions of years of traipsing through a veritable Eden, they knew not that it even existed—not to mention atoms, elementary chemicals, genes, radiation.

Although unseen, our world has long revolved round realities that determine our very existence even if we have, for most of our species' career, been utterly unaware of their fundamental influences over our everyday lives—indeed, over our every conscious moment. We think we see, we know what's around us, but, in reality, most of what is goes on unperceived.

(l.- r.) David, Doug and Jeandelle* (Luick) Olesen;* head of Doug's wife, Deb, behind Barb's husband, Tom; Lorraine (Luick) Jones with then-boyfriend Chuck Ryan, Dad, Chuck Olesen, Gramma, back of Barb's head, Wayne* & Sheranne* (Luick) Joyns*, Mom standing, right; Easter 1977 at Ashlawn Farm (*names altered)

So, too, has it been with our families—the invisible, socio "basic element" of each of our inner, emotional worlds. Researching, reliving and now recording my paternal family's history, I know that it is true in my case: things unseen yet right in front of us the entire time have dictated our past-determined fates. As with gravity and electricity, we mortals are blind to some of the most essential dynamics flowing within and between us as human beings—and that blindness binds us. Wanting to be free, we first have to "see," to truly understand what we've chosen until now not to know or even acknowledge.

It has been that quest, to comprehend the genesis of why my family is the way it is, that has so intimately and intrinsically propelled me through space and time for over half a century. That was the basic question that unwillingly led me from Ashlawn Farm so long ago and kept me hunting like some modern nomad, seeking shreds of truth in a colorful, often confusing cosmos of fake gods and false starts. It has been the search for why my family is the way it is that has ultimately fed my hungry chase for clues as to why I am the way I am—but not just why, but *who* I am.

———

One is always well advised to watch for what one wishes.

I wanted to know who I am. So, I began digging into who my family had been. Easily enough I uncovered stories, shadows, patterns that resurfaced repeatedly:

When I was a boy… and when my mother was a girl… and when her father was a boy… as all three of us were growing up at Ashlawn Farm over a span of more than eighty years, various periodicals such as illustrated farmers' almanacs, plat books, county atlases or business directories would appear on a regular basis. Lined with paid ads or featured sponsors, they a.) supplied would-be buyers with useful information, even as they b.) offered businesses an oft-consulted forum to reach rural readers. Given their desire to please both groups, the publishers of such local-focus advertising normally took great care to appear non-partisan and non-sectarian, and avoided broaching potentially-provocative social issues so as to not offend anyone and thereby lose sales. Well—at least "normally."

Given this age-old, profit-driven policy, the following article that appeared in the *History and Business Directory of Wright County, State of Iowa* seems all the more surprising and daring. Printed in 1870 by a certain J.H. Stevenson, it documents beyond doubt that not everyone was a fan of at least clan-head Henry Luick, if not Belmond's entire first-founders family. Risking alienating dozens of households which otherwise might purchase his directory, Stevenson felt it more important to poke a finger on the printed page and make a point than to protect the sensibilities of his roster of regular readers. Or, perhaps, sensing a general, popular dissatisfaction with Henry & Co., the publisher assumed more might be *gained* by giving the Luick patriarch a black eye than might be lost by briefly disavowing public propriety. In any case, the resultant parody swiped at the standing of not only of Wright County's one-time judge, but his whole house. And, as Tony Luick has noted, the piece "appears to be quite a departure from the rest of the book, which is in narrative form but more fact than satire."

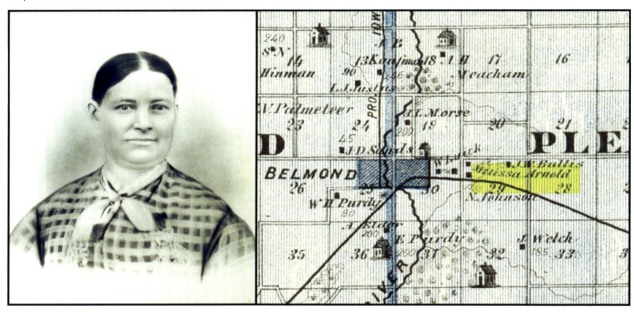

Melissa (Overacker) Luick Arnold; her farm outlined in yellow on 1875 plat book map

For the sake of clarity and ease of reading, I "out" here the characters, who in the original version were all assigned aliases, likely over fear of liability for alleged defamation. The real players in this parody are:

"Mr. Doolittle"	Charles Johnson
"Mr. Domore"	Henry Luick
"Mrs. Doolittle"	Lydia Lathrop Johnson
"Mrs. Domore"	Melissa Overacker Luick
Doolittles' daughter	Irene Johnson, Lydia's daughter
Domores' son	Sylvester Luick, Henry's son

We were furnished with a little piece of history concerning one of the first settlers of this township, which probably ought to be omitted, but owing to the strange and almost incredible transaction it reveals, we are constrained to publish, taking the responsibility however by omitting real names and putting forth the facts in our peculiar style. The history of the circumstances we are about to write runs something in this wise:

During a certain year, there came to settle in Pleasant township a man whom, for convenience sake, we will call by the name of Mr. Doolittle [alias for Charles Johnson]. This is not his real name, however, and if there happens to be a citizen in the township bearing such a name he will know that it is not him that is meant.

This much in way of explanation, and now to narrate what befell Mr. Doolittle. He was one of those fortunate creatures who had the good luck to be possessed with a very charming wife. For many years Mrs. Doolittle [alias for Lydia Lathrop Johnson] had reclined on his noble bosom, and during all this time they had sailed together on the sea of wedlock, (which by the way were not a few for Mrs. Doolittle had borne him several children, one of whom was a lovely girl) calmly and peacefully, she ever acting the part of a true and faithful wife. After a long and peaceful voyage, without anything transpiring to interrupt or disturb the mutual felicity that each seemed to enjoy, a breaker arose which destroyed their happiness forever.

Convenient to where Mr. Doolittle resided lived a gentleman whom we will call Mr. Domore [alias for Henry Luick]. This man may have been either a preacher, a teacher, or a doctor, or, he may possibly have been a — judge. From his good judgment concerning a woman's beauty we rather incline to the belief that the latter was his profession. Be this as it may, certain it is that Mr. Doolittle's wife took his eyes notwithstanding the fact of his having a wife of his own. In this age of Woman's Rights and Free Love, we don't know that he was much to blame, for the charms of Mrs. Doolittle were truly irresistible. It is evident a thought of the Tenth Commandment never entered his head, or if it did, it is equally certain he utterly disregarded it, for he did covet his neighbor's wife, and the image of the lovely Mrs. Doolittle was continually before his eyes night and day. He struggled hard and long to overcome the enchanting smile and fascinating features of the charming creature who had taken possession of his soul, but all to no avail, for strive or struggle how he would he could not flee from her, and even in his sleep her image haunted him. At length his state of mind became insufferable and awaiting an opportunity when he could find his enchantress alone he rushed to her frantically, and, falling on his knees, eloquently told the story of his passionate, earnest, true, deep, and burning love. No blame can be attached to the fair Mrs. Doolittle if her heart was moved by his piteous tale, for it was of such a soul-stirring nature and delivered in such a pathetic manner that stronger hearts than hers must have yielded to such an outburst of burning, passionate love. He told her that he adored and worshipped her; his life would be nothing but a blank without her; she was the idol at whose shrine he ever knelt, and all that the infatuated "Mr. Domore" required to make earth a paradise was the sweet angel, Mrs. Doolittle. Needless to say such earnest pleadings completely won over the affections of Mrs. Doolittle, and throwing herself into the arms of Mr. Domore, she sobbed out "Dearest, I am thine!"

Arrangements for further movements were made, when Mr. Domore took his departure from the presence of his idol with a soul filled with boundless joy. All the necessary preparations being made, one beautiful morning, just as the sun was shedding his first beams over the mountain tops, by a preconcerted arrangement, this couple met, at a place by them understood and agreed upon beforehand, and after a long, loving embrace, started for Missouri; Mr. Domore leaving his wife to mourn his loss, and the charming Mrs. Doolittle leaving her husband to repine over her departure. After an absence of two years their hearts longed to return again to the place where their first love began, and agreeable to both, they came back once more to the old familiar scenes.

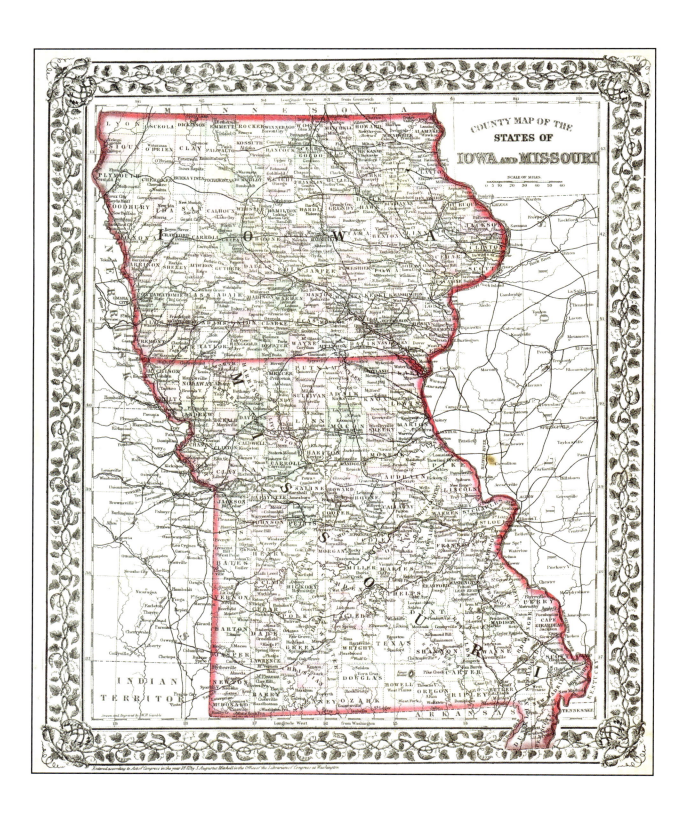

While they were gone, however, Mr. Doolittle, feeling deeply vexed at his wife taking such a long visit without consulting him on the subject, had rushed to the court and obtained a bill of divorce. It is a mystery to us how he could have the heart to do such a thing on such a frivolous pretense. However, the absent couple returned, and no sooner had the distracted Mr. Doolittle caught Mrs. Doolittle's first smile than he ran and clasped her in his arms, and good natured soul that he was, all was forgiven on the instant.

Mr. Domore, likewise, returned to the embrace of his first wife. Hearts like Mr. Domore's and the fascinating Mrs. Doolittle's, so congenial to each other, were not to be long sundered, however, and scarcely a month expired when Mr. Domore one day, about noon, drove over to Domores' and taking Mrs. Doolittle in his wagon started for parts unknown. Mrs. Domore [alias for Melissa Overacker Luick] now discovering that her lord had once again become estranged from her, and that she was completely banished from his affections, sought the only remedy to be had in such cases, that of being separated from him for life according to law. Pending the decree, Mr. Domore turns up once more, this time leaving his charmer in Franklin county, and scarcely had Mrs. Domore obtained the decree of separation than Mr. Domore returned to where his fair enchantress was, and married her.

It appears that this spirit of congeniality which existed between Mr. Domore and Mrs. Doolittle was not confined to those two alone, but was inherited by their offspring, for we find that some time subsequent to this, Domores' son and Doolittles' daughter became twain in one flesh, while poor Mr. Doolittle took to his bosom a new comforter, and the much wronged Mrs. Domore, forgetting all her troubles, seized upon the first opportunity that presented itself of burying all her grief by becoming the wife of someone else.

Now, gentle reader, you may be a little anxious to know what has become of the characters of this portion of my history. At the present time, from all we can learn, Mr. Domore and the Mrs. Doolittle that was, are living in the full enjoyment of perfect bliss in some region agreeable to both; while Mr. Doolittle, after living a long time in solitude, mourning over the beautiful bird he had so long cherished and cared for, emerged from his seclusion and mated with another, with whom he now resides, in the pleasant locality of Belmond, in perfect peace and harmony. The younger Domore, with the daughter of Mrs. Doolittle, are living in a state of uninterrupted felicity, joy, and blessedness; and the prospects are that the future generations of the Luicks and Johnsons, all around, are destined to enjoy countless years of unbroken happiness and great prosperity.

Lydia Maria (Lathrop) Johnson Luick and ailing Henry Luick, 1890s

At around the end of America's Civil War Henry Luick and Lydia Johnson did, indeed, flee Iowa one early morn on a romantic, two-year retreat in Missouri—as the citizen-judge well knew to do, leaving a legally-safe state line between now-criminal them and their still-lawful mates back in North Central Iowa. And, just as in the parody, after returning—supposedly repentant—to their respective spouses for less than a month, the duo left them once again, this time irreversibly, to start a new life in Oskaloosa.

In case the stage upon which this drama unfolded was not cluttered enough, the farce's plot thickened. It was in all innocence that Lydia's eleven-year-younger sister—the widowed Sarah Jane (Lathrop) Baker—married Henry and Melissa's oldest son, Michael Henry, in 1865. Finding his new daughter-in-law's older sister, Lydia (married to Belmond's master-carpenter, Charles Johnson) too alluring to resist, Henry ditched his frontier-worn wife of over two decades, mother-of-nine Melissa, for his delicious neighbor lady, Lydia, who seems to have borne but two babes in her child-creating career.

Sarah Jane (Lathrop) Baker Luick in her Belmond-area kitchen and era-typical parlor, 1890s

To complicate the webs connecting the adults in the Luicks' later shared, short-term domicile in Oskaloosa even further, Henry and Melissa's 20-year-old son, Sylvester, married Lydia's daughter, Irene Marie Johnson, on 25 September 1868—a week and a day after Irene turned eighteen, a month before her mother and Henry legalized their illegitimate relationship.

Depending on which of the two birth years given for my great-grandfather one believes, my Grampa George was eleven or twelve years old when his long-ailing grandfather, Henry, succumbed to "Bright's disease"—a slow, unforgiving death from kidney failure, known today as nephritis. Before the head of his familial line forever left us, did little George get to know *his* grampa well—perhaps even a little too well? At least on one level, it would seem so. Some eight decades after Henry's deceitful act, as if operating from the same secretive playbook, George did as his Gramps had done: He abruptly ran away with a neighbor's wife and laid low in Missouri a few years.

"That bastard!"

But, waita second: Great-Grampa George wasn't the only one in the Luick line. To learn the identity of a few of the others, listen to this broken record one more time, straight through:

- During the latter years of the American Civil War, Henry Jacob Luick gets to know neighbor's wife (Lydia); falls helplessly, irreversibly in love with same, betrays existing partner (Melissa) over time, runs away to Missouri for two years in the hopes of making it all work out in the end. Ultimately, Henry prevails despite great drama and strife; he remains with proclaimed Great Love for over three decades, for rest of his life, 'til death.
- During the later years of research into this familial pattern, Louis Lee Luick's grandson, Gary, reveals that Louis' father, Henry, "didn't give Louis any land 'cause of his son's womanizing."
- During the later years of the Second World War, George Michael Luick gets to better know a neighbor's wife (Olga); falls helplessly, irreversibly in love with same, betrays existing partner (Lorena) over time, runs away to Missouri for about twenty years in the hopes of making it all work out in the end. Ultimately, George

prevails despite great drama and strife; he remains with proclaimed Great Love for over three decades, for rest of his life, 'til death.
- During the later years of the Second World War, Donald George Luick gets to know hired girl (Lynann); falls helplessly, irreversibly in love with same, betrays existing partner (Charlotte) over time, (resultant daughter says, years later, he) sends now-pregnant hired girl away to Nebraska for a short time in the hopes of making it all work out in the end. Ultimately, Donald prevails for at least a short time despite great drama and strife; he remains in contact with secret Great Love for over three years, till she marries (by "coincidence?") Donald's wife's cousin's son.
- During the later years of... well, do your own research on that one.
- During the later years of the Second Iraq War, Michael Luick-Thrams gets to know organic-garden manager's love interest (Rock); falls helplessly, irreversibly in love with same, betrays then-current German boyfriend (Holm) over time, makes clandestine trips to Missouri for over two years in the hopes of making it all work out in the end. After great drama and strife, Michael still hopes genuine, lasting love ultimately will prevail; he wishes with all his heart to unite with a Great Love for rest of this life, 'til death.

Will it happen?

my namesake at a Midwest outdoor event, 1950s; me at Frank Lloyd Wright's estate Taliesin, 1990s

Stay tuned—and buy next book.

―――

When I first arrived in Berlin in July 1993 I had neither the intent nor the desire to wade into earning another academic degree. At first solely to please grumpy, visa-granting Prussian bureaucrats, however, I registered to pursue doctoral studies in history at Humboldt Universität that fall. Initially an unenthusiastic student, the focus of my dissertation—refugees from Nazi-occupied Europe who found a safe haven abroad, 185 of them at the Quaker-run Scattergood Hostel in my native Iowa—swiftly took on a life of its own and, as they say, "the rest is..."

When my *Doktorvater*, my doctoral advisor first forced me to attend the *Kandidatenseminare* of which he so happily sat as the celebrated head, I inwardly fumed and watched the clock for the much-anticipated conclusion of each week's doctoral-candidates' seminar. Although an arrogant, contrary student at the onset, I gradually began to appreciate the essential differences between advanced historical studies in the United States, versus those in newly reunited Germany.

Even though I first found the idea of *Geschichtswissenschaft*, of "historical science" a contradiction in terms—"*How* could one ever approach a humanities subject like one would a 'science'?"—I began to grasp that the occupants of centuries-old Old World ivory towers might just be on to something. Once I found the intellectual courage to suspend my native culture's understanding of what constitutes "historical study," I allowed myself to be challenged by the academic premises of a foreign-albeit-adopted one. I unexpectedly found the keys I needed to open door after door to the secrets long guarded by generations of my father's family. Among other useful tools for living deeply let alone thinking widely, I learned that distilling probing first questions often bears more insight than spinning what one might think, in an excited moment, to be pat, "final" answers.

Still, the immature young man I was at the beginning of my doctoral studies protested: "What is 'scientific' about studying human behavior, as observed over time? People are human beings, not mathematical equations, chemical reactions or masses to be measured and weighed."

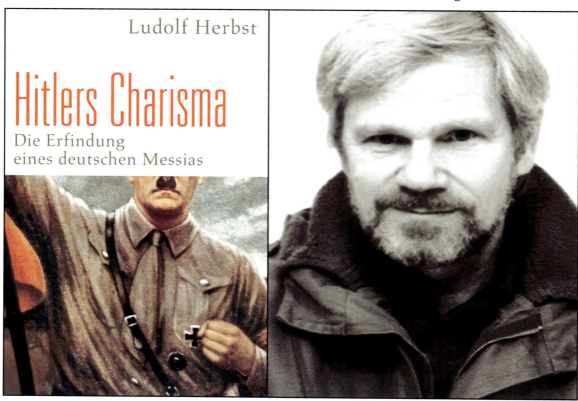

Ludolf Herbst and his signature book, in English Hitler's Charisma: The Fabrication of a German Messiah

"*Ah-h-h*" my sponsoring *Professor Doktor*, Ludolf Herbst, stalled, visibly pondering how to help me see what I resisted as a possibility, "yes, that. If a thing happens once, you see, it's an 'event.' If it happens twice it's a 'trend'" he explained. "Thrice a 'pattern' worthy of study and four times a 'phenomenon' on which to base a hypothesis. The fifth time a thing takes place" he paused, leaning back into his over-stuffed desk chair and glancing out his office window overlooking Berlin's Bebelplatz, where Nazi fanatics once had burned "degenerate" books, "it's 'the truth.'"

As "scientific" historians seek patterns made plausible by proof, my family's multi-generational trail of woeful misjudgments and pain-sowing missteps offers many. Where to start?

The parody from 1870—despite being wrapped in now-quaint, obtuse language—provides documentable proof that already in the Victorian era, Luick men in America were deserting their sworn marital duties. Thus, we modern observers can see that at least Henry's wandering eye created lasting suffering. What price did the whole family pay when not only two of Melissa's five sons but her own husband of twenty-two years married Lathrop-Johnson women? Census records show that Louis lived with Henry and his new wife, Lydia, in Oskaloosa in 1870—but we also know that as a sixteen-year-old boy he joined his mother, Melissa, a few years later when she and her second husband, abolitionist pastor John Arnold, trekked to California, reportedly via covered wagon. To what degree did such divided allegiances tax young Louis' heart and head?

His grandson, Gary, claims Louis forfeited a share of his father Henry's fortune due to "womanizing." (Ol' "Mad Bobcat" had plenty o' money to spread around: Not only did he make savvy land deals, beginning with buying John Beebe's cabin for pocket money and continuing with advantageous land sales to many of Belmond's early settlers, but Henry reportedly had inherited a sizeable windfall from his nobly-descended mother's people back in Swabia. From the looks of well-dressed Lydia, this German-immigrant boy left his widow sittin' mighty pretty when he died—slowly and painfully, from a disease that all the wealth in this world could not disarm.) We also know that when Louis married Mary Louisa Hunt in autumn 1881, she already had a child at the time of their betrothal, little three-year-old Anna Leora, sired by Louis or, more likely, a man named Elias Ross, who was a decade older than she when Elias married Mary on 15 August 1876 in Calaveras County, California. Despite whatever constellation hung over their early married lives, Louis and Mary went on to have eight children who—excluding Anna's and typhoid-fever-stricken Ethel's deaths—lived on average to be 89.29 years old.

While we lack any signs of marital strife between them, we know from newspaper articles as well as family recollections that at the end of the Second World War Louis and Mary's third of five sons, George Michael—my great-grandfather—left his wife of forty years, Lorena Ethel Jenison Luick, much in the same way that his grandfather, Henry, had left his grandmother, Melissa: suddenly, supposedly unexpectedly and southerly—for Missouri. The same patterns, separated by eight decades, seem striking for their similarity, down to the most intricate details.

George's only son, Donald, had at least one, documented extra-marital relationship, although more were rumored. The on-going contact he had with hired-girl Lynann Maloy—apparently from fall 1943 to spring 1949—resulted in at least one baby being born and caused Charlotte unending torment till the day she died. Taken from first-person testimony, not idle second-hand speculation, this claim comes from Sheranne, who stated that during her dying mother's hallucinations, Charlotte screamed at times "Get Lynann out of here! Get her *out*!"

And, my own relational deceptions are broached above: Let's let that admission suffice for now.

———

Besides what seemed to be an inherited predilection among Luick men to abandon our mates—either literally and permanently, or emotionally (even if we stuck around bodily) and in stints, while they conducted extra-marital relations—years of family-history research has revealed other unhelpful patterns in our lineage, such as that of unplanned pregnancy. Per Herr Herbst's "five-times-a-truth" formula, a swift survey solely of Charlotte's immediate pedigree reveals the following:

- Her mother, Charlotte Esther (Moorehead) Juhl, gave birth to Gramma's older brother, Delbert Dwayne, less than eight months after "Young Lottie" married Nicholas Paulsen Juhl.
- Nick's second wife, Bertha Mae (Hadsall), gave birth to baby Cleo four and one-half months after their wedding. Nick's widow referred later in life to that father of at least eight as a "reprobate."

- Charlotte's "older sister," her mother's youngest sister Della Ann Moorehead, married Lawrence Hughes at age 16 and gave birth to their first child, Ivan, five months after their wedding. Della would ultimately raise seven children as a single, unemployed mother, and tap social assistance and help from family members.
- Gramma gave birth to her oldest child, my aunt Lorraine Marie, fifteen weeks "early" after marrying my grandfather, Donald George Luick, at Iowa's "shotgun-wedding chapel" extraordinaire in Nashua, known in the past to have fudged dates on wedding certificates to accommodate "impatient cupids."
- Donald and Charlotte's first child, Lorraine, conceived her first child at age 15 and then gave birth to Mickie exactly one month after marrying Robert Lewis Jones, age 21. Lorraine ultimately raised seven children as a single, unemployed mother, tapping social assistance as well as help from family members.
- Donald sired at least one child with his and Charlotte's hired, in-home helper, Lynann Maloy, who came to work for them in fall 1943 when she was 17; she left the Luick home by fall 1944, pregnant. Donald fathered her daughter, Lois, who was born May 1946, when Lynann was 19.
- Lynann's mother, Mattie Steward of Hatchechubbee, Alabama had given birth to Lynann eight months after she married Lynann's father, William Jefferson Maloy—who later murdered Mattie as little Lynann watched.

Be the records accurate and rumors true, less than three months after marrying him on 26 October 1843, Melissa Overacker bore Henry Luick a son, Michael Henry, on 22 January 1844. On another branch of my paternal family tree, Alvina Sprague (Jennison) gave birth to her and Joseph Bud's first child, Charles Earl, seven months after they married, on 29 March 1851. And, local legends have it that cousin Cloe Jenison once conceived an unplanned pregnancy with a man who promised to marry her *if* she "got rid" of their illegitimate baby. Unwilling to abort it (then a severe violation of several laws) she is said to have gone to New York, carried the baby to term, and gave it up for adoption. She then returned to Iowa—only to have the man she supposedly loved brutally brush aside all hope of marrying out of hand.

Cloe Jenison, circa 1920

Despite any appearances to the contrary, I'm not interested in morally judging this cascading trail of out-of-wedlock conception and unplanned pregnancies. To the contrary, I offer it as a cautionary tale, a warning distilled out of what often became ultimately unwanted, legally-tied and thus locked-in long-term partnerships based on inadvertent marriage. An alternative might have been better considered: time-tested unions freely undertaken, independent from whatever role child bearing might or might not later play in a couple's career. We're talking here about real freedom—to be in a relationship, or not; freedom to simply be, without being coerced by unplanned or inauspicious child-bearing.

In addition to a generations-long tradition of mating by default upon becoming pregnant out of wedlock, my Luick lineage has the habit of making "problematic" family members "disappear." Besides being exceptionally life- as well as truth-denying, making relatives effectively invisible simply does not remove a problem: It makes it—and them—only harder to face. Reacting to people, past events or potentialities by acting as if the things we don't approved of don't exist, denies the fuller truth of who we have been, who we are now and who we might yet become, both as family forever bonded by blood, as well as individuals, born alone and destined to so die.

Bud, Charlotte, Lorraine, Jeandelle & Sheranne, early 1970s; scene from Moorehead daily life, early 1920s

In phone interviews with my aunts Jeandelle or Sheranne, with my mother, siblings and numerous cousins, each family member I asked seemed to genuinely believe that their mother[in-law] or grandmother grew up in George and Lottie Moorehead's home as the sole child in the house. (At least on this one, my aunts presumably told the truth as they knew it: Jeandelle was only six years old and Sheranne not yet born when their great-aunt proved to be a serial-murderer with a ghastly track record.) Likely as the searing truth behind the cold-blooded facts truly was too horrific to bear, Charlotte had simply sanitized tales of her childhood home to omit any mention of a girl who'd grow up to poison at least the two youngest of Della's seven children, if not her second husband and his parents, too.

Had our cousin Tony Luick not discovered Della's deeds on-line, none of us would have ever known about that sister of Gramma's dead, tragedy-victim mother, nor what Della's mental health suggested about that of the people who produced Charlotte. We would not have fully understood why Gramma was the way she was or why she acted the way she often did. In effect, after decades of digging, I finally uncovered at least a few of the ghosts Gramma might have been chatting with as she stood at the lonely kitchen window of her farmhouse and looked out over a quiet, secret-swallowing prairie.

Already well-practiced in the art of editing oral histories 'til inconvenient truths disappear, just over a year after Della's second child, innocent Merle, "succumbed" to a late-night drink laced with poison, Charlotte did away with Lynann's unwanted baby—at least as far as any of us grandchildren ever knew. She did not do so in isolation, however, but with the collusion of her entire immediate family. When my newly-wedded mother asked Bud about rumors she'd heard in nearby Thornton, my then-young father answered her merely with a non-answer. A half-century later, during the sole phone interview that Jeandelle grudgingly granted me, she chanted each time to my repeated questioning about that or related incidents: "I can't tell you; I have no idea; I wouldn't have a clue; I honestly do not know."

Sheranne on Santa Claus's lap, late 1940s

In confusing contradiction, only weeks earlier, Sheranne had sworn that "They all knew what happened with Dad and the hired girl! It was no secret—the whole town knew!" And, when I broached the matter with Donald's sister, Velma's, three children, all were aware of having an extra-marital cousin. For years, my mother had hinted at elusive rumors. My cousin Barbara's family also "had heard something about Donald and some hired girl," yet all claimed to know nothing more or specific. Again, were it not for Tony in faraway Orlando following up on a tip I'd gotten from a relative (who I assured would remain anonymous), I could not have called "little Lois" sixty-eight years and two weeks after the birth of the baby all those involved tried so hard, so long to make "not have happened."

―――

Lois' illegitimate birth was the earliest but not the last in the Luick-Juhl clan. Coming together some eight years after Bob had walked out on Lorraine and their seven children, the formerly married couple conceived a ninth child (although no longer living a shared life). Bob wanted nothing to do with it, but Gramma helped Lorraine carry the fetus to full term, then supported her when my aunt surrendered the newborn to adoption upon birth.

My cousin Barbara and I have spent a lifetime trying to understand who we are and how we got to be the way we are. In the process, we have confronted deeper truths behind the often unhealthy dynamics that seem to pulsate through our family's shared generations. At the same time, we both have been blessed by unexpected, often improbable treasures that seemed to appear as if by a miracle. In the case of her long-lost youngest sibling—for example—Barbara had submitted a letter to the adoption agency as a teenager asking to be put in contact with her youngest sister. Forty-one years later:

> The adoption agency contacted me about the sister who had read my letter and wanted to get in touch with her biological family. Little did she know that I was just one of her seven siblings who were eagerly hoping to find her!

And, as Barbara happily added,

> Soon, after my youngest sister reappeared in our lives, all five of our surviving mutual siblings reacted positively. They all traveled to Missouri last August to meet her. I was "there" via SKYPE and the whole thing was so beautiful, so healing and it felt so right. We all welcomed her, our sister, into our family.

Barbara Lee (Jones) Noonan, 2008

I feel gratified that, improbably, even a child born out-of-wedlock (to a couple which could not even successfully care for their seven existing children), ultimately could be rejoined with her family forty years after her birth. At the same time, if only all adult-age reunions between siblings separated as children could run so flawlessly!

The first time I called Lois—on the U.S. Tax Day 2014, our annual national date to publicly state and, if possible, square outstanding sums—I invited her to consider contacting the two, still-living half-sisters she didn't know she had until a few minutes earlier. When I proposed that she do so, she wavered. After a few awkward, silent seconds she confessed "The idea frightens me."

"What frightens you about it, Lois—that they might reject you?"

"Yes" she responded reflexively. "Yes, that's it."

"Don't forget, though—you're guiltless, after all."

"What you mean?" she wondered.

"No one can be blamed just for having been born, you know."

"Yes" she echoed softly, almost absently, pretending to be convinced, "that's right."

It seemed so easy, so effortless to preach that line to Lois—but believe it myself? Forget it.

———

It would have been one thing, had my father always acted heartlessly and physically aggressive towards me. Me being me—a Luick, of hearty pioneer stock and all that—I'd like to believe that somehow I'd have muddled through. That having undergone years of therapy, or maybe experiencing a religious conversion, or just embracing a moment of grace, the Mike Luick that I didn't become would somehow, to some degree, have "gotten over it." I'd hope that at some point that Mike Luick (the straight-acting, born-again Christian, Republican-activist Iowa farmer that I almost became but then, at the last moment, didn't) would have arranged himself with the idea that his father had, "Well, drove him hard all right—*real* hard." Perhaps, in some parallel universe that ultimately hardly counts, that Mike Luick would have quickly come to terms with growing up at the hands of a raging lunatic.

This one, though, did not.

Well, not at first—and not without constant, continuing effort. It took some time to own my own abandonment, to come to terms with the solitary state that resulted from having been "erased" from a family that didn't have a clue how to deal with a queer, clever, curious kid.

It would have been one thing, had my father always acted heartlessly and physically aggressive towards me. As it was, that's not the way this Mike Luick's life unfolded. Instead, weaned at an early age on Old-Testament Methodist Sunday-school lessons, I extrapolated what

me (squatting, left) with other Iowans lobbying Congress, mid-1980s

I'd been taught about looming biblical figures to the larger-than-life ones in my own, little-kid world. I assumed that just as Adam and Eve first had a fun time in that nifty garden—least ways, 'til apple-harvest time, when everything started going wrong after some mythical moment brought to you and me by a wily, talkin' snake—at some point, sompthin' I hadn't noticed (and sure as dickens didn't understand) had happened that displeased My Earthly Father. Just as our Heavenly Father had cast Adam and his lady friend outta Eden, from that mysterious moment on Daddy had withdrawn all the tenderness, all the love that he'd shown me so easily before. It was exactly *that* "fall" from which I've never fully recovered.

Dad's inexplicable banishment of me from his heart was abrupt and total—and palpable, even if unspoken. As such, it left me inconsolably confused. The first time I tried, solo and free-style, to ride a bike, I immediately fell down. Eventually, though—after tipping over uncountable times—I peddled up and down the lane that tied our lonely farmyard to the gravel road already beckoning me. Yes, I'd mastered staying upright on a two-wheeler, but Dad's bizarre, brutal behavior held me hostage. To vent, I cursed God—even while pleading "What have *I* done? Why does he hate *me*? What have *I* done? *Why* does Dad *hate* me so?"

As I peddled up and down that driveway, in my mind a scratched, Kodachrome home movie flickered with images of Dad as a young man lifting me to the ceiling—both of us content and relaxed—rolling me between his big, sturdy hands. Then, with a *swoosh*, he'd let me drop halfway to the floor. At that point, I wondered where had that playful daddy had disappeared? And, I wondered, where had I disappeared—where had *I* become lost and invisible?

me, Dad, Deb & Dave, Christmas at Ashlawn Farm, 1965

I well know the dangers of being too close to a thing to understand it, let alone face it enough to name it. My whole family does. We watched Gramma Luick—unable to make sense of or peace with her own biography—die a protracted, miserable death from two cancers and one broken heart, over eleven hellish weeks one hot summer at Ashlawn Farm. Unable to embrace her life, she could not accept death.

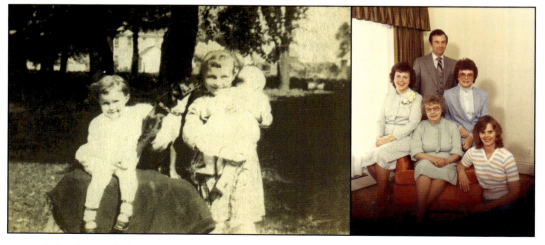

June Fuller & "Lottie" Juhl, 1920s; Lorraine, Charlotte, Bud, Jeandelle & Sheranne, 11 April 1982

Charlotte Luick's dark last days unfolded like this:

Mom had been on her ruptured back for five weeks before a doctor was willing to operate on it. Afterwards, she lay on a wheeled bed, bivouacked in the living room as cancer-stricken Gramma Luick occupied the folks' darkened bedroom for nearly a quarter of a year, unalterably refusing to surrender a life she had not, in over eighty-four years, found a way to live unburdened.

Despite having to nurse two bed-ridden family members as well as run what was left of our family's farm, Dad and his sister, Jeandelle, took flawless physical care of them both. They cooked for and fed them, washed them and their endless laundry, shopped for food and drugs even while they juggled bill payments along with the legal paperwork associated with concluding a human life. As Mom was able, she tried to take care of the caretakers.

On the Fourth of July 1997, my then-boyfriend Ingo and I flew from Berlin's Tegel airport to Minnesota's Twin Cities. I had just, two days earlier, successfully defended my dissertation at Humboldt Universität and was returning to Iowa to oversee the second printing of my first book, *Out of Hitler's Reach: The Scattergood Hostel for European Refugees, 1939-43*. Having reserved the flights for my three-month summer sojourn in the American Heartland eons earlier, I could not have known that my stay stateside would coincide with my Gramma Luick's earthly demise.

I drove down Ashlawn Farm's long, dusty lane, parked, took a deep breath, then braved my way into the farmhouse my great-grandfather Christian Ludwig Thrams had built seven decades before. I did not know what to expect. What I found, however, was worse than I had imagined. Dad's younger sister, ever-mad-an'-mean Jeandelle, and her sweet-but-kowtowing husband, Chuck Olesen, had driven their massive mobile home from the deserts of Arizona to the steaming cornfields of Iowa to be on-hand as Charlotte slowly checked out of a difficult, heart-rending life. When I walked in, they and my parents had just finished a quick breakfast.

"Oh, hi, Mike" Dad offered absently, not looking up from the *Globe-Gazette*, spread-out over the crowded kitchen table. "Was the car workin' all right on the way down from the Cities?"

"Yeah—all's well" I replied, then turned to my mother and wanted to know "but where's Gramma? How's she doin'?"

"She's Okay" Jeandelle answered before Mom could. "She's sleepin'."

"Jeandelle" Phyllis countered timidly, "I was just in there: I think she's awake now."

Dad and one of his favorite pastimes, scouring the Globe-Gazette

"No" my aunt barked hollowly, although she'd obviously been parked at the kitchen table for some time, "she's not"—and so it would go, the whole summer.

"Okay" I said, "I get it." As I carried my bag toward the door to the living room I bid over my shoulder "I'm gonna go upstairs an' change my clothes." As I left the tension-cooking kitchen, I heard the four slowly stand from the crowded table and begin to busy themselves with the immediate and unimportant, so as to avoid the long-term and fundamental.

Knowing I was bein' naughty, I quietly set my bag at the bottom of the stairwell door, then tip-toed towards the hospital bed the folks had set up in the ground floor's spare room. As I neared, I first smelled creeping rot, then saw Charlotte's pale, sunken cheeks and dull, flattened hair. She was awake.

At least, her eyes were open, but she did not blink. She only stared blankly toward the diffused light coming through the nearby north window, gazing into nothingness.

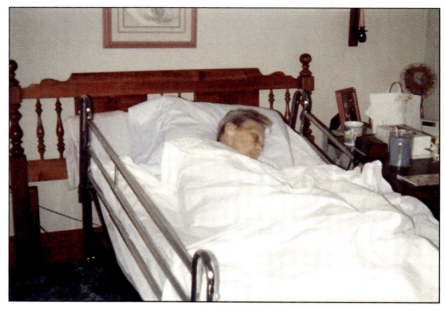

Sheranne said she asked Gramma before taking this photo, and that "Ma was restin', not sleepin'." I deliberated long before using it, but…

I was not upstairs very long, changing clothes in the big guestroom that once had been Dave's and my shared "boys' room" back when we were kids. Still, by the short time I returned to the low-intensity-warfare battlefield our family's farmhouse kitchen had become, Dad had gone outside to do chores and Uncle Chuck to the Olesens' yacht-sized camper to file away freshly-folded laundry. Wanting to be helpful, I picked up a towel and began drying breakfast dishes that Jeandelle was washing by hand at the sink. She stood looking out the window in the direction of the old orchard, laid out a hundred years earlier along the driveway.

As I carefully laid a dried glass on the cluttered counter, my father's sixty-year-old sister turned to me and grilled "Who's that out in the car?"

"Where do you mean?" I asked, pretending not to know what my long-unseen aunt was wanting to know.

"There," she nodded with her gray-haired head, as both hands and forearms bore fluffy dish-soap-bubble foam halfway to her elbows. "Out there" she growled, "at the end of the driveway!"

"Oh" I said softly, "there." I looked over Jeandelle's bent shoulder and glanced at Mom,

vocal Jeandelle, staid Bud and coy Lorraine Luick, circa 1940

Ingo hiding out in Mason City's Central Park, July 1997

who—as she wiped off the folks' round, solid-oak kitchen table—motioned "no" with a wagging face and mute-but-moving lips. "That's Ingo" I blurted out, with as much nonchalance as I could feign.

"What's an 'Ingo'?" Jeandelle demanded, glaring a look through me as if I weren't there.

"That's my boyfriend—from Berlin. I left him in the car to nap 'cause he's from the former East an' only speaks German, Russian an' a bit of *Bierstube* Vietnamese. So, I thought it'd be…"

"Well, wasn't that a lovely idea?" Jeandelle mocked. "It's such a beautiful thing, now, isn't it?"

I looked at her, the coffee cup I was drying suspended in mid-air, unsure if she was being serious or provocative. "*Huh-h-h*?" I hummed. "What's a 'beautiful thing'?"

"Yeah, we're here workin' our butts off an' you bring your lil' German honey with—"

"Hey, you two" Mom shouted as she squeezed between us and pushed us apart. "Just stop it, *now*!" Shoving me towards the back door, she added "Some beds along the driveway need weeding, Michael."

the flower beds I weeded along the paddock as Judy pulled in the drive

Stunned, having never seen my mother act so assertively, I froze, gawping at an aunt I long had been convinced was deeply wounded, but now suspected to be inherently nasty. Still, Jeandelle's mean and demeaning behavior shouldn't have surprised me: I'd suffered from her older brother's most of my life.

In the late '80s, I was living in Omega House—already then a 20-year-old commune in a turreted Victorian mansion with broad, fan-shaped stained-glass windows in Minneapolis. I'd recently come out to Dad, at Easter 1986. I would have done it years earlier but when I told Mom at Thanksgiving 1982 that my heart longed to find a man with whom to share life, between angry sobs she warned "Don't tell your father about this—he'll ban you." When I told David and Debbie by the following Christmas, my brother said "Don't tell Dad you're gay, 'cause he'll beat you or your boyfriend." Our older sister infantilized our father further with "Don't tell Dad what you are—he'll have a nervous breakdown!" Three and a half years later, though, on Easter Sunday, when I finally told Bud Luick that his wisecracks about his youngest son "finally findin' a girl" were fully misplaced, it was Mom's prophecy, of the three, that hit the raging bull's eye.

me & Mom on Omega House's back deck, Minneapolis, late 1980s

Half a year later, in fall 1986, I deliberated a long time while planning a short trip to Ames and Des Moines to visit college-day friends, until finally one early morning I hesitantly dialed the phone number in Iowa assigned to my family more than half a century ago.

"Hello" Mom answered after just two rings.

"Good morning!" I offered, as cheerily as I could muster.

Silence.

"Mom" I checked, "you there?" No response. "Hey, it's me—Michael."

Her lips rustling against the mouthpiece, she whispered "Wait." Then, I heard her shout "What'd you say, Bud?" across the room. I recognized Dad's booming voice in the distance. Likely, he was headed out the kitchen door, post-breakfast, to do the morning chores. I could make out my father's bellowing buzz, but no audibly distinct words. After the back door slammed I heard a weak "Ye-e-es?"

"Hi, Mom" I began again. "How are things at the farm?"

After an awkward moment of no response, she quietly bid a tentative "OK, I guess."

Realizing midwifing small talk was going to be impossible, I cut to the chase: "Look, I'm drivin' to Ames next week and would like to see you."

No response.

I pushed on: "So, I thought I'd call and ask if I should stop by on the way south."

Hearing nothing on the other end, I asked "Mom—you still there?"

A faint "Yeah" seemed to be all Mom could manage to get past her lips.

The '80s—the decade of The Big Chill, *but not only on the big screen.*

"Well, should I stop—or not?"

Wanting to believe that she'd shoot back "Yes, of course," I was all the more floored when she said "Well, I got to ask you dad."

"*Uh-h-h*" I back-peddled, "can't you make that decision on your own?"

"No" she replied, tersely yet void of any detectable emotion.

"Well, if you think it wouldn't be a good idea for me to stop by the farm, what if we, what if you and I met at Perkins at The Lake or, say, for a walk on the beach at State Park?"

"I dunno" Mom said, sighing softly.

Before we hung up—which wasn't too long after her non-committal, soul-deflating "dunno"—we neither made a plan for following up with a decision nor spoke about the matter ever again. And, I never forgot how my mother's cold shoulder made me feel.

———

Happily, at that time my friends made me feel a whole lot better about myself than my family.

One of them was Gordon Weil. To this day, he's a real character. And that's why I love him, still.

As he tells it, he was "the only white, Jewish boy growing up in an all-black, Baptist neighborhood in South Chicago in the Sixties." Gordon's biography has always been unique.

As a single mother working at the University of Chicago, Joyce Weil's two sons attended (per half-tuition) its renowned Laboratory School, founded in 1896 by visionary, reform-educator John Dewey. Gordon's brother, Jason, later married a beautiful African-American woman, and pursued a fancy career and much money. In contrast, preferring a simple life, Gordon moved to Minneapolis and lived at Omega House for fourteen years. Taking up meditation, vegetarianism and biking to his job at the University of Minnesota's epidemiology department every workday (even in the dead of winter, even during the Upper Midwest's serial snow storms) he still cuts a fit figure.

"Gordon has such beautiful, auburn hair" Mom swooned the couple times she came to visit during the four and a half years I lived at the commune. Gordon's trademark hair, however, only hinted at his hybrid lifestyle.

Sharing a thirst to experience, reflect, understand and grow, Gordon and I enrolled in a course offered one winter by the U of M-campus' YMCA titled "Eight Weeks to Live, Eight Weeks to Die."

Interviewed thoroughly first, each of the dozen or so participants was assigned a fatal condition less likely to occur in each participant's case. Being heterosexual and of Jewish origin, for example, the staff assigned Gordon HIV rather than, say, Tay-Sachs disease; being gay, they gave me a brain tumor rather than HIV, and so on. Once we'd familiarized ourselves with our individual diseases, we lived for two months as if we truly did have but eight weeks before we would die.

Accompanied by trusted companions—Gordon by his elementary-school-teacher girlfriend at the time, Linda Martin from New York, and me by my then-best-

Nina, me, Gordon and Linda at Omega House, late 1980s

friend, artsy San-Francisco-born Nina Brahmin (both of whom were fellow Omegans) we prepared to surrender the lives we had had up to that time, even to the point of visiting a cooperating funeral home to order our burial or cremation, complete with selecting a coffin or urn and planning a personalized memorial service: What would we like said or sung, who should come—or not; where? We kept daily journals to document our "ultimate journey" and met as a group one evening a week for two months to compare and deepen the process.

At the end of those two profoundly powerful months, our perceptions of dying as well as living were forever altered. We and our companions met for a "final farewell." Long after what was, in effect, the commemorative celebration of a life we still had a chance to change, the lingering legacy of that entire course would stay with us a lifetime.

Weeks later, thoughts of my own, unavoidable mortality trailed close behind me. One day, unable to buck a whim, I picked up the phone in Omega's big, deserted dining room and greeted my startled mother with a hearty-but-forced "Hi, Mom!"

Quickly plowing past the initial awkwardness of resuming a life-long dialog between what had become, at least for the time being, an estranged mother and her strange son, I told her about what an enriching experience "Eight Weeks" had been. At the end, I also asked her "So, Mom—if I were to ever have a terminal disease, could I come home? Would you care for me as I died?"

While my mother hesitated to answer, I held my breath. When she finally confessed, quietly, "I'm not sure" I realized anew that death is not only a physical phenomenon.

The Luick family's self-selected entrée to "*Amerika*" was a choice slice of bloody physical violence, served on a bed of rage, garnished with a hint of capital punishment. For just desserts, there followed years of wandering from place to place—except for Louis & Co. ever restless, forever enticed by the delicious morsels that always lay just beyond the next horizon, never staying in one space "too long." Heinrich ran away to the New World; generations of Luick men kept running for years—including me. Wherever we have gone, we have taken a mean gene with us.

My historian-writer "reader," Iowa-born Alan in Berlin, has asked repeatedly why I don't "go deeper into [my] victimization, into having been beaten as a boy, into [my] own biographical narrative more." Well, why *is* that? Mainly because the narratives we tell and retell become the narratives we believe, then live out—over and over the years, until and only if we're able to re-record the ever-playing tape in our heads, a tape full of the static inherited from those who weren't done with their own lives' theme songs, but happily instilled in us a few loose tunes to carry, too. Besides, despite any appearances to the contrary, this book really isn't about me but, rather, the people who made me "me."

Dave, Mom, Dad, Deb and me, the afternoon of Gramma's funeral

A veteran of (counted together, minus much-welcome breaks) X-many years of therapy, I've repeatedly faced and named my own internalized reflex to react explosively to a range of settings, people or experiences, almost none of which require a rageful response. My father, however, lived a different story. Yes, he mellowed as he aged: Just before he died, I saw Dad genuinely smile a couple times and even once or thrice let a belly laugh escape over his usually taut lips. That blessed redemption, however, came late—long after my nearly two decades spent under his angry roof, tottering on egg shells, always within his stinging striking range.

Save for the eight years during which we spoke but once (for about ten tense minutes) I stayed in contact with my father my entire adult life despite his having happily done without his queer second son ever appearing at his door, insisting on interaction. In all that time, I never heard Luwarren Myrle "Bud" Luick utter a single sentence even closely resembling "I have a problem with managing my rage." Instead of ever naming his own shadows, we only heard in quiet hours stray bits about Dad waking up, covered with sweat, having dreamed again that Donald was at the foot of the bed. Sadly, Bud mirrored his father's wholesale displeasure with most anything

(l. to r., back row) Dad, Mom, Deb & her now-deceased husband Gerry Wass, Omegan Gerry Tyrrell, Gordon Weil, Nina (name altered) Dave, me & then-boyfriend Bruce; (front row) Ian & Jared Wass, Gramma with hands on Jamin Wass' shoulders; Easter at Omega House, late 1980s

Son ever did. (When, while still in high school, Dad drove his new car into a ditch and totaled it, Donald asked "How's the car doin'?" but made no such inquiry about his only son.) Like Dad, Grampa seemed to know everything about all things. In the case of both men, though, based on what they were willing to share, they seemed to know themselves least.

I wonder now—now that both my father and his father are long gone and, by all but a handful of mortals, forgotten—what a difference it might have made, had Bud and Donald been able to face their own wounds, let alone those they caused to so many others. I assume that while for them painful (especially for the men but also for the women of their "greatest" generation) and unimaginable—doing so would have meant better, less miserable lives not only for their battered children and long-suffering wives, but for their own pitiable, broken selves.

As it was, the Bud Luick that could have been, but wasn't, remained a shining, unattainable vision. The one that was—at least the man I knew growing up—used recurring rage like his never-met maternal grandfather, Nick Juhl, and his likely little-known auntie, Della, used booze—as a medication, a tranquilizer, a buffer from emotions, from situations, from a life with which none of them could cope. Populated with pious, officially tee-totaling Methodists, the Luick-Thrams house hardly could have accepted alcoholism, but my pre-women's-lib mother tolerated her husband's ranting and raving, his scolding and raging far, far too long.

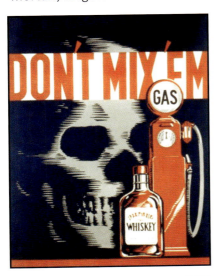

WPA anti-drunk-driving poster, 1937

"Phyl an' Bud" soon after they met, fall 1952 in Iowa, and celebrating half a century together, 2004

They both were products of their time—and of their parents' imperfect child-rearing as well as their own childhoods. As Nick Juhl's granddaughter, Bud's cousin Janet Gullickson Dahlby says, "We are what we come from." When I witnessed our barn walls shake, as the shovel or pitch fork Dad had thrown at my brother Dave hit the walls instead, they must have resembled the ones our Aunt Lorraine recounted when our "Grampa Luick used ta throw things at yer dad—he'd yell so loud an' hurl stuff with such a force, the wallsa the barn wud shake."

Dad's own, sketchily told accounts of how Donald man-handled him as a boy left no doubt that he'd been beaten routinely—assumptions later confirmed by his older sister, Lorraine, and mother, Charlotte. Whatever happened to "little Buddy" as a little boy, it couldn't have been good. When I finally cornered Jeandelle for a sole interview for this book, only once did she depart from her script of "I can't say; don't know; haven't a clue." That one exception happened abruptly, wholly unexpectedly, when I mentioned Lorraine's and Sheranne's reports of Donald beating Dad. "How would they know" she countered bitterly, "what was going on in the barn?"

"They said they could hear and see it going on—"

"They weren't there" Jeandelle angrily interrupted, "They was in the house, havin' a good time, playin' where it was warm an' dry. Me an' Bud, we was outside at age five an' six, pullin' the hay down from the mow with pitchforks taller than we was, feedin' the cattle corn an' silage we had ta carry in big bushel baskets from the shed or silo an' sprinkle 'long the bottom o' the bunks. What would they've known 'bout any o' that? They was in the house, enjoyin' the good life."

Norma "Jean" Luick with her nieces, Jeandelle & Lorraine, and nephew Bud on his pony, circa 1940

As kids, we Luick children and our folks spent many an oppressive, pre-air-conditioning summer night laid out like shroud-draped corpses in a long, evenly-spaced row in front of our buzzing Army-surplus fan. We sought enough relief from the merciless heat to finally fall asleep. Unlike the miserable, sultry Midwest summers stuck in my memory, on the morning I was ordered out to weed flower beds around my family's farmhouse, the weather was pleasantly dry, tolerably warm. Despite the depressing drama unfolding inside, I enjoyed being outside in the sunny, verdant yard, under what was left of the once-towering grove of ash trees Christ and Lydia Thrams had planted a century earlier. And, I felt grateful to be distracted by the mindless work of plucking soft, supple plants out of unresisting Iowa loam.

Suddenly, I was yanked out of drifting thoughts by the grinding of car rubber on spikey gravel. Turning towards the driveway behind my hunched shoulders, I slowly stood up and wondered *Who the hell's this, showing up so ungodly early?*

As the little, road-worn car pulled to a sharp stop, it sent a billowing bank of chalky dust towards the barn. I recognized the driver getting out even as I thought *No, it can't be—*

"Michael!" Judy screamed, "I've been pondering if you might not be related to these 'Luicks'!"

"Indeed" I smiled, running over to the robust-but-aging woman scurrying in my direction. Her long arms stretched heavenwards and slightly shook as we embraced and enjoyed a lingering hug. Right away, I *had* to know "What brings *you* here, stranger?"

Stepping back an arm's length, Judy looked me over. "You look great, Michael—absolutely great!"

Judy in front of hospice where she worked as chaplain, summer 1997

"Ya" I puffed breathily, "the miracles of modern face cream!" Genuinely stumped, I wondered "Seriously, now, Judy Brutz—what in this ol' wide world are you doin' *here*, of all places?"

"Haven't you heard?" she marveled.

"Heard what?"

"I'm now. The hospice chaplain. Assigned to Charlotte. As she—"

"As Gramma dies?" I finished my old friend's halting sentence. "I'm so glad you are—but, how does a clergy-less Quaker end up becoming a 'chaplain' of anything, my dear?"

"Look" Judy whispered as she peered past my ear, towards the house, "we gotta talk. Can we meet for lunch?"

"Sure—I'd love to! Jus' tell me when an' where: I'll be there."

As she pressed on, making her way up the crumbling sidewalk, towards the house, she shook her head and muttered under her breath "Incredible, Michael—truly incredible…"

That talk came soon.

―――

After my eyes adjusted to the dark den that I always found the Clear Lake Perkins to be—having worked there as a waiter for a year while a senior in high school—I spied Judy, wildly waving to me from a secluded corner table.

Like me never one to waste words, as I slid along the bright-orange-upholstered bench to sit next to her, she demanded "Michael, *what* is that all about?"

Although I knew precisely what my old friend from my undergrad days (at what at the time I referred to as "Iowa Straight University") wanted to know, I picked up one of the two over-sized menus left by the cute lil' number who had seated me. I pretended to peruse the entrees. "What's what all about, dearie?" I asked.

Judy ran her fingers through her thick and wavy graying hair. She shook her head. "You know, I've worked with a lot of families since taking this job, but I can't remember ever working with one so blocked as yours."

"Really?" I asked, pointing to a yummy-looking casserole pictured on the menu, oozing with golden-baked cheese, on a bed of colorful Mediterranean veggies. "This one sure looks good, doesn't it?"

"Really" she confirmed, "it's amazing." Her three-word reply left me unclear as to whether she was referring to my crazy family or the tasty casserole.

Closing the bill of fare, I asked "What exactly about my quirky kin do you find so amazing?"

"Well, for starters, that your aunt, Jeandelle, *never* leaves me alone with your grandmother. *Every* time I go out to your folks' farm, I'm never left alone with the person dying—which is standard hospice practice. Charlotte's approaching death's about her, after all—not only them."

Pushing the menu away I looked at Judy and confessed "Well, I'm not surprised, to be honest."

"Why do you think Jeandelle—and Bud, too—won't let me speak to your grandmother one-to-one? What do you think they're afraid of?"

Mom, Jeandelle, Gramma & Sheranne after Lorraine's funeral, 1995

Judy finally opened her menu and began to scan it. "Think they're afraid Charlotte's gonna say something she 'shouldn't'?"

"Oh, you mean like deep, dark family secrets?" I sat up straight, pulled back my tight, heavy shoulders and noted "There are more than enough to go around!"

Judy didn't respond; she only stared at me, as if expecting me to spill some choice family beans.

"Can't learn from the past if ya can't talk 'bout it, huh?" I held my breath as I asked "Is there more?"

"Well, as weird as it sounds, I don't have the feeling that Charlotte's consciously acknowledged that she's dying—despite the doctors' diagnosis of not just one but two kinds of cancer eating through her." Judy paused to monitor my reaction, but seeing none, continued "And the other thing that's so striking is that in absence of acknowledging what's really happening, of accepting that her life is ending, the emotional processing, the grieving that would relieve them all of such tremendous pressure, just isn't happening." Again Judy watched me, but I kept a stone face. "Michael" she shook her head, "instead of real, spontaneous emotions, when I call on your family it's like there's this big black hole in the room, sucking them all in, all the time."

Lorraine, Gramma, Dad, Jeandelle & Sheranne, early 1990s

I shrugged popping shoulders and begged off with "Look, Judy, if I knew I'd tell ya, but I'm not sure, myself, what dark demons Jeandelle and Dad are so carefully keeping watch over, or what's stoppin' Charlotte from lettin' go. *Ach*, I don't understand any of them" I sighed, looked out the window and saw the sinking sun soak the trees and lawn in bright light. "If I knew why my family is the way it is, I wouldn't have left my family's home so screwed up so many years ago, would I've?"

At first she mumbled "I might just have a sandwich." As she laid down her menu, though, Judy looked up at me, studied my face, smiled, then recalled with gusto,

"Yes, you did arrive in Ames pretty burdened."

"Aw, come on, Judy" I whined, "I was jus' a kid."

"David and I had just come to town a short time before you arrived to study—was it?—history."

"It was first anthropology, then history."

"Hadn't you just returned from living a year in Germany?"

"It was in England, actually."

"Anyway, I was working on my—"

"On your doctoral degree."

"That's right" she nodded her head, smiling, "in human development and family studies."

"Well, if ya ever needed a case study in family pathology, ya sure as heck got one now!"

"Thanks—but my degree's already hangin' on the wall, Michael," Judy smiled.

Stopping to order, she sipped on the sweating glass of iced tea, then added "I remember when you first arrived among the Ames Quakers. You were so young, so full of life—"

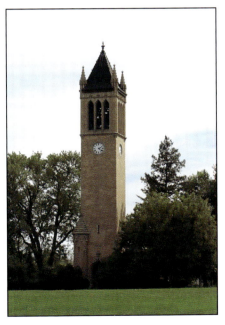

ISU's Campanile on Central Campus

me as ISU campus activist, and in white hat with then-partner Tim in blue cap, August 1983 march on DC

"That I was" I interrupted to concur, "but—*ouch*! If I'd only known then what I know now."

"But even then, I wondered what it was that kept you so restless, that kept your mind constantly busy, always asking, trying to dig deeper, looking for something vague yet defining." Judy's voice trailed off as she looked around the restaurant filling with diners. "Michael" she added apologetically, "as long as I've known you, you've been searching for something that just wouldn't let you go."

"Nor I would let go of" I interjected, self-consciously.

"It's been gratifying, though," Judy assured me, "watching you develop over these past ten years."

"Try fifteen, Judy" I corrected her.

"Oh—my! Has it been *that* long?"

"Indeed." I sipped some tangy, chilled cranberry juice.

"You know, Michael, yours is a mixed inheritance."

"What is, Judy?"

"Remember when you and I addressed FGC in Boone, North Carolina that time?"

"At Friends General Conference, as guest speakers during that evening program on—what was the subtitle?—the 'roots and legacies of family dysfunction' or some such, as I recall. That was the summer of eighty-seven," I guessed, at which Judy shook her head to the negative. "No?"

"No, it was eighty-eight. FGC 1987 had been at Oberlin, in Ohio. Boone was 1988."

"Yeah, sure. Anyway" I nudged Judy in the arm, "you spoke about your research into abusive behavior among Quaker families, which didn't win you many points with some Quakes very quickly—"

"And, you, my friend?" Judy butted in. She feigned bopping me on the nose, "You spoke about having been beaten as a boy, and the process of forgiveness, of finding peace amongst the bruises."

"Yeah" I faintly whispered, "I remember." The sweet, flirty waiter came and set our food on the table, then I added "That was a big step, you know—to talk about such intimate, upsetting things in front of a couple thousand people."

"It sure was" Judy beamed. "But, you moved them and touched something in them, too. I know. I saw it happen. The healing came through naming the previously unacknowledged." Judy then lowered her head and looked me lovingly in the eye. "It was palpable—and profound."

———

After my talk with Judy, I hurried back to Ashlawn Farm to check on the latest misery.

As I trotted into the house and entered the living room, I found Grampa Donald's last surviving sister, old Aunt Velma, and her jolly husband, Uncle Hans "Jake" Jacobsen, sitting stiffly across from dying

Gramma Luick. Riding shotgun, Jeandelle hovered in the background, pretending to be busy with paperwork or something equally unimportant spread out on the buffet.

Oren Hanson, Velma (Luick) & Hans Jacobsen, an aunt, Jean (Luick) Jackson, Albannis & Madge (Jenison) Mayhew, Mona (Jenison) Hanson, Donald & Charlotte (Juhl) Luick, 1950s; Velma & Hans' 1946 wedding

With plump, nearly-blind Hans quietly sitting beside her, Velma was saying "We thought we'd stop by, as we had ta go to The Lake ta get some groceries—"

Charlotte didn't move—not so much as a muscle…

"—an' wanted ta come an' see how ya were doin'—"

…nor said a thing.

"—but can't stay long."

Having swiftly run out of nothing to say, hollow-eyed Velma waited, her sagging face's expression frozen, her mouth hanging ajar.

Nothing. Gramma just stared. No, she "glowered," really—straight ahead, right through the Jacobsens as if they weren't there. She did not speak, but we could hear her, loud and clear.

Everyone but Jeandelle—who continued busying herself with nothing atop the buffet—looked at shriveled, silent, motionless Charlotte. And waited. Again, though—nothing.

Gramma didn't say a word. Or move. Or show any further emotion on her gaunt face.

Finally—mercifully, really, for Gramma as well as us, her helpless audience—mad Jeandelle brushed the papers on the buffet into a sloppy pile, strode across the room and took a stiff-backed position behind the little lump of darkness that once had been my spry, lively granny.

"We're glad you could come by" my aunt declared flatly to no one in particular. As she bent at the knees and began to squeeze together the slumped bundle in the chair in front of her, she lied "Ma sure does appreciate visits."

―――

The late afternoon of Velma and Hans' aborted mid-day visit, I returned to Ashlawn Farm from running an errand at The Lake and found the house mostly empty save for Mom cooking dinner and, for a change, Gramma sitting at the kitchen table, albeit again perfectly still and speechless.

"Chuck an' Jeandelle are out cleanin' the camper" Mom said, stirring a big pot of something unidentifiable on the stove, "an' Dad's taken an ornery mare to an auction over in Waukon." My mother distractedly added a dash of salt to her mystery creation on the back burner, then added "She wasn't producin' any good colts anymore anyway—an' he'll be back in time for supper."

Just then the phone rang. Mom dashed into the dining room to answer it. Left alone with the chicken coop open and unguarded, this fox snuck in and sat down next to silent Charlotte.

At first I simply looked at Gramma, who seemed to not see me. Following her locked gaze over the round, newspaper-cluttered table, across the breakfast nook and out the bay window, I wanted to know "What ya lookin' at, Gramma?"

Expecting no answer she surprised me with an immediate-if-lifeless "Nothin'."

"Are you watching those colts prancing about in the old orchard?"

"Ya" she lightly puffed, "I am." With effort, she swallowed. "They live so free—an' happy."

"I'm glad you can enjoy 'em, Gramma. They're cute—an' this time of day is so pretty, now that the sun's lower an' the air's coolin' down a bit."

My grandmother did not move but just stared out the wide window. Fearing that Officer Olesen soon would be back on her beat and shoo me away, I grabbed my chance while I still had it.

"Look, Gramma" I ventured, "I'm sure it's hard for you—for all of you—right now, but you have good, constant care and are surrounded by people who love you." The woman who gave birth to the man who afforded me the same neither looked at me nor acknowledged my presence. I pressed on: "It's a coincidence, you know, that I'm back here this summer, Gramma. I'm *so* glad that I could see you."

five well-developed foals with two mares grazing in paddock, 1990s

"Why?" Charlotte suddenly, but almost inaudibly challenged.

"Well-l-l" I stammered, "'cause if I'd missed seeing you, I would have regretted that the rest of my life." Taking her limp, cold hand in mine I confided "You've been such an important part of my life, Gramma—you have no idea."

Still not looking at me, the frail shadow of a woman I once thought I knew said matter-of-factly "When I'm over this, I'm gonna have a lot more energy." She swallowed with visible difficulty, then added "I've got a lot ta do back home"—deep breath—"when I git ta feelin' better—real soon."

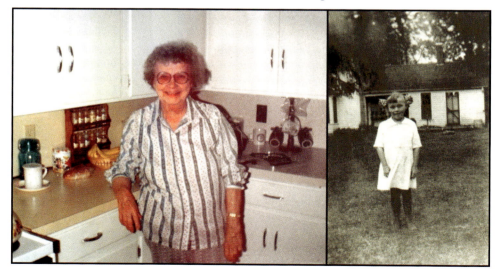

Gramma in her kitchen in Thornton, 1985; "Little Lottie" in the yard in Rockwell, 1920

As it was the first time we'd spoken alone since I'd arrived, only now did I realize where my grandmother was—or wasn't—in the process of finally letting go of a life she'd somehow missed living fully and freely.

Tears welled up in my eyes. I simply whispered "I love you, Gramma."

At that moment, Charlotte lifted her head a bit, blinked and smiled slightly. Wondering what she was looking at, I peered out to see the frisky colts romping round their grazing mothers. Then, as I repeated "I love you," the back door opened, and Gramma dropped her smile, along with my clasping hand.

―――――

Needing to meet periodically in Iowa City with the publisher of my book, conduct interviews with former POWs, give programs at local libraries or museums, tend to non-English-speaking Ingo during his partially hidden three-week stay and generally carry out the business that had brought me Stateside in the first place, I could only irregularly stop by Ashlawn Farm that busy, eventful summer.

One day, I arrived and immediately found myself to be invisible—but happily so, as I was thus able to dispassionately observe a turning point take place in my family's history much as one would watch a good flick or reality TV show: transfixed, but uninvolved. As if following a hand-held camera team, I saw Dad sitting at the round kitchen table, having just come in from doing morning chores. He poured himself a cup of Mom's ever-thin coffee. As he spun the lid back onto the thermos Jeandelle entered the room, having just checked on Gramma. Surely, the two siblings had discussed this game's-end scenario at least once before, as their exchange took place with the same, terse matter-of-factness as if they were discussing doing a load of laundry or warming up leftover chicken soup.

Without saying anything else Jeandelle strode up to the table's edge, placed her hands flat on its thickly varnished oak surface, looked Dad square in the eye and said, without a trace of emotion, "I think it's time."

My father, looking up at her for the shortest eternal moment imaginable, replied, "I'll call 'em."

From that second on, nothing remained the way it had been before I unwittingly found myself in the middle of a game-changing-but-muted familial tsunami. Within what felt like a few minutes an ambulance arrived, two men in white suits loaded the wee worldly bit of what was left of Charlotte Adelia (Juhl) Luick into their cavernous vehicle, then sped down the driveway, turned on two wheels onto the empty road and headed off to Mason City's Hospice of North Iowa. Within minutes of the ambulance passing the front gate Bud and Jeandelle had erased every trace of Gramma's months-long presence in my family's house. The hospital bed: disassembled and out the back door. The bedding: already in the humming washing machine. Her clothes and few personal effects:

Charlotte, visibly frail and taxed, getting dressed at Sheranne's, 1990s

boxed up and ready to be driven to Mason City that afternoon. The assorted pill bottles, thermometer, bed pan… the whole kit and caboodle: same. And, Chuck and Jeandelle's colossal camper? Packed and in the dry flash of a dying eye, also rolling down the driveway, headed to the Olesens' long-vacant split-level on The Lake.

With nary a tear shed nor any visible sign of an emotional response to the latest developments, in shortest order my father and aunt had restored the Luick home to "normal"—whatever that was—and, per looks at least, it seemed as if in our house vanishing Charlotte had never been.

———

No one else seemed to have any say in how Gramma spent her final earthly hours. Not my mother (her sole daughter-in-law for over forty years); not Charlotte's youngest daughter, Sheranne (effectively erased from the equation through then-recent charges by Bud and Jeandelle, based on documentable fact or not, of having "embezzled" some $80,000 from their mother over a couple years' time); none of Charlotte's many grandchildren. It was completely in keeping with how our Luick family had been ruled for decades—maybe a century, maybe even more. Secrecy, carefully choreographed crises and the control of information needed to make sound decisions or take effective action, have been the primary strategies to establish and maintain power in our family for generations.

Sheranne and Charlotte, mid-1980s

While of course parents cannot let (especially young) children rule a shared home, consistently excluding others' needs, well-being or wishes (those of minors or individuals of majority age) constitutes intra-familial tyranny. The one who gets to continually choose the music and constantly call the tunes to which all others always are forced to dance is a tyrant. The lives of the self-appointed leader, along with the lives of those dependent on that leader are diverted forever by decisions made solely by the leader. In heavy-handed tyrannical family systems, few are consulted, even fewer heeded.

Melissa and Lorena were the last to know, for example, that first Henry then, some eighty years later, his grandson George had been planning to slip outta town and slide into completely new lives—with other women. Still, being abruptly dropped as second in command profoundly and forever affected, respectively, the lives of young Louis and his even younger Luick siblings as well as, later, George and Lorena's adult children and their offspring.

Charlotte, for another, likely found out about Lynann carrying Donald's baby inadvertently or late in the story, yet for years thereafter had to watch her step every time she dared show her face on Thornton's Main Street. According to Sheranne "everybody knew about everything," yet by Barbara's and my generation, no one seemed to know a thing about anything of import that had ever happened in our family. Such a cynical, insulting farce, although at least some of us grandchildren could smell the sickening rot of festering lies in the air and feel the lingering chill of cloaked deceit in our very bones.

In any event, rolling crises kept us on our toes—and, by the fact of our involuntary dependence, compliant if not always complacent. Ol' Heinrich Luick's thrashing of some cocky nobleman might have made him feel better—at least for a few, adrenalin-soaked seconds. Three entire Luick households, including mates and children and their most precious personal effects, though, were sent packing on short notice—regardless that Heinrich and Katherine had been pleading for permission to emigrate for half a decade before the famous beating occurred.

Gramma clowning, Deb & Gerry at Ashlawn Farm, Christmas 1982

In early Belmond, his son, Henry Junior, might have fancied lovely Lydia (Lathrop) Johnson who lived next door, but their two-year, pre-marriage honeymoon in Missouri could not have gone unnoticed by Charles Johnson or jilted Melissa back on the Iowa prairie. Once the missing couple resurfaced from the Show Me State and went through the motions of seeking amends for a month, only to prove to be soulmates after all, the subsequent romantic realignments meant multiple divorces and new marriages, not to mention Melissa's ping-ponging from Iowa to Michigan, back to the "Beautiful Land," then on to California via covered wagon. All the while "Mad Bobcat" Henry was havin' a sweet ol' time with his new sweetie, multitudes were in crisis-management mode for months, then years. Who had the peace o' mind to appeal for reason or justice when all were preoccupied with playing by new rules enacted by someone else, by default?

Examples of avoidable, "managed" crises are aplenty in the lives of under-employed Louis, ever-moving George and aggressive-but-silent Donald, but we need not look to history's annals for case studies. My intelligent albeit poorly educated father mastered manipulation through crisis already as a boy. He had to. How would he have survived his similarly intelligent, power-savvy father? (Did someone say "anger management?" According to Sheranne, as a little boy my father would fly into fits of rage so rabid that Gramma would take him outside during such tantrums, hold him under the pump and souse him with freezing water "'til he cooled off." Not to be outdone, his kid sis Jeandelle—again, per Sheranne—"would fly into temper outbursts so bad, then carry on an' carry on so Dad had no choice but ta set her down on a kitchen chair an' keep her there 'til she'd stop.")

Dad with his cherished cherry-red Chevy in the house yard, circa 2000

By the time he headed a household of his own, my Dad could create a new crisis every day. Not enough money? Rage against the banks! Not enough rain? Rage against the weather man! Not enough pre-mixed pig food? Rage against Ralph from the Farmers Co-op, who (supposedly) forgot a phoned-in order! Not enough commodities-price support? Rage against Jimmy Carter! Not enough of any ol' thing? Jus' *RAGE*!

Rage an' rage an' rage on, Dad—RAGE till yer whole world turns cardinal red… then rage some mo'… an' then jus' a lil' mo'… till ya jus' can't rage no, *no* mo'!

And in that state, the rager loses any shred of responsibility for his own role in investing capital wisely, buying adequate crop insurance, remembering to order pig feed early enough in advance of an approaching holiday, or diversifying crops to accommodate expectable declines in one crop's prices. During one of those endless daily rages, all connection to that "humiliating" not-knowing, that "impermissible" imperfection or that "inexcusable" fallibility disappears.

An' if *that* rage don't fly, Daddy's gonna kill a mockin' bird, lil' guy! He's gonna beat yer head an' kick yer ass, he's gonna slap yer face, then rub it in muddied grass. He's gonna rage while ya git a smack on the back with a busted shovel; he's gonna rage on an' on, even while ya run ta that lil' farm hovel. "Go on an' be yer Grandma T's apron-string joy—ya lil' sissey; ya Mommy's Boy!"

P.S:

Dear Daddy,

I forgot somptin'.

I can git

pretty crazy-angry

sometimes, too.

Be well,

Mike

———

Bob Fairweather was waiting already in Iowa City for me to come round and approve the corrected galleys for the reprinting of *Out of Hitler's Reach*—and Ingo needed to connect with my boyish girlfriend from Clear Lake High, LJ, for a ride to the Chicago airport. She was en route to some "women's music fest" in some secluded Michigan meadow. The morning summer sun was shining so seductively, and the car was full of gas for a change. All were waiting, all was ready—but I needed to stop by the Elizabeth Muse Norris in-patient unit. At the hospice. In Mason City.

Leaving Ingo in the sun-soaked car, I made my way to Gramma's room, empty save for her barely-breathing tiny self. I entered the room as quietly as I could, hoping to be able to swiftly sneak away yet honestly say "I stopped by—I really did." But just then my last living grandparent opened her heavy eye lids—only half-way—but enough to see that a shadowy figure floated near the foot of her bed.

"Oh, Gramma—you're awake?"

Her dried-out face nodded,

Hospice of North Iowa in Mason City, summer 1997

almost imperceptibly, to the affirmative.

"I just wanted ta stop by, as I'm on the way to Iowa City to—" I began but, choking on my own hollow inanity, cut to the chase with "—to say good-bye."

Charlotte's eyes opened wider and followed me as I hesitantly made my way to her bedside, one unsure step after the other.

"I know it's early morning, Gramma, so I'm sorry if I've awakened you."

"That's... all... right" she moaned breathily.

"But, I didn't want to leave town without comin' round."

"We're... gonna... go ta lunch" she announced in padded, whispered segments.

"What?" I cocked my confused head. "Gramma, what are ya talking 'bout?"

"When I... get outta here... we're gonna go... ta the Chit Chat... on Main Street... in Thornton." She fought to find a deeper breath with which to finish her burdened sentence, "We'll get... one of those... pizza burgers"—exhaling weakly—"you... always... liked."

Gramma, Jeanette & Lorraine visiting me in Ames, Iowa, fall 1982; Gramma with my folks at Christmas, 1990s

Torn, wanting to let her have her truth yet honor the opposing one I perceived in that same shared moment, I slowly, quietly protested "But, Gramma? Do you know? Where you are?"

"It doesn't matter" Charlotte moaned again. "The girls up front... are dears"—shallow breath—"but I don't need... ta be here."

Just then I heard Judy's words waft through the darkened room: "We die the way we've lived."

"But" I began to cry, "Gramma—"

"There's been... a mis..."—cough—"...take. Ya know... I'm gonna be"—deep breath—"okay."

"—don't ya see-e-e?" As that long vowel hummed over my teeth, I bit my lip and said no more. Instead, I gently reached between the bed rails and fumbled under the flannel sheets till I found what remained of my grandmother's frail fingers. Squeezing her thin hand I bent over and kissed her scaly forehead, then wiped a loose strand of hair from her chalky, sleep-filled eyes.

"Get some rest, Gramma—an' go, knowin' that I love you."

"Okay" she rasped, "you... too."

I turned and, although I wanted to run, I ploddingly placed one leaden foot in front of the other until I was out the door and well down the hall. Then, I buried my face in my shaking hands and sobbed like I hadn't wept in ages.

———

The galleys were now checked and ready to print, but the call came too late. Gramma had died. Early morning. Alone.

Yes, I could come: I'd leave Iowa City after breakfast and be in Mason City that afternoon.

When I pulled into the drive at Ashlawn Farm the barnyard was full of cars, mostly ones I didn't recognize. Jeandelle stood in the door, barking orders where to put the endless offerings friends and neighbors kept bringing by and dropping off—bowls and bags, plates and trays of Midwest specialties baked, roasted, marinated, jellied or fried. Mom, I found, was further inside.

I'd only been gone a week but much had happened. "Gimme an update, will ya?" I begged.

"It wasn't dignified" was all she could say, at first.

"What ya mean, Mom?"

"To the very end Charlotte could not, would not accept that she was dying. We tried to lead her there, but she would *not* say it. She refused to go."

I could only shake my head, sad and in disbelief.

"The night before she passed, Bud's mother finally did call her pastor, in Thornton."

"Oh, she did?" I lit up, eager to hear what I had hoped to hear—that Gramma's soul had departed this world peacefully, despite everything.

"All she could muster at that point was to whisper 'Can you come? I'm dying.'"

When my mother stopped speaking and simply stared at me, I waited, then asked "So, did he?"

"No" Phyllis said softly, adding, as if to excuse a shepherd from abandoning his flock in its hour of gravest need, "it was the middle of the night."

"*Uh-h-h*, isn't that his job?"

"Don't start, Michael."

"Well, I'm jus' sayin'."

"As it was, by morning they found her—dead."

back row: Maude (Campbell) Breeding, Lelia (Campbell) Kew, Winnie Campbell, Jennie (Moorehead) Fuller, Charlotte Juhl, Ann (Kew) Moorehead, (behind Ann) George Moorhead, Jr.; middle: Ernest Campbell (standing, far left), Lottie (Campbell) Moorehead, Edrice Breeding, Jennie's mate Herb Fuller, Cleo Breeding, Gus Campbell, Lorna Campbell, George Moorehead, (on cellar door) Paul Breeding; front: Lowell Campbell, Della Moorehead, Stanley & Evan Breeding; outside Breedings' home in Union Township, Cerro Gordo County, Iowa; summer 1914

———

"In English the word 'project'" explained the rather rotund, white-bearded man sitting at the head of our oblong circle of entranced listeners, "has two main forms. Pronounced 'pro-JECT' it's a verb, but spoken out loud as "PRO-ject" a noun. Both come from the Latin '*pro + jacere*,' to 'throw forth.' And that, my friends" John Croft declared as he opened his hand and threw a few small stones onto the dirt floor in front of us, "is exactly what this week's workshop's all about."

So began a "Dragon-Dreaming" workshop I attended one summer at Sieben Linden, an environmentally focused residential community consisting of some 150 souls living on the gentle, pastoral plains between Berlin and Hannover. An Aussie with years of experience working closely with Australian aborigines as well as many other "peripheral" native groups, John has distilled both their ancient wisdom and his own, decades-long experience with social-change projects Down Under, in Europe, the Americas, Africa, Asia and elsewhere.

Already impressed by his diverse résumé and up-beat personality, I found my attention commanded even more at his casting of a handful of pebbles into the midst of the rapt circle of participants. "A 'project,' then," John continued "is a 'projection' of the self—or a collection of selves, the focus of a set of people working in concert. Given the darkness and light that is in each of us" he noted rather seriously, "a project can be a source of evil—the Third Reich comes to mind—or of good, such as an ensemble of players, an orchestra performing together, for example to bring Mozart's brilliance off the page and into the hearts of millions."

John sharing wisdom about Life, the Universe and...

John passed his eyes round the circle to see if we were still with him. Seeing we were, he warned "Because our limited human brains have a hard time putting dualistic dynamics into one image large and complex enough to accommodate both concurrently, we like to split the world in black or white, to write off various parts of its whole as 'evil' or 'good'—but forget it: There's some of *each* in everything! That includes" he raised his voice and slowed his speech, "in *ev-e-ry* project." As he said it, a shudder went through me, for I had observed or, sadly, survived too many crash-and-burn projects.

Seeing some of us shift uneasily in our stiff chairs, the experienced facilitator softened his tone. "The pyramids truly are a wonder of the ancient world. They are so amazing that some have claimed we humans aren't capable of constructing such colossal structures—certainly not then, with sticks and ropes. 'They must be the work of aliens' these critics claim. Indeed, the pyramids came out of us—and are great projects, right? Well, sure—*if* you were a pharaoh or an Egyptian priest overseeing the whole thing. If you weren't, if you were one of the tens, more likely hundreds of thousands of faceless, nameless slaves who lost their lives stacking those damned piles of massive rock, the pyramids weren't so great any more." Again looking at each of us, John asked "See what I mean? 'Evil' and 'good' depend on one's perspective, in whose shoes you are standing at any given moment."

Over lunch I mentioned that I had become a Quaker when I was seventeen. John exclaimed "Ah, then you are familiar with Fox's 'oceans of darkness, oceans of light' image of the world."

"Indeed" I smiled. "I've been there—and do that."

———

Sitting in Thornton's Methodist church with my siblings and their spouses in the pew behind our parents, aunts and Uncle Chuck, I bit my lip and dug my fingernails into my leg more than once. The preacher—the one who could not leave his cozy sheets to go comfort my failing grandmother as she lay fading away between her death-dusted ones—stood tall and puff-chested behind the pulpit, droning on about "How much Charlotte's Bible meant to her, how that gift from her beloved Donald guided her through her darkest hours as well as happiest moments."

Besides *Who the hell wrote this stuff?* I seriously wondered if I was the only one likely to puke trying to swallow it. *Did he even know the woman?* I tried my best to mentally check out of a service I found fundamentally disturbing—one last Big Lie to cap a life that had tottered on mountains of 'em ever since an innocent newborn's mother had succumbed to a Big Thud. *If he did*, no one bothered to fill him in on what really *took place in the Luick house.*

Finally, mercifully, Gramma's funeral ground to its mind-numbing, soul-grinding conclusion—up until the last moment built on one hollow, phony motif after another. Playing the Dutiful Grandson as best I could, I stood in the reception line next to my folks and then shook hands of dozens of people, some of whom I hadn't seen in a quarter century. All the while, I watched from the corner of my eye as Dad and Jeandelle danced around Sheranne. They had, according to Sheranne, taken her out to the Olesens' camper just weeks before and threatened to throw her "into prison" if she didn't relinquish her claim to the little left of Gramma's worldly wealth. *Classic,* I thought: *Behind-the-scene Luick intrigue to the end!*

Jared Wass in gateway to Thornton's Pleasant View Cemetery; me at Gramma's freshly-turfed grave

Once we returned from the motorcade to Pleasant View Cemetery to bury Charlotte above the little prairie town that had witnessed so much of her protracted misery, I made a point to sit with black-sheep Sheranne and her two young-adult children. Suddenly, I knew how Jesus must have felt, sittin' with the sinners: It wasn't so pretty. Contracting leprosy likely would have been less ugly than the glaring how-dare-you stares I fielded from Bud, Jeandelle & Co.

———

In the afternoon session on the first day of his week-long workshop, John Croft expounded upon the main ideas he'd presented before lunch, such as "We have an impulse—a question, a complaint, a dream, a fear, an idea—and we take that spark and 'throw forth' from the deepest part of our selves what's most present, most important at that moment. That's why" he paused, checking to see if we were getting what he was trying to help us see in ourselves, "a 'project' can both expand or exhaust a person, a family, a community. A national project, for example building pyramids or gas chambers, can give a shaky empire a focus, a shared mission that supersedes all other things: local problems, religious differences, a sour economy, political unrest, regional disasters, the ruler's recurring hemorrhoids or sagging ego—you name it."

"And war?" I asked.

"*Exactly*! There's nothing like a war to unite a people who otherwise can't stand each other, all the while fooling them into thinking that 'they' are really an 'us.'"

"Could a 'war' as a 'project'" a quiet, forty-something blonde asked sheepishly, "take place on the personal level—at the workplace or within a family?"

Smiling, John provoked her with "What do *you* think?" Not waiting for a response he added "A project—whether arising from a benevolent or a devilish leader—can unite or divide a town, a country, an agency or a family like little else. In the end" John lowered his chin along with his voice, "a project is what we make it and how we use it."

———

Having washed down my emotional woes with several plates of Midwest-church-lady potato salad and Jell-O-suspended lettuce topped with grated carrots, marshmallows and a dollop of Miracle Whip, I stood up and drifted over to the other corner of the church basement, where my immediate family sat a safe distance from sinner Sheranne and her shunned offspring.

"Jared?" I asked the nephew with whom I have always felt a special, visceral bond. "What say we drive out and look at Gramma and Grampa Luick's old place?" As his round, blond face instantly betrayed visible hesitancy I dared him with "Game, kiddo? The chance to see where your mom's people once lived won't arise twice," at which point my sister's first-born son took to his feet.

"Let's head 'em out!" my then-21-year-old nephew shouted playfully.

Driving slowly down the dusty, vacant road towards the old Luick farmstead, I abruptly stopped the car atop the tiny old bridge spanning Bailey Creek. "Tour starts here" I boomed, getting out.

photos Jared took while on the bridge near former Luick-farm pasture, soon after funeral on 13 August 1997

Jared and I tossed dusty, angular gravel over the flaking concrete railings. *PALUNK!* echoed the sharp stones as they fell into the pooling water below the bridge. I held forth: "When we kids—your mom, Uncle Dave and I, or our many cousins—used to come spend a week or so with Gramma, we'd run down here and dribble gravel into the crick for fun."

"You guys found playin' with gravel 'fun'?" Jared marveled.

Looking around, motioning with a flapping arm, I explained "It was different then—the crick's been straightened an' the grassy banks plowed up to the water's edge." Gazing out over what now was little more than a V-shaped drainage ditch, I lamented "There was still life here then. Grampa's Black Angus steers grazed in the wild-flowered pasture that bordered a meandering, vibrant crick. It wasn't a sluggish cesspool of chemical runoff" I scoffed, "like it is now."

"Seriously?" my skeptical nephew checked again. "You guys actually enjoyed jus' hangin' out here? Like," he shrugged and wrinkled his face as if he'd eaten a bitter bug, "that's it?"

"Are you kiddin', kid? It was *great*!" My hand pointing, swirling in the air, I outlined a vanished cosmos. "We hunted for crawdads over there. We fished right here, an' built a series of intricate little damns and side canals at the base of this dinky bridge—where pirates waited to fall upon unsuspecting damsels." Jared grinned. "This was a whole world of its own then. The cows over on that slope—lookin' on, chewin' their cuds—they were approachin' soldiers. And, the red-winged black birds, scolding us overhead? They were kamikaze pilots in buzzing, nose-diving planes. It was fabulous! The world here then was colorful and lively, full of surprises and little joys." I studied my nephew's face, wondering if he could fathom even a fraction of the world I tried to revive for him. "It's not like today, where kids sit in front of endless screens, overfed an' zoned out. We had to create our own fun an' find our pleasure."

"Yeah, Uncle Mike—but didn't ya say we was gonna see 'the old home place'?"

"Indeed" I conceded, unhappily aware that my homily had fallen on only half-listening ears.

After we turned the next corner, pulled up to the end of a grown-over driveway and got out of the car, Jared and I stood at the dented and chained steel gate, at first speechless and confused.

"I thought we were gonna see Gramma's old farm?" Jared complained.

"Dearest Neph" I said, barely audible, "we *are* at Gramma's ol'"—I swallowed hard—"place." Surveying the stray mounds of rubble that once had been a tidy collection of barns, sheds and other buildings, tears welled up in my disbelieving eyes. Where a proud grove had stood for decades, protecting the lives our Luicks had led here from the worst winter winds and screaming summer storms, I saw only broken stumps and scrubby underbrush. Shaking my sad head, all I could muster was a weak "I tell ya, it was diff'rent then."

Lorraine, Sheranne with Ring, Bud and Jeandelle on Donald and Charlotte Luick farm, late 1940s

Odd as it might seem, standing there next to my beloved flesh-and-bones, besides crumbling concrete and towering weeds, rotting fence posts and crusty old feed bunks, all I could see were ghosts. Of course I saw Gramma—both the worn, fallen-checked granny I had known all my life, but also the pretty young mother caught by a snapping camera shutter, all dolled up in a lace-collared cotton-print dress—as well as Grampa, that dark, mysterious figure floating through the threadbare living room, leaving behind a chilling wake as his lightless shadow swept across the linoleum floor. And, I could also see the little, unsuspecting souls they pulled into their doomed, never-resolved duel.

Somewhere among the rusting machinery and abandoned parts I spotted Dad as a little boy, already raging, without standing the entire time unable to reach the pedals of the tractor-mounted cultivator he was forced to operate from age five. There was spindly-legged Jeandelle not far behind, with her unkempt hair and flapping plaid skirt, gathering eggs and laying away toxic resentments that would poison her inner well for decades. Somewhere, 15-year-old Lorraine was meeting up with a suave Private Jones, getting an early start on what would become a lifelong career as a poverty-stricken single mother, while little late-comer Sheranne skipped circles round the clapboard farmhouse, always just a step ahead of unspeakable shadows. I had no face, no name for the unknown hired-girl or the illegitimate baby she conceived here—the aunt I wasn't even aware I had, at that moment—yet as I think back now, standing there with my foot on a heavy, unyielding iron bar, I swear I could feel the weight of things unseen and consciously not understood, yet existent all the same.

what remained of the Luick farm southeast of Thornton, circa 2000

After I drove Jared back to Thornton's Methodist church I set off, solo, across the quiet prairie, headed to Ashlawn Farm for the night. What we had seen—or, rather, not seen—of our Luick family's former farm stayed with me, though, mile after lonely mile.

I drove north over the verdant plain, the endless azure sky above. Desolate images flashed before my eyes. My mind filled with scenes of the few, ruined remains of Donald's prized, long-planned project—not just prettying up but expanding upon what his always-cashless, ever-moving parents had simply maintained as a rented farm. Unable to enlist Gramma wholeheartedly into his project, Grampa had recruited my young father and others to help him, leaving his estranged wife to pick out wallpaper with Phyl. Still, Donald had thrown forth an ambitious vision and realized much of it. Yet as we buried the wife he neglected in the process, only shards of his all-consuming project survived.

Luick farm in foreground; Ashlawn Farm on horizon, upper-right

Just as I exorcised the last mental pictures of that sobering scene, the car passed Dad's birthplace, the old Moorehead homestead where Gramma and Grampa Luick first started farming—and the haunting film in my head began flickering all over again. Ghosts of famine-fleeing John Moorehead and his English-born, thatched-roof-raised wife, Ann Kew, floated afore my tired eyes, followed by their handsome, death-beleaguered son, George. Somewhere in the foggy background I sensed once-petite Big Lottie lumbering about, gasping. Just beyond the car window lay the few shattered outlines of what had been a home on the prairie. My family had toiled so hard and endured so much to build it: grasshopper plagues, unstoppable epidemics, deadly blizzards, droughts, usurious merchants, collapsed prices—the whole, decades-long drama.

Leaving Europe—hungry Ireland and crowded Swabia, defeated Denmark and class-entrenched England—our family had thrown forth all its few worldly treasures to buy tickets, then put all its surviving dreams and sustaining vitality into a massive family project: to plant a new life, together, in the rich soil of the New World. Problem was, we brought with us age-old weaknesses, foibles and foolishness. It sabotaged us too often, leading us to not always live up to our own high ideals. Failing ourselves, then, we new "Americans" also failed each other.

———

Upon reaching Ashlawn Farm's gate, I turned down the driveway. I spotted the last handful of horses from Dad's one-time large herd. Watching them for a moment, peaceably grazing in the old orchard, I thought "*Ach*, they're the last strands of yet another project that has both delighted and distracted."

A thrown-together dinner of brought-by dishes was followed by obligatory small talk with Mom while drying dishes. We were all exhausted after such a dark and eventful day. I had to rise first-thing the next morning to return to Iowa City to retrieve newly-printed books. I bid the folks a weary "Good night," turned in and swiftly drifted off to a deep sleep.

I awoke too early the next morning—during the tender dawn, but before sunrise. As chirping birds searched for new friends, I had the uncanny, unmistakable feeling of a heavy presence in the room. I cast my half-closed eyes around the dim room: I saw nothing. Yet, the air was so still outside; not even a ripple of a breeze or the quiver of a leaf on the motionless ash trees broke the stillness.

Just then the handful of mares in the orchard raised their heads. Their skittish colts jumped sideways as a powerful, solitary wind blew across the yard and upwards into the guestroom window. It set the curtains fluttering and the small, brass pagoda-shaped wind chimes hanging between them clanging.

The gust startled me, having come out of nowhere. I pushed myself up off the mattress and looked out the window, towards the orchard. As I watched the

bathed in Light

horses begin to calm down, I did not hear but rather physically felt Charlotte's bodiless voice sing softly "Now I am light," then disappear forever.

"I am Light"

---

postscript: into Everlasting Light

    I didn't have much time.
    Don Bancroft was waiting for me at the Belmond Historical Society's museum. We had a lot to do, in too short a time, before Christian and I set off for archives in Des Moines and Iowa City, enroute to our flight from Chicago back to Dresden. It'd been a full but quick visit to "water the roots." Like every pilgrimage to my Midwestern homeland, the month had flown by in a blur—pleasant, but frenetic.
    Still, I wanted to "jus' drive by" the old Luick farm southeast of Thornton, having already stopped briefly at Pleasant View Cemetery to pay respects at Gramma's and Grampa's graves, and having driven meditatively down the skeletal remains of what once was a vital Main Street.
    With gravel spitting from the spinning wheels, I flew over the prairie, down the long, straight ribbons of county roads dissecting what had become, over the past half century, one vast plain covered not by a palette of colorful crops but solely a monotone carpet of "corn-an'-beans."

Barely slowing down to check if an unlikely vehicle might be approaching from the right or left at the last intersection before reaching the ol' home place, I barreled on towards my goal, expecting to squeal to a sudden stop as soon as I saw the old gate posts pop out on the left.

The next thing I knew, though, instead of the remnants of the Luick farm appearing next to the road, my grandparents' neighbors' place to the east emerged from the sea of corn. I shook my head, as if trying to dislodge a mirage from my disbelieving eyes. Having braked, I rubbernecked to check *Where the hell'd their place go?* before executing a tight, three-point turn.

As I idled back west, however—my eyes keenly combing the topography, searching for clues to where I'd somehow overlooked the piles of broken concrete, jumbled fieldstones and scrap wood atop rotting tree stumps I'd seen the last time I'd ventured here, with nephew Jared the afternoon of Gramma's funeral seventeen years earlier—but I saw nothing other than towering cornstalks.

The forgiving prairie, though raped and subdued, offers stray bouquets.

Then, it hit me:

Why, they've bladed off every atom of what little had remained of our farm so they could plant even more beans an' corn—the greedy bastards!

Disbelieving my own conclusion, I pulled to a stop where a narrow dirt bridge spanned the ditch—clearly marking the end of what once had been the long driveway where sad-eyed Tammy, widowed Gramma's snippy Shetland Collie, used to wait for Grampa to return—in vain.

Absently turning the key until it finally clicked into "off," I hesitantly opened the heavy door, took a deep breath and stepped out onto the simmering gravel surface of the utterly empty road. Slowly standing on the frame of the rental car, I looked out over the undulating field and imagined where the barn once sat... the grove stood... and the windmill spun under the prairie sun. As I swore I heard a stray hog-feeder lid faintly clang shut—tucked somewhere among the secret-swallowing rows of cloned corn plants—my eyes followed the horizon, along the tops of the algae-green tassels, until they reached the spot where the farmhouse would have stood.

The first thing I thought of was those stairs—specifically the crook of the stairs, where the witch was always waiting for me, next to the window sill full of dead flies. For a second I felt afraid, then remembered that it was all but a distant, ancient memory—a powerless ghost unable to touch a grown man now gray at the temples, sporting a softening belly. No longer a clueless kid tossed about by parents or their parents acting out unconscious scripts, I had a choice. As such—although mesmerized by the lure of things once precious but now lost—I forced myself to step down from the chassis, get into the car, start the engine and simply slowly drive away.

Forgetting for a few more moments all thoughts of Don waiting in Belmond, I sat motionless as the car drove itself down the road, my mind locked in a parallel cosmos somehow visually far away yet consciously close and all-present. All I could see before me was a mental parade of swirling quasars and shimmering stars, flaring comets and iridescent nebulae. As a plethora of planets and myriad moons spun through my head, I sat motionless in that hot car, stared straight ahead, oblivious to all other things. In my mind's eye, I watched as a vast cosmos exploded with spiral arms and galactic halos, meteor showers and solar winds… a multitude of gigantic forms in a complex universe.

Just then, I recalled the morning after Gramma's funeral, when that brief breeze spooked the mares and their foals in the paddock, then tickled the chimes hanging in the room where I half-slept. And, I remembered then "hearing" Gramma's silent yet crystal-clear voice affirm "Now I am Light."

Gradually awaking from my stupor, I realized the car had reached the pavement leading back to Thornton. After managing to actually stop and look for traffic, I pulled onto the highway. As the car sluggishly gained speed, I felt well aware of how short Gramma's life was—how soberingly short *all* our lives are—in the cosmic scheme of things. I also felt humbled, having just seen how all traces of the center of her and Grampa's adult-life universe had been so casually, so easily and yet totally erased.

A dry knot formed in my throat as I pondered how long the fruits of my own earthly efforts would be traceable in this dizzy, careening world of ours after I, too, rejoin the Light.

Over verdant, yielding plains, hangs our nearest star.

Just as deep sadness settled upon me, a verse from my childhood religious training rang through me:

All the things we see will disappear; what we hope for is eternal.

———

To be continued in:

Oceans of Darkness, Oceans of Light—a Pentalogy:
Volume II: *Chasing Restless Roots: The Dreams that Lured Us Across America*, with conclusion about the *populi*: my disappearing people

Volume III: *Tap Roots Betrayed: How Our Dreams Got Derailed in America*, with conclusion for the *polis*: my derailed country

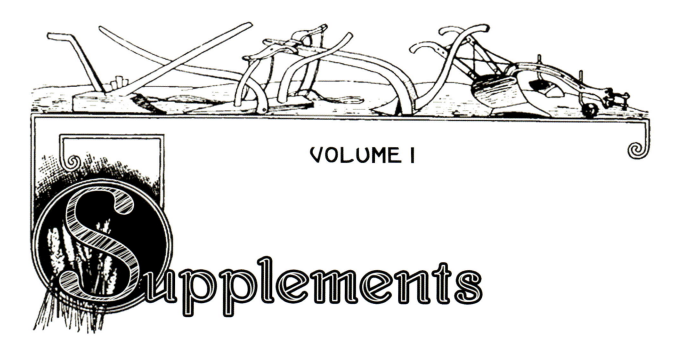

Volume I
Supplements

Born to a Quaker family in Upstate New York in 1828, Benjamin F. Gue grew up on a farm that served as a station on the Underground Railroad. At the age of ten he lost his father, but ran the farm with his mother and younger brothers. In spring 1852, a brother and he came to farm in Scott County, Iowa, near the Mississippi River. Active in Republican Party politics, he served as first a representative (1858-'62), then a senator (1862-'66) and finally vice-governor (1866-'68) at the Iowa Statehouse. Moving to Des Moines in 1872, with his son he published a newspaper, *The Homestead*. The year before he died in 1904, he published his *History of Iowa from the Earliest Times to the Beginning of the Twentieth Century*, numerous passages, photographs, sketches and maps from which appear throughout this pentalogy.

A sample passage from *History of Iowa* suggests how well-read and deep-thinking Benjamin Gue was:

Nature's supreme laws of never-ending change from one degree of development to another, seem to pervade the universe. Man [or woman] in all ages has been slowly reading these immutable statutes, unwritten, and only to be known through careful observation and patient investigation.

A little gained by one generation handed down to another, since the first appearance of [people] upon the earth, has made the sum of human knowledge. For how many ages on some other far off planet human intellect has been slowly pursuing the same great study we have no means of knowing.

Here the astronomer has discovered the existence of other worlds, has carefully computed their size, has measured their distance from the earth and each other, has observed their motion, their satellites, and learned some of the laws which govern them. He has even constructed a plausible theory as to how these planets were formed from the original elements...

Notes

Notes